Additional Praise for
The Crisis of Crowding

"What causes systemic risk in economic markets? What are the signals that there could be problems? How do you prevent systemic risk? And how should we change our risk management practices to take this risk into account? Chincarini looks at the financial crises of the past 15 years—starting with a comprehensive analysis of the Long-Term Capital Management crisis in 1998 and ending with the Euro-debt crisis of 2012—and argues convincingly that the central risk in these crises was accentuated from within the financial system rather than from external economic forces (it includes the best analysis I have read on the LTCM crisis). This bold new theory has important implications for both industry practices as well as for new regulations. It is essential that we learn the lessons from the past (or else we will repeat the same mistakes). Chincarini's book should be required reading for anyone who wants to understand and help prevent financial crises."

—Eric Rosenfeld, Co-Founder of Long-Term Capital
Management and JWM Partners

"Chincarini connects the dots between LTCM, mispriced risk, the 2008 financial crisis, the flash crash, and the Greek debt crisis. The instability created by crowded trades, interconnected financial institutions, and too much debt is the recurring theme. For those interested in understanding the quantitative approach to investment, the section of the book focused on LTCM is a very useful reference. It contains, for example, a comprehensive inventory of the types of trades LTCM had entered into and an inventory of lessons learned. This book is not only a useful history of recent financial crises, but a treasure trove of insightful quotations from interviews with many luminaries among modern financial practitioners and academics."

—Robert Litterman, Former Partner and Head of Risk Management at Goldman
Sachs; co-inventor of the Black-Litterman Model

"Chincarini returns to the proverbial crime scene of a decade earlier to find the origins of the crisis of 2008. Based on new interviews with key players and his own analysis, the book argues that the LTCM collapse of 1998 should have been the early warning signal of fragility in the financial system rooted in the fact that holders of sophisticated financial products so often just end up copying each other's behavior. It also provides a cautionary tale about the unintended consequences of financial regulations. Chincarini's book, which combines a narrative style with an overview of economic fundamentals, should be on the reading list of anyone interested in the roots of our financial meltdown."

—Austan Goolsbee, Former Chairman of the Council of Economic Advisers to
the President; Professor of Economics at the University of Chicago

THE CRISIS OF CROWDING

Since 1996, Bloomberg Press has published books for financial professionals, as well as books of general interest in investing, economics, current affairs, and policy affecting investors and businesspeople. Titles are written by well-known practitioners, BLOOMBERG NEWS® reporters and columnists, and other leading authorities and journalists. Bloomberg Press books have been translated into more than 20 languages.

For a list of available titles, please visit our Web site at www.wiley.com/go/bloombergpress.

THE CRISIS OF CROWDING

Quant Copycats, Ugly Models, and the New Crash Normal

Ludwig B. Chincarini

BLOOMBERG PRESS

An Imprint of

WILEY

Published by John Wiley & Sons, Inc., Hoboken, New Jersey.
Published simultaneously in Canada.

For general information on our other products and services or for technical support, please contact our Customer Care Department within the United States at (800) 762-2974, outside the United States at (317) 572-3993 or fax (317) 572-4002.

Wiley also publishes its books in a variety of electronic formats. Some content that appears in print may not be available in electronic books. For more information about Wiley products, visit our web site at www.wiley.com.

Library of Congress Cataloging-in-Publication Data:

Chincarini, Ludwig B.
    The crisis of crowding : quant copycats, ugly models, and the new crash normal / Ludwig B. Chincarini. – 1
        p. cm. – (Bloomberg)
    Includes bibliographical references and index.
    ISBN 978-1-118-25002-0 (hardback); ISBN 978-1-118-28271-7 (ebk);
    ISBN 978-1-118-28438-4 (ebk); ISBN 978-1-118-28480-3 (ebk)
    1. Financial crises–United States–History–21st century.   2. Global Financial Crisis, 2008–2009.
3. Long-term Capital Management (Firm)   I. Title.
    HB37172007 .C46 2012
    330.973'0931–dc23

                                                                        2012003587

10 9 8 7 6 5 4 3 2 1

Dedicated to the late Angus Butler. We're still undefeated.

Preface

My initial motivation for writing this book was to clarify many of the misunderstandings surrounding financial failures and crises. After a collapse, we are often given incorrect versions of what happened, and this leads us to make mistakes again in the future. Therefore, even if a lot of work is required, it is best to get the story straight.

This particular story begins with the failure of Long-Term Capital Management in 1998, continues to the financial crisis of 2008 as well as the Flash Crash of 2010, and ends with the ongoing European debt crisis. I hope to show that all these events are connected and might have been avoided. These events all involved crowded trading spaces, where risk models did not take into account either the presence of crowds through valuation or their actions. Prices in many of these instances were determined by the holders of the securities rather than fundamentals.

When LTCM collapsed, many people tried to explain what had happened, but in an effort to make the story easier to grasp, it was distorted, and so were our own perceptions of the financial world. As a result, an opportunity to improve the financial system was lost and bigger crises occurred.

Still, it is never too late to learn. Thus, in the first part of the book I retell the LTCM story with the help of many conversations with the partners of LTCM and access to a wealth of proprietary data. Also, I decided to tell the story from a financial point of view rather than a personal one, so as to understand the real lessons that we should have learned in the historic LTCM collapse.

The second part of the book goes through the financial crisis of 2008 in detail. While other books on the crisis have focused on the personalities and the inside stories, this book focuses mainly on explaining what happened in a straightforward way. There is something for everyone. Some technical bits for more specialized readers and simpler bits for more general readers. This part of the book includes the Quant Crisis of 2007, the collapse of Bear Stearns, the implosion of Freddie and Fannie and Lehman Brothers as the housing bubble burst, and finally, the collapse of Liar's Poker king, John Meriwether's new fund, JWMP. I also discuss the lessons we should learn from the financial crisis.

The third part of the book speaks about some of the same elements of crowd behavior that snuck into the May 2010 Flash Crash—when Apple stock traded briefly for $100,000 per share—and on to the continuing debt saga in Europe, which started with the Greek crisis.

Throughout the book, I sprinkle in excerpts from my interviews with many of the people who were on the front line of the crises, including five LTCM partners: Eric Rosenfeld, Chi-Fu Huang, Hans Hufschmid, and Nobel prize winners Robert Merton and Myron Scholes. I also spoke with numerous bank authorities, like Sir Deryck Maughan, former Vice Chairman of Citibank; Andrew Crockett, former head of the BIS; Jimmy Cayne, former CEO of Bear Stearns, and the founders and CEOs of many leading hedge funds, including Goldman Sachs Alpha fund. These are supplemented by numerous other sources—testimonies, court documents, newspaper articles, and previous books on the crises—that helped me understand and explain what had happened.

For completeness, I also provide an online appendix (www.wiley .com/go/crisisofcrowds) that goes through all aspects of the U.S. economy before, during, and after the financial crisis of 2008. There are other online appendices on policy reactions to the crisis, including a detailed analysis of Dodd-Frank, a detailed analysis of unconventional policies offered by the Federal Reserve, a brief analysis of government policies such as Cash for Clunkers, and an overview of the most recent global regulatory standard for bank capital, Basel III.

I had originally planned to write a small research paper on the financial crisis, but two people inspired me to write a whole book: Eric Rosenfeld and Chi-Fu Huang. Eric has been a friend for many years. He has taken time to come to speak to my students several times about LTCM. Not only did many students learn from his guest lectures, but I, too, learned a lot more about finance. He was patient with me throughout the process of writing this book, sharing his time, his data, his contacts, and his wisdom. Chi-Fu Huang also supplied his time, thoughts, and data. He also provided key insights into parts of the book, especially Chapter 12, The Absurdity of Imbalance.

I would also like to thank other people who supplied key insights into various events described in this book, including Cliff Asness, Steve Blasnick, Mark Carhart, Jimmy Cayne, Pierre-Olivier Gourinchas, Mark Hooker, Hans Hufschmid, Eric Scott Hunsader, Ray Iwanowski, Ken Kroner, Deryck Maughan, Michael Mendelsohn, John Meriwether, Sandor Strauss, Anthony Valukas, Cliff Viner, Chris Ward, and those people who chose to remain anonymous.

A few people took the time to read my long manuscript and give me their feedback, which helped me improve the book. These people include David Bieri, Mark Schroeder, Daehwan Kim, and Peter Sasaki. I would also like to thank Andrew Crockett for his insights and detailed comments and for reminding me not to be such a hedgehog.

I thank Anthony Gonzalez and Matt Walkup for giving their excellent research assistance. They never gave up no matter how difficult things got and thirsted for knowledge. Other research assistance was provided by John Wick, Jason Blauvelt, Andrew Oetting, Bridgette Adams, Jing Wen, James Lambert, Coady Smith, Evelyn Khalili, and Saw Jae Won. For data help, I thank Alexey Polishcuk, Wayne Passmore, Terry Lobes, David Blitzer, Michael Rappaport, Kristof Starzynski, Lisa Finstrom, Sabya Sinha, Salvatore Bruno, Robert Mc-Cauley, Sabya Sinha, and Andrew Dialynas. For useful discussions, I thank Jim Barth, Bob Litterman, Wayne Ferson, Carl Hopman, Viral Acharya, Bob Mc-Cauley, Mark Schroeder, Wolfgang Chincarini, Chris Kawasaki, James Angel, Chris Lalli, James Hamilton, John Taylor, Steve Ross, Robert Whitelaw, Ross Waldrop, Kevin Brown, Bryan Bashaw, Dennis To, Jacob Gyntelberg, Stefan Avdjiev, Silvio Contessi, Gregg Berman, Claudio Borio, Kostas Tsatsaronis, Mathias Drehmann, and Frank Fabozzi. Thank you, Morgan Ertel, for trying.

I thank Pam Van Giessen for putting up with me over the years and taking a leap of faith with me on this book, Evan Burton for helping to make this book a reality, Judy Howarth and Melissa Lopez for editing, Michael Freeland for his cover design, and Simone Black and everyone else at Wiley for their support.

I wrote this book all over the country, but the place that most inspired me was Berkeley, where I had studied as an undergraduate. I thank the Royal Ground Coffee of Albany, California, for letting me live in their cafe. At times they must have thought I was a homeless person. The Aroma Cafe in Studio City, California, the Coffee Bean in Claremont, California, and the P.F. Changs in Rancho Cucamonga, California, also allowed me to work for long periods of time and for that I am grateful.

If you would like to send me suggestions or comments on the book, please send them to my e-mail address below with the subject line: Book Comments. If you were involved in any of the events I describe, please let me know as well, and perhaps I can include your story in the future. If you are an instructor that uses this book as a supplemental text in your class, please let me know and I will add you to the acknowledgements.

Ludwig Chincarini, CFA, PhD
chincarinil@hotmail.com

Cast of Characters

Herbert Allison: President and COO of Merrill Lynch during the LTCM crisis. Appointed President and CEO of Fannie Mae in September 2008 and is currently the Assistant Secretary of the Treasury for Financial Stability of the United States.

Madelyn Antoncic: Managing Director and Chief Risk Officer at Lehman Brothers during the financial crisis.

Cliff Asness: Co-founder and CEO of the quantitative hedge fund AQR Capital Management. Previously was Managing Director of Quantitative Research at Goldman Sachs.

Ben Bernanke: Chairman of the Federal Reserve during the crisis of 2008.

Lloyd Blankfein: CEO and Chairman of Goldman Sachs.

Steve Blasnik: President and CEO of Parkcentral Capital Management, a relative value hedge fund that managed Ross Perot and other investors' private wealth.

Warren Buffett: Billionaire investor and CEO of Berkshire Hathaway.

Erin Callan: Managing Director and Head of Hedge Fund Investment Banking; Chief Financial Officer, 2007–2008.

Mark Carhart: Former co-head of Quantitative Strategies and Global Alpha hedge fund at Goldman Sachs.

Jimmy Cayne: Chairman of the Board of Bear Stearns during the financial crisis. Former CEO of Bear Stearns.

Ralph Cioffi: Managing Director of Bear Stearns Asset Management and head of two Bear Stearn hedge funds that collapsed in 2007.

Jon Corzine: Former CEO of Goldman Sachs and Meriwether's classmate at the University of Chicago. Also served as Governor of New Jersey from 2006 to 2010 and former CEO of MF Global.

Christopher Cox: Chairman of the SEC during the financial crisis.

Jim Cramer: Host of *Mad Money* television show, author, and founder of Street.com.

Andrew Crockett: Former CEO of the Bank for International Settlements from 1994 to 2003. Currently President of J.P. Morgan International. Knighted by Queen Elizabeth in 2003.

Jamie Dimon: Former President and co-CEO of Smith Barney Salomon. Currently CEO of J.P. Morgan. At Salomon when arbitrage group was shut down, which may have helped trigger LTCM crisis.

Chris Dodd: United States Senator from Connecticut during financial crisis. Co-author of Dodd-Frank bill.

Rudi Dornbusch: The late MIT professor of international economics. The mentor of almost every well-known international economist, including Paul Krugman, Ken Rogoff, Jeffrey Sachs, and many more.

Stanley Druckenmiller: Former lead portfolio manager of the Quantum Group from 1988 to 2000, the George Soros hedge fund.

David Einhorn: President of Greenlight Capital, a long-short value-oriented hedge fund.

Antonio Fazio: Governor of the Bank of Italy at the time that the Bank of Italy invested with LTCM.

Eric Felder: Managing Director and head of Global credit products at Lehman Brothers during the financial crisis.

Barney Frank: Democratic member of the House of Representatives from Massachusetts. Co-author of the Dodd-Frank bill.

Paul Friedman: Chief operating officer of Bear's fixed-income division.

Richard Fuld: CEO and Chairman of the Board of Lehman Brothers during the financial crisis.

Timothy Geithner: President of the Federal Reserve Bank of New York during the financial crisis. Currently, Treasury Secretary of the USA.

Michael Gelband: Managing Director and global head of fixed income who was asked to leave in 2007.

Alberto Giovannini: Senior strategist at LTCM. Currently CEO and founder of Unifortune SGR.

Ace Greenberg: Chairman of the Executive Committee of Bear Stearns during the financial crisis of 2008. CEO of Bear Stearns from 1978 to 1993.

Alan Greenspan: Chairman of the Federal Reserve from 1987 to 2006.

Joseph Gregory: President and Chief Operating Officer of Lehman Brothers up to the collapse.

John Gutfreund: CEO of Salomon Brothers until 1991.

Victor Haghani: Principal at LTCM and JWMP. Headed LTCM's London office and also very influential trader.

Gregory Hawkins: Principal at LTCM and JWMP. Nicknamed the Hawk.

Larry Hilibrand: Principal at LTCM and JWMP. One of the most influential traders at the firm.

Chi-Fu Huang: Principal and head of Toyko office for LTCM. CEO and CIO of PGAM from 1999 to 2009. Head of Fixed Income Derivatives at Goldman Sachs with Fischer Black from 1993 to 1994.

Hans Hufschmid: Principal at LTCM. Responsible for foreign exchange trading, among other things. Currently CEO of GlobalOp.

Ray Iwanowski: Former co-head of Quantitative Strategies and Global Alpha hedge fund at Goldman Sachs.

Bob Jones: Former head of the Quantitative Equity group and Global Equity Opportunities hedge fund at Goldman Sachs.

Mitch Kapor: Founder of first commercially available spreadsheet program, Lotus 1-2-3 (the precursor to Excel). Business partner of Eric Rosenfeld.

John Maynard Keynes: British economist who first mentioned ideas of quantitative easing.

Alex Kirk: Managing Director and global head of high-yield and leveraged loans at Lehman Brothers during financial crisis.

William Krasker: Principal at LTCM. Modeler at LTCM.

Arjun Krishnamacher: Principal at LTCM and JWMP.

Ken Kroner: Head of Blackrock's global market strategies overseeing the quantitative hedge fund group.

Jim Leach: Republican member of the U.S. House of Representatives for Iowa during LTCM crisis.

Dick Leahy: Principal at LTCM and JWMP. Handled mortgage trading and co-managed with Meriwether the Macro fund at JWMP.

Ken Lewis: CEO and Chairman of Bank of America during the financial crisis.

John Mack: CEO and Chairman of Morgan Stanley during the financial crisis.

Deryck Maughan: Chairman and CEO of Salomon Brothers from 1992 to 1997, Vice Chairman of Citigroup from 1998 to 2004, Vice Chairman of the NYSE from 1996 to 2000, and currently partner at KKR.

William McDonough: President of the New York Federal Reserve during the LTCM crisis.

James McEntee: Principal at LTCM and former Chairman of the Board and co-CEO of the government bond trading firm Carroll McEntee & McGinley. Meriwether and McEntee shared a love for horses.

John Meriwether: CEO and founder of Long-Term Capital Management and JWMP. Vice-Chairman of Salomon Brothers from 1988 to 1991.

Robert Merton: Principal at LTCM and Professor of Finance at MIT. Winner of the 1997 Nobel prize in economics.

Euoo Sung Min: Chairman of the Board and Chief Executive Officer, Korea Development Bank.

David Modest: Principal at LTCM. Managing Director at Morgan Stanley and J.P. Morgan and currently at the Soros Fund.

Samuel Molinaro: CFO of Bear Stearns during Bear Stearns collapse.

Paul Mozer: Salomon Brothers trader who made illegal bids in the Treasury auction causing Meriwether and Gutfreund to resign from Salomon.

Peter Muller: Former head of Morgan Stanley's Process Driven Trading group.

David Mullins: Principal at LTCM and former Secretary of the Treasury. Principal role to raise capital and raise credibility of LTCM.

Roger Nagioff: Managing Director and appointed Global head of fixed income in 2007.

Hank Paulson: Treasury Secretary of the United States during 2008 and former CEO of Goldman Sachs.

Chuck Prince: CEO and Chairman of Citigroup from 2003 to 2007. Resigned in 2007 due to the poor performance of mortgage-related products.

Franklin Raines: CEO of Fannie Mae from 1999 to 2004 and Vice Chairman of Fannie Mae from 1991 to 1996.

Julian Robertson: Founder of the very successful hedge fund Tiger Management.

Eric Rosenfeld: Principal at LTCM and JWMP. Meriwether's right-hand man.

Myron Scholes: Principal at LTCM and PGAM. Winner of the 1997 Nobel prize in economics.

Alan Schwartz: CEO and President of Bear Stearns during 2008.

William Sharpe: Professor at Stanford University and co-inventor of the CAPM. Won the 1990 Nobel in economics for his work on asset pricing theory.

Robert Shustak: CFO of LTCM. Currently CFO and COO of the hedge fund founded by Sanford Grossman, QFS.

James Simons: Founder and CEO of Renaissance Technologies, one of the most successful quantitative hedge funds. This hedge fund also suffered during the Quant crisis. Simons was a mathematician prior to his entry into finance.

George Soros: Founder of Soros Fund Management. Famous for his hedge fund bet that the British pound would devalue.

Warren Spector: Co-President of Bear Stearns and Head of Mortgages and Fixed Income.

John Thain: Chairman and CEO of Merrill Lynch during the financial crisis. Former CEO of the NYSE and President and co-CEO of Goldman Sachs.

Bob Upton: Former Treasurer of Bear Stearns.

Cliff Viner: CIO of the hedge fund named III.

Paul Volker: Former Chairman of the Federal Reserve from 1979 to 1987. Chairman of the Economic Recovery Advisory Board. Promoter of the so-called Volker rule under Dodd-Frank.

Sandy Weill: Former co-CEO of Smith Barney Salomon. CEO of Citigroup from 1998 to 2003. Was instrumental in creating Citigroup and eliminating Glass-Steagall.

CHAPTER 1

Introduction

Since the beginning, it was just the same. The only difference, the crowds are bigger now.

—Elvis Presley

Humans are a social species, grouping together to do everything from waging war to attending cocktail parties. This desire to be with others also occurs in the financial markets. Some portfolio managers follow whatever investments are in vogue, mostly because bucking the trend doesn't pay. If the trend continues and they haven't followed it, they could look like idiots. If they follow it and it doesn't continue, they simply join the herd of other wrong-headed investors.

At other times, portfolio managers create an innovation. This innovation usually makes abnormally large returns, so others desperately want to copy the strategy. These copycats eventually learn the ropes and begin trading money in the same fashion. At first this leads to even more profits for the early innovators, because others buy more and more of their trades.

The copycats create a side effect, however: They crowd the space. The strategy's future returns depend increasingly on the copycat's behavior.

Oftentimes copycat investors make their trades on borrowed money, which amplifies both their positions and their risks. Modern risk-measurement models generally ignore the presence of copycats and the resulting crowded spaces, which often leads to underestimations of risk. A shock to the system can lead to sudden, sometimes large asset price moves, which can cause panic and failure among the institutions involved in that investment space.

In the past 20 years, globalization, technology, and increased leverage have made the effects of overcrowding more apparent and dramatic. In fact,

1

market crashes are happening more regularly than in the past, with nearly every crisis labeled a 100-year event.

The stock market crash of 1987 was likely the first crisis caused by modern-day crowding. The financial industry had popularized dynamic portfolio insurance, which involved protecting investors from losing money on their portfolios. Many institutions offered this protection by selling the market when it went down and buying the market when it went up. This practice can work quite well if only a small portion of the market pursues these strategies.

But if that proportion grows too large, crowding the space, the market may destabilize. As the market falls, the large group sells its positions, pushing prices further and further down and sometimes leading to a crash. In 1987 there were too many copycats, too much crowding, and too many models that didn't adequately account for this crowding.

The next big crisis came in 1998, eleven years later. It involved Russian markets and the failure of Long-Term Capital Management (LTCM), a well-known hedge fund. In 1994, Long-Term Capital was one of the largest hedge funds. Managers used technological and quantitative techniques learned at Salomon Brothers to sublime perfection. They were the new financial juggernauts, and everyone wanted a piece of their amazing performance.

Soon other institutions, including the proprietary trading desks of Goldman Sachs, Morgan Stanley, Lehman Brothers, and multiple new hedge funds, began to reverse engineer LTCM's strategies, all of which involved leverage. The lucrative relative-value bond arbitrage investment area became very crowded. Quantitative copycats saturated the space. Risk models were no longer accurate, because they didn't capture this crowding and its potential effects. Heavily leveraged positions meant that small moves could destroy an entire firm in a short period of time.

In July 1998, one of the large institutions, Salomon Brothers, began closing its copycat positions. In August 1998, the Russian government defaulted on its bonds. The shock occurred as the relative value funds were scrambling to survive. LTCM was on the brink of bankruptcy; many feared that this would shatter the financial system, just as with Lehman Brothers in 2008. The Federal Reserve stepped in and coordinated a private solution to prevent chaos.

In 2000, Internet stocks traded at ridiculous multiples. The crowd rushed in and the bubble formed. By April 2000, the bubble began to crash. The NASDAQ dropped by 70%. Yet despite investors' dramatic losses, the aftereffects were comparatively mild, mostly because of the limited amount of leverage in Internet stocks. This put some brakes on the crash.

From 2000 to 2008, every aspect of the U.S. economy got more and more involved in a massively leveraged trade: real estate investing. Instead of involving just traders, as most crowding does, the subprime lending bubble featured politicians, greedy home buyers, mortgage brokers, real estate agents, banks, investment banks, and quasi-government organizations Freddie Mac and Fannie Mae.

Investment banks took outright positions in real estate and also created, sold, and traded derivatives based on housing values. Hedge funds also took various bets on real estate market segments. Insurance companies joined the space by offering insurance to the crowded investors. Rating companies joined the greed train and issued AAA ratings as fast as they could write the three letters and cash the checks. Even the media pushed us forward with talk of rising home ownership, rising stock markets, and good times.

Like the Internet bubble of 2000, this bubble kept growing. Almost everyone was crowding this trade and using unprecedented leverage. Some home owners took leveraged investing to new heights by putting zero money down and enjoying a leverage ratio of infinity.

Risk models were glaringly inadequate. They used historical data, which didn't include the enormous amount of crowding and overvaluation that existed by 2008. It was only a matter of time before we saw the worst crash since the stock market crash of 1929: the 2008 financial crisis. The massive exposure to a collapsing bubble combined with leverage and short-term borrowing created an unprecedented shock to quantitative hedge funds. Known as the Quant Crisis, this destroyed Goldman Sachs's star hedge fund.

The crisis gave us a spectacular show: the historic collapse and rescue of Bear Stearns, a government rescue for Freddie Mac and Fannie Mae, hundreds of bank failures, Lehman Brothers' bankruptcy, a market-wide lending freeze, the failure of a whole host of hedge funds (including John Meriwether's new fund, JWMP), and unprecedented marketplace interventions from the U.S. government and Federal Reserve.

Three years and a depression later, the markets had slightly recovered. On May 6, 2010, between 2:42 P.M. and 2:47 P.M., the Dow Jones dropped by 600 points, then rose 600 points by 3:07 P.M., events known as the Flash Crash. Procter & Gamble stock dropped by 37% in that short period. What happened? Was a leveraged crowded space wreaking havoc again?

From 2001 to 2008, banks around the world lent money to Greece, assigning it a risk level very similar to that of countries with more discipline and higher productivity, such as Germany. The crowded space kept Greek interest rates at unrealistically low levels, and the Greeks were happy to borrow to fund consumption—until the crowd realized that Greece was a mess.

This is the story of the crisis of crowding. The story begins in 1998 with Long-Term Capital Management's fascinating collapse and tries to explain the ways in which crowds and leverage demolished one of the most successful hedge funds in history. The failure of LTCM had many lessons for the financial community and for society at large, but no one paid much attention—perhaps because disaster was ultimately averted. Ignored lessons formed a large part of the basis for 2008's financial disasters, only this time with more leverage, more participants, and a series of policy mishaps.

PART I

The 1998 LTCM Crisis

All human beings are interconnected, one with all other elements in creation.
—Henry Read

The 2008 financial crisis really began 10 years earlier, with the collapse of the famous hedge fund Long-Term Capital Management (LTCM). LTCM was not an ordinary hedge fund. It was a large financial intermediary with a vast amount of technology and a lot of very experienced, intelligent managers.

LTCM's enormous, consistent success seemed evidence that it was possible to tame the financial markets with sophisticated experience and quantitative tools. Some people were jealous of LTCM's success. Others were inspired, as it showed them that traders could understand and manage the financial markets.

Suddenly, in just two months in 1998, LTCM stood on the brink of bankruptcy. The firm would have failed without an emergency cash infusion and rescue from a consortium of investment banks. The rescue brought cheers from those who envied LTCM and cries from those who wanted to become LTCM, plus a lot of stories that weren't even true.

Many of LTCM's trades were clever. LTCM's experience in the financial markets was second to none. Its risk-management framework was on a par with state-of-the-art systems, but the firm underestimated the danger posed by crowds. Lured by LTCM's success, other investors had entered the firm's investment space. LTCM's risk management failed to measure the ways that these crowds changed investments' return and risk. With leverage and quant copycats running for the exits, LTCM found itself trapped in the fire.

CHAPTER 2

Meriwether's Magic Money Tree

We're sucking up nickels from all over the world.

—Myron Scholes

The Birth of Bond Arbitrage

In 1974, John Meriwether, having just received his MBA from the University of Chicago, went to work as a government bond trader at Salomon Brothers. In those days, bond trading was not a quantitative endeavor. Traders bought or sold bonds they thought looked good or bad. John Meriwether realized that bond pricing was highly quantitative and saw that, if he could tap into this quantitative pricing, he could not only outperform his industry peers but make lots of money as well.

He slowly began recruiting top talent, hiring both highly trained quantitative and old-fashioned traders. He went to MIT, Harvard, and other places to find experts in economics, finance, and other sciences. He planned to teach them the basics of bond trading and then tap their intelligence to find ways to mathematically model various fixed-income products, find inherent mispricings, and make money on them. Some of his hires included Larry Hilibrand, who had just finished a master's degree in mathematics from MIT and was hired in 1980. Dick Leahy, with a BS from Boston State College, worked at Merrill Lynch and then joined Meriwether in 1986.

Eric Rosenfeld, a PhD in economics from MIT, was working at the time as a professor at Harvard Business School. Meriwether called to ask if Rosenfeld had a bright student who would like to come to Salomon. Rosenfeld was sick of teaching case studies and grading exams and asked Meriwether if he could try the job. He left Harvard 10 days later and never went back.

Rosenfeld's interest in using quantitative techniques to exploit profitable opportunities started when he was an MIT undergraduate in the early 1970s. He enrolled in a statistics class with the famous econometrician Jerry Hausman. Hausman needed a summer research assistant to help build predictive models for NFL football games. For the previous 12 years Rosenfeld had collected NFL football game data, including the game's day of the week, which team was home or away, the Las Vegas betting spread, whether the game was played on turf or grass, and each team's winning percentage at the time of any given match. The pair used this data to build an econometric model to predict the winning margin on NFL games, then bet on games. The model worked during the two-year project; then both researchers moved on to other things.

Many recruits had interesting backgrounds independent of their financial experience. Eric Rosenfeld and fellow MIT student Mitch Kapor created a regression program at MIT to help Eric with his PhD dissertation. They eventually called the program VisiPlot and sold it alongside the first spreadsheet program, VisiCalc. They sold the rights to a software company for about $1.2 million.

Rosenfeld went on to teach at Harvard Business School, while Kapor went on to work for that software company. Realizing that one product could combine all their concepts and find a huge market, Kapor launched Lotus 1-2-3, the first commercially available spreadsheet program. His company became Lotus Development and eventually made Kapor a billionaire.[1]

Victor Haghani, who had just received a BS from the London School of Economics, joined the firm in 1984. Gregory Hawkins, a 1982 PhD in economics from MIT and a professor at UC Berkeley, was hired in 1985. Known as Hawk to his trading partners, Hawk was in Rosenfeld's fraternity at MIT.[2]

William Krasker, a 1978 PhD in economics from MIT and a Harvard professor with an interest in arbitrage possibilities, was hired in 1987. One of the quirky strategies he examined was whether buying wine in the current year and storing it for later consumption was an economical way to drink quality wine. He found that, on average, buying and storing wine has a return on investment that's very similar to that of Treasury bills.

Arjun Krishnamachar, a 1987 Wharton business school graduate, came to Salomon in 1988. Hans Hufschmid, with a BA from the University of Southern California and an MBA from UCLA, came to Salomon in 1985. Myron Scholes, a PhD from the University of Chicago and a professor at MIT and Chicago, became a managing director of Salomon in 1991, as well as co-head of the fixed-income sales and trading department. Finally Robert Merton, a PhD from MIT and a Harvard professor, arrived in 1988 as a senior advisor to Salomon Brothers.

The whole quantitative team worked in fixed income, but focused on slightly different areas. Haghani was a bond arbitrage trader, Hawkins worked in bond arbitrage and mortgages, Hilibrand worked in bond arbitrage, Hufschmid worked on the UK fixed-income arbitrage desk and then moved permanently to the FX trading desk, Krasker worked in fixed-income arbitrage, Krisnamacher worked on the derivatives trading desk, Leahy was head of mortgage trading, and Rosenfeld was the co-head of the bond arbitrage group.

Meriwether cherished the quantitative discipline and frequently invited prominent scholars to give talks at Salomon Brothers. He also mingled with freshly minted PhDs at the American Finance Association conferences, always looking for bright new talent.

This small group of traders generated more profit for Salomon Brothers than did the firm's investment banking services, asset management, private wealth management, and all other divisions combined.

Figure 2.1 shows the profit and losses (P/L) of the Meriwether trading group and the rest of Salomon Brothers.[3]

The profits were mind-boggling. From 1990 to 1992, Salomon Brothers' investment banking, client services, and brokerage activities posted losses every year. The firm as a whole returned a profit only because of Meriwether's small team and their innovative work. Meriwether group profits from 1990 to 1993 were $485, $1,103, $1,416, and $416 million respectively, versus mainly losses from the rest of the firm of –$69, –$67, –$26, and $1,159 million. Figures from after 1993 compare Salomon with LTCM. Remember that some members of the Meriwether group had remained at Salomon to run that proprietary trading group.

In 1988, the team's success propelled Meriwether to a perch as Salomon's vice chairman. His traders were fiercely loyal to Meriwether, in part because he shielded them from office politics and in part because he handsomely rewarded their hard work. Meriwether negotiated a deal in which his group kept 15% of the profits they generated and awarded bonuses from that reserve. In 1990, Hilibrand was the talk of the industry with his $23 million bonus. At $20 million, Hufschmid's 1993 pay package was larger than that of Deryck

FIGURE 2.1   Profits of Meriwether's Proprietary Trading Group at Salomon versus the Rest of the Firm

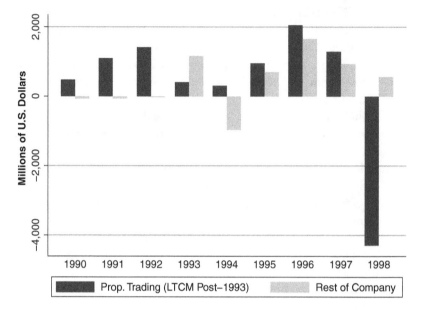

Note: For 1998, the LTCM P/L is computed as the –92.04% year-to-date performance through October 1998.

Maughan, Salomon Brothers then-CEO. Team members grew quite rich, and others in the firm were envious.

Then in 1991, the Salomon fixed-income trading group was involved in a Treasury auction scandal. Acting independently, a trader named Paul Mozer made false bids on behalf of clients in a Treasury auction. In particular, he bid for more Treasury securities than allowed for any primary dealer by pretending that the securities were for clients.[4]

Paul Mozer was not part of Meriwether's arbitrage group, and Meriwether had nothing to do with Mozer's bids. Even so, he would suffer for Mozer's actions. John Meriwether and company CEO John Gutfreund became the scapegoats, ultimately taking responsibility for Mozer's stunt.

An SEC investigation eventually led to Gutfreund and Meriwether's resignations. The two settled civil charges that they had failed to properly supervise their employees by paying fines of $100,000 and $50,000, respectively. In addition, Gutfreund agreed to never run a securities firm again and Meriwether agreed to a three-month suspension. Salomon Brothers paid $290 million to settle charges arising from the bidding scandal.

The firm itself made comparatively little from the illegal bids, estimating that its illegitimate profits were between $3.3 million and $4.6 million. Meriwether, the last of the three to resign, complained to friends that he was unfairly made a target of the investigation.

Warren Buffett, a major shareholder of Salomon though his Berkshire Hathaway fund, became Salomon's interim CEO for about six months. During this period, Buffett seriously considered having the firm declare bankruptcy. The Treasury had determined that Salomon would no longer be able to participate in bond auctions. Buffett and other senior management believed this would destroy the firm. After Buffett's personal appeals, the Treasury agreed that Salomon could bid on Treasury auctions, but not for customer accounts.

The Dream Team

After leaving Salomon, Meriwether spent three years considering his next move. On February 24, 1994, he launched Long-Term Capital Management (LTCM) with $1.125 billion in capital, making it the largest start-up hedge fund to date.

More than $100 million came from the partners themselves, especially those who came from the proprietary trading operation that Meriwether had headed at Salomon Brothers.

Meriwether and Rosenfeld originally asked Warren Buffett to invest. After all, Buffett was familiar with Meriwether's group, and Berkshire Hathaway had owned about 20% of Salomon Brothers stock. (Though Buffett publicly claims that he doesn't like derivatives, he likes derivatives when others use them to make him money.) Nevertheless, Buffett declined to invest money in LTCM.

Meriwether and Rosenfeld then asked UBS for investment funds and perhaps the use of their facilities. UBS refused.

The pair had hoped that Goldman could raise money for them, particularly as Jon Corzine was an old buddy of Meriwether. At the time, however, Goldman did not market third-party funds.[5] Merrill Lynch eventually led the team to seek LTCM investors.[6]

The new company was not without its detractors. During the firm's road show, Andrew Chow, the vice president in charge of derivatives for Conseco Insurance, told Nobel prizewinner and LTCM partner Myron Scholes that "You're not adding any value. I don't think there are that many pure anomalies that can occur."[7]

"As long as there continue to be people like you, we'll make money," Scholes reportedly replied.

LTCM's founding partners included Victor Haghani, Gregory Hawkins, John W. Meriwether, Robert C. Merton, Eric Rosenfeld, and Myron S. Scholes. Another founding member was James J. McEntee. He had been chairman of the board, co-CEO, and co-founder of the bond-trading firm Caroll McEntee and McGinley from 1969 to 1983, when it was sold to Marine Midland. In 1988, he formed the investment firm McEntee and Associates. An old friend of John Meriwether, McEntee had experience in both starting a firm and bond trading. At LTCM he was a directional bond trader.

Chi-Fu Huang taught finance at MIT. The Salomon arbitrage team had wanted to approach Huang before starting LTCM, but felt that their close ties to MIT precluded poaching faculty. But when Huang left MIT to work in Goldman Sachs's fixed-income area with Fischer Black, LTCM hired him soon after to run their Tokyo office.[8]

The new firm hired David Modest, who has a PhD from MIT, from the Haas School of Business, where he was a professor. At LTCM he built the firm's relative value equity business and was actively involved in financial technology management and in mentoring strategists.

Robert Shustak, with a BA in accounting from Queens College and prior experience in Salomon's financial division, was LTCM's new chief financial officer.

David Mullins, a PhD in economics from MIT and the former assistant treasury secretary under President George H.W. Bush was the firm's salesman. Mullins had already enjoyed an impressive public career. Secretary of the Treasury Nicholas Brady asked him to run the Brady Commission, which investigated the causes of the 1987 U.S. stock market crash. (They found that derivatives and dynamic hedging of portfolio insurance may have been to blame.)[9] Mullins helped resolve the savings and loan crisis with the Financial Institutions Reform, Recovery, and Enforcement Act (FIRREA) and the formation of the Resolution Trust Corporation (RTC). In 1990, President Bush nominated Mullins to a four-year term as vice chairman on the Federal Reserve Board of Governors. He left for LTCM in 1994. His presence brought greater credibility to LTCM's capital raising campaign and also opened many doors, including those of some central banks.

Later, other partners joined, including Dick Leahy, Larry Hilibrand, Arjun Krishnamachar, Hans Hufschmid, and William Krasker.

Myron Scholes and Robert Merton, who had been associated with Salomon and who would eventually win the 1997 Nobel Prize in economics, also joined LTCM as limited partners. But though Merton and Scholes had influenced Salomon's practices, LTCM's core trading strategies were those of Meriwether and his team. Scholes and Merton helped with the firm's marketing. Half of the founding partners had previously taught finance at major business schools, which helped the firm develop creative finance ideas.

Every organization has war generals and ordinance generals. Meriwether, Haghani, and Hilibrand were the war generals. I was not that. I was the ordinance general. I was involved in marketing—this is ordinance. I didn't know how to trade strategies initially—I learned this over time. But I was not in charge of fighting the war. Neither was Bob Merton. I did a lot of research on equities and strategies. I built a huge credit facility for LTCM. This helped improve after-tax returns with assets in the UK. It had to do with utilizing the OIC structure in the UK. Because of tax discrepancies between dividends in different countries, a legal vehicle was set up that was able to make the company more tax efficient.

—Interview with Myron Scholes, July 9, 2011

I was one of the first four people to start LTCM with Meriwether, McEntee, and Rosenfeld. I had no desire to become a partner. I just thought it was interesting to do this. I presumed that to be a partner, it would be a 150% job. The whole period building the company was fun. I wrote the marketing plan for investors. People came throughout the year. None of the ex-Salomon traders were asked to come. They just came because they were excited by the opportunity. The modeling stuff was the same trades as were done at Salomon Brothers. I looked over the models, but wasn't actively involved in them.

—Interview with Bob Merton, July 9, 2011

I remember the first time I visited LTCM headquarters in Greenwich, Connecticut, in a building with a beautiful view of the lake. Eric Rosenfeld was the first person I met. I wore a suit, but he wore slacks and a collared shirt with its top buttons open. That was dressed up by his office's standards, he told me. John Meriwether, by contrast, wore an elegant collared shirt and an ascot. "So you're the Italian kid?" he asked me. That whole day left me feeling energized and inspired. I wasn't alone. Financial market professionals were increasingly convinced that this talented group of intellects had mastered the financial markets.

Early Success

LTCM's initial success mirrored that of the Salomon team. Figure 2.1 shows LTCM's profit and loss (P/L) from 1994 to 1997. It was amazing. *Business Week* featured a cover story calling LTCM traders the "Dream Team," citing their record at Salomon Brothers. Their performance at LTCM was just as impressive. It was as if Meriwether and his 140 employees had a magic money tree.

The Sharpe ratio is an important, risk-adjusted tool for comparing the performances of different investments or portfolio managers. The higher the ratio, the better the portfolio manager. (See Box 2.1.) Table 2.1 shows that, before 1998, the LTCM fund had a Sharpe ratio five times that of the standard returns of U.S. Treasury bills and bonds.

Box 2.1   The Sharpe Ratio

The Sharpe ratio measures the return of a portfolio minus the risk-free rate divided by the portfolio's standard deviation. It is a risk-adjusted return measure that assists in comparing different portfolios or investments, even in the presence of leverage. If portfolio A has a higher Sharpe ratio than portfolio B, then there is no amount of leverage that can make portfolio B as good as A. Sometimes hedge fund returns are distributed non-normally. In these cases, a better measure is the Sortino ratio, which is similar to the Sharpe ratio but divides excess return by the semistandard deviation rather than the standard deviation.

Consider a golf analogy. Suppose an average amateur golfer plays with a top pro golfer such as Phil Mickelson. On every hole, Mickelson drives his ball further than the amateur does. Think of this as the portfolio's net return. It's important, but it's not enough to judge who's a better golfer. Distance matters, but so does accuracy. How often do drives land in the fairway? The Sharpe ratio is essentially drive distance divided by the variation of the drive distance from the center of the fairway. It lets us compare two golfers. It probably goes without saying that Phil Mickelson had a lower variation than the average amateur, and a much higher Sharpe ratio. He is clearly the better golfer.

The LTCM portfolio, consisting mainly of fixed-income instruments, had a Sharpe ratio almost double the S&P 500 during a period in which the United States had one of the strongest bull markets in history. Amazingly enough, the average returns of LTCM were 27.76% (net of fees), and 37.45% gross with a volatility of 8.96%. The S&P 500 average annual return was

TABLE 2.1 LTCM Returns versus Standard Asset Classes

	Average	S.D.	Sharpe	Max	Min
LTCM Net	27.76	8.96	2.54	8.41	−2.92
LTCM Gross	37.45	11.72	2.77	11.64	−3.85
S&P 500	22.25	11.48	1.50	7.96	−5.60
Treasury Bills	5.04	0.14	0.54	0.49	0.29
10-Year Govt. Bonds	7.66	7.07	0.38	6.38	−3.93
30-Year Govt. Bonds	10.08	10.75	0.48	9.57	−5.42
Corporate Bonds	8.09	4.45	0.70	3.67	−2.65
High-Yield Bonds	9.69	3.73	1.27	2.82	−2.94
Oil	7.72	22.79	0.12	14.48	−15.94
Gold	−6.79	8.19	−1.43	4.79	−6.43
Silver	5.08	21.16	0.01	15.23	−9.26
Real Estate	15.98	10.50	1.05	10.39	−3.70
World Equity	13.07	10.48	0.77	6.19	−6.67
World Bond	6.67	4.52	0.38	3.55	−2.34
Emerging Equity	−3.29	18.70	−0.44	12.41	−16.41
Emerging Bond	16.64	17.13	0.68	10.70	−13.16
Relative Value Hedge Fund Index	11.54	2.55	2.57	2.04	−0.66

Note: Average is the annualized mean monthly return, S.D. is the annualized standard deviation of monthly returns, Sharpe is the annualized average returns of the LTCM fund or the asset class minus the average monthly return of the risk-free rate divided by the monthly volatility of the LTCM fund or the asset class. Max and Min represent the maximum or minimum monthly return, respectively. The returns are measured from March 1994 to December 1997.

22.25% with a volatility of 11.48%. Even through one of the hottest bull markets ever, this fixed-income money tree left the S&P 500 in the dust.[10]

Continue the comparison across a host of major asset classes high-yield bonds, real estate, gold, silver, world bonds, or world equity and the story is the same. The LTCM money tree was the best deal around.

More than that, LTCM added diversification to many investors' holdings. The LTCM portfolio had a low correlation to many standard asset classes that an investor might already hold. Only the HFRI Relative Value Index, which is a diversified index of relative value hedge funds and not really investable, had a Sharpe ratio in the same ballpark as that of LTCM.[11]

LTCM's returns from 1994 to 1997 were impressive, but it wasn't the leverage per se that boosted them above the average. Other asset classes could not have been leveraged to achieve the same high return with a similar level of risk. The leverage raised the absolute return to investors, while keeping the ex-ante risk much lower than that of comparable asset classes.

New money raced into the fund (Figure 2.2), which closed to new capital in 1995 and grew to $7.5 billion in capital by the end of 1997. Given the

FIGURE 2.2   Growth in LTCM Assets Under Management from March 1994 to December 1997

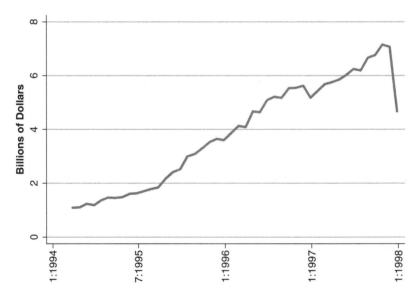

Note: Includes Dividend Distribution of $2.7 Billion in December of 1997.

lack of additional opportunities, the partners paid a dividend of $2.7 billion, leaving fund capital at $4.8 billion as 1998 began. This increased fund leverage and excluded many investors, which would later come back to haunt LTCM.

Success always breeds two types of audiences: those who admire the success and those who envy it. LTCM's early success was widely admired. It increased industry recruiting from the hard sciences, as well as from economics and finance. It nudged many portfolio managers, traders, and investors to more accurately quantify their beliefs. (The arbitrage group at Salomon Brothers used to give recruits difficult quantitative problems, including the now-common duration-neutral yield curve trade [see Box 2.2].)

In those days, though, most bond traders used crude techniques. Salomon was at the frontier of advances in bond trading. Its trading department boasted Meriwether and his quants; the fixed-income research department had Martin Liebowitz, who published *Inside the Yield Book* in 1972. Frank Fabozzi, an author and former professor of finance at MIT, argued that the book "transformed the bond markets." It offered one of the first mathematical approaches to bonds used by practitioners.[12]

The strong fixed-income research department, led by Liebowitz and others at Salomon, and the intellectual traders in Meriwether's group helped create current standard practice for most bond portfolio managers around the world. In fact, the spread of these quantitative techniques may have gradually diminished attractive opportunities in bond arbitrage.

Box 2.2 Salomon Arb Group Interview Question

Question: Your portfolio group strongly believes that the yield curve is going to flatten very soon. It could be that short-term rates will rise or long-term rates will fall or some combination of the two. Suppose also that you have three instruments available: a 30-year zero-coupon bond, a 1-year Treasury bill, and a cash account. Suppose the modified duration of the 30-year is 28 and the modified duration of the 1-year is 1. What strategy should you pursue to benefit from your beliefs?

Suggested Solution: The investor would ideally like to have no interest-rate exposure, but take a view on the flattening yield curve. Thus, one would like to hedge parallel yield curve shifts, but take advantage of the nonparallel moves. One way to do this would be to buy long bonds and to short short-term notes (e.g.,

(continued)

(*Continued*)

buy the 30-year Treasury and short the 1-year note). You would also like to match the duration and price of the positions, to be neutral to interest rate movements and have a net zero investment position. Thus, you should probably go long on very high-coupon long bonds (lower price) and short the lower-coupon notes (higher price). This is similar to creating a market-neutral market exposure by shorting one stock and going long another stock.

The goal is to be duration neutral so that you are not exposed to the majority of interest rate movements, but still express your view that the yield curve will flatten. Thus, you would like $D_p = w_{30}D_{30} - w_1D_1 = 0$, where D_p is the modified duration of the entire portfolio, D_1 is the modified duration of the 1-year bond, D_{30} is the modified duration of the 30-year bond, w_1 is the weight of the portfolio in the 1-year bond, and w_{30} is the weight of the portfolio in the 30-year bond. Modified duration measures the approximate percentage change in the price of a bond for a given change in interest rates.

Rearranging the equation, you find that your relative weights will be related to the ratio of the durations $\frac{w_1}{w_{30}} = \frac{D_{30}}{D_1}$. Thus, if you go long \$1 million long bonds, you will need to short \$28 million notes. But this also implies that you have \$27 million extra on hand. In this example, you would have to reinvest the \$27 million in overnight instruments. Theoretically, your bet on the broad part of the curve would be opposite your bet on the curve's short area.

The envious were mainly people without quantitative ability: portfolio managers and bond traders who relied on gut instinct and other crude methods. It was natural for them to be skeptical of LTCM. If the new firm's practices caught on, after all, their very existence in the financial markets was threatened.

Other critics took issue with LTCM's staff. Hilibrand was arrogant, they said, and Meriwether was too quiet.

For what it's worth, I don't recollect Hilibrand as arrogant. He always took time to talk to me. Of course, his mind went 100 miles per second, and he could challenge anything you said. During a lunch meeting I heard him think out loud about a variety of ways to consider taxes on equities and other instruments. He raced through one idea after another, comparing different tax instruments to options. He had lots of ideas, delivered them quickly, and had a strong presence in the room. I thought he was motivated and smart.

Maybe he was a bully to some, as some journalists surmised. Eric Rosenfeld described Hilibrand's influence:

> Hilibrand is brilliant. He is extremely quick and very convincing. The reason that he had a lot of influence is because he had very influential arguments and lots of experience. He could not just ram his arguments down sixteen very smart people. Everyone weighed in.
>   —Interview with Eric Rosenfeld, September 9, 2011

John Meriwether was often quiet, which some interpreted as antisocial or arrogant. I think he was simply a shy person in many respects. Self-protection may have been important to a guy made famous in Liar's Poker.[13]

I have spoken with other partners over the year, including Robert Merton, Myron Scholes, Hans Hufshmid, Chi-Fu Huang, and Dick Leahy. None of them were arrogant. All of them are busy and some appear very confident, which can both give the impression of arrogance. I always found Eric Rosenfeld quite humble during our many conversations. When I complimented him on fund returns in 1996, he replied, "We have really been lucky. Things have gone better than expected."

Of course, not everyone was hostile or jealous. Many enjoyed their success and admired it as one might admire Einstein's work. Everyone who has ever seriously worked in financial markets has looked for the Holy Grail that consistently makes money. Many people believed LTCM had found it.

CHAPTER 3

Risk Management

Man cannot discover new oceans unless he has the courage to lose sight of the shore.
—André Gide

The General Idea

At the core of LTCM's success was a risk management system intended to enhance the power of LTCM's trade-constructing skills. A portfolio manager might find a good strategy with a high return and low risk and make the trade. LTCM took this idea further by considering potential investments *in combination*, thereby changing the way arbitrage was done. They asked a basic question of their portfolio: If we can find many different arbitrage or relative value strategies that all look individually attractive, might they look even better when combined in a certain way?

Basic statistics tells us that, if lots of individually attractive trades are diverse, meaning that their returns don't move together, a portfolio that contains them all will have a return that's similar to that of the individual trades, but with much lower risk.[1]

The benefits of this combination depend on each trade's expected return, each trade's volatility, and the average correlation between trades. Perhaps the most important part of this construction is the average correlation between trades. If this is close to zero or even negative, the portfolio will have a smaller and smaller volatility as more trades are added.

In finance, we use the symbol ρ to represent correlation. Thus, LTCM tried to find trade combinations with a very low ρ.

A golf analogy may help explain why this works. Both amateur and professional golf players commonly compete in four-ball matches, with each match between two teams of two players. All four players play their own balls throughout the match; at the end of each hole, the lowest score on each team is that team's score.

Which team is likely to win the match? It depends on three things. First, how good is each player? This is analogous to a trade's expected return. If the two golfers on team A are both better than those on team B, they are more likely to win.

Second, how consistent is each golfer? If a golfer is sporadic, it's difficult to predict whether that player's team will win any given match, particularly against a more consistent golfer. This is analogous to a trade's volatility.

Finally, the correlation of the golfer's scores on each hole is very important. A team with two golfers whose performance on any given hole is very correlated is not as attractive as a team with two golfers whose performance is negatively correlated or uncorrelated on any given hole.

This is because both players will make mistakes. On any given hole, when player 1 makes a mistake, ideally player 2 will score well. The winning team has the lowest individual score on the hole, so such a pair may do very well. This is negatively correlated performance and gives a team the best chance of winning. An ideal four-ball pairing combines two very good golfers with high consistency and low or negative performance correlation with each other.

Similarly, LTCM wanted a portfolio of trading strategies that would perform very well with very low risk. They constructed their portfolio with the best trades that they could find—those with high returns and low risk—that had very low correlations to each other. Of course, there is a limit to how many trades LTCM could find with these qualities. They typically searched for about 50 different strategies with these characteristics.

Leverage

Once LTCM found a group of strategies and created a portfolio, that portfolio typically had reasonable average return and risk, plus a very high Sharpe ratio. LTCM traders then leveraged the portfolio, scaling the average return and volatility to a desired level. Leverage amplifies both return and risk. Box 3.1 describes the dangers of leverage.

Box 3.1 Why Is Leverage Dangerous?

Leverage can greatly enhance a portfolio's nonleveraged returns if the portfolio return is greater than the borrowing rate. If the return is less than the borrowing rate, however, leverage amplifies the losses. For example, suppose you invest $100 million in a security, but you borrow half of that, giving you a leverage ratio of 2. At the end of the loan, you will have to pay back $50 million plus interest and you will gain or lose $100 million times the return of the security. Thus, if this investment loses 5%, you actually lose 10% (or $10 million), plus the interest cost on your capital. Leverage multiplies the losses by approximately the amount of the leverage ratio.

Suppose you can borrow at 1% and your portfolio's realized return varies. If your leverage ratio is 5 and the trading portfolio loses 1%, you lose 9%; if the leverage ratio is 25, you lose 49%. If the portfolio loses 5%, then at a leverage ratio of 5, you lose 29%; with a leverage ratio of 25, you lose 149%! In fact, with a 5% loss, any leverage greater than 16.8 would force the fund to go bankrupt, owing more than it has. What's more, lenders may decide to stop lending to a fund, forcing a leveraged portfolio to sell positions, further exacerbating its losses.

Measuring Risk

Measuring risk is difficult. Portfolio returns come from a return distribution. That distribution may include a −100% return, which means losing the entire portfolio. Thus, one way to measure risk is to measure the worst-case scenario: losing everything. That doesn't tell us very much about more typical risks.

A more useful risk measurement uses a portfolio's value-at-risk (VaR). This measure gives an estimate of the largest losses a portfolio is likely to suffer in a given period in all but truly exceptional circumstances. The calculation depends on a host of inputs, including the portfolio's expected return, the portfolio's volatility, and the fund manager's degree of confidence in the largest loss.

Oftentimes the inputs, like the expected return, volatility, and trade correlation, come from historical data. Return distributions are assumed to be normal.[2]

Using these techniques, we could postulate how LTCM's risk might have looked at any time before their 1998 collapse. Suppose LTCM had 50 trading strategies in its portfolio, with an average annual return of 6.70% and an average annual volatility of 2.33%. LTCM measured trade correlations at 0.1. This implies that the entire portfolio, without leverage, would have an expected return of 6.70% with an annual volatility of 0.33%.

This hypothetical portfolio looked very attractive from a risk-adjusted return perspective, but LTCM altered the return-risk profile with leverage. Their leverage ratio at the beginning of 1998 was 28, which created a portfolio with an expected annual return of 35% and an annual volatility of 22%.[3]

A simple VaR calculation shows that, with a leverage ratio of 28, the portfolio's maximum one-month loss would be $58 million. In 99 out of 100 months, the portfolio's loss would not exceed $58 million. One could argue that this was a reasonable amount of risk to assume for a $4.8 billion portfolio.

There is a caveat, however. The average correlations, the ρ, could be higher than LTCM estimated, even as high as 1. In that scenario, the VaR would jump to $1.96 billion over a one-month period and LTCM would lose 40% of the fund.

If actual trade volatility also turned out to be higher than predicted, the losses could be substantially greater. For example, if the correlations between trades rose from 0.1 to 0.3 and the volatility of each trade doubled, the VaR over a one-month period would rise to $2.21 billion.

Correlation was a crucial input in the LTCM risk management system.

The ρ

If the realized correlation, or ρ, is much higher than the predicted ρ, the fund's risk will rise sharply. It is worth examining the components of this correlation.

Economics

Two strategies may be correlated because they are linked in some direct, economic fashion. For example, one-year Treasury yields and two-year Treasury yields are very linked economically. If the Federal Reserve lowers interest rates, then it is likely that yields on both the one-year and the two-year notes will decrease. In fact, yield correlation here is very high, at 0.9947.

It is more difficult to accurately understand economic links between more complex investments. Quite idiosyncratic instruments will be very uncorrelated across regions and continents, but this can change over time as the world becomes more integrated or as underlying economic drivers change. For example, you might not expect housing prices in Ireland and the United States to be correlated. Generally, real estate is a local phenomenon.

But if world interest rates are at an all-time low, this will affect mortgage rates in all countries. That may affect buying, and therefore housing prices, in many countries in exactly the same fashion.

Suppose we use historical data to measure ρ between two trades and find that it is low. We must understand whether economics suggests that it should be low, and we must also postulate the two strategies' economics, both now and over the course of the trade. This isn't easy, but it's important. LTCM used both experience and statistics to measure these correlations.

Copycats, Puppies, and Counterparties

Unlike the physical world, the financial markets obey laws that are not universal. Especially in the short run, the laws depend on other traders' actions.

If I drop a round ball from the Empire State Building, I can accurately measure the time it will hit the ground. If I repeat this experiment hundreds of times, the ball will land at nearly the same moment, every time.

If I measure the price of a particular bond that will definitely pay $100 in one year (assume no default risk), it should trade very close to 100 no matter which reasonable model I use. But if a sufficiently large number of traders don't want to hold that bond, its price could theoretically fall as low as $0.01. Buy the bond at $90 and, even though the expected one-year return is 10%, you'll have a current mark-to-market return of −99.99%.

If you cannot hold this position until maturity, a great trade could turn out to be a horrific trade. The prices in financial markets depend on economic value and on other traders' actions. With rational traders, economic values should be close to perceived values, but if traders act on other constraints or other objective functions, perceived value and economic value may differ greatly. This is not always easy to foresee.

Various market players, including mutual funds, hedge funds, commercial banks, investment banks, and others, have a variety of constraints, perceived values, and goals. As they act on these, they may distort short-term prices.

Three types of players are relevant to LTCM's situation. The first are the *copycats*. These are the vast groups of arbitrage trading funds that began emulating the trading strategies developed by Meriwether and his group at Salomon that were brought with Meriwether to LTCM.[4]

The Salomon arbitrage group, which Meriwether and his boys had left behind, was the first copycat in line. But there were others, including Goldman Sachs Asset Management internal proprietary trading, Convergence Asset Management, which launched in January 1998[5], other proprietary trading groups at other major investment banks, and hedge funds.

The second group is the *puppies*. These are small traders in hedge funds, investment banks, or even mutual fund shops, who saw LTCM's success and tried to place similar trades on a much smaller scale to improve their portfolio's Sharpe ratios. Puppies are typically first to get scared and exit positions. If they know the "big dog" is about to sell a position because of financing constraints, they may not understand the position's value or may have a horizon that is too short to wait for a more usual trading situation. They exit the positions so they don't get clobbered when the major players begin selling.

During August and September 1998, a market saturated in copycats and puppies changed expected risk and caused spreads to move severely against LTCM. Market participants of course understand that they affect other participants, but they may also underestimate the effect they can have on stable relationships across strategies when other players are placing the same types of trades.

Granted, it's very hard to estimate what impact additional players may have. When copycats and puppies began closing positions due to fear and other reasons, a self-fulfilling crisis may have emerged. Copycats and puppies expect others to reduce their positions, and many other traders do just that. This leads to further losses and stress on leveraged positions.

The third group of players is the *counterparties*. These investment banks and other institutions extended lines of credit to LTCM or were the counterparties to some of their over-the-counter transactions, such as swap trades, repo transactions, and other OTC derivatives. These counterparties played important roles in the risks of LTCM's trading positions a variety of ways.

Counterparties can change their behavior to reinforce LTCM's difficulties. A haircut is one way of doing this. In finance, a haircut is a percentage subtracted from the market value of an asset used as collateral. The size of the haircut reflects the perceived risk associated with holding the asset.

For example, a hedge fund has a U.S. Treasury bond that it wishes to use as collateral in a repo transaction. If the bond is worth $100,000, then the counterparty might lend the hedge fund $98,000, taking a 2% haircut. A mortgage-backed security might take a bigger haircut, perhaps 10%. If the hedge fund doesn't pay back the loan, the counterparty will sell the security in the marketplace. The haircut provides some protection against counterparty risk and adjusts for security liquidity.

A counterparty could also raise capital requirements. If a counterparty worries that LTCM's default risk has increased and so raises the capital required for any given transaction on its reset date, this by definition creates greater strain for LTCM, which must either supply the counterparty with more capital or go bankrupt.

If LTCM wished to neutralize or exit a position, any counterparty could mark the trades to a higher-than-market price, leading again to more losses as LTCM attempted to exit or roll over its positions.

A counterparty with a hedged position with LTCM as one of its hedge counterparties may realize that, if LTCM fails or doesn't fulfill its obligation, the hedge won't work. The counterparty may offset its LTCM trade by taking a new position with another counterparty, further exaggerating price movements that happen in the wake of economic shifts or changing fundamental values. An LTCM collapse could create a huge domino effect in the financial markets, even without any net risk to the financial system due to the web of unknown interconnections with counterparties.[6]

When copycats, puppies, and counterparties crowd a trading space, their actions—regardless of the presence or lack of any underlying economic changes—may lead to an increase in correlations across strategies, or even to an increase in any given strategy's individual volatility. By acting together, even inadvertently, these market players can be very powerful.

A collective action and resulting correlative increase could be particularly hard on a company such as LTCM if rumors spread that the company may be in financial trouble. The news will make investors want to exit their trades. Things can be even worse in a general crisis, where all market participants might rush to find liquidity. That causes more forced selling, which increases individual trade volatility for everyone.

LTCM's Actual Risk Management Practices

We've summed up the broad outlines of LTCM's risk management practices. At any given time, LTCM had 50 or more trades in place. According to LTCM partners, individual company trades were sound.[7] The mistakes occurred in LTCM's portfolio construction.

Diversification

LTCM typically considered two types of correlations between strategies: short-term correlations and long-term correlations.

Company traders assumed that its portfolio's long-term correlation numbers were very low, because the trades were very diverse economically. Short-term correlations were higher, they believed, due to their dependence on other players and on price movements that had more to do with herd trading mentalities and less to do with economic fundamentals.

The firm measured the correlation of these strategies at about 0.1, and sometimes even lower, over the prior five years. Despite this, they typically ran their risk management models with a correlation as high as 0.3, to provide a level of safety.[8]

LTCM did not run models with an even higher correlation because they believed that, even in the short run, there was a limit to how high these correlations could be. They assumed that, if trades moved too far away from their fundamentals, other risk arbitrageurs would rush in. In 1998, they learned that this assumption was wrong. During every day of August and September, every one of these so-called diversified, unrelated trades lost money.[9]

In addition to using its broad risk management framework, LTCM also performed stress tests to help it guess how individual events might affect the portfolio. The company tested for a huge stock market crash, a government bond default, a currency devaluation, and other hypothetical events.

LTCM purchased insurance on risks that were hard to hedge. For example, in 1995 LTCM had a large swap position in Italian government bonds. Traders worried that the Italian government might default, so they purchased a credit default swap (CDS) to protect their position.

Operations

LTCM had a few other risk management practices. Realizing that their business was primarily about the convergence of trades over a longer time horizon, they called the firm Long-Term Capital Management and required investors to lock up their money for three years. That reduces liquidity, something investors generally dislike. However, in this case it was in the investor's best interest, because redemptions could mean selling potentially profitable positions at a loss to all fund investors.

LTCM typically held a large fraction of its equity capital as excess liquidity, parked in cash and short-term government securities. This was the result of LTCM's working capital discipline, which sought to avoid the need to liquidate positions in case of adverse financing conditions in all markets.

LTCM tried to match their financing to trades' expected duration, rather than depending on shorter-term financing that would require a rollover, subjecting the firm to counterparties' whims. For example, if a trade was expected to converge in three months, LTCM tried to finance the trade with a three-month contract, arranging these contracts as far as six months out in a practice called *term-financing*. (Counterparties wouldn't usually accept further-out contracts.)

LTCM had two-way, mark-to-market provisions on all its over-the-counter contracts. This avoided any need to shut down a profitable trade because of one-sided margin calls. A trader might be short interest rates on one side of a position and long interest rates on the other side of the position. If overall interest rates decline, one side of the position loses money and the other side makes money. If the margin were marked to market on only one side of the trade, the trader would have a financing problem—even though the trade had not lost money.

This problem famously caused the Metallgesellschaft failure in 1993. Traders built an oil arbitrage in longer-dated oil forward contracts and hedged the position by rolling over short-term oil futures contracts. The latter require daily mark-to-market on the futures exchange, but the former do not. As the price of oil moved against them, the traders had to meet margin calls on the futures, without receiving any profits from the forwards, which were not marked to market. This precipitated Metallgesellschaft's collapse.[10]

LTCM created emergency credit lines to use if markets slid into temporary chaos and traders required additional capital.[11]

Twelve LTCM partners, who were also on the management committee, made up the firm's risk management committee. LTCM partners later admitted that it might have been better to have a separate group offering independent risk monitoring of the trade portfolio.

Overall, though, LTCM's risk management structure was well thought out and ahead of its time in many respects. Its major weakness was in the assumption that correlations were unlikely to move higher than 0.3. Events would prove this wrong, even though there had been sensible reasons to assume this correlation ceiling. Ultimately, LTCM underestimated the behavior and consequences of copycats in crowded spaces.

The Raw Evidence

LTCM's partners believed that the firm's system maintained and controlled its risk. They leveraged their portfolio to achieve a target volatility of around 20%, similar to the S&P 500. The actual realized volatility of the fund's gross returns before August 1998 was 13.64% annually. In other words, before the Russian and LTCM crises, LTCM's realized volatility was lower than its stated target. Table 3.1 shows the standard deviation of daily profit and loss in millions of dollars, as well as the monthly net and gross return volatility.

LTCM's return volatility was highest in 1994 and was lower from 1995 to 1997. It spiked dramatically during the extreme losses of 1998. The annualized monthly return volatility in 1998 was 95%. There was no evidence before

TABLE 3.1 Actual Volatility of LTCM's Daily and Monthly Returns

	Entire Period	Before Crisis	1994	1995	1996	1997	1998
Daily P/L[a]	53.66	38.64	17.78	32.97	41.54	46.68	94.85
Monthly[b]	239.98	172.79	79.51	147.45	185.77	208.78	424.19
Annualized	851.83	613.35	282.23	523.40	659.42	741.09	1505.71
Monthly Gross Returns[c]	13.46	3.94	4.80	2.45	3.68	2.28	27.65
Annualized	46.61	13.64	16.61	8.50	12.76	7.90	95.80
Monthly Net Returns	13.15	3.23	3.65	1.88	2.80	1.71	27.53
Annualized	45.55	11.20	12.65	6.52	9.69	5.91	95.37

[a]P/L stands for profit and loss. These are the standard deviations of daily profit and loss in millions of dollars.
[b]The monthly standard deviations are computed by taking the daily standard deviation and multiplying by $\sqrt{20}$ and the yearly standard deviations are computed by multiplying the daily standard deviation by $\sqrt{252}$.
[c]The monthly gross and net returns are annualized by multiplying the monthly standard deviation by $\sqrt{12}$. Before Crisis is estimated from February 1994 to July 31, 1998.

August 1998 that suggested that LTCM was taking risk higher than what it had told investors.

Although many people later claimed that LTCM had a ridiculous amount of leverage, the company's leverage was consistently between 20 to 30 before the collapse. Figure 3.1 shows LTCM's actual leverage.

The company's leverage does show some patterns over time. During this period, the peak leverage was 31 in March 1996 and the absolute balance sheet peak was $139 billion in May 1996. Within a given year, leverage typically declined over time as returns accumulated within the fund. On the last day of each year the firm gave investors the right to receive a dividend, which altered the firm's leverage. Note the large jump in leverage at the end of 1997, when LTCM returned a large amount of capital to investors, pushing leverage from 18.3 to 27.7. This was still less than the firm's highest leverage—31.2—seen in 1996.

Only during August and September 1998 did LTCM report extreme leverage, causing many to accuse LTCM of carelessness. High leverage was a

FIGURE 3.1 LTCM Monthly Leverage from March 1994 to December 1997

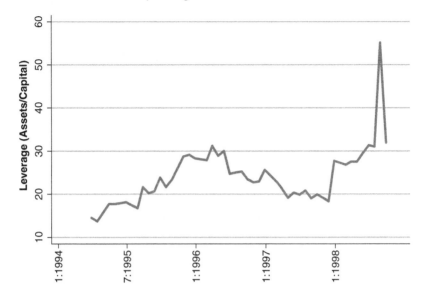

direct result of the accelerated equity depreciation. Leverage increased to 55 at the end of August and was even higher during some days in September, but returned to 32 by the end of September in response to new capital.

LTCM's leverage ratios and financing terms were similar to those of other institutions involved in capital market intermediation. These institutions included wholesale securities firms, capital market-oriented banks, and some units of insurance companies and finance companies.

Table 3.2 compares, as of end 1997, consolidated balance sheet leverage and off-balance-sheet notionals for LTCM's fund and two other institutions of roughly similar size: a major wholesale securities firm (Lehman Brothers) and a major capital-market-oriented bank (Bankers Trust).[12] These two institutions showed similar leverage ratios and greater total gross notionals.

LTCM's balance sheet looked enormous, but it was very similar in size to balance sheets at other banks, including Morgan Stanley. The main differences between these banks and LTCM was that LTCM concentrated its positions in government securities and repos, while the other banks owned a more diverse list of security types.

Repos are agreements in which a financial firm borrows money from another bank and puts up collateral, making the loan cheaper. LTCM used the repo market to borrow funds that it used to purchase both Treasury and mortgage-backed securities.

TABLE 3.2 Consolidated Balance Sheet of LTCM, Lehman Brothers, Bankers Trust

| Assets | Value LTCM (MM $) | Percent of Total Assets | | |
		LTCM (%)	Lehman (%)	Bankers (%)
Cash	1,071	0.83	1.87	5.60
Government and Agency Securities	61,965	47.96	21.78	7.88
Equities	1,331	1.03	7.17	5.65
Corporate Debt Securities	692	0.54	7.18	5.80
Mortgage and Mortgage-Backed Securities	640	0.50	7.55	0.00
Derivatives and Other Contractuals	2,903	2.25	5.51	12.61
Money Market and Other Instruments	0	0.00	1.48	14.20
Reverse Repurchase Agreements	56,720	43.90	28.74	13.68
Securities Borrowed	0	0.00	9.32	11.96
Receivables from Brokers, Customers, and Others	3,890	3.01	8.46	4.97
Other Assets	2	0.00	0.94	17.65
Total Assets	129,214	100.00	100.00	100.00
Liabilities and Equity				
Government Securities Sold Short	48,394	37.45	10.68	3.13
Equities Sold Short	591	0.46	2.83	3.76
Corporate Debt Securities Sold Short	49	0.04	1.46	0.00
Money Market Instruments and Other Sold Short	0	0.00	5.15	0.37
Derivatives and Other Contractuals	7,906	6.12	4.86	12.16
Repurchase Agreements and Securities Borrowed	60,597	46.90	46.83	12.75
Payables to Brokers, Customers, and Others	6,429	4.98	9.13	5.11

TABLE 3.2 *(Continued)*

Liabilities and Equity	Value LTCM (MM $)	Percent of Total Assets		
		LTCM (%)	Lehman (%)	Bankers (%)
Long-Term Debt	580	0.45	13.36	10.40
Short-Term Debt	0	0.00	0.00	13.95
Other Liabilities	0	0.00	2.71	34.15
Total Liabilities	124,546	96.39	97.02	95.78
Equity Capital	4,668	3.61	2.98	4.22
T.L. and E.C.	129,214	100.00	100.00	100.00
Leverage		**28**	**34**	**24**
Off-Balance Sheet Items				
Interest Rate and Fixed-Income Derivatives	1,189,322	9.2	8.73	8.16
Foreign Exchange Derivatives	28,606	0.22	3.157	5.8
Equity Derivatives	34,942	0.27	0.267	0.41
Other	0	0	0.068	0.08
Total Gross Notional Amount	1,252,870	9.69	12.22	14.448

The balance sheets are as of December 1997 for both Bankers Trust and LTCM, and as of November 1997 for Lehman Brothers.
Sources: LTCM and company financial statements.

LTCM had $1.2 trillion total in off-balance-sheet items. Its ratio of off-balance-sheet items to total assets was smaller than the same ratio at Lehman Brothers and Bankers Trust. Many of the off-balance-sheet items contained "dead swaps," or "immunized" instruments, which have only a small directional risk.[13]

The Basel Committee publishes regulatory guidelines for bank risk levels.[14] These guidelines are for individual countries' regulatory bodies. In the United States, the Federal Reserve requires that bank holding companies hold a minimum level of capital.[15] Measuring a bank's capital-to-asset ratio helps predict its stability, in that a bank with more capital will find it easier to stay solvent in the face of investment losses.

Table 3.3 compares the total risk-weighted capital ratio (total capital divided by risk-weighted assets), Tier 1 capital ratio (equity divided by assets), and leverage ratio (total capital divided by total assets) for LTCM versus other major institutions at the end of 1997. In terms of total risk-based capital and Tier 1 risk-based capital, LTCM had a much higher ratio than did some very well-known financial institutions. LTCM's risk-based capital ratio was also higher than the average of all bank holding companies (20% versus 12%). However, LTCM's leverage ratio was on the low side (3.61%)

TABLE 3.3   LTCM's Risk-Based Capital versus Other Institutions

Institution	Total CR	Tier 1 CR	Leverage Ratio
J.P. Morgan[a]	11.90	8.00	4.40
First Chicago NBD	11.70	7.90	7.80
Bank America	11.56	7.53	6.81
Bankers Trust[a]	14.10	8.30	4.40
Chase Manhattan	11.64	7.90	6.03
Deutsche Bank[b]	10.60	N.A.	N.A.
Long-Term Capital Portfolio, LP	20.49	20.49	3.61[c]
BHC Minimum Requirements[d]	8.00	4.00	3–5
Average of All BHCs[e]	12.00	9.00	7.10

Note: The Total CR is the risk-weighted total capital ratio. The Tier 1 CR is the Tier 1 capital ratio. The Leverage Ratio is the firm's equity capital divided by the value of total assets.
[a]Earlier adopter of the market-risk component of the risk-based capital measure of the capital adequacy requirements.
[b]Deutsche Bank is subject to German regulatory capital adequacy guidelines and the European Community Capital Adequacy Directives.
[c]LTCM's capital at the end of 1997 was $4.668 billion and its total assets were $129 billion, giving a leverage ratio of 3.61%. Prior to the dividend distribution of $2.7B, its capital ratio was 5.70%.
[d]BHC stands for Bank Holding Company.
[e]Average of BHCs from Hirtle (1998) and the other data from LTCM.

compared to several other banking institutions and to the average of all bank holding companies (7.10%). Had LTCM not returned capital to investors at the end of 1997, its capital ratio would have been 5.70%—much more in line with other investment banks. In some respects LTCM's capital ratios looked solid to regulators. After paying a large investor dividend, however, the firm's leverage ratio was on the low side, but still greater than regulated minimums.

LTCM's risk management involved measuring portfolio risk based on the economic and statistical links between trades. It also looked for solid operational structures designed to efficiently handle short-term cash flows. LTCM's risk management system did not consider the link between trade correlation and crowding levels in particular trades, which could stress even a sound operational system.

How did LTCM select and execute individual trades? The answer reveals much about both LTCM and the pressures that brought about its downfall. It's to this detail that we now turn.

CHAPTER 4

The Trades

As a portfolio management company, LTCM was characterized by its trades: a group of apparently diversified positions with very small absolute returns, even smaller variance, and very low correlations with one another. This strategy gave them three distinct advantages over their competition.

LTCM selected trades that had very small absolute returns. Many market players, including large institutional traders and money managers, avoid these trades altogether. A dearth of trading left some natural mispricing in these securities. To make the absolute return attractive to investors, LTCM had to use substantial leverage. Some people refer to this strategy as "picking up nickels in front of a steamroller."

Many of LTCM's trades required simple, clever mathematics to strip out unknown risks and focus on the arbitrage. Investors typically take on all trade risks. Buy a company that exports most of its goods to another country, for instance, and you'll take the fall if the company is poorly managed or the exchange rate shifts, but not in your favor. To focus on just the management risk, an investor uses other transactions to take the foreign exchange rate risk out of the trade. LTCM worked to remove the risks that didn't interest them, or on which they didn't hold strong opinions. In doing this, LTCM traders' mathematical abilities and experience gave them a comparative advantage over other investors.

LTCM constructed very creative financing terms. It profited from trades that looked impossible from a conventional lending perspective because they found clever ways to finance their deals.

LTCM's repo swap arrangement is just one example of the firm's creative financing techniques. Just as banks won't lend a home owner a home's full value, hedge funds can't typically borrow the full value of their collateral in a repo swap. The difference between the loan amount and the collateral value is called a haircut, and it's based on the deal's perceived risk and the collateral's likely liquidity. Before LTCM launched its fund, it negotiated hard to get zero-haircut swap transactions from its counterparties. That let LTCM make margin trades that would have been unaffordable for other hedge funds.

The Japanese warrant trade illustrates another clever LTCM financing idea. The 1990s saw some incredibly cheap Japanese warrants associated with small-cap Japanese stocks. (A warrant is an option to buy company stock at a fixed rate for a set amount of time. It's often associated with a company's preferred stock or bonds.) The warrants traded at a lower price than they would be worth if exercised.

There were institutional reasons that the warrants were cheap. Japanese companies issued debt with warrants attached. The warrants traded actively in Switzerland, but the stock traded only in Japan. Many of these companies had done quite well, so their stock prices went up. Warrant owners wanted to exercise the warrants and take their profits. To do that, though, they would have to exercise the warrant in Switzerland, then sell the stock in Japan. It was easier to just sell the warrants in the Swiss market at a price that reflected the hassle of exercising them.

As the warrants were trading at less than their intrinsic value, an arbitrage firm might have bought the warrants and short sold the related stocks. The strategy could have worked in the United States, but it was difficult to borrow these small-cap Japanese stocks, and to short sell a stock that it doesn't own, a firm has to borrow it first.

LTCM came up with an exact solution. It bought a basket of small-cap stocks in the JASDAQ (Japanese Association of Securities Dealers Automated Quotations Index) with cheap associated warrants and shorted the JASDAQ futures contract. The hedge wasn't a perfect one, because LTCM's short position was on the whole index, and the basket was only a subset of Japanese stocks.

So LTCM made a total return stock swap with another bank. The bank paid LTCM the return on the basket of the other stocks in the JASDAQ and

LTCM paid the bank 30 basis points. The resulting trade had zero risk and essentially no profit or loss, apart from transaction costs and the 30 basis-point financing cost.

Then LTCM borrowed the Japanese stocks *from themselves* and shorted them while also buying the associated cheap warrants. This innovative financing scheme let LTCM borrow nonborrowable stocks and take advantage of an arbitrage opportunity. They called it *index art*.

LTCM's portfolio consisted mainly of fixed-income trades with a smaller fraction in equity-related trades.[1] The firm tended to group trades into two broad themes: *relative value* trades and *convergence* trades. Both types typically involved being long one security and short another security, so as to hedge out various risks. In both trade types, LTCM typically believed that it had identified one or more overvalued securities, which traders would short, and one or more undervalued securities, which traders would go long.

Convergence misvaluations were expected to correct themselves within a specified time frame. Relative value trade misvaluations might or might not correct themselves, and by no specific date.

For example, a convergence trade might involve buying bond A and selling bond B. Bond A was currently much cheaper than bond B. On a specific future date, however, a legal system change would give bond A the same characteristics—and the same trading price—as bond B.

In a situation where bonds A and B are very similar but bond A is cheaper, a relative value trade might involve buying bond A and selling bond B. The reasons that bond A is trading lower than bond B are expected to die out over time, but not by any particular, known date.

In addition to these bread-and-butter trades, LTCM also took *directional* bets, which are common among long-only portfolio managers. A trader might be long Russian bonds, thus taking a direct bet on the behavior of Russian interest rates.

Table 4.1 shows the majority of LTCM's August 1998 positions, which consisted of multiple trades under a general strategy. At that time the short U.S. swap spread, the European cross-swap trade, and the short volatility trade were by far LTCM's largest trades.

Many of these trades had both a liquid component and an illiquid component. (A liquid security is one that can easily be bought and sold near its last traded price, such as a Treasury bond. An illiquid security is one that might be hard to buy or sell; its purchase price may move significantly from the last quoted price.)

TABLE 4.1   The LTCM Portfolio in August 1998

Trade	Name	Trade Type	Profitable When:[a]
	Interest Rate Related Trades		
1.	**U.S. Short Swap**	C	U.S. Swap spread narrows.
2.	**Euro Cross Swap**	C	Euro Swap spread minus UK swap spread to increase.
3.	Long U.S. Mortgages	RV	Mortgage spread narrows or remains constant.
4.	Swap Curve Japan	RV	10-year swap spread minus 7-year swap to decrease.
5.	Italian Swap Spread	C	Italian swap spread narrows.
6.	Fixed-Income Vol.	RV	Long-term volatility rises relative to short-term volatility.
7.	On-the-Run	C	On-the-run bonds cheapen versus off-the-run bonds.
	Equity Related Trades		
8.	**Short Equity Vol.**	RV	Long-term volatility rises relative to short-term volatility.
9.	Risk Arb Portfolio	C	Company merger deals complete.
10.	Equity Rel. Value	C	Mispriced securities converge.
	Directional		
11.	Emerging Market	D	Interest rates on Brazilian C bonds and Russian Euro bonds decline.
12.	Other	D	Included short some high-tech stocks, closed-end fund strategies, convertible and preferred strategies, currency trades, index arbitrage, high-yield, index inclusion trades, and yield curve trades.

Note: LTCM positions as of August 1998. Data obtained from a combination of Perold (2000) and conversations with former LTCM partners. The largest trades are in bold. C represents convergence trades, RV represents relative value trades, and D represents directional trades.
[a]Many trades made money if the respective instruments' relative values did not change.

The Short U.S. Swap Trade

LTCM traders made many swap trades during the firm's lifetime. A plain vanilla interest-rate swap is a basic transaction in which one party agrees to pay a floating interest rate to another party over a specific time period, and the other party agrees to pay a fixed interest rate over the same specific time period.

Of course, LTCM traders didn't use the vanilla version. They made money on the swap spread: the difference between a swap interest yield that represents the cost of borrowing between banks, and the government bond yield, which is the government's cost of borrowing.

This spread varies over time depending on the economic climate, the types of investors in the marketplace, and various investment cycles. Figure 4.1 shows the 10-year swap spread in the United States since 1991. This represents the difference in yield between 10-year swaps and 10-year U.S. treasury bonds. The figure also shows the spread's 3-year and 1-year moving averages.

FIGURE 4.1 The Historical Behavior of U.S. 10-Year Swap Spread

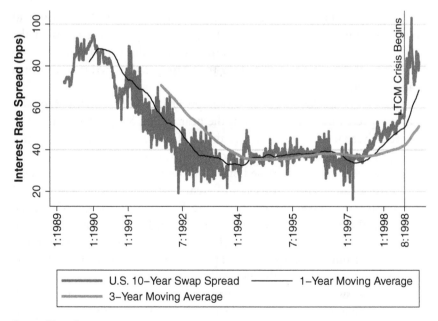

Source: Bloomberg.

LTCM typically used swap trades at various maturities, from 1-year all the way to 30-year maturity, and might be long or short the swap spread at any given time, depending on their models and other motivations. (A long swap trade profits when swap spreads widen; a short swap spread trade profits when swap spreads narrow.[2]) LTCM partners referred to a long swap spread as a view that swaps are expensive relative to treasuries. A short swap spread, by contrast, is often considered a view that swaps are cheap versus treasuries.

Depending on marketplace interest rates, a swap spread trade can offer attractive returns.

A bond portfolio manager might look at a swap spread of 50 basis points, expect that it will widen further, and so go long the swap spread. LTCM typically looked at LIBOR versus repo before making that trade, and might have avoided it if the expected financing gains were too small compared with the spread.[3] (A repo transaction is collateralized lending: One party lends cash to another party in exchange for a bond. The repo rate is the interest rate LTCM paid on the cash it borrowed in exchange for a bond offered to a counterparty as collateral. LIBOR is an acronym for the London Interbank Offer Rate. This is the interest rate that LTCM received on the swap in a long swap spread transaction.) If the spread between received LIBOR and paid-out repo stays wide, the trade is more profitable, even if the swap spread moves against the position.

LTCM traders considered how they thought the LIBOR-repo spread would evolve over time, as this would create future financing terms. If the LIBOR traded above repo and LTCM believed that this would continue into the foreseeable future, then going long the swap spread looked favorable on a financing basis.

Next, LTCM asked why the swap spread was at its current level and what it expected the spread to do in the near future. Swaps were marked to market daily, so if the trade moved against LTCM, traders could hold it until convergence as long as they could pay the daily margin calls.

If the swap spread remained steady throughout the life of the trade, LTCM made the positive carry (the difference between LIBOR and repo). If the swap spread widened over the trade's life, LTCM made the spread plus the gains from the widening. If the spread narrowed, LTCM made the positive carry, but lost on the spread on a mark-to-market basis. But if LTCM could hold the trade until maturity, the final profit and loss would be related to the financing carry. These were the basics of the long swap spread trade.

The short swap spread trade's return is approximately equal to the spread, minus financing, minus the spread change. Typically the swap spread is positive and the financing involves paying LIBOR and receiving the reverse repo rate. Because the reverse repo rate is usually less than LIBOR, short swap spread financing is typically negative. The spread change can be negative or positive, depending on what actually happens to the spread over time.[4] If the swap spread widens, the short swap spread trade loses. If the swap spread narrows, the swap spread trade gains. Suppose the initial swap spread was 17 basis points and that repo minus LIBOR was −20 basis points. The trade would have what LTCM called negative carry: Regardless of the spread change, spread minus financing equals −3 basis points. If nothing happens, the trade loses 3 basis points per year.

If the swap spread narrowed, as traders expected, then LTCM could unwind the trade at a profit. If the spread did not change, LTCM would lose the small negative carry amount, multiplied over time.

The trade carried two risks. First, if LIBOR rose dramatically over repo, then trade financing would become more expensive, costing more than 3 basis points per year. Second, if the swap spread widened, rather than narrowed, LTCM's two-way mark-to-market would force the firm to supply additional cash to one side of the transaction. With sufficient capital, however, they could hold the trade until the spread became favorable again, until they could no longer bear the losses, or until maturity.[5] In theory, this trade cost LTCM just the interim financing plus the initial spread, but it required the firm to hold the position until maturity. If the swap spread widened by a large amount and the company could not continue financing the trade, LTCM would lose a lot.

As an example, consider a one-year short swap spread trade, a swap with one year-end payment, a one-year repo, and a shorted one-year Treasury bond. The swap spread could widen enormously in that year. If LTCM could make all the mark-to-market margin calls, however, then by year's end it would have paid just the initial swap spread and the financing cost. In this example, the firm would lose 3 basis points.

This was the reason that LTCM tried to structure swap spread trades with *term repos*. Typical repo transactions are done overnight and are rolled over every day, by mutual counterparty consent. LTCM knew that its business relied on convergence and wanted to minimize financing problems caused by adverse circumstances, so it secured long-term financing. Ideally, it would have wanted to finance for a maturity close to that of its trades, but this was not available in the marketplace. Instead, the firm contracted term repos of three and six months, far longer than the norm.

LTCM generally had two-way mark-to-market on this trade, so that if rising interest rates forced the firm to put cash into the swap half of the trade, LTCM would receive this cash from the repo side of the trade (provided repo rates also went up). The company's only cash flow exposure was to the swap spread movements. With counterparties typically requiring zero haircuts, this trade usually required no cash outlay, making it even more attractive than it would be to a typical bond manager.

LTCM used both long and short swap spread trades. The long swap trade was better in several ways. It usually had positive carry, and its worst-case scenario was one in which swap rates converged to treasury rates. A short swap trade was more risky. It typically had a negative carry and, in theory, its spread could widen indefinitely. LTCM began August 1998 with a large position in short U.S. swap spreads.

Did this trade make sense in August 1998? Figure 4.1 shows the 10-year swap spread in the U.S. bond market.

By January 1, 1998, the 10-year swap spread had widened to 55 basis points, higher than the 3-year average of 42 basis points and the 1-year average of 46 basis points.[6] It made some sense to short the swap spread, but the trade wasn't wildly attractive, particularly given its negative financing.[7]

By August 4, 1998, the spread was 65.8 basis points. Since 1991, only five other days had a spread greater than this: 67 basis points on May 30, 1991; 68 basis points on June 28, 1991; 71 basis points on November 7, 1991; 68 basis points on December 31, 1991; and 68 basis points on January 1, 1992. LTCM likely thought that the spread would narrow, as it had in the past.

That didn't happen. On September 18, 1998, the 10-year spread was at 97 basis points.[8]

This short swap trade caused LTCM large losses. In noncrisis circumstances, this may have been a good trade, depending on the spread and expected LIBOR-repo evolution. During crises, however, markets clamor for liquidity, and this is generally not a good trade.

The European Cross-Country Swap Trade (Short UK and Long Europe)

In 1998, LTCM believed that European swap spreads were too narrow, compared with United Kingdom swap spreads. The firm wanted a position that would let it profit from this view. It accomplished this with a combination of swap spread trades in different currencies.

LTCM constructed a position short UK swap spreads and long both German and French swap spreads. The trade made money if the difference between UK spreads and European spreads narrowed. The key was the relative value, not the swap spreads' overall direction.

The company used both economic logic and statistical analysis to choose this trade. In 1998, the single European currency was coming around the corner. Bond market prices reflected market optimism about the change, and UK spreads had widened quite a bit relative to European swap spreads. LTCM believed that the relative movement was overdone.

In early 1998, the UK swap spreads traded around 48 basis points; a combination of German and French spreads traded at about 23 basis points, a difference of 25 basis points (see Figure 4.2). By the beginning of August 1998, the spread was still high at 23 basis points. Since 1995 the average spread had been 10 basis points and the spread's daily standard deviation had been 8 basis points. The spread had reached its largest value prior to 1998—24 basis points—on September 4, 1997. The spread's short history indicated that it was trading at its high end, and that combined with LTCM's views about the Euro to persuade them of the trade's merits.

The Russian crisis, when Russia defaulted on its debt and devalued its currency, had a disproportionate effect on the UK spreads. By October 5, 1998, the spread was 71 basis points. LTCM's large position took enormous losses.

FIGURE 4.2 The Historical Behavior of the 10-Year UK Swap Spread versus the Europe Swap Spread

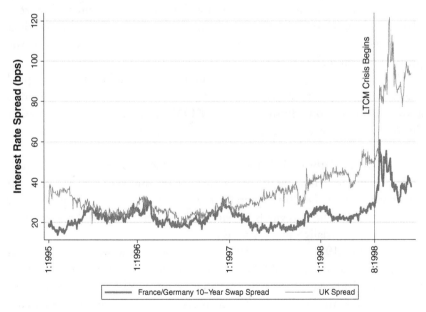

Source: Bloomberg.

Long U.S. Mortgage Securities Hedged

For relative-value hedge funds, trading a collateral-backed bond versus a Treasury bond is a staple trade. A collateral-backed bond is any bond that has underlying collateral supporting its payment: a mortgage, credit card, or automobile, for example.

LTCM typically used mortgage-backed securities. The firm would go long on mortgage securities such as bonds issued by Freddie (FHLMC), Fannie (FNMA), or Ginnie (GNMA) or a bond backed by a pool of mortgages.[9] LTCM hedged the interest rate risk by shorting some other security, such as Treasuries or swaps.[10]

The trade was essentially a short spread trade but with a spread equaling the mortgage yield minus either the government yield or the swap yield. LTCM was typically short this spread trade because a pool of mortgage bonds typically has a higher yield than do either LIBOR or Treasury bonds. That gave traders a positive yield pickup for an instrument that was in effect backed by the U.S. government.[11]

Mortgage-backed securities have higher yields than other securities for several reasons. They offer a premium to investors who take on credit risk. The underlying mortgage borrowers may default on their loans and cause losses for the mortgage-backed security's owner.

These yields are also higher because the bond can be prepaid, particularly when interest rates decline and many home owners refinance their mortgages. In that situation, an investor receives less than the bond's true price appreciation.[12]

LTCM used proprietary prepayment models to adjust mortgage pool yields to account for estimated prepayment risk. The remaining spread is known as the option-adjusted spread, or OAS. LTCM determined whether the bonds were cheap or expensive after considering them on an option-adjusted basis.

LTCM regularly traded this spread from 1994 to 1998, because these trades, even after adjusting for prepayment, were quite attractive. Figure 4.3 shows the Freddie Mac 30-year and Fannie Mae 30-year mortgage spreads over Treasury yields. The two yields are virtually the same because the companies are offering essentially the same product.

From June 1996 to August 1998, the average spread was 55 basis points with a standard deviation of 5 basis points, making this trade very attractive. As long as yields stayed constant, a trader could make 55 basis points with very low risk, as the Freddie and Fannie mortgage pools were both very secure

FIGURE 4.3 The Option-Adjusted Spread of Freddie Mac and Fannie Mae Mortgages over Treasuries by Maturity

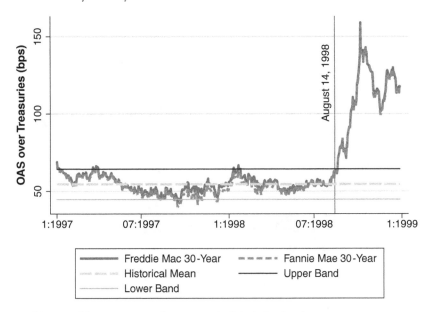

Note: Upper and Lower represent the two standard deviation bands.
Source: Bloomberg.

and implicitly backed by the U.S. government.[13] If the spread declined, traders made an even larger return. LTCM might close out the position and realize the profit immediately or even take the opposite position and go long the spread.

By August 1998, the spread was at 55 basis points, around its two-year historical average. Its highest two-year point was 69 basis points and the typical movement was 5 basis points. LTCM held a short spread position, looking forward to an attractive profit with very little risk. LTCM's financing arrangements were such that, even if the spread widened a little, the trade would eventually make money if the company held onto it.

Unfortunately, a mortgage-market tsunami struck in August and September 1998, and LTCM suffered tremendously on this trade. By August 31, 1998, the spread had moved to 84 basis points. On September 22, the spread was at 111 basis points.

How did this happen? Did LTCM rely on too short a horizon to measure trade risk? Or were these highly unusual mortgage spread jumps? Often

FIGURE 4.4   The 30-Year Mortgage Rate Minus 30-Year Treasury Rate

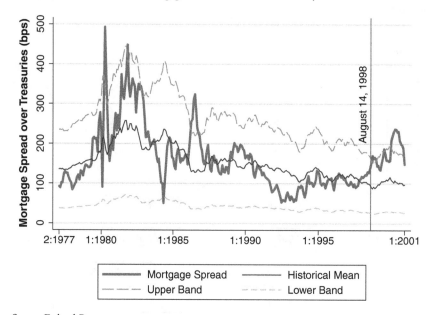

Source: Federal Reserve.

financial innovations don't offer a long history with which to measure risk. This was the case with OAS spreads.

To get a better sense of how mortgage spreads behaved over time, compare 30-year conventional mortgage rates to 30-year constant maturity Treasury bills from 1977 forward. The juxtaposition shows that, from the middle of July 1998 to the end of December 1999, the monthly mortgage spread rose by two standard deviations. (See Figure 4.4.)[14]

According to this longer-term measure, the spread increase was large, but not as large as it seemed when compared against a shorter horizon.[15]

The Box Spread in Japan

LTCM's models indicated that the three-year swap spread seven years forward in Japan was too high. Traders constructed a position that reflected their prediction that the 10-year swap spreads would tighten versus the 7-year swap spreads.[16]

The overall trade was hedged against general interest-rate movements and focused on taking the specific relative value bet—the change in the relative swap spreads—that interested LTCM. In relative value lingo, this trade was known as being short the box spread.[17] The trade can be accomplished by going short the 10-year swap spread and going long the 7-year swap spread. Or one could do the opposite, known as being long the box spread.[18]

Figure 4.5 is a graph of the 10-year Japanese swap spread minus the 7-year Japanese swap spread. It shows that the 10-year spread increased significantly versus the 7-year spread from July 1997 to July 1998, and was also higher than both the 1-year and 3-year moving averages. To LTCM, this spread looked rich. For this and other reasons, they shorted the box, making a trade that would make money if the spread decreased.

The major risk of this trade was that the relative spread of the 10-year minus the 7-year could widen, rather than narrowing or remaining constant. Even if the spread remained constant, this trade had positive carry.

In August and September 1998, this trade went against LTCM—just like all the others. The spread was around 1 basis point on July 28, 1998. By September 30, it was out to 18 basis points.

FIGURE 4.5 The Historical Behavior of the 10-Year Swap Spread Minus the 7-Year Swap Spread in Japan

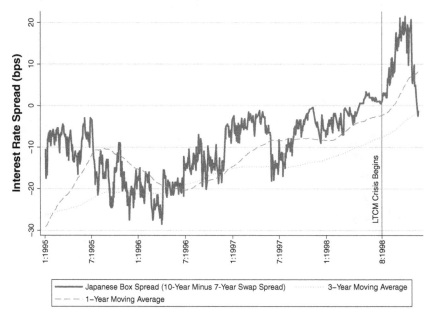

Source: Bloomberg.

The Italian Swap Spread

The Italian bond market has always differed a little from most fixed-income markets. The long end of the Italian yield curve often trades at odds with conventional pricing.

Swap yields are usually higher than government bond yields, because investors require compensation for taking the credit risk associated with swaps. In the 1990s, Italian swap yields were lower than Italian government bond yields, also known as Buoni del Tesoro Poliennali or BTPs (see Figure 4.6).

There were some logical reasons for this. The long end of the Italian market was not as actively traded as is the U.S. debt market, so its pricing was less efficient than that of both the U.S. long bond market and the Italian swap market. Investors expected to be paid for taking on political risk. Italy has always carried a large debt, and there is some uncertainty about its interest rate payments.

Perhaps most importantly, Italy levied a 12.5% withholding tax on foreign owners of Italian bonds. Owners could recover the withholding tax by filing

FIGURE 4.6   The Historical Behavior of the 10-Year Italian Swap Spread

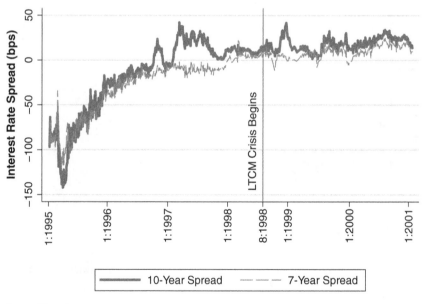

Source: Bloomberg.

the right forms, but many institutions found this a hassle and didn't bother. That left friction in the marketplace.

LTCM constructed an institutional arrangement that let the firm go short the swap spread. The trade offered a constant income stream from the higher yield on Italian bonds. As this anomalous spread converged, traders would turn a profit on the converging spread. It was a beautiful trade that other firms had also discovered.

The Italian government announced in March 1995 that it would suspend this withholding tax. The trade converged. In 1997, the tax was eliminated and the market has traded more or less normally since then.

> It was one of our biggest trades in the early 1990s. We weren't the only ones doing this, virtually everyone was doing this trade. By 1998, our positions in this trade were small.
> —Interview with Eric Rosenfeld, October 4, 2011

LTCM's Italian tango didn't end after the lucrative tax arbitrage trade. Even in 1997, the Italian 7-year maturity bonds were still trading at a discount to the swap. In the 3-month area of the curve, Italian swaps were trading much higher than short-term Italian government bonds (BOT or Buoni Ordinari del Tesoro). LTCM believed that, with time, this anomaly would also disappear as the Euro replaced the lira in 1999 and as Italian capital markets grew more efficient.

Reflecting this belief, LTCM entered into a short swap spread trade, one that was slightly more complicated than a typical swap spread trade. The firm entered into an OTC swap contract with a counterparty in which both parties paid each other a floating interest rate, which varied according to market conditions. LTCM paid the counterparty LIBOR and the counterparty paid LTCM the Italian government yield plus 40 basis points.[19]

If the spread tightened over time, LTCM would make money. It could also unwind the swap transaction and realize an immediate profit.

Suppose LTCM initiated the swap contract on January 22, 1998. On this date the spread was around 40 basis points. The 3-month LIBOR was 6.08% and the 3-month BOT was 5.68%.

According to the swap agreement, LTCM paid the counterparty the current LIBOR rate and the counterparty paid LTCM the Italian bond rate plus 40 basis points. At the beginning date, the trade had a net value of zero, because LTCM paid and received the same interest.

Now suppose that over time, as LTCM expected, the LIBOR-BOT spread narrowed. LTCM would receive more than it paid in interest. LTCM could then hold on to the agreement and receive an ongoing income stream, or close out the position by entering another swap that would lock in all the discounted profits.

In fact, by July 10, 1998, the spread had decreased to −2.5 basis points. LIBOR was 4.875% and the BOT yield was 4.9%. LTCM received an interest payment of 5.30% (the government yield of 4.90 plus 40 basis points) and paid a yield of 4.875% (LIBOR). The firm made a net gain of 42.5 basis points on the trade at every payment date.[20]

In 1998, these were not large trades in the LTCM portfolio. It does, however, illustrate LTCM trades that used practical financing techniques to provide liquidity to a rather perplexing inefficiency, while simultaneously bringing the firm substantial profits.

Fixed-Income Volatility Trades

A volatility trade bets on how volatile an asset's returns will be. The bet can be a simple one, based on a belief that the volatility will be higher in the future than the market believes, or that it will be lower in the future than the market believes. It could also combine views about relative volatilities. Appropriate trade construction often involves sophisticated financial engineering to remove unwanted bets. In the late 1990s, financial products that bet solely on long-term volatility didn't yet exist. Instead, LTCM traders constructed deals that took a net view on volatility while eliminating other risks.

In order to understand LTCM's volatility trades, some option theory review is helpful. An option gives a holder the right to buy or sell a security at a set price within a given time period. Call options give the holder the right to buy a security at a given price, while put options give the holder the right to sell a security at a given price. For example, suppose you wish to buy a call option on the S&P 500. There are many ways to buy this option and many types of call options to buy. You could buy the option through your brokerage, from an options exchange such as the Chicago Board Option Exchange, or from a bank.

If the S&P 500 is at 1,000 and you buy a call option to buy it at 1,000 with two years to expiration, you have two years to decide whether to buy the S&P 500 at 1,000. Clearly you will do this at some point if the S&P 500 trades above 1,000. A put option works in reverse.

A security option's price is related to many things: the price at which you can buy the security (also known as the strike price), the time you have to decide whether to use the option (also known as time to maturity), the volatility of the security's returns, prevailing interest rates, and the underlying security price. Both call and put options cost more when volatility is higher or time to maturity is higher. A lower strike price, a higher underlying security price, and a higher interest rate cause call options to be more costly. The reverse is true of put options.

Security price volatility is the important link for this trade. A call and put option give the holder the right to buy or sell a security at a given price, so the higher the security's volatility, the greater the chance that the security's price may move above or below the strike price, letting the investor make a profit. That's why higher volatility means a higher option price. With a formula that relates an option's price to the underlying security's volatility, a trader could convert the option's price into a volatility consistent with that price. This is called *implied volatility*. The Black-Scholes formula, discovered in 1973, is most commonly used for this purpose. It is named after one of LTCM's principals, Myron Scholes, and the late Goldman Sachs partner Fischer Black.

LTCM made volatility trades in both fixed income and equities. In the fixed-income arena, they noticed in 1998 that the implied volatility of 5-year options (i.e., options with five years to maturity) on German-denominated swaps was trading much lower than actual realized volatility. Option prices were trading with an implied volatility of 3 basis points per day, while the realized volatility in the marketplace was closer to 5 basis points. These were essentially options on German interest rates, and the market's volatility assessment was out of step with actual movements in German interest rates.[21]

LTCM wanted to go long on volatility at the 5-year mark. Traders hedged the position for interest rate risk, using interest-rate swaps and other short-term options. In other words, LTCM used additional financial instruments to remove all the risk the firm didn't want, including risk associated with interest rates going up or down. The company wanted to focus its bet.

To execute this trade, one might buy 5-year call options on 10-year swaps in Deutschemarks and sell 1-year call options on 10-year swaps in the right proportion to hedge away unwanted risks, such as risks from overall interest rate movements.

Figure 4.7 graphs the difference between the implied volatility of 5-year options and 1-year options. When this went up, LTCM made money. When this went down, LTCM lost money.

Around June 1998, the implied volatilities of short-term and long-term options were about the same. Then, as LTCM predicted, the implied volatility on the 5-year increased, making LTCM profits. Then came the Russian crisis,

FIGURE 4.7 The Difference between Implied Volatility on 5-Year Options and 1-Year
Options on 10-Year Euro Swap Rates

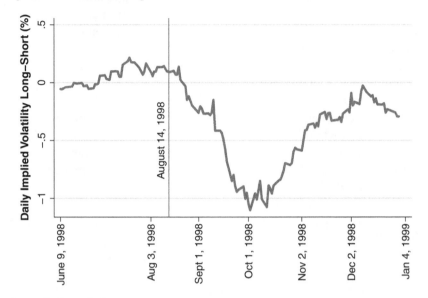

Source: Goldman Sachs.

when Russia defaulted on its debt. The volatility spread crashed and took
LTCM's position along with it. The same volatility spread collapse took place
in the 2008 crash. In market crises, the short-term volatility of fixed-income
instruments typically rises much faster than does longer-term volatility.

The On-the-Run and Off-the-Run Trade

One of the most fascinating trades LTCM made is now commonly known
as the on-the-run/off-the-run trade. This trade depends on institutional bias
and the Treasury bonds' regular auction cycle. LTCM used this trade in a
variety of countries and with bonds of various maturities, but the concept
always remained the same.

   To understand this trade, it's helpful to know a little about institutional behavior. The U.S. government constantly sells debt to finance U.S.
operations.[22] The U.S. government issues debt of varying maturities, from
one month to 30 years.

   Auction schedules for these securities vary by security type and government needs. For example, the one-month Treasury bill is auctioned every

week, so every week there is a brand new one-month Treasury bill. The 30-year bond is auctioned less frequently. In the 1990s, the 30-year bond was issued about twice per year. In recent times, however, the 30-year bond has been issued every month.

Traders call a newly issued government bond an on-the-run (OTR) bond. Other, less recently issued bonds are called off-the-run (OFR) bonds.

Many fixed-income mutual fund managers, traders, and other market participants prefer to hold the latest issued government security. The latest issues are usually benchmark bonds in many indices, and many mutual fund managers rebalance their portfolios by selling OFR bonds and buying OTR bonds. Partly because of this, OTR bonds are the most heavily traded bonds of a particular maturity.

As a result, very closely related OTR and OFR bonds have different yields. Suppose the U.S. government issued a 30-year bond six months ago and now issues a new 30-year bond. One bond is a $29\frac{1}{2}$-year bond and the other is a 30-year bond, but they are the same kind of instrument. Yet the 30-year bond will trade at a lower yield than the $29\frac{1}{2}$-year bond. Higher demand for the OTR bond pushes its price slightly higher and its yield slightly lower.

LTCM saw this as another classic opportunity to profit from an inefficient space, one created by institutional and other constraints. LTCM would purchase the cheap OFR bond, and short sell the expensive OTR bond, and wait for the normal business pattern to continue. When a new 30-year bond appeared in six months, the previous 30-year bond would become OFR, the liquidity premium would disappear, and LTCM would make a profit.

LTCM financed this trade using as little capital as possible. That made the trade more efficient and profitable.[23]

The minute they put this trade on, it gave LTCM two profit sources. In the 1990s, OFR bonds typically had higher interest payments than OTR bonds, giving LTCM a net positive yield. As time passed, the two bonds' prices converged until, by the time a new OTR bond was issued, they traded at roughly the same price.

See an example of one of these trades in Figure 4.8. The figure shows the difference between the yields of an OFR and an OTR U.S. Treasury bond. LTCM bought the OFR bond issued on May 17, 1993 and sold the OTR bond issued on February 10, 1994.[24] Initially, the OFR bond's yield was 12.82 basis points higher than the OTR's yield. Six months after issuance, however, the yield difference between the old 30-year bond and the new 30-year bond

FIGURE 4.8   The On-the-Run, Off-the-Run Typical Convergence

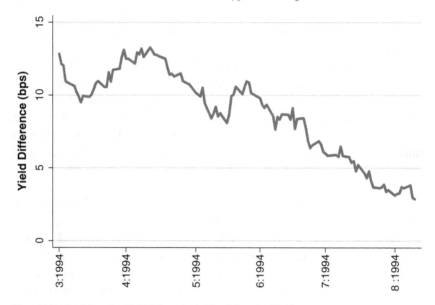

Note: 02/15/23 Maturity Yield Minus 08/15/23 Maturity Yield.

converged to 2.87 basis points. At about that time another new 30-year bond was issued, on August 11, 1994.

This yield convergence meant price convergence and a profit for LTCM. The same pattern occurred continuously until 1998, with this trade forming a stable, income-producing part of LTCM's portfolio. But once again a reasonable trade with solid history began performing erratically in August and September 1998 (see Figure 4.9).

In earlier years the spread had never been higher than 15.72 basis points. Yet by October 17, 1998, the spread was as high as 28.5 basis points—81% higher than any prior peak.[25]

This was a very unusual move in the spread and, more importantly, just the opposite of what valuation would suggest for two bonds that are almost exactly the same instruments.

The spread's extreme movement forced the shorted bonds' prices up and the long bonds' prices down, giving LTCM a mark-to-market loss on the trade. A trade that had never risen more than 4 basis points from its starting position had risen by four times this amount. This meant huge losses for LTCM. By November 1998 the spread had recovered, perhaps because the copycats and crowds had settled down. It was too late. LTCM had been roasted.[26]

FIGURE 4.9 The On-the-Run, Off-the-Run Trade Explodes

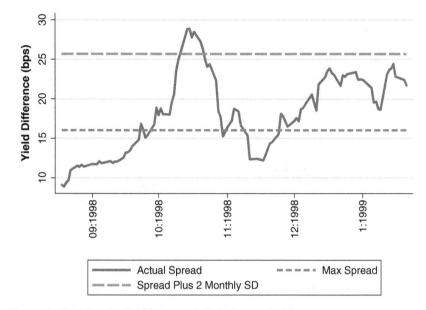

Note: 11/17/27 Maturity Yield Minus 08/15/28 Maturity Yield.

Short Longer-Term Equity Index Volatility

Though LTCM concentrated mainly on fixed income, they also had a collection of equity trades. Within this area, LTCM used its knowledge of option pricing theory and experience in financial market mechanics to find opportunities, using ideas similar to those they used to find fixed-income volatility trades.

In the equity markets, there are many call and put options that have a maturity of two years or less. Longer-term options, however, are really only available over the counter (OTC), which requires calling an investment bank and asking for a quote on a longer-dated option. The longer-term option market is much less liquid. Traders tend to quote options based on implied volatility, just as in the fixed-income markets. In general, options cost more when market participants believe that future volatility will be higher.

For example, if S&P 500 returns become more volatile or have a higher standard deviation, then an option to buy (call option) or sell (put option) the S&P 500 becomes more valuable, because there is a greater chance that the holder can take advantage of a beneficial price movement.

In 1998, LTCM's pricing models showed that long-term equity options were trading at very high implied volatilities. In other words, banks were charging very high prices for longer-maturity options, relative to short-term options.

LTCM believed that this was due to investor demand for long-term insurance protection and a low supply of these options in the marketplace. At the time, many retail investors demanded longer-term insurance protection for their investment portfolios, and thus drove up prices.

LTCM traders had many ways to take advantage of their view. Overall, they tried to sell expensive long-term options and then dynamically hedge the unwanted risk with futures and short-term options. In option lingo, they wanted to be delta-neutral: focused only on the idea that equity index volatility would be lower than the level market prices implied, with no exposure to equity market price shifts. If volatility turned out to be lower than implied during the five years after the option changed hands, LTCM made a good profit.

LTCM sold options that were priced as if volatility would be as high as 20% per year in the coming years. Historical data, however, suggested that volatility would be only 10 to 13%.

To focus their bet as precisely as possible, LTCM constructed straddles. A long straddle position consists of buying one call option and buying one put option. The position makes money if equity indices go up or down a lot.

LTCM traders took the other side of this position: They sold a call and sold a put option to another commercial bank. The firm was short the straddle. In option lingo, a short straddle position has a very high negative vega value.[27]

Vega measures the movement in the position's value for a 1% change in volatility. If actual volatility turned out to be lower than the implied volatility of the selling price, LTCM made money over the next few years. But if volatility spiked up, the position would lose money.

This was a frequent trade for LTCM, one it began using in 1994. The firm might be long volatility or short volatility at any given time. In August 1998, LTCM was short volatility. If the major index return volatility remained close to historical averages, or even a bit above those averages, LTCM's positions would profit. They shorted these straddles on equities across the world, including the stock markets of the United States, Germany, France, and England.

LTCM's positions involved two risks. If volatility turned out to be higher than expected, the trade would lose over time. The trade also had an illiquid component. Though some of LTCM's hedging was in the very liquid short-term market, the firm was also short illiquid options that depended on the behavior of a small handful of counterparties. If these counterparties altered their behavior suddenly—asking for more collateral, for instance, or marking prices much higher against them—the market was not large enough for LTCM to seek alternatives.[28]

LTCM's aggregate vega on these positions was about $50 million. That implies that LTCM received an option premium of about $1.01 billion for selling the straddle.[29] According to LTCM partners, they had a vega of $25 million on the S&P 500 and another $25 million vega shared in the European equity markets. LTCM's idea was good, but in August and September 1998 it was not practical.

Figure 4.10 plots the implied volatility (according to market prices) of 12-month options on the S&P 500 and the Nikkei, as well as the rolling 20-day and rolling 5-year historical volatility of the S&P 500.

It's clear that the Russian default and LTCM's crisis pushed both short-term actual volatility and one-year options' implied volatility sharply up. On August 3, 1998, the implied volatility on short-term options was 24%, 20-day historical volatility was 16%, and 5-year historical volatility was 12%. By August 31, these three numbers rose to 32%, 32%, and 13% respectively. By September 30, they rose to 34%, 35%, and 14% respectively.

FIGURE 4.10 The Implied Volatility of 12-Month Options on the S&P 500 and the Nikkei 225

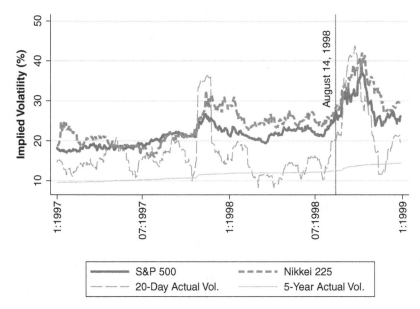

Source: Goldman Sachs.

LTCM was short volatility—and volatility had shot through the roof.

But not all of LTCM's positions were in short-term options. The company had shorted long-term options with various counterparties. In most crises short-term option volatility rises much more than long-term volatility, but LTCM's options were being marked at volatilities around 45%. Why was this?

The overall market panic was partly responsible. Fear was high, and that was expressed in short-term volatility numbers. But why was long-term volatility even higher? The illiquid nature of this market was partly to blame, as was market interconnectedness. Other traders knew that LTCM was short volatility. As rumors spread that LTCM might be in trouble, counterparties worried that they would not get paid and marked volatility higher as a cushion. For every one percent volatility increase, LTCM lost $50M. Dealers' long-term volatility marks on the trade went up 25% from where LTCM had sold it. This alone cost LTCM $1,250 million (50 times 25) on a mark-to-market basis. When all was said and done, LTCM lost a total $1,539 million on this trade. As one trader described it:

> When it became apparent they were having difficulties, we thought that if they are going to default, we're going to be short a hell of a lot of volatility. So we'd rather be short at 40 than 30, right? So it was clearly in our interest to mark to as high a volatility as possible. That's why everybody pushed the volatility against them, which contributed to their demise in the end.
> —Interview with trader, October 1999 (Dunbar 1999)

The short-term crisis had driven LTCM out of the marketplace. Had LTCM's trade been a rational one? Fast-forward to August 2003, five years after the LTCM crisis. The S&P 500's historical volatility turned out to be about 22%. The options that LTCM thought were cheap in 1998 were actually fairly priced. Even if LTCM had survived, the trade would not have made money for them, though their losses would have been much more manageable.[30] The 1998 risk models didn't include crowd interconnectedness or the price of liquidity during a crisis.

Risk Arbitrage Trades

Risk arbitrage, also known as merger arbitrage, is a trading strategy used by many hedge funds. In this strategy a trader invests in companies going through a merger, spinoff, acquisition, or similar event.

The most typical trade begins when two companies announce their merger (or similar event). Risk arbitrage attempts to profit from the merger's completion or failure. Risk arbitrage funds may also take speculative positions in companies that traders think might be bought out or become the subject of a bidding war, but these transactions are the minority. The overwhelming majority of transactions involve trading on companies whose deals have already been publicly announced.

Stock deals and cash deals are the most common trades. In a stock deal, one company buys another in exchange for shares of the acquiring company. In a cash deal, the acquiring company pays cash for each share.[31]

For example, on September 15, 1999, Microsoft wanted to acquire the company Visio. For every share of Visio, MSFT offered to pay 0.45 shares of Microsoft stock. It was a friendly deal and Visio's CEO was happy with the offer. On the first day of trading after the announcement, Visio's price was $39.875 per share; Microsoft's price was $92.625 per share. If one believed that the merger would go through, Visio's price should have been $41.6825 (0.45 · 92.625). The price was below that. The difference between the merger price and the stock's actual trading price is called the *arb spread*. This arb spread was $1.806.

The arb spread exists because there is always a chance that a deal will not go through as scheduled. Even if both companies are very enthusiastic about the merger, there is always a chance that the deal will be delayed, the price renegotiated, or the merger completely abandoned. A deal could take longer than estimated to consummate, tying up capital that could be earning interest. Or regulators could disapprove of the deal for antitrust reasons.

The more the market believes a deal will go through, the smaller the risk-arb spread. If the deal does break, relative prices usually fall to preannouncement levels, giving traders a large negative return.

Risk-arbitrage trades work like this. A trader buys a certain number of Visio shares. For every Visio share, the trader shorts 0.45 shares of Microsoft and waits until the merger is finally completed. If all goes well, the trade will make a $1.806 profit per share traded. It's not a pure arbitrage because there is a risk that the deal will change or evaporate. It is a quasi-arbitrage.

LTCM created a portfolio of 30 to 40 of these trades. They were not LTCM's specialty, so the firm mainly focused on risk-arb trades with a very small discount—trades where the market thought the deal was very likely to close on time and so the target company's trading price was very close to the deal's actual offer price. LTCM preferred stock deals, which are generally considered less likely to break up.[32]

Before the LTCM crisis, most of the market wasn't aware that LTCM was making risk arbitrage trades. When other hedge funds and the media found out, they criticized LTCM for venturing away from its core business.

They specifically criticized LTCM for trading deals with very small arb spreads (deals with a high probability of success) because potential gains were so small compared to potential losses on an abandoned deal. LTCM was aware of these concerns and made risk-arb deals for two primary reasons.

First, LTCM was able to finance the trades with zero haircuts using total return stock swaps. Second, risk-arb strategies had a very low correlation with other typical LTCM trades. Choosing low-correlation trades was a central feature of the firm's risk-management system.

Figure 4.11 shows a risk arbitrage portfolio's performance.[33] The index depicts the performance on a $100 initial investment from January 1997 to January 1999.

This portfolio did quite well throughout 1997 and most of 1998: up almost 18%. When Russia defaulted on its debt and the LTCM crisis began in August and September 1998, this strategy suffered as well. The strategy might seem to have nothing to do with either the Russian default or the LTCM crisis, yet from August 17, 1998, to October 8, 1998, it fell by 10%. Even this atypical portion of LTCM's portfolio performed horribly in the crisis.

FIGURE 4.11   A Diversified Risk Arbitrage Portfolio Index

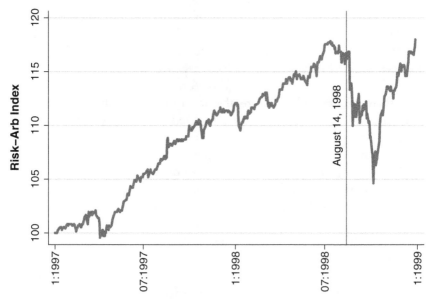

Source: Bloomberg.

LTCM's losses in this space weren't due to inexperience. LTCM suffered in risk arbitrage, as did all experienced risk arbitrage traders in August and September. Most of them had a trade on the merger of Tellabs, Inc. and Ciena Corporation. On August 21, 1998, Tellabs announced that it might reduce or change its offer for Cienna. Cienna shares fell 45%. That's the equivalent of an atomic bomb in risk arbitrage. That failed deal alone cost LTCM $160 million.

Equity Relative-Value Trades

Equity relative-value trades are another class of beautiful arbitrage possibilities. These trades work like this. A trader finds two securities that are very similar but are trading at different prices for some understandable reason. The trader buys the cheap security, short sells the expensive security, and waits for the two prices to converge. LTCM had a portfolio of these trades, as did many other hedge funds, including proprietary trading desks such as the Salomon Arb group.

A typical relative-value trade might involve companies whose operating assets were held by two distinct, publicly traded companies, each with equivalent economic claims on the operating assets: the same or similar voting rights, profit shares, and dividends. Many times one of the companies traded at a discount to the other company, even though it had the same value.

Traders worked to understand the discount motivation. Maybe one group of buyers bought one security in one country and another group bought it in another country, both for tax reasons. The investors' different objectives could create a price divergence.

If LTCM grasped the logic behind the divergence and thought prices would eventually converge, they put on the arbitrage.[34]

In August 1998, LTCM had a very large position in an equity relative-value trade: the Royal Dutch-Shell trade. LTCM was not the only one with this trade. One Salomon arb trader at the time said, "Everyone had that trade on."[35]

Royal Dutch Shell was a dual-listed company, based on an agreement between Royal Dutch and Shell to be independently incorporated in the Netherlands and England, respectively. In 1907, the companies merged their interests on a 60 to 40 basis while remaining separate, distinct entities. When the company assigns profits, they credit 60% to Royal Dutch and 40% to Shell. By that math, Royal Dutch should be worth 1.5 times as much as Shell.

If this isn't true, the market is not valuing these companies correctly. LTCM might react by going long the cheaper shares and going short the more expensive shares.

Traders would discuss reasons a price discrepancy might exist, as well as whether catalysts might bring the prices back in line. In this case, LTCM believed that different investor clienteles had caused the discrepancy. (U.S. pension funds received a full withholding tax refund on Royal Dutch, but not on Shell. UK taxable corporations received 80 percent of Shell dividends, but only 69 percent of Royal Dutch. LTCM thought that an April 1999 change in British corporation tax law would make Shell more attractive for many tax clienteles.)

There was also a possibility that the dual share class would be combined into one share class in the near future, pushing the two share prices to converge and making LTCM ever more eager to do this trade.[36]

LTCM went long Shell and short Royal Dutch using a zero-haircut total-return swap.[37]

This trade had some other advantages. Because Shell received the same dollar dividend for a much smaller share price, the trade had a dividend pickup. All else being equal, the swap favored being long Shell by about 35 basis points per year. However, the swap had a financing fee of 70 basis points per year. If the two share prices did not converge, LTCM would lose 35 basis points on this trade every year. And if the misvaluation increased, LTCM would also lose money on the swap payments.

The upper chart in Figure 4.12 shows the percentage premium of Royal Dutch over Shell.[38] At the beginning of 1998, Royal Dutch traded at a 10% premium to Shell. The market valued Royal Dutch 10% more than it should have, compared to Shell.

The bottom graph shows LTCM's position starting at 100 in January 1998. The position decreases throughout 1998 and also during the LTCM crisis. From January 2, 1998, to August 3, 1998, the Royal Dutch premium moved against LTCM, going from an overvaluation of 8.13% to an overvaluation of 12.84%. In August and September, things got worse. By September 8, 1998, the overvaluation was 16.03%. By September 8, LTCM had lost 11% on this trade. The trade would eventually go LTCM's way in the next few years, but it didn't in 1998.

LTCM was a long-term player, designed to wait out discrepancies, but market movements did not let it wait beyond 1998. Markets eventually became rational. If LTCM had waited, the trade would have yielded 10% as the stock price discrepancy disappeared.[39]

FIGURE 4.12 The Royal Dutch-Shell Relative Value Trade

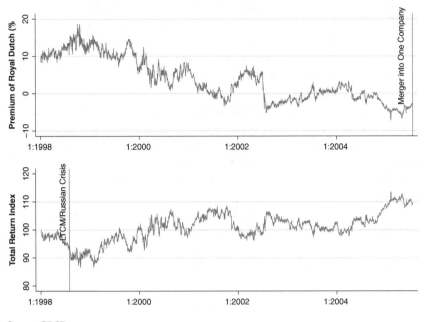

Source: CRSP.

On July 20, 2005, Royal Dutch and Shell merged into one company. Share values aligned almost perfectly, making the convergence trade successful for anyone able to hold the position long enough.[40]

Emerging Market Trades

The majority of LTCM's trades were in fixed income, relative value, and convergence, but the company also had about 20% of its portfolio invested in directional bets. In addition to making equity arbitrage trades and combined on-the-run and off-the-run trades, which look for misvaluations and create trades hoping these misvaluations will be corrected, LTCM also took straight bets on interest rate direction, just like so many other portfolio managers.

For example, LTCM was long Brazilian C bonds, long-term Brazilian government bonds that were payable in U.S. dollars. They were created after the restructuring of Latin American debt in 1994, when the Brady Plan worked to help Latin American governments solve their debt crisis. LTCM's partner, David Mullins, had been a key figure in the administration that created the Brady Plan. Now his team was buying the resulting debt.

(Brazilian government debt is very different from U.S. government debt. It offers high yields, but also high risk. When markets crash, Brazilian debt behaves more like equity than fixed income and usually crashes very fast. Latin American countries have frequently defaulted on their debt, causing large losses on these bonds. For example, after Mexico devalued its currency in December 1994—the so-called Mexican Peso crisis—Brazilian C bonds dropped by 50%.)

LTCM also bought Russian government bonds denominated in Euros. Emerging economies had a history of devaluing their currencies. Debt payable in dollars or Euros was thought to be more secure—if, of course, the country didn't default altogether.

LTCM's direct exposure to Russia, Brazil, and other countries was a small part of its portfolio and was not the principal reason for its troubles. Nevertheless, even these trades did poorly during August and September 1998 (see Figure 4.13). Between January 2, 1998, and August 31, 1998, the Russian

FIGURE 4.13   Russian Bond and Brazilian Brady Bond Return Indices

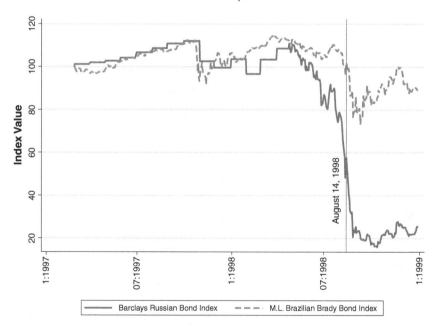

Source: Datastream and Bloomberg.

trade lost 76% and the Brazilian trade lost 20%. By the end of September the losses were 81% and 21% respectively. LTCM lost a total of $278 million in emerging market direction trades in 1998.

Other Trades

LTCM had many other trades. The company got agency security exposure by being long interest-only strips of agency-backed pools of fixed-rate residential mortgages, known in the industry as IOs. LTCM hedged the interest rate risk by using swap contracts. This was essentially a mortgage trade.

LTCM also purchased AAA-rated tranches of structured products backed by commercial mortgages and paid fixed rates on swaps, taking advantage of the yield spread. This is also a mortgage trade, one that caused a lot of trouble for hedge funds in 2008.

LTCM's fixed-income portfolio included butterfly yield curve trades. A butterfly trade is typically one in which a trader is long the 30-year bond and the 5-year bond, but short the 10-year bond. The trade is neutral to general interest rate movements, but takes a view that the yield curve will become more hump shaped. A trader could take the other view by changing the long positions to short positions. Either view could apply to any part of the yield curve, not just the 5-10-30 combo.

In 1998, LTCM had a relative butterfly trade on in Germany and the UK. LTCM executed this trade in the swap market. In the UK, it paid fixed interest on the 20-year and 3-year area of the curve, and received fixed in the 7-year area. In Germany, LTCM executed the opposite trade. These trades were structured to benefit from changes in the relative shape of the two yield curves, but were hedged against overall interest rate movements and curve steepening or flattening. LTCM hoped to profit from a mispricing of 21 basis points with this trade.

LTCM engaged in preferred-common arbitrage trades with Japanese banks. The firm was long Japanese banks' preferred shares and short the common stock. These preferred shares were generally trading cheap because their implied options were mispriced.

The fund also made convertible arbitrage trades, where LTCM was either long or short on corporate bonds and short or long the same company's common stock. The trades were constructed to maintain an overall zero exposure to stock price movements and to take advantage of mispricings between certain stocks and their convertible bonds.

LTCM made other directional trades, including being short Japanese government bonds when the bonds' interest rate reached 2% in 1997.

The Portfolio of Trades

By August 1998, LTCM's portfolio had lots of strategies that appeared to be economically and statistically uncorrelated.[41] The firm's portfolio consisted mainly of relative value and convergence trades in the fixed-income swap and bond markets of OECD countries.[42] These trades were constructed to profit on temporary distortions between security prices.

There were some disturbing trends, however. LTCM was aware of some, but not necessarily aware of others.

Though the majority of LTCM's portfolio was in core relative-value and convergence trades, the fund had ventured into less lovely territory. For example, the portfolio had about 20% in directional bets. These trades looked uncorrelated to the core portfolio, but they didn't offer the same competitive advantages that LTCM had in its other trades, such as inevitable convergence and favorable financing.

Two of LTCM's largest trades didn't look nearly as beautiful as the others. In 1998, LTCM was short the U.S. swap spread. The trade's logic has already been discussed, but not its two distinct dangers. In a world crisis the swap spread would tend to widen as traders fled to quality and switched holdings from interbank debt to U.S. government debt. The spread's widening could be unlimited, as could potential losses.

The long swap spread trade, which LTCM also used from time to time, seemed to have a much more protected downside. If the spread was 20 basis points, then one might argue that the most swap spreads could decline is to zero, not more.[43] The short swap spread trade is a convergence trade in theory, but it didn't seem as good as a long swap trade.[44]

The short long-term volatility trade was a short on marketplace volatility. LTCM used the trade when it found long-term volatility very expensive relative to the way it actually behaved. In a crisis, however, volatility typically shoots through the roof. In that case, LTCM would suffer tremendously on a mark-to-market basis, even if they were right about the expensive options in the long run.

LTCM knew these trades weren't perfect, but may have kept them on in the interest of diversification. But crowds were developing, and that was affecting trades. With every call to a dealer, with every cocktail party between dealers, and with every quant trying desperately to reverse engineer LTCM's success, word traveled and more investors copied LTCM's moves. The beautiful trades were getting ugly, with smaller expected profits and a new danger: the danger that copycats might rush for the exit at inopportune moments and cause dramatic changes among trade correlations. That's just what happened in August and September 1998, when Russia defaulted on its debt, the copycats ran for the exits, and the *Titanic* of hedge funds sank into the chilling water.

CHAPTER 5

The Collapse

> *. . . the market knew something that our formula didn't know . . .*
> —Fischer Black, 1973

By the start of 1998, LTCM was *the* superstar hedge fund. It had just given a large sum of capital back to its investors, and entered 1998 having had an enormous amount of success.

The returns for the first part of 1998 were −1.26%, 1.24%, −0.30%, and 2.74% respectively: up and down, with no clear direction. LTCM seemed set for a quiet year.

The events that brought down LTCM are shown in Figure 5.1. The end began with unusually bad months in May and June (see Figure 5.2). Salomon's arbitrage trading group closed and the Russian government defaulted on its debt, both unexpectedly. By the fall, LTCM's survival was in question.

Early Summer 1998

In May, LTCM had its greatest monthly loss ever: −6.74%. The firm had substantial losses in June, too: −10.14%. Until then, LTCM had never had back-to-back losing months. LTCM partners canceled their summer vacation plans to sit down during the first two weeks of July and carefully analyze their situation. The partners saw nothing obvious. No large trade created the losses. The losses were spread out through every trade in the LTCM portfolio.

FIGURE 5.1 Timeline of LTCM Collapse

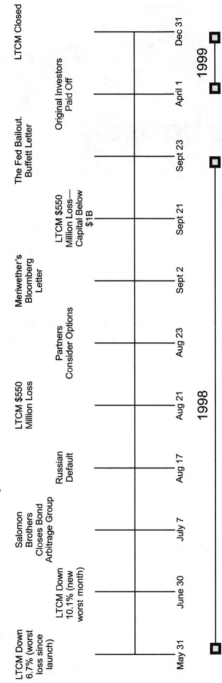

FIGURE 5.2   LTCM Gross Monthly Returns in 1998

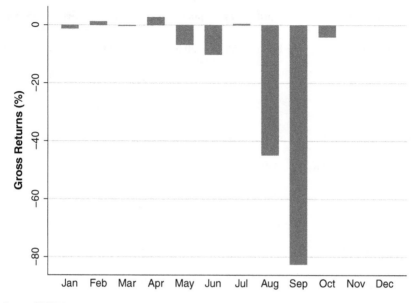

Source: LTCM.

Table 5.1 shows the LTCM portfolio's actual losses by month during 1998. Though almost all trades were losing money, the biggest losses occurred in the firm's bread-and-butter fixed-income relative-value trades. Without any single obvious culprit, the partners chalked up the poor returns to the market's sometimes-random nature.

> That was a real signal that the correlations were breaking down, but we missed it because we focused on a trade-by-trade analysis. This, combined with the portfolio rebounding by 7% through mid-July, allowed us to chalk it up to bad luck. As a precautionary measure, we still reduced the risk of the portfolio by about 10%.
> —Interview with Eric Rosenfeld, September 28, 2010

The Salomon Shutdown

In November 1997, Traveler's Group bought Salomon Brothers. Soon after, Traveler's bought Citicorp. Sandy Weill, the firm's new CEO, was in the midst of merging the new firm, Salomon Smith Barney, with Citicorp and wanted

TABLE 5.1 LTCM Losses by Trade Category in 1998

Trade Category	Jan–April	May	June	July	August	Sep	Jan–Sep
Holding Companies[a]	−89.6	−58.6	−30.6	1.2	−38.4	−70.2	−286.2
Auction Strategies	12.4	4.2	−0.3	1.2	0.7	0.0	18.2
Closed-end Funds	6.6	3.6	−4.6	4.7	4.1	−1.9	12.5
Convertibles and Prefs	80.0	22.8	2.8	50.1	−10.6	−53.5	91.6
Currency Relative Value	0.0	0.0	0.0	0.0	−1.4	−3.1	−4.5
DEM Swap Options	−6.4	−5.9	1.2	−61.4	104.9	−73.4	−41.0
Directional Trades	−48.8	−89.4	−72.7	−12.3	−56.8	−90.9	−370.9
E.M. Directional[b]	5.7	−34.4	−31.9	−12.3	−180.2	−24.9	−278.0
E.M. Relative Value	1.9	−4.9	−2.7	2.9	−119.6	−29.3	−151.7
Equity Volatility	−133.5	−26.3	5.8	−38.8	−356.4	−764.6	−1313.8
Fixed-Income Relative Value	132.8	1.7	−259.5	36.4	−829.8	−710.0	−1628.4
High Yield	36.8	−8.7	4.6	−0.6	−62.4	−69.7	−100.0
Index Arbitrage	33.4	−30.7	40.4	−15.4	−4.9	−15.6	7.2
Other	5.9	1.9	−2.0	1.8	2.6	−6.6	3.6
Risk Arbitrage	2.9	7.5	108.6	46.1	−168.2	−0.4	−3.5
S&P Inclusion/Reweight	−32.9	−66.2	−30.4	−5.7	−56.2	−11.9	−203.3
Turn of Month	0.7	−0.6	−2.6	3.7	−8.9	−0.1	−7.8
Yield-Curve Trades	19.4	−64.5	−88.3	−14.9	−69.8	3.2	−214.9
Total	27.4	−348.5	−362.2	−13.3	−1851.3	−1922.9	−4470.8

Note: Losses are in millions of U.S. dollars.
[a]These trade types involved buying and selling different classes of securities, such as A and B shares of the same company, with perhaps different voting, tax, and other rights.
[b]E.M. stands for Emerging Market positions.
Source: LTCM.

to scale back Salomon's proprietary trading arm. On July 7, 1998, Salomon officially shut down its U.S. bond-trading group. The co-chiefs of Salomon Smith Barney, Jamie Dimon and Deryck Maughan, stated that the arbitrage group had lost around $100 million in the second quarter and that "the U.S. capital markets have matured and the opportunity for arbitrage profits has lessened over time while the risks and volatility have grown."

Jamie Dimon, co-head of Salomon Smith Barney, had earlier described overall profits from the former Salomon's bond trading business as "fabulous" and said that the firm would not scale back its commitment to the business. Dimon saw the arbitrage group as Salomon's crown jewel. He wanted it at all costs, but Weill didn't want the risk. The two didn't see eye to eye on many things, but Weill got his way and the group halved its positions.[1]

Salomon's shutdown was surprising, but no one suspected the impact it would have. The dealer desk liquidated about half of Salomon's positions, a process that took a couple of months. The Salomon Arb group's positions were very similar to LTCM's positions. After all, John Meriwether had created and trained this team before leaving to start LTCM. By selling similar positions, Salomon might have devalued LTCM's trades. This was the first sign that part of the crowd wanted to leave the party.

By mid-July LTCM had seen no backlash from Salomon's bond portfolio sale. In the last week of July, however, LTCM lost 7%, bringing their monthly performance to a mere 0.48%. In August, Salomon's continuing sell-off kept hurting LTCM positions. LTCM's portfolio suffered heavily in August—and more was coming.

The Russian Default

On August 17, 1998, the Russian government and the Central Bank of Russia issued a joint statement announcing that the ruble-dollar trading band would expand from 5.3 to 7.1 Russian rubles per dollar to a band of 6 to 9.5 Russian rubles per dollar. The Russians also announced that Russia's ruble-denominated debt would be restructured and that it was imposing a 90-day moratorium on paying some bank obligations, including certain debts and forward currency contracts, to prevent a mass Russian bank default.

Russia had devalued its currency and defaulted on its debt, handing domestic and (especially) foreign investors a giant investment loss. Markets had expected a devaluation of some sort, and the Russian stock market dropped in the days before the announcement. Even so, market participants had not expected an outright default.

From August 17 to August 25, the ruble steadily depreciated on the Moscow Interbank Currency Exchange, or MICEX, moving from 6.43 to 7.86 rubles per dollar.[2]

On August 26, the Central Bank terminated ruble-dollar trading on the MICEX, and the MICEX did not fix a ruble-dollar rate that day.

On September 2, the Central Bank of the Russian Federation decided to abandon its floating peg policy and float the ruble freely. By September 21 the exchange rate had reached 21 rubles to the U.S. dollar, worth almost a quarter of its value a month earlier.

Russia's unexpected default and devaluation caused panic throughout the financial world. Lehman Brothers almost went bankrupt in 1998. Its share price fell by 60% between the Russian announcement and October 5, 1998. Lehman's Richard Fuld wrote an internal memo.

> While, unfortunately, these fictions continue to circulate, I want you to know that this firm remains strong and stable ... [the firm has] been in contact with various regulators as part of an investigation into the source of these rumors, and the possibility that they may be economically motivated.
> —Richard Fuld, CEO of Lehman Brothers, October 6, 1998
> (McGeehan 1998)

Other banks and markets were also in trouble. From August 21, 1998, to September 3, 1998, Bank of America was down 16% with $220 million in losses from Russia. Bank of Boston was down 8% with losses of $10 million from Russia. Bankers Trust was down 23% with around $260 million losses from Russia. Chase Manhattan was down 14% with charge-offs of $200 million, Citicorp was down 19%, J.P. Morgan was down 20%, Morgan Stanley and Bear Stearns were down 23%, and Salomon Smith Barney was down 19%. (Goldman Sachs was not yet a publicly traded company.) Everyone suffered between August 17 and October 1, 1998.

LTCM's August losses were staggering, with the portfolio down 44.78%. It is hard to know how much was attributable to the Salomon arbitrage group shutdown, how much to Russia's indirect effects, and how much to other factors. LTCM's portfolio was down 2.11%, or about $78 million, on the day that Russia defaulted. LTCM's historical profit-and-loss volatility on any given day was about $38 million, so this was a big dip.

The next few days brought a string of smaller losses. Extreme losses began on Friday, August 21, when LTCM lost $552 million, $160 million of that on a merger arbitrage play—the Ciena Tellabs merger—that fell short. On the following Monday, the firm lost another $220 million. On Tuesday, it shed $129 million.

LTCM's losses seemed to be a symptom, one caused by crowds of other traders unwinding positions similar to the firm's favored investments. LTCM lost money on 14 of 18 business days from July 22, 1998, to August 14, 1998. How many losses did the exodus cause, and how many were the fault of a general panic about problems in Russia and Asia?

Jim Cramer of *Mad Money*, along with many other market participants, seemed to believe that massive bets on Russia had caused LTCM's losses.

> Let's stop the pretense that these guys were good at all . . . their returns sucked. [LTCM were] . . . clowns . . . their returns ex-this year . . . were disappointing given leverage . . . The money they [the consortium] will have to put up reflects a fraction of what they ultimately will have to put up because the only stuff that Long Term still had left was completely unsaleable . . . These have to be unwound at hideous losses to whoever is holding the bag. These guys had a massive bet on Russia, just massive. Idiots. Stop calling these guys rocket scientists. They were hopelessly out of their league, doing things that your mother would have told you were just plain stupid.[3]
> —Jim Cramer, September 28, 1998 (Cramer 2008)

From August 17, 1998, to September 21, 1998, LTCM's daily losses were uncorrelated with Russian stock returns, Japanese stock returns, U.S. Treasury returns, U.S. high-yield bond returns, world bond returns, and mortgage bond returns. LTCM's total losses from directional trades in emerging markets reached $278 million (Table 5.1), a small fraction of its total losses. LTCM's losses had nothing to do with massive Russian exposure.

Were LTCM's losses generated by the Salomon arbitrage trading group's shutdown? This is hard to say, because the exact timing of Salomon's liquidation is not known. In total, Salomon may have closed down a portfolio as large as LTCM's portfolio. The Russian default announcement on August 17, 1998, may have accelerated the sell-off. How much did Salomon dump on August 21, 1998, the day that LTCM lost the most? (See Figure 5.3.) And how did the behavior of other copycats exaggerate the price moves in this trading space?

Whatever the reason for the losses, LTCM had to do something fast.

The Phone Calls

Fund capital had fallen from $4.131 billion at the end of July to about $2.930 billion by the close of business on August 21, 1998. LTCM partners realized that it would be prudent to raise more capital.

Eric Rosenfeld left for a 10-day vacation on August 21, 1998. It became a one-day vacation. All the senior partners gathered to discuss the situation on

FIGURE 5.3 The Daily Profit and Loss of LTCM in August and September 1998

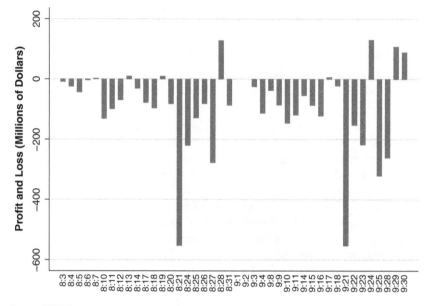

Source: LTCM.

Sunday night, August 23, 1998. The partners decided to sell some of LTCM's positions, including the U.S. 10-year swap spread position, which was trading at a virtually unheard-of 21 basis points. Next, they would hire an investment banking firm to help them raise more capital.

That weekend they hired J.P. Morgan to seek $1.1 billion for a closing by August 31. J.P. Morgan would also invest $100 million of its own money in exchange for 15% of LTCM. From August 24 to August 28, LTCM lost another $581 million, so the firm raised its capital target to $1.4 billion.

Meriwether approached Merrill Lynch's Herbert Allison to tell him that the opportunities were large and the fund just needed more capital, which might have sounded like a double down plan. He asked if Merrill could invest between $300 and $500 million. Merrill refused.[4]

Eric Rosenfeld called PaineWebber, but it said no. John Meriwether met with Stanley Druckenmiller, the chief strategist and CIO for George Soros. It seemed that the Quantum Fund might contribute $500 million to the fund-raising efforts. LTCM also approached Julian Robertson of Tiger Management, but he declined.

On August 26, Eric Rosenfeld and John Meriwether asked Warren Buffett for money. The next morning, Larry Hilibrand went to Omaha, Nebraska, to talk to Buffett. Buffett declined to invest because he thought the portfolio was too complicated. Myron Scholes called William Sharpe, another Nobel prizewinner in economics, to ask him for money from a family office that Bill Sharpe was advising. Again, LTCM's trades looked too complicated.

Despite the many negative responses, it seemed that LTCM had enough commitments for capital. On the anticipated closing day, August 31, George Soros's Quantum Fund pulled out its large stake: $500 million. That was it. LTCM was desperate.

Who would LTCM call next? In the end, a letter would seal its fate.

The Meriwether Letter

LTCM ended 1997 with $4.668 billion in capital; the partners controlled a little more than $2 billion. At the end of July 1998, the capital was down slightly to $4.132 billion with a leverage ratio of 31 (and a capital ratio of 3.22%). By the end of August, the capital had declined by 55% to $2.281 billion (and a capital ratio of 1.82%). The partners normally issued monthly investor reports around the 10th of every month.

With such extreme losses, the partners felt it was their fiduciary duty to tell their investors earlier. On September 2, 1998, Meriwether drafted a letter, which was sent to LTCM's approximately 100 investors via the company's two fax machines.[5] By the time they reached investor number 60, Bloomberg had posted the letter for every trader to read.[6]

The Meriwether letter caused a panic in the fixed-income markets, publicizing LTCM's troubles and giving copycat traders an engraved invitation to leave the trades they had modeled on LTCM's deals. It's hard to know whether September's losses would have been less had Bloomberg never posted the letter.[7] Asked why LTCM didn't wait to tell investors, LTCM founder Eric Rosenfeld responded:

> You're there in August, you've lost half your capital. You are way out of control in terms of risk, but you're okay in terms of riding out the positions. We felt it was prudent to sell positions and raise additional capital. When you raise additional capital, you have to let people know what they are buying into, which may have caused more problems. Playing chicken didn't seem the right thing to do.
>
> —Rosenfeld interview, September 2, 2010

After the announcement hit Bloomberg, LTCM lost money for nine consecutive days, bleeding a total of $972 million. The damage was done. LTCM continued looking for the capital infusion it so desperately needed.

Meriwether turned to Vinny Mattone, a close friend at Bear Stearns, a Brooklyn native of Italian descent, and a classic old-style trader. Mattone had known Meriwether at Salomon and was one of the main reasons LTCM chose Bear to clear its trades. Unlike the Meriwether team, Mattone trusted his gut feelings about the markets. Meriwether told Mattone that LTCM had lost half its capital and asked Mattone for advice.

> You're finished. When you're down by half, people figure you can go down all the way. They're going to push the market against you. They're not going to roll your trades. You're finished.
> —Vinny Mattone to John Meriwether, August–September 1998
> (Lowenstein 2000)

On September 17, LTCM ditched J.P. Morgan and hired Goldman to raise its capital. LTCM asked Goldman to sign a nondisclosure agreement (NDA), but Goldman refused. LTCM went ahead anyway, given the dire circumstances. The two companies agreed that Goldman would get 50% of LTCM in return for raising needed money. Goldman immediately went looking for potential investors, including Michael Dell, CEO of Dell Computers. Goldman co-CEO Jon Corzine told the Federal Reserve that LTCM was weak, but that Goldman was trying to raise money for it.

During this period, all kinds of potential investors came to examine the books at LTCM's Greenwich headquarters. Visitors included Goldman Sachs, J.P. Morgan, Merrill Lynch, Salomon Brothers, and UBS. Goldman and J.P. Morgan had the most detailed look at all of LTCM's positions. No one invested. Some banks seemed interested only in uncovering LTCM's positions in order to bet against them. A few days after Goldman's visit, LTCM had its biggest one-day loss, dropping $553 million on September 21, 1998.[8]

Even worse news was on the horizon. Bear Stearns, LTCM's clearing agent, would stop processing trades if LTCM's capital fell below $500 million. This was Bear's standard clearing procedure, even though Bear and LTCM had never signed a formal agreement. Jimmy Cayne told Meriwether to use his emergency credit lines. The largest was with Chase for somewhere between $200 and $500 million. This helped capital stay just above the $500 million level, but Bear told LTCM that after September 23, Bear would no longer clear LTCM's trades. LTCM couldn't run its business without a clearing agent. Without one, bankruptcy was the firm's only option.

LTCM and Chase called New York Fed President William McDonough in early September to alert him to the company's potential difficulties.[9] A delegation from the New York Federal Reserve and the U.S. Treasury visited the fund on Sunday, September 20, and realized that LTCM's situation was quite bad.

Peter Fisher, the number-two man at the Federal Reserve Bank of New York, believed that some of the recent market volatility came about because LTCM had been forced to sell positions to shore up capital. He realized that, if LTCM were to liquidate, it would be "in the eye of the hurricane."

On September 23, 1998, the New York Federal Reserve invited LTCM's primary creditors to discuss a rescue package. Those present agreed to inject new capital into LTCM and mount a rescue if no one else took over the fund. The counterparties included Bankers Trust, Barclays, Bear Stearns, Chase, Deutsche Bank, Lehman Brothers, UBS, Paribas, Salomon Smith Barney, J.P. Morgan, Goldman Sachs, Merrill Lynch, Credit Suisse First Boston, Morgan Stanley Dean Witter, and Societe Generale.

On Wednesday, September 23, the group learned that the fund had another offer, one that would expire at lunchtime. The offer was from Warren Buffett.

Buffett's Hostile Alaskan Offer

As the group met that morning, a faxed offer arrived. Warren Buffett, Goldman Sachs, and AIG offered a total of $250 million for LTCM.[10] In exchange, they would supply the fund with $3.75 billion. The team had about an hour and a half to respond.

Existing shareholders, including Wall Street banks and LTCM partners, would have lost everything in this deal. Buffett (on vacation with Bill Gates in Alaska at the time) was not trying to help LTCM. He was making a low-ball offer to a group of desperate fund managers.

The partners were unable to accept the proposal as it was crafted. The fund had approximately 15,000 distinct positions, each a repo or swap contract with a credit counterparty. Transferring those positions to the Buffett-led group would require approval from all counterparties. Of course, all LTCM's counterparties would prefer Warren Buffett as a creditor, especially when the other choice was a nearly bankrupt hedge fund. Even so, there was no way to get complete approval in an hour. Nor was there any certainty that Buffett (or anyone else) understood and could deal with LTCM's complex positions.[11]

The Buffett offer upset many of LTCM's bank creditors, who were unhappy that Goldman Sachs had worked on this behind their backs.

The partners rejected the offer and proposed that all of LTCM's bank creditors contribute capital to LTCM so it could continue to manage and liquidate the fund in an orderly fashion. This would be a better deal for banks, investors, the financial markets, and even LTCM's partners.

The Consortium Bailout

> This agreement was not a government bailout, in that Federal Reserve funds
> were neither provided nor ever even suggested.
> —Alan Greenspan, October 1, 1998 Testimony to the House

The consortium bailout was among the most controversial aspects of LTCM's collapse, but it was probably the wisest solution. Ten years later the market saw Lehman Brothers fail without a coordinated bailout. LTCM's collapse perturbed the markets a bit, but they recovered quickly after the coordinated rescue. After Lehman's collapse, by contrast, interest rates on commercial paper and short-term lending skyrocketed, creating imbalances on both Wall Street and Main Street.

Merrill Lynch's Herbert Allison was lead investment banker, and banks contributed according to how much risk each had with LTCM. Bear Stearns and Lehman did not want to put up as much capital as other participants. Bear Stearns paid nothing, claiming that clearing LTCM's trades had already given them too much exposure—a clever excuse, and one that Bear Stearns stuck with, despite protests from other creditors.

Jimmy Cayne was making a pure business decision. He had millions of his own money still invested with LTCM. He also was on good terms with LTCM partners, playing poker and golf with Meriwether and Rosenfeld frequently. The participants in the room were shocked. The Fed officials took Jimmy into a room to speak with Merrill Lynch CEO David Komansky. Komansky barked at Jimmy. "What the !@#$ are you doing?" Jimmy replied, "We never had any risk with LTCM. You were the banks that gave them zero haircuts and piggybacked on their trade ideas. We are a clearing agent, a vendor. If we should inject capital, then why isn't AT&T here?" Komansky and Cayne agreed that Cayne would return to the big room and explain LTCM's status and why Bear would not contribute.[12]

> They're in compliance. They paid everything on time. We paid everything
> for them on time. I don't see any chink in their armor. I don't see anything at
> all. But I also don't see a responsibility on our part to partake in something

that we had nothing to do with ... You all had something in common. Number one, you all gave them no initial margin requirements. Number two, you all piggybacked. Who's kidding who? ... Bear Stearns is not where you are. As a matter of fact, we took, as it turns out, the worse clearance deal in the history of clearance deals.
—Jimmy Cayne, former CEO of Bear Stearns (Cohan 2009)

Eventually 14 creditors injected a total of $3.625 billion. Bankers Trust, Barclays, Chase, Deutsche Bank, UBS, Salomon Smith Barney, J.P. Morgan, Goldman Sachs, Merrill Lynch, Credit Suisse First Boston, and Morgan Stanley Dean Witter each contributed $300 million. Societe Generale contributed $125 million; Paribas and Lehman Brothers each contributed $100 million. Bear Stearns contributed nothing.[13] LTCM's partners retained their jobs, but would be overseen by a steering committee made up of consortium members.

The bailout used no public money. The Fed simply coordinated private entities, hoping to avoid a larger crisis such as the one that Lehman's failure precipitated. The Fed helped coordinate a temporary capital injection by the private market to aid with an orderly liquidation of LTCM.

McDonough described the rescue eloquently at the time:

If you save a baby from getting hit by a truck and the baby gets slightly bruised, you're going to get some criticisms for the bruises. The baby we were concerned about was the credit markets, not Long-Term Capital. And we think the risks were worth it.
—William McDonough, President of NY Fed (Schlesinger 1998)

On September 25, 1998, William Meyer, former President of Credit Suisse, described the bailout:

The [bond] markets have basically shut down already, and you would have had serious risk of some carnage here ... [had Wall Street firms not been bailed out.
—William Meyer (Siconolfi 1998)

The LTCM bailout was widely misunderstood as a purely company rescue. But counterparties and investors would have lost the most from LTCM's collapse. The bailout really rescued LTCM's partners, its investors, its counterparties, and averted further market imbalances.

Too Big To Fail

What's true for the gods, isn't true for the cows.

—Rudiger Dornbusch

After the consortium injected $3.625 billion into LTCM in exchange for 90% of the fund's value, partners and employees stayed to clean up the mess. They had told the consortium that it would take at least three years to wind down all positions. They finished the job in just one and a quarter years, between September 1998 and December 1999.

The atmosphere at LTCM was less than joyous. The partners had lost most of their net worths; some of them even owed banks money. Their dream of taming the markets was shattered. They could have chosen to walk away and forget the disaster. Instead, they stayed at LTCM with no bonuses and reduced salaries of $100,000 to $200,000.

Fund partner Hans Hufschmid recalls that this period was a "... pretty harsh experience ... what was amazing, is how unified the group stayed and didn't bitch and moan. There was no finger-pointing."

Rosenfeld recalls some of the innovative approaches LTCM used to pair up and close hundreds of billions of dollars in swap positions.

For an example, suppose LTCM had bought a cheap 10-year bond and hedged it by paying fixed interest on a 10-year swap with a 5% fixed rate. Six months later the bond revalues and the fund sells the bond, leaving an open swap position that LTCM would like to close. Buying back the swap—in other words, entering a new swap position to receive a fixed rate on a 9.5-year swap—is one way to close the trade. LTCM could go back to the counterparty and ask them to sell this to the fund, but that counterparty might not be the best swap seller for the opposite side of the transaction. LTCM could approach another counterparty for a look-alike swap, but there are associated frictions and costs. Most of the market is set up to price fresh, on-the-run swaps such as a 10-year swap. A counterparty will charge for the specialized pricing it will have to construct for a 9.5-year swap.

Instead, LTCM found innovative ways to close their positions. In this case, the fund might buy a pristine 10-year swap. The two swaps (old and new) are similar but opposite, and so cancel one another's risk exposure, becoming what are called dead swaps. According to an LTCM partner, there is still a "remaining amount of annuity risk and tail risk, but these are essentially offsetting positions."

LTCM had a $1.2 trillion book of dead swaps, which they auctioned to the investment banks. For example, suppose LTCM had a swap with UBS receiving 5% and paying floating; the other swap had Goldman Sachs paying

4.9% and receiving floating. Anyone with a high bid could purchase the position, but Goldman Sachs and UBS had the biggest incentive to buy. By purchasing, they could remove LTCM as the middleman and face the other side of the swap directly. Over the next year and a quarter, LTCM paired its dead swaps and sold them off. In the end, Rosenfeld says, "We cleaned out the dead swap portfolio with almost no losses."

> I am pretty proud of what LTCM did after the crisis. We stayed around and cleaned up the mess we made. We didn't bitch and moan. We told the consortium it would take 3 years to clean out the portfolio, but we got it done in 15 months.
> —Rosenfeld interview, September 28, 2010

Just after April 1999, LTCM partners went around the world telling investors what had happened and apologizing for August and September's extreme losses. Some people saw this as an attempt to lay the groundwork for the next fund, but there was also a lot of genuine remorse.

Why Did It Happen?

Why did this seemingly well-behaved system collapse? Many factors may have contributed, and it's difficult to discern the most significant.

There were several minor causes. Perhaps Meriwether managed LTCM too democratically. Hufschmid recollected that "We would have discussions on anything and everything with everybody. It was one person, one vote, even though some people were much more qualified than others. An organization should have one person who listens to everybody, but ultimately someone has to decide to go left or right."

Conflicts of interest may have contributed. Some employees were more interested in the firm's performance; asymmetric compensation policies meant that others were more interested in individual portfolio performance. There was no system that gradually transferred company ownership from old employees to new ones, and that reinforced traders' tendency to put their portfolios above the overall company's health.

LTCM's risk management framework was a strength and a weakness. Traders were more likely to take on marginal trades because they believed that the diversified portfolio protected them.

> When we came into 1998, I didn't like a lot of our trades. They were very marginal. I didn't do anything about it. I thought with our diversification, it

would come out in the wash. There was a general notion that if these trades were standalone trades, we would not have put them on. Diversification fooled us.

—Hans Hufschmid interview, September 30, 2010

Diversification may have also encouraged less experienced, more theoretical traders to make experimental trades.

There were only about 4 people at LTCM who had substantial trading instincts, something that got at times lost in a larger group. Furthermore, we had academics who came in with no trading experience and they started modeling away. Their trades might look good given the assumptions they made, but they often did not pass a simple smell test. There was pressure on them to come up with trades, which often resulted in poor trade selections. The partners with good trading instincts were John, Larry, Victor, myself, and also Eric and Greg. Of course, others like Myron, Bob, or David Mullins had no trading experience.

—Hans Hufschmid interview, September 30, 2010

Tension may have existed between the firm's traditional, experienced traders and its quantitative theorists. That led to less efficient overall portfolio management.

There are lots of lessons you learn. One is that it is very hard to mix hunters and farmers. LTCM was characterized by hunters. Hunters don't always tell the truth, whereas academics are more inclined to do this. Hunters don't want to be evaluated, want to do things on a gross return. Don't want to respect others. They marginalize others. This makes it very hard to run a business. The AIG and Merrill Lynch failures also suggest that it is hard to control hunters. They don't disappear. It's a very big problem. For so long, LTCM was doing well. There was a lot of beef and thus everything was great. In times of abundant bison, hunters look great, while others look bad. We paid people more and more on what they killed; however, there was no real measurement on why the money was being paid. This goes on today in other institutions. It's like dealing with one's children. If senior management ask the hunters how things are going, their natural inclination is to say everything is fine. They want to keep their capital and do more hunting. In general, it's a major problem that needs to be addressed.

—Myron Scholes interview, July 9, 2011

Although these causes contributed in small ways, the major direct cause for LTCM's failure had to do with crowding and a flight to quality in the trades.

TABLE 5.2 Correlations and Standard Deviations of Strategies, Pre-August 1998 and Post-August 1998

Trade	σ_{pre}	σ_{crisis}	ρ_{pre}	ρ_{crisis}
Trade 1	1	1.90	0.08	0.32
Trade 2	1	1.89	0.04	0.18
Trade 3	1	2.34	0.11	0.30
Trade 4	1	1.16	0.00	0.11
Trade 5	1	3.47	0.18	0.37
Trade 6	1	2.13	0.18	0.33
Trade 7	1	1.34	0.10	0.12
Trade 8	1	3.94	0.17	0.29
Average	1	2.27	0.11	0.25

Note: Correlations are computed from LTCM's inception in February 1994 until July 31, 1998 and then from August 1, 1998 until October 1, 1998 for pre and post respectively.
σ_{pre} normalized the standard deviation of each strategy to 1 prior to the crisis; σ_{crisis} is the ratio of the volatility during the crisis to that of precrisis. Correlations both before and during the crisis are the average correlations of the strategy with all other strategies. Trade 1 is the short U.S. swap trade, Trade 2 is the European cross swap trade, Trade 3 is the long mortgage trade, Trade 4 is the Japanese box trade, Trade 5 is the short equity volatility trade, Trade 6 is risk arb trade, Trade 7 is the equity relative value trade, and Trade 8 is the long emerging markets trade.

To understand what happened to LTCM, it's helpful to look at the fund's trade portfolio, described in Table 4.1.[14] Table 5.2 shows each LTCM trade's standard deviation and the trade's average correlation with other trades both before and during the crisis. Standard deviations precrisis are normalized to 1.

This table shows that both trade correlations and the standard deviation of each trade increased during the crisis.[15] The average daily correlation more than doubled from 0.11 to 0.25 and the average standard deviation more than doubled, going from 1 to 2.27. The average correlation between the short swap trade and all other trades increased from 0.08 before the crisis to 0.32 during the crisis.[16]

Trade correlations over a three-day horizon did double in August and September, but this doesn't tell the full story.[17] Before the crisis, strategies' average monthly correlation was 0.05. In August 1998, however, every strategy had a negative monthly return, implying a correlation of 1. In September, 6 of the 8 strategies had negative monthly returns.

The increase in correlations across strategies *and* every strategy's overall increase in risk caused LTCM's failure. Both were most likely caused by a flight to quality, away from less liquid instruments such as mortgage securities, off-the-run securities, and swaps. The moves carried more weight because a group of similar traders simultaneously exited similar positions.

LTCM had strived to maintain position secrecy, but the partners knew that most of their proprietary strategies had been copied. The crowding had severe consequences in 1998.

> Everyone else started catching up to us. We'd go to put on a trade, but when we started to nibble, the opportunity would vanish.
> —Rosenfeld in Lewis (1999)

> It ceased to feel like people were liquidating positions similar to ours. All of a sudden they were liquidating our positions.
> —Richard Leahy in Lewis (1999)

> The few things we had on that the market didn't know about came back quickly. It was the trades that the market knew we had on that caused us trouble.
> —John Meriwether in Lewis (1999)

> They went down because the exit door got very crowded.
> —Jimmy Cayne interview, former CEO of Bear Stearns,
> February 15, 2012

By the end of September 1998, LTCM was owned and operated by 14 consortium members, plus LTCM's former partners. The hedge fund that could do no wrong had failed, for several reasons. It had underestimated the possibility that all of its strategies could simultaneously move against it in a crisis. It had not anticipated strategies' behavior in the presence of lots of quant copycats, nor the crowd's behavior during market shocks. Some of its largest trades weren't as beautiful as the trades that had made LTCM so successful. The short swap trade was vulnerable to a market crisis and had a large downside. The short volatility trade was also vulnerable to a crisis in which short-term and long-term volatility spiked and liquidity was very low. Together, these two trades cost LTCM a total of $2.9 billion.

LTCM's partners survived to trade another day. But how did LTCM's investors and counterparties fare when the fund collapsed?

Appendix 5.1   The John Meriwether Letter

Some things are better left unsaid.

—Daryl Hall

(The following is a reformatted version of a letter issued by
John W. Meriwether, Chief Executive Officer Long-Term Capital
Management as it appeared on Bloomberg.)

September 2, 1998

To Investors in the
Investment Vehicles of
Long-Term Capital Portfolio, LP

Re: Impact on Net Asset Value of August Market Conditions

Dear Investor:

As you are all too aware, events surrounding the collapse in
Russia caused large and dramatically increasing volatility in
global markets throughout August, capped by a last-day decline in
the Dow Jones Industrial Average of 513 points. The resulting
dislocations in markets and greatly increased uncertainty have
driven investors to safer and more liquid assets. With increases
in both risk and liquidity premia -- investment funds widely,
many Wall Street firms, and money-center banks have reported
large trading losses with resulting sharp declines in their share
prices. Investors everywhere have experienced large declines in
their wealth.

Unfortunately, Long-Term Capital Portfolio (``Fund'') has
also experienced a sharp decline in net asset value. As you know
our formal procedure for releasing our official net asset value
normally takes about ten days after month end. Following our
usual practice to give you an early estimate of the Fund's
performance, it is down 44 percent for the month of August, and
52 percent for the year-to-date. Losses of this magnitude are a
shock to us as they surely are to you, especially in light of the
historical volatility of the Fund. The losses arising from the
event-driven major increase in volatility and the flight to
liquidity were magnified by the time of year when markets were
seasonally thin.

The losses in August occurred in a wide variety of
strategies, distributed approximately 82 percent in relative-
value trades and 18 percent in directional trades. Emerging
markets across both trade categories accounted for 16 percent of
the month's total losses in the Fund. Within emerging markets,
holdings involving Russia accounted for less than 10 percent of
total losses.

A distinguishing characteristic of the Fund's investment philosophy has always been that its returns are generally expected not to exhibit systematic correlation with the returns on global bond, stock and currency markets. August saw an accelerating increase in the demand for liquidity in nearly every market around the world. Consequently, Government bonds have been the best performers, while small-cap common stocks and other relatively illiquid and risky instruments such as high-yield bonds have performed poorly. Many of the Fund's investment strategies involve providing liquidity to the market. Hence, our losses across strategies were correlated after-the-fact from a sharp increase in the liquidity premium.

The majority of the Fund's risks are in our core investment strategies; that is, convergence, relative-value and conditional convergence trades in the U.S., Japan and the larger markets of Europe. Although we have hedged risk-exposure components that were not expected to add incremental value to performance, large divergences in August occurred in many of our key trading strategies that resulted in large losses. The use of leverage has accentuated these losses.

With the large and rapid full in our capital, steps have been taken to reduce risks now, commensurate with our level of capital. We have raised the risk-return tradeoff requirements for positions. Risk and position reduction is occurring in some strategies that do not meet the new standard. This is a prudent step given the level of capital and uncertainties in the market place.

On the other hand, we see great opportunities in a number of our best strategies and these are being held by the Fund. As it happens, the best strategies are the ones we have worked on over many years. We will focus on these high expected return-to-risk positions and, thereby we can manage them more aggressively.

A cornerstone of our investment management philosophy is the availability and efficiency of financing to support the long horizon for many of our investment strategies. Our capital base is over $2.3 billion, and it is quite liquid. Our financing is in place, including secured and unsecured term debt and long-dated contractual arrangements. These term arrangements provide time to reduce our positions, if needed, as markets become more settled. We continue to work closely with counterparts.

Investors in the Fund provide long-term equity capital that can only be withdrawn in multi-year stages at each year-end. This capital allows the Fund to secure stronger term financing and contractual agreements. It also provides greater flexibility to adjust positions, given changes in the level of its capital. The first date that any investors can withdraw capital is year-end 1998 and that potential withdrawal is less than 12 percent of the capital of the Fund. The principals of LTCM represent over a third of the capital of the Fund. To provide a solid foundation for the Fund and to capitalize on the materially richer investment opportunity set, LTCM is in the process of seeking to raise additional capital.

The poor performance of the Fund, year-to-date and especially in August, has been very disappointing to us all. However, I would ask in assessing performance going forward, that you keep in mind that the Fund's relative-value strategies may require a relatively long convergence horizon. The expected horizon for convergence on our trades range from six months to two years, or even longer. Implementation of these strategies involves large positions that take significant time to accumulate and to reduce efficiently. The convergence return pattern of these core strategies normally implies that the day-to-day volatility is much greater in proportion to time than the month-to-month or year-to-year volatility of their performance. This does not imply, however, that the reported short-term performance of the Fund is in any way an inaccurate or invalid measure of actual returns. The mark-to-market valuations on positions in the Fund reported to you are always derived from actual dealer and broker quotations.

The Fund returned approximately $2.7 billion of its capital at year-end 1997 when it appeared that the existing investment opportunities were not large and attractive enough to warrant its retention. Many of the trades had converged producing profits and were unwound. Over the past several months, however these trades that had converged once again diverged. The Fund added to its positions in anticipation of convergence, yet largely because of last month's market events, the trades diverged dramatically. As a result, the opportunity act in these trades at this time is believed to be among the best that LTCM has ever seen. But, as we have seen, good convergence trades can diverge further. In August, many of them diverged at a speed and to an extent that had not been seen before. LTCM thus believes that it is prudent and opportunistic to increase the level of the Fund's capital to take full advantage of this unusually attractive environment.

With limited expectations, the Fund has been closed to new investment since July 1995. Many of you have asked to add to your investment in the Fund. Since it is prudent to raise additional capital, the Fund is offering you the opportunity to invest in the Fund on special terms related to LTCM fees. If you have an interest in investing, please contact Richard Leahy at Long-Term Capital Management (203-552-5511) for further information.

I cannot close without telling you about the remarkable performance of the LTCM employees during this particularly difficult month. Over the first four years of the Fund, we had the great good fortune of consistent return performances resulting in larger-than-expected returns with lower-than-expected volatility. We expected that sooner or later that this good fortune could not continue uninterrupted and that we as a firm would be tested. I did not anticipate, however, how severe the test would be. I am happy to report the magnificent performance of our employees operating as a team - administration,

technology, operations, legal and strategies - coordinate d across
our Greenwich, London, and Tokyo offices during this extrem e
period. August has been very painful for all of us, but I
believe that as a consequence, LTCM will emerge a stronger an d
better firm.

Sincerely,
John W. Meriwether
Chief Executive Officer
Chairman of the Management Committee

(ns) PN

-END-

Appendix 5.2   The Warren Buffett Letter

Wall Street is the only place that people ride to in a Rolls Royce to get advice from those who take the subway.

—Warren Buffett

HIGHLY CONFIDENTIAL

September 23, 1998

Mr. John Meriwether
Chief Executive Officer
Long-Term Capital Management, L.P.
One East Weaver Street
Greenwich, CT 06331-5146

Dear Mr. Meriwether,

Subject to the following deal structure, the partnership described below proposes to purchase the assets of Long-Term Capital Management (and/or its affiliates and subsidiaries, collectively referred to as "Long-Term Capital") for $250 million.

To purchaser will be a limited partnership whose investors will be Berkshire Hathaway for $3 billion, American International Group for $700 million and Goldman Sachs for $300 million (or each of their respective affiliates). All management of the assets will be under the sole control of the partnership and will be transferred to the partnership in an orderly manner.

This bid is also subject to the following:

1) The limited partnership described herein will not assume any liabilities of Long-Term Capital arising from any activities prior to the purchase by the partnership

2) All current financing provided to Long-Term Capital will remain in place under current terms and conditions.

The names of the proposal participants may not be disclosed to anyone. If the names are disclosed, the bid will expire.

This bid will expire at 12:30 p.m. New York time on September 23, 1998.

Sincerely,

Warren E. Buffett   Maurice R. Greenberg   Jon S. Corzine

Agreed and Accepted on behalf of Long-Term Capital

_____
John Meriwether

Copy of the $250 million offer for Long-Term Capital Management

CHAPTER 6

The Fate of
LTCM Investors

> *Prosperity is not without many fears and distastes; and adversity is not without comforts and hopes.*
>
> —Francis Bacon

Most of LTCM's investors were large institutions: commercial banks, asset management funds, pension funds, and insurance companies. (See Table 6.1.) These represented 93.9% of LTCM's investor base. Individuals represented only 3.6% of the firm's outside money. Other securities firms contributed another 2.5%.

Five investors had LTCM stakes of more than $100 million, 15 investors had between $25 and $99 million, and 55 investors had less than $25 million in the fund. Investors came from all over, but were mainly from Europe and the United States.

After the bank consortium acquired most of LTCM in a down round of financing,[1] they paid off LTCM's original investors, cutting checks by April 1, 1999.

Original LTCM investors, therefore, have fund performance histories from February 1994 through April 1, 1999. Although 1998 was a disastrous year for the fund—$1 invested in January 1998 was worth 8 cents by September 23, 1998—original investors were eventually paid 10 cents on the dollar for that year's performance, losing a total of 90% for 1998. But in earlier years LTCM's performance was extremely good and the firm paid substantial investor dividends, including $2.7 billion at the end of 1997. That greatly

TABLE 6.1 Investor Profiles in LTCM

	Percent of Investor Base
By Investor Type	
Commercial Banks	69.30
Investment Funds	13.60
Pension Funds & University Endowments	6.10
Insurance Companies	4.90
Individuals	3.60
Securities Firms	2.50
By Investor Size	
$100M and over (5 investors)	43.00
$25–$99M (15 investors)	33.00
Under $25M (55 investors)	24.00
By Geography	
Europe	58.50
United States	24.10
Asia	12.70
Other	4.70

Note: Investor types are as of December 1997.
Source: LTCM.

improved net investment performance. Of 100 investors, only 12 actually lost money and only 6 lost more than $2 million.

Ironically, the investors who lost money were preferred investors. They were allowed to keep their money in the fund at the end of 1997, when LTCM made its large forced dividend. At that time, LTCM's original investors received all their profits to date. From 1998 forward they could only keep their original investments in the fund.

The fund's strategic investors were institutions that could add value beyond their investments. In China, these investors might help LTCM navigate through closed markets; in Korea, they might help finance LTCM's positions; in Latin America, they might give LTCM insight into new government regulations. UBS, for example, helped complete innovative transactions with LTCM, helping all LTCM investors. LTCM let strategic investors retain both their original investments and profits to date in the fund from 1998 onward.

Investors that invested after the first year and lacked strategic value were paid back in full and forced to exit the fund in 1997. Preferred investors remained in the fund after the forced distributions and consequently lost more when the crisis hit.[2]

The median investor had a 19% annualized return from LTCM's inception until its close. By comparison, the S&P 500 had an annualized return of 25%, a treasury bill index returned 5.1%, a 10-year government bond index returned 7.8%, a high-yield bond index returned 8.4%, gold returned −5.5%, a world equity index returned 16.4%, a world bond index returned 7.1%, an emerging equity index returned −4.8%, and an emerging bond index returned 11.2%.[3] The median investor did reasonably well, compared to other investment alternatives.

UBS lost a great deal in LTCM's failure. UBS was interested in LTCM's counterparty business; it also had lots of cash to invest in LTCM, but the fund was already closed to investors.

In autumn 1997, LTCM and UBS negotiated a deal for LTCM's partners to buy an at-the-money 7-year call option on $750 million notional of the LTCM fund from UBS.[4]

The call option's price was $293 million. Again, a call option buys the right to purchase a given instrument at a given price. In this case, it gave LTCM's partners the right to buy the LTCM fund at a given net asset value (NAV). If LTCM's NAV increased, LTCM partners would have greater fund exposure and make more money. If the fund went down, the partners had limited losses.

UBS wrote the call option, so its situation was different. If LTCM did well, UBS would lose money on the option. If LTCM performed poorly, UBS would gain the option premium.

In exchange for this, LTCM let UBS invest around $266 million directly into the fund.[5] UBS got a desirable investment; LTCM got a cheap way to lever management's fund exposure with downside protection.

By purchasing a call option on LTCM, its partners leveraged their personal stakes on the upside if LTCM did well, which most of them expected it would, while limiting the downside to the $293 million option cost. The trade also let LTCM invest further in the fund without having to worry about a conventional loan's mark-to-market requirement. Most of the premium was invested in LTCM, so LTCM did not have to shell out a large amount of cash. The deal even deferred taxes until the option's maturity, letting partners pay taxes at the lower capital gains rates, not higher income tax rates.

If LTCM's NAV never increased, UBS would make a cool profit of $293 million. If LTCM's NAV continued to rise, UBS would be short an in-the-money call on a notional amount of $750 million. UBS could have an unlimited loss on their books over the option's 7 years, depending on how much LTCM's NAV rose.[6]

Other banks had refused to write this option. Swiss Bank Corporation, for instance, thought it was "too much of a risk because it couldn't be hedged." That wasn't quite true. The call option was difficult, but not impossible to hedge.

According to the contract, LTCM let UBS hedge the call option by investing directly into LTCM. In option jargon, this is known as dynamic hedging, or delta hedging. A call's writer can hedge the position by borrowing some cash and investing that in the underlying security—in this case, the LTCM fund. In theory, a dynamic hedge requires continuous adjustments. In practice, daily (or even less frequent) adjustments may be enough. UBS's contract let it dynamically hedge its position every month, with a one-month lag.[7]

UBS didn't make those monthly adjustments. Instead, it simply over-hedged the position. In a call option hedge, delta's smallest value is 0 and its largest value is 1. At most, UBS needed a total investment of $750 million in LTCM (a delta of 1) to create an adequate hedge. Most of the time, the hedge could be smaller than this. UBS decided to hedge the option by investing $800 million in the fund, in addition to its $266M investment, giving a hedge ratio larger than 1.[8]

UBS saw the written call as an income stream from a firm that they believed would not lose money. The UBS position was like a covered call, long the stock and short a call option. Investors often pursue this strategy when they believe an investment's downside is low and they can get extra revenue by selling the call option.[9]

When LTCM collapsed, UBS lost $626 million from its LTCM invest-ment. It lost 90% of its $800 million investment, 90% of its $266 million investment, gained 10% on the $300 million consortium injection, and re-ceived an option premium of $293 million.

Credit Suisse had a similar option position, to the tune of $150 million notional.[10]

The Bank of Italy was one of LTCM's highest-profile investors. Bank of Italy Governor Antonio Fazio received much criticism for this investment. After all, central banks typically keep their foreign exchange reserves invested in very safe assets, such as short-term government bonds. But the late 1990s saw a general push for central banks to be more aggressive with their bank reserves and seek higher-yielding assets. Some central banks did this by investing in swaps and U.S. agency securities and by extending duration on the yield curve.

In 1994 the Bank of Italy decided to place 1% of its reserves in high-risk investments. Its portfolio was $27 billion. It invested a total of $100 million in LTCM, or 0.3% of its foreign exchange reserves, later loaning the firm $150 million. The bank earned profits of $120 million on its investment in LTCM, and the bank consortium bailout paid back their loan with interest. Ignoring cash flow timing, the Bank of Italy made about 20% on its LTCM investment, plus loan interest. It would be hard to claim negligence around such a small amount, even if the bank had lost every dime.[11]

LTCM had other notable investors when it collapsed. It is hard to know how much they may have lost or gained over the entire time their investment was in LTCM. They include Dresdner Bank (about $145 million); Sumitomo Bank (about $100 million); Credit Suisse (around $55 million); Merrill Lynch employees' deferred payment program (around $22 million); Liechtenstein Global Trust (around $30 million); Bear Stearns executives, including Jimmy Cayne, Warren Spector, and Vinny Mattone (about $20 million total); PaineWebber chairman Donald Marron (about $10 million); McKinsey & Co. executives (about $10 million); Prudential Life Corporation (about $5 million); Bank Julius Baer; Republic National Bank; St. John's University Endowment Fund; Credit Agricole; some large funds of funds; and the University of Pittsburgh.

In addition to fund investors, other groups had direct financial ties to LTCM. One was the large group of counterparties with which LTCM had conducted its over-the-counter trades. LTCM paid all its counterparties everything it owed. LTCM also paid its margin calls to as many as 60 counterparties on any given day. These counterparties never had any losses.

The bank consortium that injected $3.625 billion on September 25, 1998, in exchange for 90% of the company made a 10% return, or $362.5 million, on their investment by the time the fund closed in December 1999. The fund was actually up 25% by April 1, 1999. Rather than slowly liquidating positions so the market could handle the large volume, the bank consortium chose a faster liquidation path, lowering its eventual returns.

Fund partners were the last group with a significant LTCM investment. Despite popular suspicions, the partners did not walk away with a profit when the bank consortium infused LTCM with capital. LTCM partners had contributed personal funds to the fund's management company, which in turn borrowed more than $200 million to leverage partners' stakes.[12]

Individual partners also borrowed to increase their personal fund stakes. Credit Lyonnais made a total of $34 million in personal loans to partners. Lawrence Hilibrand and Hans Hufschmid personally borrowed $24 million and $14.6 million, respectively; Arjun Krishnamachar and Gregory Hawkins borrowed $2.7 million and $1.3 million, respectively.[13]

When the bank consortium made its capital infusion, the management group owed a total $180 million. Between September 1998 and December 1999, when the partners steered the fund to a tranquil closing, their incentive fees helped pay down their debts.

At the beginning of 1998, the partners controlled $2 billion of the roughly $4.8 billion fund. When the fund closed in December 1999, the partners still owed $60 million. The bank consortium forgave this remaining debt.

All told, LTCM's partners lost more than 100% between January 1998 and the fund's close in December 1999. It's hard to know how the partners fared over the fund's entire history.

> Every partner was different. So it's hard to say. There were no fees for investing partner money. It was such a good perk that most people bought in to it. Generally, older partners kept some money out, while younger partners invested all and borrowed to invest more. My gut tells me that as a group, we were net negative over the entire existence of LTCM. Most people walked away with less than they started with. However, some people did buy homes with some of their profits and walked away with those. And some had individual personal debt due to borrowing to invest and had to work it off. Everyone worked it off.
> —Eric Rosenfeld interview, September 2, 2010

The partners were wiped out and the investors had taken big losses. All they had left, it seems, were the lessons the failure offered them: lessons in managing hedge funds, pricing risk, and maintaining transparency, as well as lessons that applied to the whole financial system.

CHAPTER 7

General Lessons from the Collapse

Periclum ex aliis facito tibi quod ex usu siet.[1]

—*Heauton Timoroumenos*

Innovation and volatility are linked, so it's impossible to protect society from individual firm collapses and bouts of systemic risk. Even so, broad lessons can be learned from LTCM's failure, lessons that are important for individual financial institutions and for the financial system as a whole. Ignoring these lessons was, in part, the cause of a much greater systemic financial collapse in 2008 and 2009.

Interconnected Crowds

Risk and liquidity depend on the trading space's saturation and interconnectedness.

Market movements aren't independent of the players who make them. Most of modern finance has produced models that either assume that all security holders behave the same way, or that horizons are all of a single period. The real world contains many investor types, all trading based on different constraints and opinions. A trade's long-run returns may differ substantially from its short-run returns precisely because traders have different agendas and motivations. Investor behavior does tend to converge during a crisis, a

101

factor that helped cause LTCM's failure. Variously motivated traders copied LTCM's trades, then sold positions out of panic or inexperience.

Some academics have tried to model this behavior, but most finance theorists and practitioners avoid this very important issue.[2]

Tackling this issue means estimating what fraction of the current market is invested in various trades—not a simple task. A good model also requires an understanding of each security's return and risk characteristics and how these change as differently motivated players react to market changes. Good models could generate more complicated security-price distributions, but might also ultimately measure risks more accurately.[3]

Risk models' failure to account for crowding and interconnectedness also played an important role in risk misvaluation during 2008's financial crisis.[4]

VaR

There are limitations to VaR, stress testing, or any other risk management system.

LTCM's risk management system rested on selecting a portfolio with a large number of low-volatility trades, all with very low correlations to one another. The portfolio had a very low estimated value-at-risk (VaR) before the fund collapsed in August and September 1998.

Extremely large directional bets often bring down traders and hedge funds, but this wasn't the case for LTCM. LTCM's failure illustrates some of the limitations of VaR analysis and stress testing—as well as the impossibility of stress testing the unimaginable.

VaR analysis is nothing new. In its simplest form, it involves using a return process's standard deviation to estimate how much a trader or portfolio manager might lose if one event or another takes place. As a risk management tool, VaR became popular in the late 1990s with the development of J.P. Morgan's Risk Metrics program. Soon, other banks also sold their clients risk-management systems.

VaR measures the historical variances and covariances of asset classes or individual instruments, then uses this to infer, given an investor's current investment position, how much a portfolio might lose if one or more rare events occur. The most basic system assumes that returns are distributed normally, so an analyst can use a simple scaling factor to infer the fund's worst-case losses.[5] VaR can be misleading when returns are not normal, with fat tails. In that case, the portfolio has a much larger chance of losing a lot than the normal distribution predicts.

VaR became popular in the 1990s, and almost immediately people began criticizing the use of VaR in cases that assumed normal distributions. VaR was also criticized for assuming that returns' historical variances and covariances would be good predictors.

The critics offered no simple alternative, and so many practitioners continued using historical variance-covariance estimates. LTCM is a case in point. It measured historical correlations and even performed stress tests using slightly higher correlations. However, analysts never asked what would happen if strategy correlations reached 1.

One lesson from the LTCM crisis is this: Given that VaR has deficiencies, consider scenarios in which correlations approach 1. This is not a foolproof risk management system, but it is certainly more conservative. Supplement it with alternative risk measure approaches.

LTCM's failure also illustrates the danger of crowded spaces and the endogeneity of risk. Most VaR systems use historical data and ignore the investment space's current players. But a position's actual risk depends on a trade's current and potential investors. Hold positions that no one else would naturally hold unless a huge price change made them more attractive, and historical measures mean nothing. By definition, any attempt to liquidate those positions will entail huge losses.

In some markets, it's easy to see this. In the natural gas futures market, Amaranth Advisors LLC sometimes owned more than 90% of the open interest on a natural gas futures contract. Selling that position may clearly have resulted in a large price movement.[6]

For LTCM, spotting this saturation was much more difficult. LTCM bought and sold relatively liquid contracts from other banks in the over-the-counter (OTC) market. In the OTC market it is very difficult to get an idea of how many investors are operating similar trades. The opportunity's size is the only real signal. If the spread historically had been 30 basis points and now it is 15 basis points, the market may be saturated with other traders. It's difficult to find the right points of comparison for both the historic and current spreads. Should an analyst look at the trade as of three months ago? Five years ago? If the opportunity is smaller, smaller than what? Risk managers should try, even though very difficult, to measure risk's interconnections, especially as related to crises.

VaR is based on standard risk measures, such as standard deviation, and that could create self-fulfilling crises. A series of rapidly decreasing prices in an asset class or a position may lead to a higher measured volatility, which then may lead to investors cutting those positions to bring the VaR in line with limits. Suppose a bank has a position of $100 million on security A. The historical volatility is 20% and the critical value used to measure VaR is 2.33. The VaR for the investment horizon is VaR $= -2.33 \cdot 0.20 \cdot 100 = \$46.6$ million. Suppose that is the maximum allowed. If a severe price movement pushes the position to $90 million and volatility to 22%, the VaR may change to VaR $= -2.33 \cdot 0.22 \cdot 90 = \$46.1M$, plus the loss of $10 million. The total at risk is now $56 million, and the bank's managers may ask the trader to reduce the position—causing further price declines.

Consider a particularly extreme example, beginning with a bond that will pay $100 with certainty at the end of the time horizon. Suppose the risk management system measures a rolling 30-day return volatility for use with VaR.

Simulate a process for the trade's 60-day price movement return, assuming a daily mean return of 0.04% and a daily volatility of 1.2649%.[7]

On the 60th day, we change the trade's return process to have the same daily volatility, but a daily negative return of –4%. This is a bit like a sudden, mass rush to sell the security. The trade's measured volatility rises as the selloff continues, increasing the VaR and potentially pushing bank managers to further cut their positions. That would further decrease the trade's value (see Figure 7.1).

FIGURE 7.1   Bond Value and Associated VaR as Simulated Panic in Market Begins

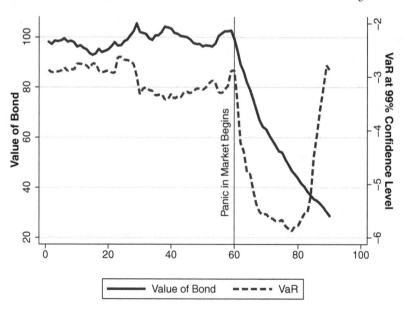

That's all despite the fact that the security will pay $100 at maturity. The closer this security gets to 0, the lower its risk should be.

Most risk management systems use historical, statistical returns to compute risk. They don't consider the trade's fundamental valuation, the space's level of crowding, or other investors' behavior.

A better risk measure might include a component that decreases as a trade's price moves away from its fundamental value. To work well, such a risk measure would need to be widely used. Agreeing on a valuation measure, however, may prove difficult.

Leverage

Leverage can lead to bankruptcy even when positions are sound.

Leverage is a powerful tool for any investor. If an investment's expected return is higher than the borrowing rate, a trader can amplify the return as a percentage of capital by borrowing at the lower rate and investing at the higher rate.

Just as leverage amplifies gains, it also amplifies losses. LTCM had identified very high Sharpe ratio trades with very low volatility. To give investors meaningful returns, the fund leveraged its portfolio. Although most of LTCM's trades were not pure arbitrages, but rather statistical arbitrages or quasi-arbitrages, it is helpful to illustrate this concept with a pure arbitrage.

Suppose LTCM had identified a bond that would pay $100 in one year with certainty. It bought the bond at $90, giving an unlevered return of 10%. The risk for the one-year holding period was zero. With no leverage, LTCM could just wait, even if the bond's price fell as low as $0.01 in the interim.

With leverage, this becomes difficult or impossible. To simplify this example, ignore haircuts and margin collateral but assume that the lender can ask for all its collateral back the minute the firm's capital reaches zero.

With a leverage of 2, LTCM could invest $180 in this trade. However, if the bond price reached $45 (a –50% return) before the year was up, the firm would effectively go bankrupt. With a leverage of 10, the firm goes bankrupt at a bond price of $81 (a –10% return). With a leverage ratio of 25, the firm goes bankrupt at a bond price of $86.4 (a –4% return). Even a small drop in the trade's price can lead to bankruptcy when a firm is extremely levered, even when the trade is guaranteed to be profitable in a known, finite period of time.

This illustration of leverage's dangers is only part of the story. Leverage requires financing, and financing requires a lender. If returns sour or marketplace rumors say the investor is doing poorly, a lender might decide to alter the terms of financing by more than would be justified from marking to market.

Marking to market is a way that lenders can safeguard an investment. If the position moves against the borrower, the lender will either require more collateral or ask the borrower to put more capital against the position. If rumors say the firm may collapse, a lender might aggressively collect new capital, forcing the firm to spend down capital and perhaps actually pushing the borrower toward bankruptcy. In fact, rumors of collapse can become self-fulfilling prophecies, as more and more borrowers hear the "bad news" and require more collateral.[8]

This can happen to *any leveraged* institution. The events of 2008 and 2009 made the LTCM failure look tame, but some of the causes were similar. Leverage and self-fulfilling prophecies played a large part in the Bear Stearns and Lehman collapses. LTCM suffered from crowd behavior in 1998; so did Bear Stearns and Lehman Brothers in 2008.

As of May 31, 2008, Lehman's shareholder equity was $26 billion; total liabilities and stockholder's equity was at $639 billion.[9] Lehman Brothers' leverage was about 24. In contrast to LTCM, Lehman Brothers had a broad array of business lines: capital markets, investment banking, and investment management. It had a heavy exposure to the housing market—about $71 billion—as of the second quarter of 2008. It did not engage solely in fixed-income trading.

But there was an important similarity between the two companies. Their leverage ratios were about the same and, just as with LTCM, rumors spread that Lehman Brothers might be insolvent. Customers withdrew funds and credit lines. In particular, hedge fund clients in the prime brokerage area began closing their accounts.

The rumors led investors to short-sell Lehman stock, and that caused a dramatic price decline: from $36.50 on March 30, 2008 to $3.65 on September 12, 2008 (the Friday before the Monday on which they announced their bankruptcy).[10]

Were Lehman Brothers' positions sound? This is still unclear.[11] Lehman's leverage combined with investor rumors to create a self-fulfilling prophecy of collapse, just as happened to LTCM.

Some have argued that LTCM's positions would almost surely have been profitable in the near future, while Lehman faced very real potential losses from its real estate exposure. Even here, the time frame may have been the only difference. The real estate market may have eventually returned to values that made Lehman's positions profitable.

Even so, one thing is clear: a levered strategy can cause even a perfectly sound firm to fail.

Should leverage be prohibited or restricted? Even beginning a discussion about that means asking another question first: What purpose does leverage serve in the financial markets?[12]

Substantially different pricing for similar goods can lead to a misallocation of resources. Suppose that the interest rate for business loans in country A is much higher than the same rate in country B, even though all the economic risks are the same. This might lead to too little borrowing in country A compared with country B.

Some investors would accept this situation.[13] An arbitrageur, on the other hand, would immediately ask why investors are not taking advantage of this discrepancy, then lend more to country A at the higher interest rates, thereby causing this differential to vanish. Without leverage, these lenders will barely move market prices. With leverage, however, they may reduce market distortion and provide efficiency.

Given sufficient arbitrageurs, of course, there would be no need for leverage—there would be enough lenders to tip the market toward efficiency. In a world with more mispricings than arbitrageurs, however, leverage might be an important tool for restoring balance.

Are there enough large price imbalances for society as a whole to care? If two identical countries had risk-adjusted interest rate disparities of 1,000% versus 2%, then the vast majority of investors would bring assets toward country A. But an extremely small disparity—just 50 basis points—might not be enough to cause a societal cost and a mass investor movement.

In general, all investors are interested in exploiting a very wide spread until they push the spread to a level (and risk) that interests only specialized arbitrageurs. If enough arbitrageurs pile into the trade, the opportunity may shrink to a dead zone with no willing participants—at least, none who know that the spread has shrunk to these unattractive levels.

Arguing against leverage as a tool for hedge funds or other money management organizations also means arguing against banks. Almost every bank is leveraged. Banks pay small interest rates on deposits and earn higher interest rates in riskier investments, including loans. The Federal Reserve requires banks to keep a minimum of 10% of those deposits as reserves.

Banks can lend their remaining deposits, so many banks invest 90% of depositors' money. Banks also have shareholder equity. A bank's leverage is measured as the ratio of its total assets to its total equity.

For example, as of December 31, 2009, Capital One had total assets of $171,597,613 and shareholder equity of $26,605,676, for a leverage ratio of 6.45. Generally this leverage is small enough to avoid disaster, because banks often invest in relatively safe assets, and because banks receive a large spread between what they pay on deposits and what they receive on investments. Capital One's consumer loan yield is 10.37%; it pays out 2.02% on deposits.[14]

Bank failures occur all the time, not just in times of crisis.[15] Do we even need a financial system built on leverage? This is a very difficult question, one worthy of future research. Certainly a leveraged banking system most likely leads to more lending and perhaps more growth than a banking system without leverage.

Without leverage in the banking system, loans would depend on venture capitalists, who might charge higher rates, do less lending, and foster less growth. Or perhaps banks should all be nonprofit organizations that return profits to depositors.[16]

The safety of a given amount of leverage depends on the instrument's underlying volatility, not the actual leverage number. One investment with a volatility of 0.05% could be leveraged to 100 times and still be less risky than an unleveraged investment with an underlying volatility of 5.1%. However, it is always true that, without leverage, the maximum loss is the principal invested. With leverage, the losses can be much greater. Without capital to buffer this, leveraged losses will result in bankruptcy or lead to contagious selling, in which assets are sold to increase capital and reduce leverage. That further reduces investment prices and capital in a cycle that can continue indefinitely.

Clearinghouses

> Without a clearinghouse for common over-the-counter (OTC) products, the financial system's aggregate risk from one firm's collapse is significantly higher.

When the Federal Reserve got all LTCM's counterparties together to examine their risks, it acted to prevent worse financial trouble. A government report after the crisis noted the various problems with LTCM's web of counterparty contracts, yet failed to suggest a potential solution to these problems.[17]

> An LTCM Fund default would have caused counterparties to move quickly to limit exposures. These risk-limiting moves may have required the liquidation or replacement of positions and collateral in the many markets

where the LTCM Fund held sizable positions at depressed prices. These very actions in a market that, last September, was already suffering from a substantial reduction in liquidity could have resulted in significant losses. LTCM itself estimated that its top 17 counterparties would have suffered various substantial losses—potentially between $3 billion and $5 billion in aggregate—and shared this information with the fourteen firms participating in the consortium. The firms in the consortium saw that their losses could be serious, with potential losses to some firms amounting to $300 million to $500 million each.

Moreover, if the LTCM Fund had defaulted last September, the losses, market disruptions, and pronounced lack of liquidity could have been more severe if not for the use of closeout, netting, and collateral provisions.

—Report of the President's Working Group on Financial Markets,
April 1999

LTCM tried to keep its trades secret, in part by placing swap legs with different counterparties. Again, consider the plain vanilla interest-rate swap. Suppose LTCM created a fixed-for-floating swap with bank A and then completed another floating-for-fixed swap with bank B. Also suppose that the fixed and floating terms were exactly the same.[18] The net risk to the financial system from an LTCM bankruptcy in this case is zero. LTCM is just an intermediary. The fixed-rate payment LTCM owes to bank A could come directly from bank B, and vice versa.

But bank A and bank B have no way of knowing this. If either or both think LTCM will collapse, the bank will feel it has unhedged risk exposure and losses. If the positions are very large, a collapse could lead to spillovers, where the original LTCM collapse leads to other counterparties collapsing. That could happen even if another bank has their funds.[19]

A clearinghouse, especially one that maintains trade confidentiality, is one possible solution. Even an electronic record keeper could be helpful, though a fully collateralized exchange might even be more secure.

An electronic record-keeping system would have helped LTCM's investors. Managed by real people, such a system could serve two very important functions. First, it might be able to tell counterparties that their desire to mark-to-worst or increase margin requirements is not warranted, given the risks that the clearinghouse can observe. Perhaps it could measure firms' net risks and assure counterparties of their ability to pay. Of course, this feature could also be abused.

In a bankruptcy, the system administrator could quickly contact all counterparties and divulge net exposure. (In LTCM's case, net exposure was actually very small.) For LTCM, an administrator could have explained that most counterparties would be paid through another link in the LTCM counter-party system. Some of these contracts could be renegotiated and legal issues resolved. The record keeper could prevent systemic risk from a collapse when net risks are small, even though notional risk is large. Had this system existed during the LTCM collapse, the Federal Reserve may not have had to coordinate a capital injection. Instead, most of those banks would have met with the central clearing agency.

The lack of a clearinghouse led to Bear Stearns' near-collapse (it was purchased by J.P. Morgan for $2 a share on March 16, 2008) and worsened the effects of Lehman Brothers' bankruptcy announcement on September 15, 2008. Both caused havoc in the financial markets. Lehman Brothers, like LTCM, was an intermediary with hundreds of thousands of individual OTC transactions with banks all over the world. Even though many of those transactions might have netted within Lehman Brothers, banks' coordination failure in the face of the bankruptcy exaggerated an already bad situation.[20] A clearinghouse might have muted the market impact.

Compensation

> It's not so obvious which compensation structure is best.

The federal bank bailout created a lot of conversation about inappropriate compensation schemes in the financial sector. Many argue that compensation must be long-term—not short-term—to avoid misaligned management incentives.

Too much short-term compensation may indeed distort management incentives. However, it is not entirely clear that financial disasters can be blamed on too much of the wrong compensation.

LTCM partners invested significant amounts of their own money in the fund, even borrowing from banks to supplement these investments. It is hard to imagine managers more aligned with investor interests. The firm still collapsed. It is probably true that combining short-term compensation with longer-term compensation is better than having only one or the other, but there is no simple, foolproof way to structure compensation.

What's Size Got to Do with It?

> Size matters not. Look at me. Judge me by size, do you?
>
> —Yoda

After the 2008 financial crisis, governments and international organizations scrambled to find new ways to prevent firms that are "too big to fail." Why would the size of a financial institution have anything to do with a recession or the 2008 financial crisis?

A firm's size, the worry goes, may be associated with problems. As a firm gets very large, its management may struggle to keep track of all the firm's activities. One company division (such as mortgage-backed securitization) might take huge amounts of risk, risk the CEO can't fully understand or appreciate and that would not exist in a small firm with a simple borrowing and lending model.

Larger firms may also naturally diversify into many businesses. A large investment or commercial banking firm might have an investment banking division, a proprietary trading division, a hedge fund business, a client brokerage business, a private equity business, a private wealth management business, and so forth. The sheer number of activities makes it difficult for regulators and counterparties to understand the firm's true overall risk.

What if the hedge fund group borrowed heavily using futures contracts and lost more than 10 times its capital? The whole firm might be on the hook. For this reason, separating big banks into smaller pieces by line of business might be a good idea.

Individual agents may treat big firms differently. In a deal with a very large firm, a trader might think that the government has issued an implicit rescue guarantee and therefore the situation is less risky. Moral hazard, an economic term used to describe a situation in which a participant insulated from risk behaves differently than a participant fully or partially exposed to risk, enters the equation.

Suppose I believe that the government will bail out AIG if it is in trouble. I probably won't monitor AIG's risks very carefully. I might even do business with AIG as if it were 100% secure. Knowing this, AIG may take on a lot of risk, because that will not affect its business relationships. This increases systemic risk and the danger that market forces will not function appropriately.

Size may also be a proxy for the real focus: an institution's systemic risk. Consider LTCM again. The Federal Reserve thought an LTCM failure was a large threat to systemic risk. But in terms of assets, LTCM was about the size of Lehman Brothers and a little smaller than Morgan Stanley (see Table 7.1). It was more profitable than both Lehman and Morgan. LTCM had fewer employees than either firm. (That made LTCM's net income per employee astronomical. For 1997, LTCM's net income per employee was $8.6 million. For Morgan and Lehman it was $88,630 and $55,026, respectively.)

TABLE 7.1 Size of LTCM versus Morgan Stanley and Lehman Brothers

	LTCM	Morgan Stanley	Lehman
Net Income	$ 1.205	$ 1.029	$ 0.416
Employees	140	11,610	7,560
NI per Employee	$8,607,143	$88,630	$55,026
Assets	$ 129	$ 196	$ 129
Equity	$ 7.37	$ 6.538	$ 3.874
Contractuals	$ 1,253	$ 1,317	$ 1,516

Note: LTCM's variables are measured at the end of 1997 and Morgan Stanley and Lehman at the end of 1996. All numbers are measured in billions, except net income per employee, which is presented in appropriate units. Net income for LTCM was computed as the total gross return over 1997 multiplied by initial equity at the beginning of 1997, minus 2% of initial equity representing the cost of doing business. *Sources*: LTCM, public financial statements, contractuals for Morgan Stanley and Lehman from Perold (1999), and author's calculations.

LTCM was actually better capitalized than either Morgan or Lehman in 1996, especially considering the ratio of equity to total assets. (Of course, LTCM reduced this equity by $2.7 billion at the beginning of 1998.) LTCM's off-balance-sheet holdings, such as commodity derivatives, foreign exchange derivatives, equity derivatives, and interest rate derivatives, were similar to those of Lehman or Morgan Stanley, or perhaps a bit smaller. If Lehman and Morgan were large institutions, then LTCM was as well.

LTCM might even have been better off had it been a larger, more diversified firm. If LTCM had had an investment banking department and an asset management department, these divisions might have buffered the proprietary trading group's losses.

It is also important to separate the distinction between size and systemic risk. LTCM's specific risk created systemic risk, not so much because of its size, but because of its interwoven system of financial positions.

It was really LTCM's role as a large intermediary with many counterparty positions that made it a threat to the financial system. Its interconnections exacerbated systemic risk and its success attracted crowds—crowds that raced for the exits when rumors of trouble arrived. Nevertheless, the major banks had already begun the process of transforming themselves into disguised hedge funds.

> LTCM did something right in moving this kind of investing away from banks. They understood before anyone else how bad the conflicts of interest are and how important it is that banks concentrate on serving clients and not competing with them. But, they did not put the appropriate risk weight on the possibility of markets having multiple equilibria, with sudden liquidity dryouts. In particular, LTCM never expected that market participants (at the time, a handful, literally) could all turn against them as in a musical chairs game. The tragedy is that nobody at the time understood that all major banks were trying to transform themselves into LTCM (that is, become hedge funds), a transformation that got completed in the following years, with the results we saw in the 2008 crisis. LTCM was a very effective scapegoat, taking the attention away from the banks.
> —Alberto Giovannini interview, Senior Member of LTCM, October 20, 2011

Contingency Capital

> There is no such thing as a guaranteed emergency credit line.

Before forming LTCM, its principals learned an important lesson at Salomon Brothers. When Salomon was rocked by the 1991 scandal, they saw many banks pull Salomon's lines of credit. This also happened to various institutions during the 2008 financial crisis.

One of the principals' biggest concerns was the ability to hold positions until maturity. Interim volatility was not always important, provided they could hold positions until maturity. They learned in their Salomon days that, when the spread trades moved against them, banks might ask for more collateral through deeper haircuts.

In a business that uses large amounts of leverage to capture small returns, a sudden demand for extra collateral or a margin call could force the firm to unwind the position. That could mean a trading loss and unnecessarily increased market volatility.

When they started LTCM, the principals asked that investors keep their capital in the fund for a long period: three years. They also created two-way mark to market. LTCM typically executed one part of a trade with one counterparty and another part of the trade with another counterparty. The value of these separate trades often moved together (for example, if overall interest rates declined and the firm was long the swap spread). On a typical day, one counterparty owed LTCM cash on a mark-to-market basis and the fund owed another counterparty cash on a mark-to-market basis. If both sides were not marked-to-market, LTCM could experience huge cash demands, stressing their business unnecessarily.[21]

Then LTCM created term financing to match trades' estimated duration. All three innovations worked quite well through LTCM's life, including its failure.

LTCM's fourth modification was to set up emergency credit lines with banks. LTCM had two versions of this. The firm borrowed around $200 million from banks, just in case of emergency need.

The second credit line was a credit facility of around $900 million with 20 to 30 banks. If LTCM needed emergency borrowing for any reason, it could borrow up to $900 million to keep positions active. This line of credit was with the same banks that offered LTCM normal trade financing. The credit lines had a "no excuses" legal clause. A bank could not claim material changes or say that LTCM was in trouble as an excuse to refuse credit. LTCM paid a fee to maintain these lines of credit, but used neither until the 1998 crisis.

Before the crisis, LTCM made sure these lines of credit would actually work. The firm had debt drills, calling all the banks and asking for the emergency funds. The banks dutifully sent over the money; LTCM kept it for a couple of days and then sent it back.

When the actual crisis occurred, the majority of banks sent the money, but three or four did not. Even a legal contract to provide emergency funds is not necessarily an emergency credit line.[22] When markets are stressed, banks may not give emergency credit, either because they don't want to put more money at risk and are willing to be sued for breach of contract (LTCM could have probably sued the shirking banks, but had bigger issues to deal with at the time). Banks' financial stress might have also kept them from lending, or they might have claimed that the contract was not valid under the circumstances.

The Fed Is a Coordinator of Last Resort

> Coordination that prevents disorderly bankruptcy can be very important for the financial system.

Many people criticized the Fed for coordinating LTCM's capital injection. There was no way to know whether the LTCM rescue plan was necessary or not. Without knowing what would have followed had LTCM failed, we can only speculate. In Lehman's similar collapse, however, the market learned what disaster can occur without a lender of last resort.

> The Fed did a good job in the sense that it made no promises and it made no winks and we will give you a guarantee. They brought people together, both competitors and firms that didn't trust each other. They performed a very important coordination function. No government monies came forward. The worry was the two-way mark-to-market transactions. They recognized that to keep an entity like that together allowed the risk to be easily maintained.
>
> —Bob Merton interview, July 9, 2011

The financial system architecture should not encourage managers to take on too much risk out of a belief that they'll always be rescued. Nevertheless, it makes sense for a financial system to have a lender of last resort.

Counterparty Due Diligence

> Nothing has zero risk.

Many counterparties gave LTCM 0% haircuts on collateralized loans. This gave LTCM a huge advantage in trading, but was also irresponsible of the counterparties. The counterparties relied on LTCM's enormous reputation and on the fact that they were taking relative value bets, not outright bets.

Many broker-dealer banks also received zero haircuts. LTCM principals received zero haircuts when they traded at Salomon, as did other dealers. LTCM's zero haircuts did not have an important effect on the crisis. Haircuts became more significant in 2008, when many securities posted for collateral received very small haircuts, even though their risk was quite large. This helped firms lever their positions in the mortgage market, since they needed less capital to do so. Zero haircuts were an early signal of weak market behavior.

Spread the Love

> One's investors are one's partners.

As LTCM began losing capital, it turned to its investors for more capital.[23] Those investors were reluctant to give LTCM any more capital.

They may have temporarily lacked capital to give LTCM. Or they may have sought payback for the way LTCM acted at the end of 1997, when LTCM forced them to withdraw their money in the form of a large dividend: $2.7 billion. LTCM saw reduced opportunities; too much money was chasing too few arbitrage opportunities. Even so, the firm reduced outside investors' slices of the pie—not the partners' slices.[24]

Just as in retail, a business is nothing without customers. In a hedge fund, which has very large, limited investors, those investors are an extension of the partnership and must be treated as equals.

Quantitative Theory Did Not Cause the LTCM Collapse

A collection of tools is better than no tool at all.

Many people think LTCM's collapse was a failure of quantitative techniques or a failure of option theory, given the fund's association with Robert Merton and Myron Scholes, who won the 1997 Nobel prize in economics for their work on the Black-Scholes option pricing theory.[25] Others argue that LTCM's partners put too much trust in a well-behaved, supremely rational market, believing that their models would ultimately squeeze out money. Still others thought LTCM thought it could ignore market sentiment and other investors' behavioral characteristics in favor of financial pricing theory.

Scholes and Merton acted as consultants and marketers at LTCM. For the most part, trading strategies were in place when the firm started. These were trading ideas that built over the years in Meriwether's Salomon arbitrage group, which had been working at Salomon for 10 years and knew about sentiment, trader instinct, and models. LTCM was not a black box. At Salomon, Meriwether and his team had made the fixed-income markets more efficient by taking an amateurish way of confronting fixed income and substituting sophisticated mathematics. Before this approach some bond yields were too high and others were too low. Quantitative techniques offered a better understanding of risk and let many holders share it, lowering some yields and creating a more orderly market. Quantitative tools complemented the team's other strong suits. These financial models were not LTCM's only weapon.

Consider a rudimentary example. A portfolio manager believes that a 10-year bond is expensive and an 8-year maturity bond is cheap. The manager would like to make a trade on the two securities' relative prices and avoid exposure to overall market movements such as interest-rate changes.

A manager who ignores quantitative techniques altogether might guess that limiting the interest rate exposure requires shorting $1 of the 10-year[26] and buying $1 of the 8-year bond. Then interest rates rise by 1%. The portfolio loses money and the qualitative manager doesn't know why.

The quantitative manager uses a tool known as duration: the measure of how much a bond's price will change given a change in overall interest rates. Suppose that the 10-year bond has a duration of 7 and the 8-year has a duration of 5. For every $1 shorted in the 10-year, the manager invests only $1.4 in the 8-year.[27] This portfolio would lose approximately zero, given the same interest-rate change. This quantitative precision let the manager eliminate or avoid undesirable bets. Without quantitative tools, management is less precise. A portfolio manager using quantitative techniques can still lose money, but the manager's bets will be more precise and accurate.

> We made money as an intermediary to the intermediaries, that is, rather than face-to-face, we did it via the markets. We were not faster, smarter, or had necessarily better models than others. We had good stuff, but that wasn't the secret. It was institutional rigidities. We provided a service. With all the rules, regulations, and complexities, it is inevitable that those rules will have unintended consequences which put intermediaries in a bind. If you can loosen the constraints of that rigidity you can get a premium for that. Just like you get paid for cutting someone's lawn. People call this alpha. It was the basis of the business we were in. We had a highly experienced team and systematically used financial analysis. Risk management was much better than what others were doing at the time. We kept costs low.
>
> —Bob Merton interview, July 9, 2011

Option pricing theory was one of LTCM's tools. Option pricing theory doesn't work perfectly in the real world, but can help hedge and reduce risks when it's used properly. LTCM's principals were aware of option theory's strengths and weaknesses and did their best to apply it accordingly.[28]

LTCM never relied solely on option-pricing models or other financial models. Once the firm's models spotted deviations, LTCM principals examined them to determine whether there was an underlying economic reason for the discrepancy. Only then did they implement systematic trades. The flaw was more in LTCM's trade choices than in its hedging tools.

Three valid criticisms may stand against the LTCM quants. First, LTCM may have relied too much on models that specified deviations in security prices.

Second, many of their bets, such as the short volatility bet, involved positions in illiquid securities. When the Russian crisis emerged, traders with illiquid positions paid a very heavy price.

Third, LTCM relied too much on diversification. Diversification is still an important concept, but traders must understand how diversified trades behave in extreme circumstances. Some diversified trades did succeed during the Russian and LTCM crises. Equities did horribly, for instance, but Treasury bonds did quite well.

> Early on in the fund's history, there were a lot of possibilities to make money due to supply/demand imbalances. In the last year, these imbalances were disappearing—everyone was following these strategies. The "easier" money or intermediation money tended to disappear and LTCM had to become more directional. The fund's strategies were not rocket science at all. In fact, I never have understood the use of that phrase. The idea behind the models wasn't "genius"—it was smart people using technology to spot imbalances in the market and using some sophistication to hedge unknown factors and build positions accordingly. There was no "secret sauce" at LTCM, as people would like to believe. It was an understanding, with the help of tools, of why certain situations can make money.
>
> —Interview with Myron Scholes, July 9, 2011

Quantitative methods are a tool. It would be silly to argue that tools that help more precisely quantify risks and trades are worse than no tool at all. Relying blindly on tools without asking whether they are useful or they make sense in certain situations is absolutely foolish. In the period leading up to 2008's financial crisis, investors relied on the fact that overall housing prices had never declined by more than 5% to 10% in United States history as the basis for valuing a whole host of housing-related securities. Was this a tool used incorrectly or not really a tool at all?

Déjà Vu

> More regulation per se will not prevent further crises.

Regulators typically appear after a problem, not before. When LTCM collapsed, regulators began looking at hedge fund regulation. The SEC attempted several versions of new regulation in 2004; these ultimately backfired due to loopholes and a lawsuit. The rules would have made hedge funds register under the Advisors Act. Many new regulation proposals would not have required LTCM to file even one more document. The firm already provided many reports to many regulatory agencies.

LTCM had three offices, one each in Greenwich, CT, London, and Tokyo. All the venues were subject to regulatory oversight from that country's primary regulator.[29] Regulatory oversight included disclosure of the firm's full financial statements (including leverage and off-balance-sheet derivative exposure). Price Waterhouse audited LTCM.[30]

Even under a significant amount of financial regulation, LTCM still collapsed. It's not clear what regulations would have prevented the mess. Even if LTCM had divulged all of its practices, it is quite likely that regulators would not have known what level of leverage was reasonable or how to measure the presence of copycats and crowding.

Had LTCM's trades been transparent, it may have actually made the crisis worse. Traders might have moved out of copycat trades even more quickly. Remember, after LTCM let many investment banks into its offices to see its positions, these positions moved even further against LTCM.

Box 7.1 Lessons from LTCM's Collapse

1. Understanding saturation and interconnectedness is important for measuring risk and liquidity.
2. There are limitations to any risk management system. Risk measures should include some aspect of valuation.
3. Appropriate leverage depends on underlying volatility, but any amount of leverage with any amount of underlying risk can lead to bankruptcy.
4. Clearinghouses for OTC products may reduce systemic risks.
5. The optimal way to compensate risk-takers isn't obvious, nor is the question of how much compensation has to do with risks.
6. Understanding core problems and their causes is better than using size as a proxy for risks and problems.
7. Emergency credit lines might not be available when systemic crises occur.
8. Coordinated, orderly bankruptcy proceedings are extremely important in financial markets.
9. There is no such thing as zero risk.
10. Investors are partners, counterparties are partners, and the system is a partner.
11. Quantitative methods are not perfect and need to be improved, but they are not to blame for the crisis.
12. There is a tradeoff between regulation and innovation.

Private government access to these positions would have been useful only to the extent that government adequately understood LTCM's risks—an unlikely prospect. It seems especially unlikely that governments would have understood risks better than the intellectuals who had a large stake in the firm's success. The transparency may have led counterparties to be more cautious with LTCM, but it is not clear that this would have reduced the system risk.

LTCM's capital ratios were within the BIS capital ratio guidelines (Basel I). The Basel capital ratios may have failed to consider liquidity risk and inter-connectedness, and might also have been too low. Nevertheless, LTCM was within these regulatory guidelines.

Higher capital ratios, sometimes suggested as a cure, are the same as forc-ing lower leverage ratios, and the appropriate leverage ratio depends on a given portfolio's risk. One size does not fit all. More importantly, financial markets innovate, so there is always a trade-off between innovation and regulation. Unless innovation and progress are stifled, the future will bring more crises.

The LTCM crisis came and went without much deep consideration of the problems that it brought out in the financial system (see Box 7.1). After LTCM's failure, an Internet bubble rose from 1998 to 2000, then burst. Interest rates dropped and a new bubble formed in the housing market. Soon it would be déjà vu all over again, this time with participants from all over the U.S. economy, from home owners to government institutions. The old problems were new again, cropping up in August 2007 in the quantitative hedge fund space. Guess what? It was overcrowded.

PART II

The Financial Crisis of 2008

I remember in the circus learning that the clown was the prince, the high prince. I always thought that the high prince was the lion or the magician, but the clown is the most important.

—Roberto Benigni

Ten years after the LTCM debacle, the financial world was again in shambles.

This new crisis made LTCM's collapse look insignificant. All the lessons that the financial system should have learned from LTCM were either ignored, misunderstood, or pushed aside as investors continued chasing an elusive dream.

Before the big shocks of the financial crisis occurred, the quantitative investing community suffered a little shock, known as the quant crisis. It showed evidence of the crowding that helped bring down LTCM in 1998.

The quant crisis ended in 2008, just before the shocking near-failure of Bear Stearns, one of Wall Street's premier investment banks.

In 1998 the housing market began its steep rise. Politicians, home owners, the media, banks, investment banks, rating agencies, insurance companies, realtors, and (most of all) government housing agencies rode the greed train that created a crowded housing space and led to the greatest housing bubble in U.S. history. How did it happen? Who were the villains? Was it really Wall Street's fault? Or did a whole cast of troublemakers cause the problem, starting with liberal politicians who were eager to grant universal home ownership but inadvertently created in Freddie and Fannie, the largest hedge funds ever?

121

Soon after Freddie and Fannie Mae's failures came the most surprising and sudden of all Wall Street crashes: that of Lehman Brothers. What happened to Lehman Brothers? Should it have gone bankrupt, or did rumors and mob action bring it to its end? Regulators let Lehman fail, showing that they had forgotten a crucial lesson from the LTCM crisis. Lehman's failure brought havoc to the financial markets and suffering to everyone from small businesses to large corporations.

No one was saved. A couple of hedge funds, started by the former LTCM team, stood in the midst of the carnage. Despite all the precautions they had taken, Lehman Brothers' failure crashed them into the rocks. Once again, the world's liquidity providers had all disappeared, just when they were needed most.

CHAPTER 8

The Quant Crisis

It is easy in the world to live after the world's opinion; it is easy in solitude to live after our own; but the great man is he who in the midst of the crowd keeps with perfect sweetness the independence of solitude.

—Ralph Waldo Emerson

The 2008 financial crisis was the most shocking financial crisis the United States had seen since Black Tuesday, when the Dow Jones dropped by 12% and began the Great Depression, which saw a 27% drop in real output and a rise in the unemployment rate from 2% to 25%. No one can be certain when the financial crisis of 2008 really began, but there were early signals in June 2007 (see Figure 8.1 for a timeline of the crisis).

It was then that Bear Stearns let two of its large internal hedge funds fail. Both funds had been involved in mortgage securities. Their investments consisted mainly of mortgage-backed securities and CDOs, with 90% of their assets of AAA or AA quality.

Ralph Cioffi headed both hedge funds and described their investment strategies. "The thesis behind the fund was that the structured credit markets offered yield over and above what their ratings suggested they should offer."[1]

At the end of 2006, the two funds were valued at about $18 billion, but both were completely wiped out by June 2007. The more conservative fund, the High-Grade Structured Credit Strategies Fund, launched in 2003 and levered 10 to 1, was down 91% by the end of June. The other fund, the High-Grade Structured Credit Strategies Enhanced Leverage Fund, launched in 2006 and, assuming more risk with a leverage ratio of twelve to one, had no investor capital left.

123

FIGURE 8.1 Timeline of the 2008 Financial Crisis and Collapse of LTCM Spinoffs and Copycats

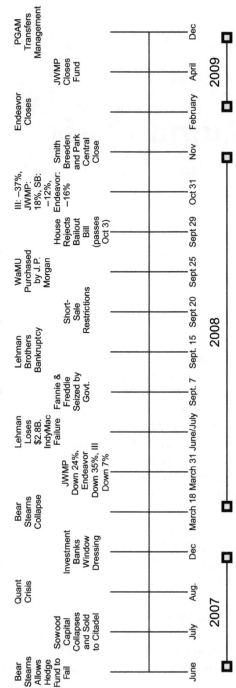

The funds were designed for highly complex operations in the mortgage markets. Though the methods were complicated, the underlying profit plan was simple: Borrow a large amount of money to make big bets on the subprime mortgage-backed securities market.

Cioffi thought collaterized debt obligations (CDOs) backed by subprime mortgages would start to increase in value over the longer term, following their recent decline.[2]

Bear Stearns was one of the biggest operators in the mortgage business, and with Cioffi's reputation, it found fund money easy to come by. Some of the world's biggest finance companies, including Citigroup, Barclays, Merrill Lynch, Goldman Sachs, Deutsche Bank, Credit Suisse, and Bank of America, extended as much as $9 billion in credit to these funds.

This credit was extended primarily through the repo markets. The hedge funds bought mortgage-backed securities and used those same securities as collateral to obtain loans.[3] The funds also raised around $1.56 billion in investor equity, including $45 million from Bear Stearns and its executives.[4]

These hedge funds had been stellar performers until spring 2007, when the mortgage-securities market began to falter. The High Grade fund's annual returns from 2004 to 2006 were 17%, 10%, and 9%. Delinquencies on loans made to risky borrowers, known as subprime mortgages, started climbing in February. The value of the securities began spiraling downward.

Investors tried to get out of the funds, but in May, Bear Stearns halted redemptions. Shortly after that, several banks and brokerage firms that had provided loans began demanding more cash as collateral. In April a Bear Stearns counterparty, Goldman Sachs, marked the securities' value from 98 cents on the dollar the previous month to 50 cents on the dollar. Other counterparties had marked them down to around 97. As others learned of Goldman's marks, they began adjusting their marks downward as well. The crowd had changed direction.

With the new marks, April's fund return went from bad, at −6%, to horrible, at −19%. As one Bear executive later reported " . . . and that game is !@#$%$@ over. By the way, the firm [Goldman] that sent us the 50 bid made a shit pot full of money in 2007 shorting the !@#$%$@ market."

Bear announced the revised losses of −19% in a June 7 investor letter. Bear Stearns told clients that "unprecedented declines in the valuations of a number of highly rated (AA and AAA) securities" contributed to June's woeful performance. Investors got less certain and more worried. Many investors started believing that no one knew the true value of these mortgage-related securities.

When Bear did not respond to requests for more capital, Merrill Lynch seized $850 million in collateral and tried to sell it, finding very few buyers and fast-sinking prices. These illiquid securities found little market enthusiasm.

> It was over. Bids were coming in at 50 cents. Merrill was selling us out. There were not bids on half the items. That's when the world woke up. That could be the wake-up call. That margin call.
> —Jimmy Cayne, former CEO of Bear Stearns (Cohan 2010)

Overcoming Cayne's resistance, Bear Stearns took over counterparties' repo positions on the less-levered fund, a move designed to relieve the stress the hedge funds felt from counterparty margin calls. On June 21, Bear announced that it would provide up to $3.2 billion for the fund to take over these counterparty positions.

The hedge fund fiasco also highlighted problems with management communication. Before going into the executive committee meeting to discuss the troubled hedge funds, Jimmy Cayne asked Steve Begleiter how much money was in the hedge funds. Steve replied $45 million. Cayne had only known about $20 million. He entered the executive committee and said, "Before we discuss what we'll do, I just found out that Bear's commitment is not $20, but $45. Does anyone know about this?" Warren Spector said, "I approved of the $25 extra. I !@#$%$@ up." According to Bear Stearns' rules, any committment greater than $5 million had to be approved by the executive committee. Jimmy didn't say anything and the room remained in silence for one entire minute.

Meanwhile the fund continued selling assets. By June 26, Bear Stearns supported roughly $1.6 billion in repo positions, held until the fund could unwind its positions and proceed with an orderly closing. Bear did not have much investor capital in the hedge fund—just $45 million—so the company could have let it fail. Bear bailed the hedge fund out to save the firm's reputation. The counterparties they saved didn't care. They were done with Bear Stearns. The firm's reputation suffered despite the bailout. Maybe Cayne was right: Bear should never have bailed out the hedge funds.

> What he [Warren Spector] didn't get was it made us the poster child for a problem in the whole industry.
> —Jimmy Cayne, former CEO of Bear Stearns (Cohan 2010)

After the news was reported, Bear Stearns shares fell 3.6%, to $134.90 on July 18, 2007. The stock was down about 14% for the year. On July 31, 2007,

Bear Stearns announced that it would close both hedge funds. As Cayne had surmised, various mortgage-related indices declined from July 13 to 18.

The Subprime Mortgage Market Collapse

Many actively traded securities and derivatives were based on mortgage returns. To get a sense of these markets, it is helpful to examine market indices that measure the health of the subprime residential mortgage market.

The ABX index is the primary measure of the value of the subprime residential mortgage market. ABX trades are based on the value of credit default swaps (CDS) on a basket of 20 subprime mortgages. When the index declines, it's more costly to insure the basket of subprime mortgages. When the index increases, it's cheaper to insure the same basket. As the ABX goes up, the subprime residential market is healthier; as it goes down, the market is less healthy.

The CMBX index is another useful measure of the real estate market's health. Similar to the ABX, the CMBX is based on CDS for an underlying basket of 25 commercial mortgage-backed securities. As the CMBX declines, it signals deterioration in the health of its basket of commercial mortgage-backed securities.

The CDX is also a popular gauge of the corporate sector's health. It trades in a variety of forms, always based on CDS of a basket of companies' debt. One possible basket is based on a portfolio of 100 non-investment-grade companies' debt. An index decline indicates that these companies' perceived health has decreased, or that the risk of holding their debt collectively has increased.[5]

It's easy to see the subprime residential real estate market's decline and the woes of the Bear Stearns hedge funds in the ABX indices movements. From July 13 to July 18, the AAA, AA, A, BBB, and BBB- versions of the ABX indices fell by −1.41%, −2.37%, −5.10%, −9.79%, and −8.11%, respectively.[6]

This decline is shown in Figure 8.2 along with the behavior of the CMBX and CDX High Yield indices. Subprime residential mortgages lost value rapidly through 2007. Commercial real estate mortgages and non-investment-grade company debt took large hits only toward the end of 2008. From the beginning of 2009 to the last quarter of 2010, both commercial real estate and non-investment-grade company debt improved, but subprime residential mortgage pools were still hurting. The lowest grade subprime mortgage pool crashed from 97.47 on January 19, 2007 to 4.236 by February 2011. AAA and

FIGURE 8.2   The ABX, CMBX, and CDX Indices

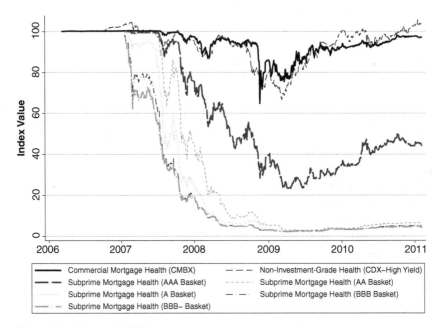

Sources: Bloomberg and Markit.

AA exposure, which Bear held, had dropped by 77% and 97% respectively by April 8, 2009. By February 2011, they were down 56% and 93%.

In July, another hedge fund collapsed due to credit problems. Sowood Capital began in late 2004, the brainchild of a former Harvard University endowment fund manager. Jeff Larson started Sowood with money from the Harvard endowment.[7]

Harvard invested first, giving Sowood $500 million. The fund invested in convertible bonds, commodities, standard bonds, and stocks. It amplified its bets using leverage.

On July 30 Sowood Capital told its investors that Citadel Investment Group was buying the Sowood Alpha Fund and Sowood Alpha Fund Ltd. The two funds had lost almost 60% of their value, and as of July 31 had a net value of $1.5 billion. According to the announcement, the funds "experienced losses mostly as a result of sharply wider corporate credit spreads," and had experienced "nonperformance of offsetting hedges." Collateral markdowns had left the funds unable to meet margin calls, and Sowood needed help.[8]

The Bear Stearns and Sowood hedge fund failures alerted markets to the possibility of spillover effects from problems in the credit and housing markets, though most investors treated the fund failures as isolated events. Then came the August 2007 quant crisis. Between August 1 and August 10, 2007, quantitative hedge funds lost abnormally large amounts of money. Some funds closed.

For example, by August 10, Renaissance Technologies,[9] the amazing algorithmic hedge fund, was down 8.7% in the first days of August and down 7.4% year to date. HighBridge Statistical Opportunities Fund was down 18% for the month; Tykhe Capital LLC, a New York-based quantitative fund, was down 20% for the month; AQR's flagship fund was down 13% by August 10; by August 14, 2007, Goldman Sachs Global Equity Opportunities Fund had lost more than 30% in one week.[10]

What Was the Quant Crisis?

A quant crisis is one that affects quantitative money managers, vaguely defined as any portfolio managers that use a quantitative system to manage trades, rather than a human-based security-picking system. The quant world includes various types of managers, including those in charge of statistical arbitrage hedge funds, many managed futures funds, and a large class of long-short or market-neutral equity funds.

This quant crisis mainly affected funds using quantitative equity strategies. In 2007, the leading quant portfolio companies were Barclays Global Investors (BGI), Goldman Sachs Asset Management (GSAM), State Street, Morgan Stanley's Process Driven Trading (PDT) group, AQR, First Quadrant, Analytic Investors, AXA Rosenberg, Panagora, Mellon Capital, Acadian, Analytic, and Numeric. The largest of these were BGI, GSAM, and State Street. The leaders and traders in many of these quant funds earned PhDs from leading schools in finance, economics, and mathematics.

In this crisis, the large negative returns seemed to disproportionately affect quantitative hedge funds, in particular quantitative equity hedge funds and statistical arbitrage funds.[11]

The value of common equity factors used to construct quantitative equity portfolios decreased in concert during this period, while their (typically low) correlations increased. Liquidity—especially in typical quant factors—completely dried up, especially during the week of August 6 to 13, 2007.

Quantitative funds have a number of common attributes.[12] Quantitative equity funds are usually market-neutral or enhanced index hedge funds or mutual funds that use computers to sort stocks by desirable and less desirable factors. They buy stocks with good factors and short sell stocks with bad factors, hoping to create a portfolio that is immune to overall market movements, but outperforms over time as desirable stocks perform better than less-desirable stocks.

Many of these funds have a value tilt, believing that it's better to own stocks that trade at low prices relative to forecast earnings. Thus, a fund might short sell stocks that trade at very high multiples to earnings (conditional on other information), while buying stocks with low prices relative to forecast earnings.

Statistical arbitrage funds, on the other hand, use statistical and mathematical models to analyze short-term, sometimes high-frequency price movements, then try to profit from short-term deviations from expected value. Traditionally, stat arb (as it's called) involves paired trades: one security bought and one sold short, based on deviations from their expected underlying relationship. If stock A is almost identical to stock B, but A performs better than B, stat arb sells stock A short and takes a long position in B, expecting that the stocks' performances will converge in the near future. These funds usually make thousands of trades with well-developed computer systems, taking advantage of price discrepancies all around the market.[13]

Over the last 20 years, the success of quantitative equity strategies slowly tempted more and more copycat funds to enter the space. The new arrivals included hedge funds, hedge fund groups, and investment banks' proprietary trading desks. The space was gradually getting crowded, but the quants underestimated the significance of this crowding.

The Erratic Behavior of Quant Factors

Quantitative equity funds construct portfolios by buying and selling stocks that have certain factors. Suppose the fund is looking for value, having found that stocks with low price-to-book ratios perform better over the long run than stocks with high price-to-book ratios. The fund would sort stocks from highest price-to-book ratios to lowest price-to-book ratios, then buy the ones with the lowest ratios and sell those with the highest, a strategy known as the value factor. A fund might do this with many stocks across many factors.

Standard Factors

Some factors are common and known to all quant managers; other factors are proprietary to individual quant funds. In August 2007, even the commonly known factors behaved oddly.

FIGURE 8.3 Common Factor Returns in 2007

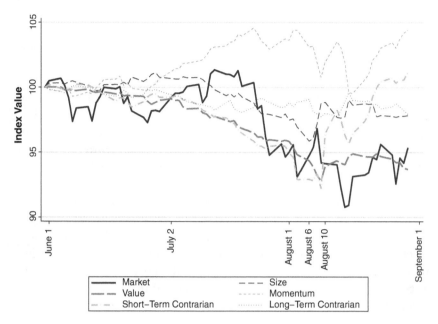

Figure 8.3 shows the behavior of some popular U.S. quant factors during August 2007, including the Fama-French factors for market, size, and value, as well as one factor for short-term reversal, one for long-term reversal, and a momentum factor.[14] Some argue that the decline in the value factor indicated that the unlevering by quant funds was primarily from stocks in the value arena.

AQR's U.S. value factor dropped 30% from the beginning of July to the August trough.[15] During the week starting August 6, 2007,[16] trading volumes for stocks on the Russell 1000 index were roughly 30% higher than average. This combined with the decline in the RevST index, a short-term contrarian indicator, to signal that liquidity was playing a role in the crisis.[17]

Many of these standard quant factors had returns that were bad but not devastating—not an issue for long-only portfolios. However, the majority of quantitative equity hedge managers use leverage. The amount of leverage varies from fund to fund, but some funds might have $8 of longs and $8 of shorts for every $1 of investor capital (a leverage ratio of 16). More typical market-neutral quant equity hedge funds might have $4 of longs and $4 of shorts for every $1 of investor capital.

With that much leverage, even small return changes can cause large movements in portfolio returns. From June 1 to August 9, 2007, the standard value factor lost 7.19%. For a market-neutral fund leveraged 8 times, this would have been roughly equivalent to a loss of 57.52%.[18] Or consider August 8, 2007, which was one of the worst historical days for the standard value factor. That day, it lost 0.75%. With a leverage ratio of 8, the loss was 6% in one day for a fund that is supposed to be market-neutral. This is huge.

Quantitative managers typically don't lever the value factor to such an extreme, since it already has a large volatility. A quant manager typically combines many factors in making leverage decisions, and a portfolio's leverage depends on underlying unlevered volatility. Even so, levered portfolios are much more volatile than unlevered portfolios.

These losses meant that counterparties asked quant funds for more capital, forcing the quant funds to either liquidate further or go out of business.

Figure 8.4 compares the momentum, value, market, and contrarian factor daily returns to the historical standard deviation of those factors to see how unusual this period was. August saw large daily moves, sometimes as much as two standard deviations. Furthermore, some of these movements ranked among the biggest declines in the last two years.[19]

FIGURE 8.4   Ratio of Daily Returns of Common Factors Divided by Historical Standard Deviations

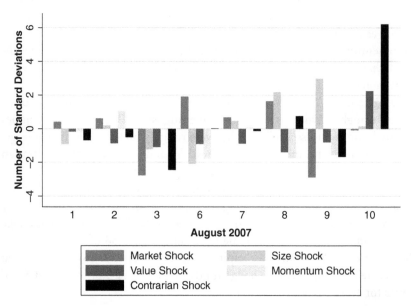

From August 2 to 8, the value factor lost money for six straight days. That was very unusual and suggests that similar funds with similar investments were exiting their positions.

Standard factor return movements during early August were unusual, but many quants experienced much more severe movements. Some less usual quant factors, such as earnings quality and valuation, moved by 10 to 15 standard deviations compared to their historical averages. What was going on?

Professional Portfolio Factors

Simple factors make good examples, but professional quantitative managers use many more types of factors, combining them into overall positive and negative signals. A professional might use standard simple factors as well as factors for earnings revision, analyst sentiment, profitability, management impact, and proprietary factors.[20] Even when quantitative managers use slightly different factors, there's generally some overlap in the stocks they buy or sell.

Quant managers crowd strategies for several reasons. They tend to use similar factors (also called alpha models). Traders quickly pick up on even proprietary factors. Their risk models are often similar, as are their transaction cost models. The optimization process traders use to create portfolios (which accounts for transaction costs) leads to professional quant portfolios that are concentrated in a few hundred similar stocks. Many of those stocks likely appear many times across many portfolios.

These concentrated portfolios moved a lot in August. Hedge fund quant factors moved between 10 and 20 standard deviations from historical norms.[21] Standard quant factors also moved by unusual amounts in August, two to three standard deviations from historical norms.

> Crowding among quants happens for several reasons, but the transaction costs model was of primary importance, as it caused us to trade similar securities at each point in time.
> —Mark Carhart interview, former co-CIO of Quantitative Strategies at GSAM and Founder of Kepos Capital, October 11, 2011

At the end of August, the quant factor aberration disappeared. That is, the factors returned to normal behavior and the funds that had held on to their positions didn't lose much.

Causes of the Quant Crisis

Some believe the quant crisis originated with multistrategy hedge funds running quantitative strategies as well as investments in highly leveraged credit instruments. When the value of these credit instruments began to fall during the subprime crisis, the funds had to raise cash to cover margin calls.

In late July, a macro hedge fund called Caxton was losing money on credit movements and foreign exchange carry positions and needed to raise cash.[22]

Caxton's quantitative equity team told senior management that they could easily raise cash by de-levering their entire quant portfolio in a single day. They took off several billion longs and several billions shorts in a day.[23]

Around the same time, Peter Muller's PDT group at Morgan Stanley was taking a beating in its quantitative equity positions. Morgan Stanley's senior management told the group to unwind their positions. That led to further price moves in the quant equity space.

Many of the equities Muller's group traded were also in portfolios held by other quantitative equity funds. Morgan Stanley's sales pushed values lower, so other quantitative equity funds took losses, sometimes forcing them to sell their positions as well.[24] The falling dominos forced even veteran hedge funds such as AQR Capital Management to reduce positions.

The situation uncannily echoed 1998. Just as had happened with LTCM, early success brought copycats. Now times were getting rough, and the copycat funds were heading for the exits.

Cliff Asness, John Liew, and David Kabiller, three former GSAM employees, started AQR Capital Management, one of the largest quant hedge funds. CEO Cliff Asness described the chaos of August.

> During the crisis, many factors that were low or negatively correlated with each other all moved together. The strategies moved in a straight line throughout the day, first up, then down. It looked like . . . someone working large orders to take down their risk . . . and then someone putting that risk back on. It was a sign that people were taking down risk in similar models. Furthermore, the most well-known quantitative factors moved the most compared to the proprietary or more esoteric factors. Some people said that returns moved by about 25 standard deviations, but what they really meant is that these movements were large compared to "normal times." It is our collective action going forward (where "our" refers to quant market-neutral managers or those employing very similar strategies) that now affects a world we didn't realize we had such influence over, and this is undoubtedly an important short-term risk factor. We have a new risk factor in our world.
> —Cliff Asness interview, CEO of AQR, October 3, 2011

A rumor spread that, as quant factors declined, Goldman Sachs began selling positions. That further exacerbated the factor movement and caused more pain.

GSAM had two quant groups: Quantitative Strategies (QS) was led by Mark Carhart and Ray Iwanowski, who were in charge of the Global Alpha hedge fund and other macro hedge fund strategies. Bob Jones headed the second group, Quantitative Equity (QE). This group managed the Global Equity Opportunities (GEO) hedge fund and other equity accounts. The two groups together were known as Quantitative Investment Strategies (QIS) and managed a total of $200 billion of the $800 billion in GSAM. The groups worked very closely and shared profits. Global Alpha hedge fund had some individual equity strategies managed by QE; GEO had some strategies run by the QS team. Were the Goldman quants responsible for further deterioration in the quant space? An anonymous GSAM trader said that Goldman was not responsible and describes events:

I think what happened is that it became a tough environment in late 2007, some funds did poorly in July and started reducing their risk. There was a fund that had a meaningful investment from an investor that had a clause that he would be able to redeem overnight if certain loss triggers were hit. They got close to that barrier and so had to begin unwinding to prepare for the client. I think this had something to do with it. Once you kick the snowball down the hill, then the large funds had no choice but to de-lever, because the big funds, like AQR, have trouble unwinding big trades in a week. So they had to start de-levering right away and this caused the self-fulfilling prophecy. Think of it as a margin requirement. Leverage is asset size divided by account equity. You usually change your leverage by changing your numerator. If you lose a lot of money, leverage starts going up rapidly and involuntarily because of the denominator. You may be subject to a margin call. You can't wait until this margin call to begin selling the numerator.[25] If you have billions on each side of a market-neutral portfolio, you cannot wait too long to begin reducing your positions. You come in on Monday, you can't wait for four days, so you start unwinding today. The big guys had to start de-levering, funds, like GSAM, BGI, Citadel, and AQR.[26] This never happened before, so there was no rule for when to cut the positions. We had to make a call as it was happening.
                                          —GSAM trader interview, October 26, 2010

Could another fund inside Goldman Sachs Asset Management—the Global Equity Opportunities fund (GEO)—have triggered the panic? Goldman started this quantitative equity fund in 2004. It had six global strategies, held about $6 billion in assets under management in its prime, and was levered about 6 times on each side.

The fund experienced its first big drawdown on August 6. The Goldman team needed to make margin and reduce risk; their first instinct was to trade down their positions. As they started doing this, they saw that the stocks they wanted to buy were moving by 10%; the stocks they wanted to sell were moving by −10%, even though the rest of the market was flat.[27]

The Goldman team realized that reducing their position would mean a large loss, big enough that they would sacrifice the equity necessary to reduce their leverage as they unwound the position because of the market impact. Alarmed by the pricing changes, the team asked its parent company to recapitalize the fund, eliminating the need to trade. On August 10, Goldman (and some of its clients) invested $3 billion in the GEO fund.

Other quantitative traders were in panic mode. Some thought Goldman was causing the market dysfunction.[28] According to Goldman, however, neither the QS nor the QE group caused the movements. Traders at these groups stopped because they saw how damaging their trades might become. Goldman's traders had begun to understand that the quant space was interconnected and fragile, just as LTCM's space had been 10 years earlier.

> When you take a lot of leverage, you need to care for the tail risk aspect. If you can't reduce the leverage quickly, it can kill you. With leverage, you have to worry about big tail unusual events. Global Alpha was more liquid and easy to take down, but the other fund [GEO] because of liquidity crunch and the crowding, was just going to take the positions down faster; there was no depth in these markets. The quant industry used to be just us, but then the other multistrategy people decided to get in because of the good returns. When they began to experience bad returns in credit, they said let's get out of the quant business, which we are less experienced in. They were heading for the exits in the quant space. We erroneously didn't plan for other people heading for the exits at the same time. We didn't realize the high correlation we would have with other shops. But the reality is that everyone studies momentum, value, etc. When you're building quant portfolios with so many stocks, 500 on the buy side, 500 on the sell side, and each portfolio manager has different constraints, different sector bets, different ways to weight the factors, you know you're correlated, but with all these differences, you can't imagine the correlation is that high. We didn't appreciate that when its time to trade positions, all of the stocks between quant funds were very similar. This hampered our ability to execute, because so many players were heading for the door at once.
>
> —GSAM trader interview, October 28, 2010

Whether it was Goldman or Caxton is not important, the point is that everyone was behaving similarly and there was no liquidity.
—State Street portfolio manager interview, December 2, 2011

A shocked, crowded space caused the quant crisis. As quantitative managers began closing positions, they put pressure on other managers to close positions or face margin calls. That pushed prices even lower.

The Shed Show

A "shed show" refers to the collapse of an entire system of interconnected units.[29] The August 2007 quant movements collapsed an ordinarily tranquil space. Many quant funds suffered throughout this period.

The Global Alpha fund had 30 strategies, involving every asset class across the globe. It had about 1.5 times the typical fund volatility for this space. Fund leverage was between 6 and 12, depending on risk. Once the fund bought fixed-income and relative-value positions, which have lower risk, fund leverage went up to about 15 to 20. Global Alpha, however, never had a funding problem, because its positions were much more liquid.

Quant space problems hit Global Alpha in August and September 2007. The Goldman group had to take down $10 billion, including positions in JGB futures and S&P 500 futures. Unlike the GEO fund, the Global Alpha market was deep and liquid in these positions and could sustain the large selling. In the end, Global Alpha was down about 38% for 2007, especially due to carry trade losses in September 2007.[30] As mentioned earlier, Global Alpha had about 20% of its portfolio invested in market-neutral quantitative equity strategies. According to traders at Goldman, this contributed to 50% of the fund's losses. The other losses were from equity value, foreign exchange carry positions, and credit losses.

Goldman's GEO fund also was hammered in 2007. According to a Goldman trader:

The fund's returns were never really that great. The first few years were good, but in 2007 the fund was down about 20%. In 2008 and 2009, the fund didn't do very well, and clients began leaving and so Goldman eventually shut down the fund. For the whole period, it was flat to down.
—GSAM trader interview, August 1, 2011

Ken Kroner, who oversees more than $300 billion in quantitative equity separate accounts under the Barclays umbrella in his position as managing director and head of global market strategies for Blackrock, describes that period:

> Virtually all quant equity funds were hit. There were significant drawdowns on the Tuesday, Wednesday, and Thursday [August 7 to 9]. The ones who stayed put for the next two weeks recovered their losses. Many of the smaller funds and newer hedge funds were closed out of their positions and had to unwind at the trough and could not experience the recovery. The organizations with good counter-party relationships were able to weather the storm, and recovered. That is, their counter-parties didn't request additional collateral. We were in constant contact with our counter-parties (multiple times per day) talking them through the crisis and we were Barclays Global Investors (BGI), but we had to talk to them all day. There was no way they would force us to close the positions. BGI did not de-lever; by the end of the month we recovered in most of the accounts. The accounts that we use internally as a measure of our success, the flagship funds, those definitely recovered. The others may have as well, but I'm not entirely sure.
> —Ken Kroner interview, October 29, 2010

Goldman's hedge funds sustained substantial damage. Mark Carhart and Ray Iwanoswki left Goldman Sachs in April 2009. They both had one-year, noncompete agreements and so spent a bit of time literally lying on the beach to recuperate. As of November 2011, Mark has launched a new quantitative hedge fund, KeposCapital, and Ray is working on a project in the pension-fund world.

Mark Carhart summarized the 2007 experience:

> Probably the most important lesson was the magnitude of commonality in the investment approach we followed across the broader investment community. Success in quant investing in the future will hinge on developing unique ideas that are differential from competitors. The second lesson is that models and approaches need to be more dynamic. When evaluating long-term historical price patterns, it's hard to appreciate how quickly the models needed to evolve. Having lived through 2007 and 2008—and the earlier LTCM crisis and the Internet bubble—I better appreciate the need for dynamic models that will have more variation in risk and signal composition.
> —Mark Carhart interview, April 23, 2010

The crowding crisis in the quant space was a bit different than the one that affected LTCM. In LTCM's situation, the crowd exited from somewhat illiquid positions, making price movements more severe. The quant crisis occurred in the equities space, which consists normally of very liquid assets. Like the LTCM crisis, though, the quant crisis hit specific strategies extremely hard while being relatively invisible to the rest of the market. The quants and their risk models missed the possibility of crowding. A member of the quantitative research team at Goldman described it:

> We saw the growth of quant assets under management, but didn't see how far these strategies had extended into statistical arbitrage desks and hedge funds. We felt our proprietary factor specifications and weightings would provide differentiation, and this was supported by historical correlations plus low exposures of other quant managers to our factors. Our individual equity positions were small, liquid, and diversified—we didn't foresee a significant liquidation event focused on similar portfolios.
> —Goldman Sachs analyst statement, December 13, 2007
> (GSAM 2007)

The Global Alpha and GEO funds at Goldman Sachs, BGI, and AQR's quantitative market-neutral funds weren't the only groups that saw losses. Many other quantitative equity money managers were in the same boat. The quantitative space continued to have losses in 2008 and 2009, perhaps because the crowd was still exiting the space.

In 2007, about half of the main quantitative equity portfolios finished down for the year. They were considerably down in August, some rebounded in late August and September 2007, and then the drift downward continued in 2008 for many funds.[31]

Many quantitative equity funds died in this period, and assets under management were much smaller than they were before August 2007. In 2008, a total of 2,494 hedge funds closed; a net total of 1,051 hedge funds went out of business. This was the first net drop in the number of hedge funds since 1996. The industry's total assets dropped by $461 billion, with the largest asset drops in the equity hedge (−34%) and relative value (−25%) categories.[32]

Even these numbers dramatically underestimate the crisis's impact. The quant space continued to suffer in 2009, when certain factors crashed. The standard momentum factor lost 54% in 2009 (see Figure 8.5).[33] As performance suffered, clients withdrew funds. State Street had not suffered much during August 2007, since it had very little leverage compared to other quant funds. Of $200 billion State Street had under management, about $20 billion was leveraged 1.5 times; the rest was not leveraged. Redemptions and poor performance left State Street with assets of $50 to $75 billion by 2011.

FIGURE 8.5   The Returns to Standard Factors in 2009

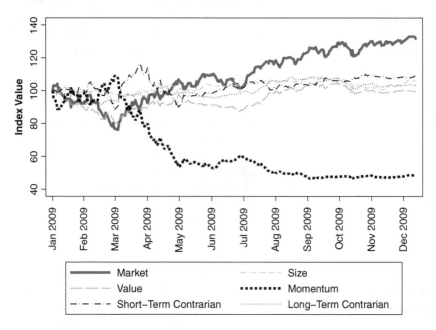

Even though many funds remain in business, they have laid off 70% to 80% of their staff, and their assets under management have dropped by around 80%.[34] At Goldman, the GSAM staff count dropped by two-thirds from 2007 to 2011.[35]

The 2007 quant crisis came and went in about 10 days, and no one really understands what triggered it or why it disappeared so quickly. The crisis's greatest lesson was that the quantitative equity space was getting crowded and that traders would need to consider the presence of copycats in the future.[36]

The market had already learned this lesson from the LTCM crisis, yet it was forgotten. Or maybe it's just difficult to measure copycats' presence and influence.

Financial experts are still working on ways to accurately measure this risk.[37] As of 2011, most risk models in the quant space have not changed.[38]

In most of the world, the quant crisis came and went without any notice. But it revealed serious problems with the mortgage market, crowded spaces, counterparty impatience, and the difficulty of holding levered positions. All of these problems got much worse just six months later, when the mortgage market soured and Bear Stearns was caught in a run on its business.

CHAPTER 9

The Bear Stearns Collapse

Those of us who have looked to the self-interest of lending institutions to protect shareholders' equity, myself included, are in a state of shocked disbelief... Yes, I've found a flaw [in my ideology of free markets]. I don't know how significant or permanent it is. But I've been very distressed by that fact.
—Alan Greenspan, former Chairman of Federal Reserve,
Congressional Testimony, October 28, 2008

A Brief History of the Bear

Bear Stearns is widely considered one of the great small Wall Street firms (despite its location at 383 Madison Avenue in New York). The company was originally formed in 1923 by Joseph Bear, Robert Stearns, and Harold Mayer as an equity trading house.

Bear Stearns survived the Great Depression and the 1929 stock market crash without laying off any employees. In the 1930s and 1940s, Bear made significant amounts of money on both the break-up of the utilities industry and the bankruptcy of many railroad companies. In 1975, Bear Stearns made a bundle by investing in New York City securities when New York City was near bankruptcy and its bond yields were quite high.

Bear Stearns's reputation as an aggressive firm began growing with the internal success of Alan "Ace" Greenberg, a proprietary trader. Some of his aggressive techniques included parking securities to facilitate the takeover of other companies.[1]

Greenberg got the nickname "Ace" while an undergrad at the University of Missouri, where he thought it would help him attract dates. He had originally started on a football scholarship at the University of Oklahoma, but transferred after injuring himself in the second game of the season. Ace also loved to play bridge. He went to Wall Street without a job, but with enough parental money to rent an apartment. He finally got a job as a clerk in the loan department of Bear Stearns making $32.50 per week. Greenberg's ambition led him to the role of CEO of Bear Stearns, a position he held from 1978 to 1993.

In 1993, James E. Cayne succeeded Ace Greenberg as CEO and Greenberg became chairman of the executive committee. Cayne had helped to guide the company toward new opportunities in investment banking and foreign markets. Greenberg was known as impulsive, but Cayne had a more cautious approach, avoiding big risks and asking consultants to enlighten his decision-making process.

Cayne was a championship level bridge player, which excited Greenberg.[2] Cayne had come to Wall Street almost by accident. He had dropped out of Purdue one semester shy of receiving his diploma, spent time in the military, and worked as a salesman for a scrap iron business. He moved to New York City in 1964 to become a professional bridge player; finances eventually pushed him to find a real job. After interviews with Goldman Sachs, Lehman Brothers, and Bear Stearns, he took a position at Bear.

In 1985, Bear Stearns became a public firm with ticker symbol BSC. It was a full-service investment firm with divisions in investment banking, institutional equities, fixed-income securities, individual investor services, and mortgage-related products.

In 1997, Bear Stearns came under investigation by the SEC for its role as a clearing broker for a smaller brokerage named A.R. Baron, which had gone bankrupt in 1996 and defrauded its customers of $75 million. Traditionally, courts had not held clearing firms accountable for losses incurred by customers of their client firms, but in this case Bear Stearns was accused of overstepping its bounds as a clearinghouse by continuing to process trades, loan money, and extend credit to Baron in the face of mounting evidence that the firm was manipulating stock prices and conducting unauthorized trading while raiding customer accounts.

The case was eventually settled in 1999, with Bear Stearns paying $51 million in fines and restitution.[3] Bear Stearns grew rapidly and did well mainly due to its prime brokerage and clearance business. It offered a wide suite of services and products to hedge funds, broker-dealers, and registered investment advisors, and had made itself as a large player in mortgage- and asset-backed securities. In 2005, Bear's Tom Morano, head of mortgage- and asset-backed securities, increased the firm's mortgage market exposure by doing its own securitizations.

> If the [traditional players] want to take on the risk of carrying all of these securities, and we're going to see a reduction of supply [to securitize], we decided we needed to get closer to the source of the collateral.
> —Tom Marano, January 10, 2005 (Sargent 2005)

Many Bear Stearns senior executives were early LTCM investors, including Jimmy Cayne, Vinny Mattone, and firm co-president Warren Spector. When LTCM was on the brink of bankruptcy and the consortium gave the firm new capital, Bear contributed no money. Although Jimmy Cayne had a very good reason for not contributing capital, since Bear had almost no exposure to LTCM, that decision may have hurt the company's image, especially with industry peers.

At the beginning of 2008, Bear Stearns leadership consisted of Chairman of the Board Jimmy Cayne, who had transferred the role of CEO and president to Alan Schwartz.[4] Ace Greenberg was on the board and chairman of the executive committee. Greenberg and Schwartz were part of the executive officer team along with CFO Sam Molinaro, Jeff Farber, Jeff Mayer, and Michael Solender. Bear was the little cub on the street interconnected with the other banks through what is known as the shadow banking system.

Shadow Banking

> When the music stops, in terms of liquidity, things will be complicated. But as long as the music is playing, you've got to get up and dance. We're still dancing.
> —Chuck Prince, CEO of Citibank, July 10, 2007

Some people refer to Wall Street as the *shadow banking system*. To understand this statement, one has to understand the basics of banking. Banks take consumer deposits and pay small interest rates.[5] They keep some deposits for customer withdrawals and mandatory cash reserves, then invest the remainder in longer-term investments, including loans. They make money on the spread: the difference between the two returns over time.[6] Banking is also known as the maturity transformation business,[7] because banks take short-term liabilities and transform them into long-term assets. This provides credit to grow the economy, but also carries risk, because banks use leverage.

Wall Street firms also borrow money on a short-term basis at relatively low interest rates and invest in a variety of securities that are a bit riskier, but provide higher rates of return. Because they are not officially banks and do not take consumer deposits, they are not regulated as banks. They're like banks in many respects, though, in that they transform short-term borrowing into long-term lending without a government backstop. For that reason, Wall Street firms are known as the shadow banking system.

Wall Street firms aren't the only shadow banking participants. The system includes a broader group of institutions and financial instruments, including government-sponsored agencies Freddie Mac and Fannie Mae, hedge funds, monoline insurers,[8] money market mutual funds, the repo market, and the credit default swap market.

In general, Wall Street firms borrow heavily, creating large amounts of leverage. Moreover, they often lower their borrowing right before reporting quarterly financial statements to make their leverage look lower than it typically is.

Window Dressing

Many commercial and investment banks end their fiscal year in November or December. Just before that, they typically deleverage slightly and sell some of their riskiest assets so they'll look more conservative when they report their financials to the Securities and Exchange Commission (SEC).

Banks also lower their debt levels before their *quarterly* reports.[9] Big U.S. banks tend to lower their short-term debt levels by 42% from a quarter's peak to its end, just before reporting to the SEC.[10]

Figure 9.1 shows primary dealers' net weekly borrowing from the first quarter of 2009 to the second quarter of 2010. There is a clear pattern of reducing risk prior to quarterly reports. The pattern is even more pronounced for some major banks, including Citibank.

Bear Stearns also practiced window dressing, lowering its leverage ratio by selling assets, only to buy them back at the beginning of the next quarter. The firm's treasurer, Bob Upton, said that this window dressing was important for keeping creditors and rating agencies happy.[11]

FIGURE 9.1 Quarterly Window Dressing by Primary Dealers

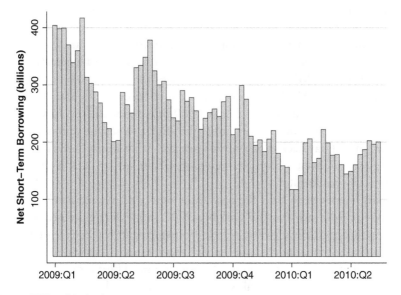

Sources: WSJ and Federal Reserve.

Repo Power

The repo system is the primary method that Wall Street firms use for maturity transformation and leverage.[12] Among Wall Street firms, Bear Stearns had been one of the most heavily involved in the repo system.

The repo mechanism is a way to borrow and invest. A repo is collateralized lending: one bank gives another a security in exchange for cash. The collateral typically takes a haircut, depending on how risky or liquid the security is. A loan might be 99% of a U.S. Treasury bond's value, but just 95% of a mortgage security's value.

Bear Stearns bought mortgage-backed securities or collateralized debt obligations, then repo'd them immediately, effectively leveraging the investments. Suppose the MBS cost Bear $100,000. When the firm gave another bank the security in a repo, Bear received $95,000. Bear effectively bought the MBS with $5,000 of its own cash and $95,000 in borrowed cash, for a leverage ratio of 20. At the end of the repo transaction, Bear (or another repo party) returns the borrowed cash, plus interest at the repo interest rate,[13] and the counterparty returns the security. Repo contracts are usually for a term of one night, so they're also called overnight repos. Every morning, both counterparties must agree to roll over the contract for another day. This is common practice and systems let this happen seamlessly.

If a counterparty is considered riskier or the underlying securities become less liquid, a lender may request more collateral for a given loan. If the lender thinks an underlying security has lost value, it may ask the repo party to give more collateral. If MBS securities drop 50% of their value, loans of $95,000 backed by a $100,000 MBS become loans for $95,000 with $50,000 worth of security. The lender will ask for $45,000 plus a new haircut, or may even stop financing the repo transaction. If the lender closes the transaction, the borrower must pay back the loan with interest. With much of the collateral's value gone, however, a borrower may not be able to pay back its loans and must declare bankruptcy.

This happened to Bear Stearns. Some repo lenders completely stopped lending to Bear. As early as October 2007, State Street refused to offer Bear anything but overnight repo. Fidelity Investments had been lending Bear $6 billion a day, then suddenly pulled all its repo transactions with Bear. Other lenders followed suit. At one point J.P. Morgan forced Bear into 20% haircuts, then repo'd the same collateral with the Fed for a 2% haircut. Bear Stearns Vice Chairman Tom Flexner said, "That liquidity facility was putting us out of business and JP was making a lot of money off it."[14] Mellon Bank told Bear that after March 12, it "might be hesitant to roll some funding tomorrow."[15]

Bear had emergency lines of credit for such scenarios, but these were not reliable, just as LTCM learned in 1998. Bear's Paul Friedman said, "The joke was that it was appropriately named a 'revolver' because the only way it would ever get used is if you'd take it and put it as a gun to the heads of the banks and say 'Listen, lend me more on a secured basis, or I am drawing down this $4 billion on an unsecured basis.'"[16]

At the beginning of 2008, Bear had $11.8 billion in equity, $383.6 billion in liabilities, and $102 billion in repo transactions. Of those repos, $70 billion were overnight repos and could be canceled at any time.[17] Bear held $46 billion in mortgages and mortgage- or asset-backed securities. Many of the securities posted as repo collateral were Level III mortgage-backed securities, which are difficult to value. (Bear posted a total of $17.25 billion in these securities.[18]) In a market panic, it would be even more difficult to value these securities, so lenders gave them bigger haircuts, just to be safe. This also happened in the LTCM crisis. Counterparties marked to worst rather than to market.

Bear's leverage ratio was close to 34. Its short-term funding (primarily repo transactions) represented 26% of its total liabilities, a number that was much higher than that of other Wall Street investment banks even before

Bear increased it by 6% beginning in January 2007. If Bear couldn't fund investments and securities by rolling over overnight repo contracts, it would have to raise capital quickly or sell assets. The crowd had been quick to snatch up mortgage securities, but now the momentum had shifted. If Bear sold its mortgage-backed securities, it would push prices even lower, which would increase the firm's capital requirements and create a cyclical demise.

Why didn't Bear's risk management committee realize the dangers of the mortgage exposure?

> I put the best people on that committee, although maybe Greenberg ran it too passively. When looking back it's so easy to point blame, but the reality is that everyone, with few exceptions, got the mortgage exposure wrong, not just Bear.
> —Jimmy Cayne interview, former CEO and Chairman of the Board of Bear Stearns, April 12, 2012

An independent analysis of Bear's risk management found that risk assessment was "infrequent and ad hoc" and "hampered by insufficient and poorly aligned resources."[19]

Warren Spector, Co-President of Bear and Head of Fixed Income, who had deceived Cayne and the executive committee regarding the mortgage hedge funds, may also have deceived the risk and audit committees of the troubles in mortgages. This was also a problem with other firms, where typically the risk management group was weak compared to the star traders of the firm.

> Spector's group generated most of Bear's profit, but he was an elitist. Many of the bond traders hated him. I think he lied to the risk and audit committee of Bear. He was losing and he couldn't face that it was getting away from him.
> —Anonymous trader at Bear Stearns interview, April 7, 2012

In fact, on August 1, 2007, Jimmy Cayne fired Spector, telling him, "I can't work with you anymore."[20]

Spector still walked away from Bear with millions.

Leading up to March 2008, Bear had moved more aggressively than other investment banks to establish a large exposure to the real estate market through mortgage loans and mortgage securities. (Bear even had its own residential real estate mortgage originator.) It financed these purchases on a short-term basis using the mortgages as collateral.[21] Because Bear borrowed heavily to buy mortgages in an overvalued housing market, it was at the crowd's mercy, set up to fail if the masses suddenly ran from the housing bubble.

The Unexpected Hibernation

> Bear Stearns's mistake, in my opinion, was that we were overleveraged.
> We had securities that were called triple-A with floating rates on them,
> so we assumed the risk on these securities was 2% or 3%. Much to our
> surprise, they weren't triple-A, and the risk was 40% to 50%. When you're
> overleveraged and something goes down by half, you've got a big problem.
> That was our problem.
>
> Ace Greenberg, chairman of Bear Stearns's executive committee,
> June 21, 2010 (Cook 2010)

The failure of two Bear Stearns hedge funds and the losses associated
with that directly cost the firm $500 million.[22] In the third quarter of 2007,
Bear reported net income that had dropped by 61% compared with the
third quarter of 2006. Bear CEO Jimmy Cayne said, "I am confident in the
underlying strength of our business and proud of the effort and determination
displayed by our employees during these challenging times."[23]

After its two hedge funds failed, S&P placed Bear on a "negative outlook."
Less than six months later, the Bear went into hibernation.

A run on the bank brought Bear Stearns down. At the end of 2007,
Bear had written down $2.6 billion in mortgage losses and its net income
declined from a year earlier by 89% due to the write-down. Bear had $11.8
billion in equity and $46 billion in mortgages and asset-backed securities.
The market was unsure how much this was really worth. If it was worth half,
then Bear Stearns was not solvent. As more and more rumors spread that
Bear Stearns would collapse, more hedge funds withdrew their prime banking
relationships, CDS spreads went higher and higher, and even the firm's ability
to finance its overnight activities proved questionable.

Credit default swaps measure the cost of insuring a company's debt.
In early 2007, the cost of insuring $10 million in Bear Stearns debt was
$50,000. By March 5, 2008, the cost was $350,000. The market was worried
that Bear-owned mortgages were overvalued, and that losses might render
Bear insolvent.

It's hard to know what started the rumors. Bear was the smallest of the
investment banks with a large mortgage exposure, which may have made it
a target. The hedge fund fiasco probably made the market less certain of
Bear. Actors within the system hurt Bear. For example, the Office of the
Comptroller of the Currency began calling banks in March to ask the amount
of their exposure to Bear. Regardless of the intention, this suggested that
these banks might want to cut their exposures to Bear. The more neutral call

would have asked the respondent's exposure to all major banks, not just the suspect one.

As the rumors spread, Bear became the focal point of a run. Short sellers attacked the stock. Eventually Bear had no financing to run its business.

Alan Schwartz, the CEO who replaced Cayne shortly before Bear collapsed, immediately pointed his finger at Goldman. He thought Goldman had started the rumors. Goldman denied this, and the SEC's investigation found nothing. It is hard to believe that Goldman wanted Bear to fail, given its business relationships with Bear. Of course, individual groups of traders may have cheered the fall. David Solomon, co-head of investment banking at Goldman Sachs, asked Bear's Molinaro if there was anything Goldman could do to help them. Molinaro told Bear treasurer Bob Upton about the call and Upton knew it was over. "That's the trumpet playing because all that means is that they want to come in and see our positions so they can trade against us and make money."[24]

Bear Stearns was one of the most levered Wall Street firms with mortgage exposure. When the housing market began to turn, rumors spread; more clients withdrew from Bear. Bob Sloan, whose firm advises hedge funds, told clients to withdraw from Bear because he was worried about Bear's survival. By March 2008, $25 billion of the hedge fund assets he advised had been withdrawn.

Large hedge funds such as Renaissance Technologies and Highbridge Capital Management began closing their prime brokerage accounts with Bear. Then D.E. Shaw pulled cash from their prime brokerage with Bear. Even the SEC, which had started a voluntary supervision program at the five major investment banks, didn't spot the trend.[25]

As clients withdrew their assets, Bear was at a loss for an explanation.

> Why is this happening? If I knew why it was happening, I would do something to address it. There is no liquidity crisis. No margin calls. It's nonsense.
>
> Samuel Molinaro, former CFO of Bear Stearns, CNBC,
> March 11, 2008 (Boyd 2008)

Former CEO James Cayne testified to the Financial Crisis Query Commission:

> [The firm's collapse] was due to overwhelming market forces that Bear Stearns . . . could not resist. The market's loss of confidence, even though it was unjustified and irrational, become a self-fulfilling prophecy. The efforts

we made to strengthen the firm were reasonable and prudent, although in hindsight they proved inadequate. Considering the severity and unprecedented nature of the turmoil in the market, I do not believe there were any reasonable steps we could have taken, short of selling the firm, to prevent the collapse that ultimately occurred.

James Cayne, former CEO of Bear Stearns,
May 7, 2010 (FCIC 2010)

Although this statement was self-serving, there was also a lot of truth in it. Bear's stock price dropped from $61.58 on March 12 to $5.91 on March 18, falling 90% in six days.[?] On March 11, 2008 Bear's liquidity pool was $18.1 billion. By March 12, the pool totaled $12.4 billion. On March 13, the pool fell sharply to under $3 billion. The SEC Chairman Cox testified to the FCIC that "At all times during the week of March 10 to 17, up to and including the time of its agreement to be acquired by J.P. Morgan, Bear Steans has had a capital cushion well above what is required." It's hard to believe that anything fundamental about Bear's business changed—but something certainly changed in the beliefs of its customers, creditors, and counterparties. Meriwether had cautioned everyone on these issues just 10 years earlier.

The hurricane is not more or less likely to hit because more hurricane insurance has been written. In the financial markets this is not true. The more people write financial insurance, the more likely it is that a disaster will happen, because the people who know you have sold the insurance can make it happen. So you have to monitor what other people are doing.

—John Meriwether, founder and CEO of LTCM and JWMP,
January 24, 1999 (Lewis 1999)

The Polar Spring

On March 16, 2008, J.P. Morgan bought Bear Stearns. In the deal every Bear share could be exchanged for 0.05473 J.P. Morgan shares, giving Bear an effective value of $2 per share (and a total value of $236 million). As part of this rescue, the Fed purchased $28.82 billion of Bear's mortgage-related securities, residential and commercial mortgage whole loans that were very difficult to sell and were potentially worth very little. This left J.P. Morgan on the hook for the first $1.15 billion in losses. Eighty-five years of independence as a Wall Street firm evaporated in an afternoon. And what a deal this was for

J.P. Morgan. The Bear Stearns building on Madison Avenue alone was worth $1.5 billion. Morgan CEO Jamie Dimon got the deal of a lifetime.

Even the market knew the deal was too good to be true. On March 20, Bear's shares closed at $5.93, likely because the market anticipated that the deal would be re-cut. Joe Lewis, Bear's second-largest shareholder, approached Jimmy Cayne, the fourth-largest shareholder, and told him that Lewis would launch a campaign against the deal unless J.P. Morgan paid more. On March 19, Lewis filed a 13-D with the SEC stating that he would contact other shareholders and other third parties to get a better deal for Bear Stearns shareholders. Jamie Dimon became worried about the lending agreement between J.P. Morgan and Bear. Bear might find another buyer at a better price.

Lewis's battle eventually paid off. On March 24, J.P. Morgan announced the new deal at 0.21753 shares of J.P. Morgan for each share of Bear. On March 24, 2010, this amounted to $10 per share (a total value of $1,180 million).[26]

Jimmy Cayne had kept much of his wealth in Bear Stearns stock. On January 17, 2007, Cayne's stock was worth $958 million. By January 3, 2008, it was worth $478 million. Cayne sold all his shares by March 27, 2008 for $61 million total.

> I was prepared to get $2 or anything for Bear as long as it prevented bankruptcy and saved employee jobs, benefits, and health insurance. All my life, I never thought about money, I just wanted to move ahead, become a leader. In the end, the pain of felt by 14,000 families was my overwhelming grief.
>
> —Jimmy Cayne interview, former CEO of Bear Stearns, April 12, 2012

Many employees lost their life savings. One former Bear employee had to take a train back from Grand Central station to Greenwich, Connecticut, and tell his wife and kids that he was unemployed because of an overzealous housing market and a run on the bank.

> I worked eight years at a firm that promoted me from the back office to investment banking. I had thousands of shares and thought I could afford to send my kids to private schools and college. It's all gone now. I think I'll probably move to Pittsburgh, see if the Federal Home Loan Bank needs anybody.
>
> —Anonymous employee, Bear Stearns, March 14, 2008 (Boyd 2008)

The average Bear employee had $200,000 in a retirement fund, but was left with $2,000 after the collapse.[27]

Bear's former CEO put the crash in perspective.

> There is no other banking system that's ever existed. The reason we have deposit insurance is because a banking system is fundamentally about raising a bunch of assets, which are short-term in nature because it's the liquidity of individuals that when aggregated become a pool that you can lend out. That is banking. [But] in this cycle the cycle froze . . . In truth, it was a team effort. We all !@#$%^ up. Government. Rating agencies. Wall Street. Commercial banks. Regulators. Investors. Everybody . . . And fifty years from now, there'll be another crisis and it'll be about some instruments that we've never heard of.
>
> —Alan Schwartz, 2010 (Cohan 2010)

When J.P. Morgan bought Bear Stearns, the Fed opened the discount window to prime dealers that very day. At the congressional hearing on April 3, 2008, Geithner and Bernanke responded to questions about why they had not prevented the run on Bear Stearns.

> Whether opening up earlier would have helped or not is very difficult to say . . . But Bear Stearns was losing customers and counterparties very quickly. They were downgraded on Friday. And we did lend them money, of course, to keep them [going] into the weekend, but it's not at all obvious to me that it would have been sufficient to prevent their bankruptcy.
>
> —Ben Bernanke, Fed Chairman, Congressional Testimony,
> April 3, 2008

> Friday morning we took the exceptional step, with extreme reluctance, with support of the Board of Governors and the Treasury, to structure a way to get them to the weekend, so that we could buy some time to explore whether there was a possible solution that would have them acquired and guaranteed.
>
> The number of customers and counterparties that sought to withdraw funds . . . accelerated that dynamic, despite the access to liquidity and despite the hope that that might buy some time. The way the Federal Reserve Act is designed, and the way we think about the discount window for banks, is we only allow sound institutions to borrow against collateral in that context . . . I can only speak personally for this, but I would have been very uncomfortable lending to Bear, given what we knew at that time . . . And I do not believe it would have been appropriate for us to take that act Sunday

night if we had not been faced with the dynamics that were precipitated by, accelerated by, the looming prospect of a Bear default.

Timothy Geithner, Treasury Secretary, Congressional Testimony,
April 3, 2008

Bear had repeatedly asked the Fed to open up the discount window before their collapse. Jimmy Cayne erupted when asked about Geithner's decision to keep the window closed until after Bear's purchase.

> The audacity of that prick in front of the American people announcing he was deciding whether or not a firm of this stature and this whatever was good enough to get a loan. Like he was the determining factor, and it's like a flea on his back, floating down underneath the Golden Gate Bridge, getting a hard-on, saying, "Raise the bridge." This guy thinks he's got a big @$%!. He's got nothing, except maybe a boyfriend. I'm not a good enemy. I'm a very bad enemy. But certain things really—that bothered me plenty. It's just that for some clerk to make a decision based on what, your own personal feeling about whether or not they're a good credit? Who the !@#$ asked you? You're not an elected officer. You're a clerk.
>
> —Jimmy Cayne, former CEO and Chairman of the Board of
> Bear Stearns (Cohan 2010)

Cayne was probably right: Uncertainty and market forces were causing runs on small banks. Why would anyone keep a prime brokerage account at Bear, when Bear might be too small to save, instead of holding money at J.P. Morgan? Banking is a system of trust. As the market grew less certain of Bear's solvency, customers ran, which helped cause more insolvency. Had the Fed stepped in and offered the capital resources it provided after Lehman's failure, Bear might not have failed.

Bear, like others after it, had a short-term solvency problem. A former CEO of one of the largest investment banks in the U.S. examined Bear before the collapse and realized that Bear needed capital. He told the Fed and the Treasury, which said that they couldn't be preemptive.[28] The Fed and the Treasury hadn't faced this situation before and didn't know what to do. It would be pleasant to hear a government official admit that—just as pleasant as it would be to hear Cayne confess his mistakes.[29]

> I was not guiltless. The buck stopped with me. I did not see that it would be so bad. But what does that mean anyway? That phrase is overused and means nothing. I can't change anything now and at the time I cannot honestly tell you that I would do anything differently. What you should know is that

I loved working there and I hated weekends. It was a great company with great people. We were a special family. Bear was synonymous with my soul. I loved Bear Stearns.

—Jimmy Cayne interview, former CEO of Bear Stearns,
April 12, 2012

As spring rolled into summer, the mortgage markets were still unhealthy. Everyone had seemed to have forgotten how the crowd had chased Bear into extinction. Lehman, Merrill, Morgan, and Goldman had also financed 10% to 20% of their assets in the repo market and had between 18% and 70% of their repo transactions as overnight repos. Lehman and Merrill had failed the Federal Reserve's liquidity stress tests in June by a whopping $22 and $15 billion, respectively. But before people focused on the investment banks again, they would focus on the problem's source: the housing market and the two largest hedge funds in the United States, Freddie Mac and Fannie Mae. Their bankruptcy was only prevented by a government bailout. That shouldn't have been so surprising. After all, their general partner was Uncle Sam.

CHAPTER 10

Money for Nothing and Fannie and Freddie for Free

If you tell grown-ups, "I saw a beautiful red brick house, with geraniums at the windows and doves on the roof . . . ," they won't be able to imagine such a house. You have to tell them, "I saw a house worth a hundred thousand francs." Then they exclaim, "What a pretty house!"

—The Little Prince

The financial market is connected to the Federal Home Loan Mortgage Association (Freddie Mac) and the Federal National Mortgage Association (Fannie Mae) in many ways. They are the biggest securitizers and purchasers of mortgages in the United States, and toward the end of the 1990s the debt they issued to finance these mortgages became very attractive to all kinds of institutions. Bond portfolio managers at investment banks, hedge funds, commercial banks, international agencies, and central banks began crowding the space, buying up Freddie Mac and Fannie Mae bonds in droves.

There were two principal reasons bond managers bought up so much of Fannie and Freddie's debt. First, the U.S. government began running surpluses at the end of the 1990s and even stopped issuing 30-year bonds from 2001 to 2006.[1] Bond traders and other institutions needed a substitute for U.S. government debt.

Second, debt issued by Freddie and Fannie paid a higher return than did U.S. Treasuries. Figure 10.1 shows the interest rate difference (the spread)

155

FIGURE 10.1   Interest Rate Spread between Freddie Mac Bonds and U.S. Government
Bonds

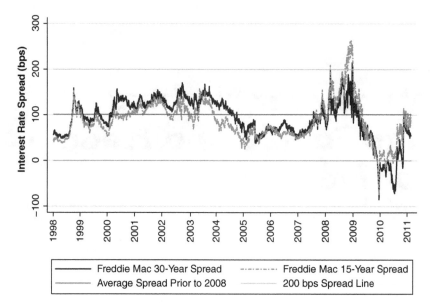

Source: Bloomberg.

between a Freddie Mac bond and a U.S. government bond. The graph shows
the spread for 15-year and 30-year bonds in basis points.

The average extra yield from owning 15- and 30-year bonds was 85 basis
points and 101 basis points more than Treasuries, respectively.[2]

If a bond manager bought a 15-year Freddie Mac bond, it paid an extra
0.85% over a Treasury. In theory, this is because Freddie Mac (or Fannie Mae)
securities are riskier than U.S. government securities. For example, in 2008
and 2009, the spread widened as the mortgage crisis grew.

In portfolio management, the goal is to achieve the highest return for
the lowest amount of risk. Toward the end of the 1990s, even central banks
wanted to earn higher returns on their foreign exchange reserves. To do that,
they moved out of U.S. Treasuries and invested more in what professional
investors call Agency securities: the bonds issued by Freddie, Fannie, and
Ginnie Mae.[3]

Portfolio managers (including central banks) bought this debt because
it offered slightly better returns than Treasuries, but with nearly identical
perceived risk. Officially, the U.S. government backed only Ginnie bonds,
but Freddie and Fannie had implicit government guarantees. The U.S.
government didn't officially back their bonds, but was their supervisor, with

the implication that, if these organizations were to find themselves in financial trouble, the government would backstop them.

LTCM sometimes went long Fannie and Freddie and hedged the interest rate risk by shorting U.S. Treasury bonds or U.S. Treasury futures. If the two securities really did have the same risk, traders picked up extra return over a longer period at zero cost.[4]

The Basic Business

To understand the role these agencies had in the U.S. housing market and how they got in so much trouble in 2008, it's crucial to understand the agencies' basic business. Ironically, Freddie, Fannie, and Ginnie began in the Great Depression. In 1934, Congress passed the National Housing Act to strengthen a deeply troubled housing market.

In 1938, Congress amended the act to create Fannie Mae, both to establish a national commitment to housing and because the government felt that private lenders were unable or unwilling to ensure a reliable supply of mortgage credit throughout the country.

In 1968, Fannie Mae split into two parts: Ginnie Mae and the new Fannie Mae. Ginnie Mae continued as a federal agency and focused on making housing more affordable for low- and moderate-income buyers.

Fannie Mae became a government-sponsored private corporation, responsible for supporting the secondary market in mortgages. Fannie Mae would be stockholder-owned and managed. The new company retired the last of its government ownership on September 30, 1968, and completed its transformation into a government-sponsored private corporation in 1970.

Around the same time, on July 24, 1970, Congress passed the Federal Home Loan Mortgage Corporate Act, which created another stockholder-owned and-managed corporation to assist the mortgage markets: Freddie Mac. The reasons for Freddie's creation were much the same as the reasons behind Fannie: the desire to commit to housing growth and the belief that private lenders would not supply an adequate amount of mortgage credit, especially to low-income buyers.

Of all three organizations, only Ginnie Mae was officially a government agency. Still, every market participant treated the others as if they were also government backed.[5]

Freddie and Fannie, which compete with one another, engage in two basic types of businesses for mortgage originators: the *swap business* and the *cash business*.[6] The swap business lets banks transfer loans to Freddie or Fannie. Only mortgage loans that are *conforming loans*—those for below a certain amount—can be transferred to Freddie Mac and Fannie Mae. The national conforming loan limit for mortgages that finance single-family, one-unit properties increased from $33,000 in the early 1970s to $417,000 for 2006, 2007, and 2008, with limits that are 50 percent higher in four high-cost areas: Alaska, Hawaii, Guam, and the U.S. Virgin Islands. Since early 2008, a series of legislative acts have temporarily increased the one-unit limit to $729,750 in certain high-cost areas within the contiguous United States.

Banks transfer loans because owning mortgages involves risk. Borrowers may not be able to pay back the loan. This is called *default risk*. Or home owners might choose to refinance the loan, typically when rates have dropped, and repay the entire original balance. This is called *prepayment risk*. By selling mortgages to Freddie and Fannie, banks get commissions for making the loans, may even earn a monthly fee for processing payments, and unload all their risk.

In the cash transaction, Freddie pays cash for a mortgage pool. The amount is based on the fair value of the mortgages minus a small guarantee fee, called a G-fee.[7] Fannie and Freddie then securitize the loans, selling them in pools to investors—usually pension funds and insurance companies—at auction. These assets are called mortgage-backed securities (MBS).

In the swap transaction, the mortgage originator gives the entire mortgage pool to Freddie or Fannie in exchange for a security that is backed by the pool of mortgages, minus the credit risk. The yield on this mortgage-backed security is a fixed yield, minus the G-fee.

Mortgage originators get either cash or a security, both of which are much more liquid than a pool of mortgages. One widely recognized security—with no credit risk—is better than a complicated pool of unique mortgages. Securitized bonds usually have a better credit rating than do mortgage pools, so a swap or cash deal also helps banks improve their risk-adjusted capital ratios.

Freddie and Fannie do not sell all the loans they buy to other investors. They retain some. As a result, both agencies need to generate cash. They do this by issuing debt commonly referred to as agency debt. Agency debt has a lower interest rate than the mortgage pools, so Freddie and Fannie make the spread between rates on the loans they hold and the debt they sell. The difference is about 40 basis points per year.[8]

Where's the Risk?

What Congress did turned out to be absolutely brilliant—it created a system that harnesses private enterprise and private capital to deliver the public benefit of home ownership. And it maximizes this public benefit while minimizing the public risk, and without spending a nickel of public funds.

—Franklin D. Raines, CEO of Fannie Mae from 1999 to 2004,
Testimony to U.S. House of Representatives,
May 16, 2000

Freddie and Fannie's risk comes in two forms. They assume all *credit risk*—the risk that mortgage holders won't pay back a loan—attached to the securitized mortgages they sell to investors. To reduce some of this credit risk, Freddie buys insurance on some portion of its mortgage pools.[9]

Investors, on the other hand, assume interest-rate risk: the risk that interest rates will rise and a set of pooled mortgages will become less valuable, or that interest rates will fall and home owners will prepay their mortgages.

Freddie and Fannie also assume a second risk, this one with respect to the mortgages that they retain. Because they own these mortgages,[10] they assume credit risk for this retained mortgage group. And because they borrow in order to buy and retain mortgages, they also assume the associated interest-rate risk. Of the two, interest-rate risk is typically far more significant, and Fannie and Freddie enter into large hedging transactions to mitigate it.

They do this because the retained mortgages produce far greater profits than the GSEs would get by selling the loans. Fannie and Freddie's government-sponsored enterprise (GSE) status gives them favorable interest rates in the capital markets, so they can make extra profits from the larger spread between what they pay for borrowing and the rate they earn on the retained mortgage pool.[11]

Most of the time, this is a slam-dunk business model. As long as mortgage borrowers pay their mortgages on time and do not default, the GSEs make money on the G-fees plus the spread between what they pay to borrow money and what they earn on mortgages.

They can lose money in two ways. Without adequate interest-rate hedging, they may lose money when interest rates change. They can also lose money if credit risk is higher than they anticipated—that is, if home owners default on their loans more often than Freddie, Fannie, or Ginnie predict.

CDO and CDO²

Is my head on straight?

—C3PO

The process of buying a bunch of securities, putting them together, and selling them to other investors is known as *securitization*. Freddie and Fannie

FIGURE 10.2   The Business Flows of Buying Mortgages and Making MBS, CMO, and CDOs

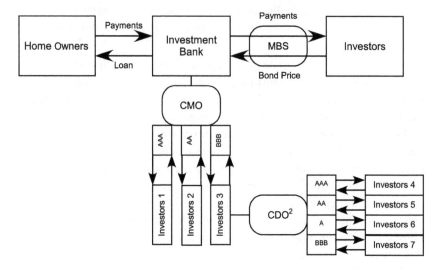

securitize mortgage loans, as do investment and commercial banks. Securitized assets include student loans, mortgages, credit card loans, auto loans, and other forms of debt. When mortgages are the underlying asset, the created security is known as a mortgage-backed security. Some MBSs are more specialized, including residential mortgage-backed securities (RMBSs) and commercial mortgage-backed securities (CMBSs). An investor who purchases a share of the mortgage pool receives a proportional share of the income the pool generates from interest and principal payments on the mortgages.

A securitizer might also purchase a mortgage pool and split its components into several investment vehicles, determined by aspects of payments from the underlying mortgage pool. These collateralized mortgage obligations (CMOs) can be greatly customized. Figure 10.2 shows a typical separation of securities within a CMO. In this situation a securitizer might create three bonds: one rated AAA, one rated AA, and one rated BBB. The ratings indicate the likelihood of default. The higher the rating, the more likely that the underlying mortgage owners will pay back the loan.

A higher credit rating also means lower prepayment risk. Consider a $100 million mortgage pool. A banker divides it into three equal tranches. The lowest tranche (BBB) gets all the prepayments and all the defaults first. Additional prepayments or defaults go to the next tranche (AA), and so on. An investor who owns the AAA tranche suffers losses only if more than 66% of the mortgage pool defaults.[12]

In theory, a CMO is also a collateralized debt obligation (CDO). A CDO is the more general form of a CMO. It can be created from a whole host of underlying bonds, not just the mortgage bonds that characterize CMOs.

Figure 10.2 shows a typical CDO created during the housing bubble between 2000 and 2008. Investors in the third group owned the CMO's BBB bonds. They split these bonds into a new CDO and sold it to other investors. Amazingly enough, some parts of that new CDO could have a AAA rating.

Why? The rating agencies may have simply gotten it wrong. Or perhaps another, more complex explanation is correct.

Investors created this CDO from the BBB tranche, which was the CMO's bottom tranche. If any mortgages in the initial security defaulted, this tranche would get them. Suppose that 50% of the mortgages in this pool would default if housing prices declined by a substantial amount. Housing prices drop by 50% and 50% of the mortgages in the original BBB tranche default. But the defaults are not total losses, because the underlying collateral—the houses—still have value. The tranche's owners will recover perhaps 50% of each defaulted mortgage's original value.

The CMO's entire value when the investor bought it was $100 million, a sum representing an underlying mortgage pool of loans against 500 houses of $200,000 each. If housing prices decline 50%, 50% of the BBB tranche default, and the recovery rate is also 50%, then the BBB tranche loses $8.33 million.

To create the second CDO, also known as CDO-squared, a securitizer might split the original BBB tranche into four more tranches with notional values of $8.33 million each.[13] As before, tranches are divided by the likelihood of defaults and prepayments. If mortgage holders behave as they did before, the top tranche could have zero losses. The default scenario will cause a total of 50% of defaults in the mortgage pool, costing investors a total of $8.33 million. The lower tranches would absorb these losses and the top tranche would not lose a dime. The highest tranche could be rated AAA while the lower tranches could be given lower ratings, as shown in Figure 10.2.[14]

An investment bank might also create a synthetic CDO, which doesn't contain any actual collateral or underlying mortgages. A synthetic CDO's value is determined by a reference group of mortgages, with values adjusted accordingly. This had two economy-wide effects. First, it gave more participants housing market exposure and therefore exposed them to subprime mortgages, which lurked within the CDOs.

Second, it created conflicts of interest. Investment banks had to find buyers and sellers for these securities, so investment banks might work with a seller to help create the CDO that the seller wanted to market. The investment bank would then turn around and sell part or all of it to a buyer. A conflict of interest arises because a complex instrument that is good for the seller may be a less reliable product to the buyer.

On the positive side, because these synthetic CDOs did not securitize underlying mortgages, they probably did not further the housing bubble. They also allowed investors to short the housing market, which may have tamed the bubble somewhat.

From 2004 to 2006, Goldman Sachs launched 63 CDOs totaling $32 billion. Between 2004 and 2007, it sold 47 synthetic CDOs with a face value of $66 billion.[15] Goldman made 0.50% to 1.50% in commissions on deal totals. It also made money taking outright positions in some deals.

Investment banks, Freddie Mac, Fannie Mae, and commercial banks created CMOs and CDOs, giving investors exposure to the mortgage markets. Layered CDOs spread mortgage risk throughout the financial system. If the assumptions underlying individual home owner or housing price behavior were incorrect, the elaborate system for creating AAA instruments would fall to pieces. During the housing bubble's mad rush, the crowd ignored inconvenient details and kept packaging these securities.

The Gigantic Hedge Fund

The GSEs rely on the interest rate spread, just like a bank or a hedge fund that borrows money at one rate and invests at a higher rate. And just like a hedge fund, the GSEs use leverage. At the end of 2007, Freddie Mac's total assets were $794 billion. These assets consisted mainly of Freddie's retained portfolio of mortgage securities, worth a total of $728 billion. Freddie's total shareholder equity was $26 billion, giving Freddie Mac a leverage ratio of 28 (728/26). Considering all its mortgage obligations, including the book of securitized loans sold to investors and therefore no longer on Freddie's balance sheet, gave Freddie a leverage of 81.[16] Fannie had a similar amount of leverage, with ratios of 20 and 80, respectively.

Remember all the criticisms of LTCM for carrying a leverage ratio of 25? Here was a government-sponsored institution with a leverage somewhere between 20 and 80 with an underlying investment in real estate. The complaints were few and muted. Officials and investors both believed that home owner default was the only real risk on these assets, and noted that historically, defaults were comparatively rare.

It was the U.S. government that created this massively leveraged hedge fund. By law, Fannie Mae and Freddie Mac had to meet the higher of two regulatory capital requirements: minimum and risk based. The minimum capital requirement was 2.5 percent of assets, which largely consist of mortgage-backed securities (MBSs) and whole mortgage loans, plus 0.45 percent of off-balance-sheet obligations, which consist primarily of credit guarantees on the MBSs sold to investors.[17]

The Office of Federal Housing Enterprise Oversight (OFHEO), the federal regulator of the firms' safety and soundness, also required both government-sponsored enterprises (GSEs) to hold an additional 30 percent in capital surplus (above minimum capital levels) to protect against uncertainty related to operating performance. That provision temporarily raised the firms' capital requirements to 3.25 percent of assets and 0.585 percent of the MBSs guaranteed by the GSEs and those held by investors.[18]

These capital ratios imply a maximum leverage of 31 for retained portfolios and a leverage ratio of 171 for mortgage pools passed through to investors (see Box 10.1). At the end of 2007, Freddie and Fannie had actual leverage ratios of 30 and 20 before considering off-balance-sheet mortgages. Add these and their leverage ratios were 81 and 68, respectively. Major investment banks, by contrast, have average leverage ratios of 33.[19] These leverage ratios were also much higher than anything LTCM considered back in 1998. With Uncle Sam's backing, the GSEs felt free to use big leverage and take big bets.

Box 10.1 The Capital Ratio and Leverage

Leverage is created whenever any company borrows money to fund its investments. An investment bank or a hedge fund may borrow short-term capital from a broker-dealer in order to invest in equities, bonds, or other instruments. For institutions such as Freddie and Fannie, leverage consists of mortgage investments, which they finance by borrowing in the capital markets. All firms have shareholder equity, consisting of capital that a firm's owners brought to pursue company business. When a company's total assets (including investments) are greater than its shareholder equity, the firm has borrowed to finance its investments. A firm's capital ratio can be measured in many ways; one method involves dividing total shareholder equity by total assets. Using this method, a company's leverage ratio equals 1/CR, where CR is the capital ratio.

As Freddie and Fannie's leverage grew, criticism centered on their retained portfolios—because of interest rate risk, not default risk. Alan Greenspan and other financial professionals worried that the GSEs might have insufficient hedges on their interest rate risk.

> The unease relates mainly to the scale and growth of the mortgage-related asset portfolios held on their [Freddie and Fannie] balance sheets. That growth has been facilitated, as least in part, by a perceived special advantage of these institutions that keeps normal market restraints from being fully effective... most investors have apparently concluded that during a crisis the federal government will prevent the GSEs from defaulting on their debt... Unlike many well-capitalized savings and loans and commercial banks, Fannie and Freddie have chosen not to manage that risk by holding greater capital. Instead, they have chosen heightened leverage, which raises interest rate risk but enables them to multiply the profitability of subsidized debt in direct proportion to their degree of leverage... Interest rate risk associated with fixed-rate mortgages, unless supported by substantial capital, however, can be of even greater concern than the credit risk. Congress needs to clarify the circumstances under which a GSE can become insolvent ...
> —Alan Greenspan, Fed Chairman, Statement to the Banking, Housing, and Urban Affairs Committee, February 24, 2004

Amazingly enough, hardly anyone was worried about the risk that would eventually seal Fannie and Freddie's fate: credit risk. This was very strange. Real estate was booming, so it was easy to argue that real estate was enormously overvalued. A drop in real estate prices could lead to high defaults and large mortgage portfolio losses.

Consider Freddie Mac's total combined mortgage portfolio at the end of 2007. (It was worth $2.8 trillion.) Suppose average housing prices dropped by 27% (this was the Case-Shiller national index's actual drop from December 2006 to December 2009). If just 3.6% of borrowed dollars defaulted, this would eat up $28 billion in equity capital and Freddie would go bankrupt.[20]

Freddie and Fannie had no incentive to behave more cautiously. The federal government continually pressured them to support the housing market.[21] Supporting housing, after all, was their mission. What's more, Fannie and Freddie's managers had a free option. If they continued to bet big on the housing market and kept earning the leveraged spread, profits would be high—and so would individual bonuses. If the housing market collapsed and the GSEs were insolvent, the government would rescue them, just as it had rescued the Farm Credit System in 1987. In economics, this is called the *moral hazard* problem. No one had a very strong incentive to be vigilant. In fact, the GSEs became slightly more enamored of risk.

Between 2004 and 2006, there was a large rise in the subprime mortgage market. Wall Street firms were securitizing these loans, reducing Freddie and Fannie's share of the total mortgage market between 2003 and 2006 (see Table 10.1). Freddie and Fannie participated in the expanded market. Every year roughly 14% to 18% of their mortgage portfolio exposure involved loans to home owners with FICO scores of less than 660, considered subprime loans.[22]

Freddie and Fannie Mae purchased about 23% of the subprime and alt-A MBSs securitized by Wall Street.[23] Figure 10.3 shows the total originations of subprime mortgages alone and those purchased by Freddie and Fannie. Freddie and Fannie's exposure to high-risk mortgages represented about 20% of their activity before 2005, but about 43% of their activity by 2007.[24] About 28% of the loans Fannie purchased did not have full documentation—a significant departure from past practices.[25]

Freddie and Fannie's push into these markets let others, including commercial and investment banks, go deeper into the same markets.[26]

In large part, Freddie and Fannie bought securitized subprime loans to fulfill their charter to support low-income housing.[27]

Lots of leverage can provide lots of profits, and the luxury of taking large risks with government protection led to very high profits indeed.

Big-Time Profits

A walk down Jones Branch Drive in McLean, Virginia, will bring you past the luxurious Freddie Mac campus. A walk down Wisconsin Avenue will bring you right by Fannie Mae, a magnificent building modeled after the Governor's Mansion in Colonial Williamsburg. The vast complexes bellowed "We are making lots of money."

From 1995 to 2006, Fannie and Freddie's average annual profits were $3.8 billion. Seven major investment banks had average annual profits of $3.3 billion during the same period.[28] In some years, Freddie and Fannie's profits swamped the investment banks' takings. In 2002, for example, Freddie made $10 billion in profits, while Goldman Sachs made only $2.1 billion. Citibank, with $15.3 billion, was the only major bank with profits larger than Freddie's haul. Goldman and Citibank have many more employees than Freddie does. In 2002, Freddie made $2 million per employee. Goldman and Citi made $108,000 and $60,000 per employee, respectively.[29]

Freddie and Fannie's profits went to everyone—especially their executives.[30]

TABLE 10.1 Total Residential Mortgage Securities Outstanding and Held by Freddie and Fannie (billions of dollars)

Year	Total RDO	Retained			Securitized			GSE Share of Total Market (%)		
		Fannie	Freddie	GSE Total	Fannie	Freddie	GSE Total	Total	Retained Portfolio	MBS Outstanding
1990	2,894	117	22	138	288	316	604	25.67	4.79	20.89
1991	3,058	129	27	156	355	359	714	28.46	5.10	23.36
1992	3,213	158	34	192	424	408	832	31.87	5.98	25.90
1993	3,368	191	56	247	471	439	910	34.35	7.32	27.03
1994	3,546	222	73	295	486	461	947	35.02	8.32	26.71
1995	3,719	254	107	361	513	459	972	35.85	9.70	26.14
1996	3,955	287	138	425	548	473	1,021	36.57	10.74	25.82
1997	4,200	317	164	481	579	476	1,055	36.57	11.45	25.12
1998	4,591	415	255	670	637	478	1,115	38.89	14.58	24.30
1999	5,056	524	324	848	679	538	1,217	40.85	16.78	24.07
2000	5,509	610	392	1,002	707	576	1,283	41.49	18.20	23.29
2001	6,103	716	498	1,214	863	653	1,517	44.74	19.89	24.85
2002	6,896	800	567	1,367	1,040	730	1,770	45.49	19.82	25.67
2003	7,785	909	645	1,554	1,301	752	2,053	46.33	19.97	26.37
2004	8,863	917	653	1,570	1,408	852	2,260	43.22	17.72	25.50
2005	10,043	738	710	1,448	1,599	974	2,573	40.04	14.42	25.62
2006	11,158	729	704	1,433	1,778	1,123	2,900	38.84	12.84	25.99
2007	11,954	728	721	1,449	2,119	1,382	3,501	41.40	12.12	29.29
2008	11,903	792	805	1,597	2,289	1,403	3,692	44.43	13.42	31.02
2009	11,683	769	755	1,525	2,433	1,495	3,928	46.67	13.05	33.62

Note: RDO indicates Residential Debt Outstanding, "Retained" shows the mortgages that the GSEs retained rather than sold to others; "Securitized" shows the number of mortgages that the GSEs securitized and sold to others; and GSE stands for government-sponsored enterprise.
Source: FHFA.

FIGURE 10.3 Origination in the Subprime Market and the GSE Share

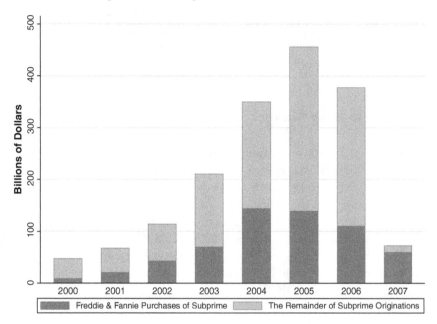

Note: Excludes Alt-A originations.
Source: Thomas and Van Order (2011).

In the five years up to 2002, Fannie paid its 20 top executives a combined $245 million in bonuses. In 2002, its 21 top executives each earned more than $1 million in total compensation.

As far back as 1996, the Office of Federal Housing Enterprise Oversight was concerned about compensation practices at Fannie and Freddie. Fannie paid outgoing chairman David Maxwell a $19.5 million lump sum when he retired in 1991, in addition to the $7.5 million salary he received in 1990. Fannie Mae Chairman James Johnson made more than $1.5 million in salary and bonuses in 1994. His counterpart at Freddie, Leland Brendsel, pulled in slightly more than $1.4 million, according to the companies' 1995 proxy statements.

Even in 2007, prior to Fannie and Freddie's government takeover, Freddie Mac Chairman and Chief Executive Richard Syron pocketed nearly $19.8 million in compensation. In 2005 and 2006, he received a total of $23.6 million. Leland Brendsel, Freddie's CEO from 1987 to 2003, pocketed around $23 million between 2000 and 2003.

Franklin Raines, Fannie Mae's CEO from 1999 to 2004, received a total compensation of $91.1 million during his reign at Fannie. Daniel Mudd, Fannie's CEO from 2005 to 2008, earned a total of $24.4 million in 2005 and 2006. In general, the market rewards risk—and the GSEs took big risks—and made big money only because of their implicit government backing.

The U.S. Housing Bubble

To understand Freddie and Fannie's collapse on September 7, 2008, it's important to recall what was going on in the housing market at the time.

In 1999, the housing market was attractive. By 2008, it was unaffordable for many. Figure 10.4 shows Freddie and Fannie's stock prices and a housing-price index for the 10 largest metropolitan areas in the United States, plus the major metropolitan areas of Miami, Washington, DC, and Los Angeles.[31]

By 2006, the housing market was a bubble ready to pop. Many people claimed there was no bubble in housing prices, including Ben Bernanke, Barney Frank, and the FDIC.[32]

FIGURE 10.4   Fannie Mae and Freddie Mac Stock Prices versus Selected U.S. Housing Prices

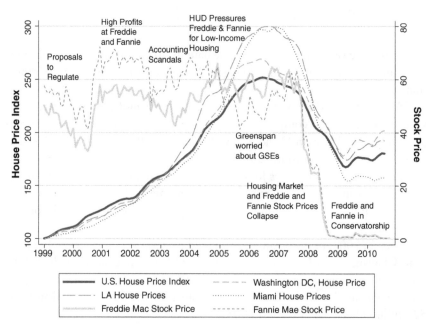

... those who argue that housing prices are now at the point of a bubble seem to be missing a very important point. Unlike previous examples, where substantial excessive inflation of prices later caused some problems, we are talking here about an entity, home ownership, homes, where there is not the degree of leverage that we have seen elsewhere. This is not the dot-com situation.

—Barney Frank, U.S. Representative, Chairman of Banking
Committee from 2007 to 2011, June 27, 2005

In fact, the Internet bubble was substantially less levered than the housing bubble. The housing bubble was levered in some cases at infinity.[33] It's very difficult to predict a bubble's end. In 2005 and 2006, I believed that there was a housing bubble and shorted the U.S. housing market by purchasing put options. I lost on both transactions because the bubble continued until 2007.

It's not always easy to identify a bubble, either. There is no perfect way to determine whether the housing market is cheap or expensive; a simple measurement offers a good starting point.[34]

Most people do not have enough money to buy a house with cash. They borrow most of the money from a bank. The home owner then makes regular monthly loan payments and eventually pays it back within a specified time frame, usually 30 years. The loan payments include principal and interest. Two financial factors influence the purchase decision: the home buyer's income and the available mortgage interest rate. Higher incomes and lower rates mean that more people can buy more expensive houses.

To measure whether the housing market is expensive, compare the relationship between the cost of owning an average home with the average income of a U.S. resident. Divide the monthly mortgage payment on the 30-year fixed-rate mortgage that would buy an average home by the average person's income.[35]

Figure 10.5 shows this measure each year. At the end of 1997, homes were relatively cheap for the average person. After taxes, mortgage payments accounted for about 22% of the average person's income. From 1998 to 2005, the cost of acquiring the average home rose dramatically, taking up 37% of the average person's income.

Home prices were the primary driver behind this change. The average single-family home in the United States cost $162,988 at the end of 1997, but $359,362 (an increase of 120%) by the end of 2005. During this same period, average income in the United States went up from $49,662 to $63,344, an increase of 27%. This bubble was not as inflated (according to this measure) as the last time houses were so expensive with respect to income. In the late

FIGURE 10.5   The Burden of Annual Mortgage Costs Relative to Average Household Income

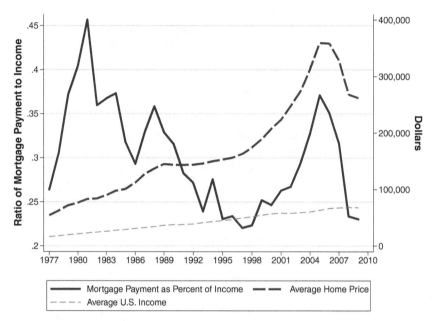

1970s, the ratio was 45%. However, in the late 1970s, the ratio was high because of very high mortgage rates, not because of an overinflated housing market.

The Circle of Greed

Everyone in the circle of greed caused the housing bubble, not just predatory lenders or Wall Street (see Figure 10.6). The circle of greed began with home owners. Realtors and mortgage lenders encouraged it. Fannie and Freddie and a host of commercial banks, insurance companies, investment banks, and hedge funds made it feasible. Politicians who wanted to win votes spurred it on, as did the regulators who failed to monitor the party and the overly optimistic rating agencies.

Low mortgage rates make housing look more attractive to potential buyers, and this bubble had very low rates indeed. Alan Greenspan and the Federal Reserve aggressively cut interest rates from 2000 to 2004, in response

FIGURE 10.6   The Circle of Greed in the Housing Bubble

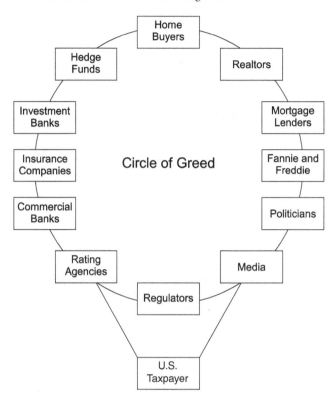

to another problem: the Internet bubble collapse in 2000 and the ensuing recession.

The Federal Reserve cut the effective Fed funds rate from 6.53% in June 2000 to 1% in February 2004 (see Figure 10.7). Over this same period, 30-year fixed mortgage rates dropped from 8.22% to 5.58%, and housing prices in Los Angeles and Washington, DC, grew by 70% and 59% respectively. After 2004, housing prices kept growing. Real estate was hot and virtually everyone wanted to get in on it.

The aggressive interest rate policy created a bubble in housing and construction. Though this would stimulate the economy in the short run, it would prove devastating in the long run.[36] The entire circle of greed was to blame—not just Greenspan. Greenspan tried to stimulate an otherwise sagging economy. No one wanted to accept that the United States might be stagnant for a while. We all wanted more.[37]

FIGURE 10.7   Greenspan Lowers Fed Funds Rate to Lift Economy Out of Internet Doom into Housing Gloom

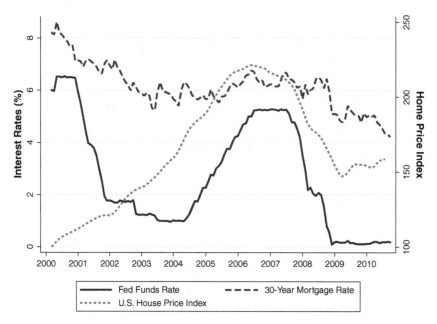

Future Fed chairman Ben Bernanke didn't see the signals that a national housing bubble was forming, either. In a CNBC interview about the possibility of a housing bubble, he said:

> Well, unquestionably, housing prices are up quite a bit; I think it's important to note that fundamentals are also very strong. We've got a growing economy, jobs, incomes. We've got very low mortgage rates. We've got demographics supporting housing growth. We've got restricted supply in some places. So it's certainly understandable that prices would go up some. I don't know whether prices are exactly where they should be, but I think it's fair to say that much of what's happened is supported by the strength of the economy . . . Well, I guess I don't buy your premise. It's a pretty unlikely possibility. We've never had a decline in house prices on a nationwide basis. So, what I think is more likely is that house prices will slow, maybe stabilize, might slow consumption spending a bit. I don't think it's gonna drive the economy too far from its full employment path, though.
>
> —Ben Bernanke, Chairman of the Council of Economic Advisors,
> CNBC Interview, July 1, 2005

Like many others, Bernanke was implicitly using a risk model that looked at historical real estate price movements while ignoring the market's current overvaluation, its composition, and the types of holders of real estate. The real estate market was overvalued by many measures, so historical real estate price behavior was not as relevant.[38]

The real estate market had become extremely crowded. Everyone was investing there, from previously unqualified homebuyers to banks, insurance companies, and hedge funds. The crowded space had increased correlations. Real estate price behavior was no longer locally independent—it became correlated across the geographical space.

Real Estate Agents and Mortgage Lender Tricks

> [No-money-down mortgages are] the most dangerous product in existence and there can be nothing more toxic.
> —E-mail from Angelo Mozilo, CEO of Countrywide, 2006

Homebuyers were the first guilty party in the circle of greed. In their search for more houses, bigger houses, and more expensive houses, the first person they called was a real estate broker. I looked at properties around the Washington, DC, area between 2003 and 2006, always with a real estate agent. Prices were out of whack with reasonable value, I told the agents, so ridiculous that they couldn't be sustained.[39] The agents always said something to the effect of "Real estate prices are always steady in this area. Washington, DC, is not like other places." In other towns, agents said the same thing, adding that I didn't understand real estate. After the bubble popped, one of them sent me the following e-mail.

> Remember me, your buyer's agent with Long & Foster? How's California? Just came across an old email and wanted to give you the credit for predicting the market "shedding." A total shed, dude! Hope all is well, and I appreciated your good-natured attitude.
> —E-mail from Real-Estate Agent at Long & Foster, May 12, 2010

Real estate agents, of course, don't get paid unless they sell houses.[40] They were selling a lot of houses, too—enough that many more people wanted to get in on the action by earning a real estate license.[41] Even new agents didn't find it difficult to sell homes. Home purchasers were so anxious to buy that bidding wars broke out and many homes sold well above their list prices. Real estate agents earn a percentage of a home's selling price, so they were quite happy to see prices soar.[42]

By 2003, housing prices had grown substantially, putting home ownership beyond many people's reach. A $300,000 loan had a monthly mortgage payment of $1,520. A $600,000 loan had a monthly mortgage payment of $3,040. For people with incomes of $50,000 to $70,000, this mortgage was unaffordable.

Realtors didn't want the party to end and this is where the mortgage lenders entered. They designed clever schemes to make homes appear more affordable so the buying could keep going. Mortgage originators make commissions every time they help someone take out a loan. A slowing housing market would have meant less money for them, so they came up with innovative ways to use nonstandard mortgages. They did this in two ways: by rearranging cash flows and by loosening lending standards.

Rearranging cash flows was relatively easy. Varying cash flow sequences can offer a single rate of return.[43] A mortgage rate is simply the implied rate of return from a series of monthly mortgage payments paid over the life of the loan. The present value of this payment sequence should equal the value of the loan used to purchase the target property.[44]

Many loans ask the borrower to pay the same amount every month—but there's no reason that payments must be equally spread across the loan's term. Enter the *graduated payment mortgage* (GPM), which lets the borrower pay very little in the loan's first few years, but a lot more in later years. For example, a $600,000 loan might carry a monthly mortgage payment of just $500 for the first three years. After year three, however, monthly mortgage payments would rise to $3,561. If the home owner's income had not substantially increased in three years, the borrower would find the loan unaffordable and would need to sell or default. It played into everyone's greed by making homes look affordable. With a conventional 30-year fixed-rate mortgage, the same house would have meant a monthly payment of $3,040 from the beginning of the mortgage. Most homebuyers would not have been able to afford this and would not have bought the property.

A friend of mine fell for this trick. In 2006, she owned a small apartment just outside of Washington, DC, She had a decent job and made about $60,000 per year. A realtor convinced her to rent her place out and buy a new condo in the heart of Washington, DC, plus another home in Maryland, all for the same mortgage payment amount she paid on her small apartment. I asked her what she would do in three years if her income didn't change; she said she would sell the properties. But what if the properties are worth less than you owe, I asked? Unlikely, she replied. She lost everything in 2009, undone by her own greed.[45]

Adjustable-rate mortgages (ARMs) were another way to make home ownership more affordable. As its name implies, an ARM's interest rate varies with interest rates in the overall economy. *Hybrid* ARMs were common during the housing bubble. These had a fixed interest rate for some period of time—perhaps a year or more—then charged a variable rate pegged to a reference index rate such as U.S. Treasury yields, the Fed Funds rate, or the London Interbank Offer Rate (LIBOR).

A 2/28 hybrid ARM was a common offering. For the first two years, this loan's monthly payments were lower than monthly payments would have been for a standard 30-year fixed-rate mortgage for the same amount. To make up for this, payments must be higher after year two, even if the reference interest rate doesn't move. If the reference interest rate goes higher, borrowers would make even higher mortgage payments. Greedy borrowers took the risk that their homes would become unaffordable. Early year "teaser" rates drew them in.

They also took on interest rate risk. Individual home owners were essentially running their own levered hedge funds. If interest rates went down, they made money. If interest rates went up, they lost money, sometimes to the point of losing their investments.

Hybrid ARMs gained substantial market share during the housing bubble. In 1999, 2/28 hybrid ARMS were only 6% of all subprime mortgages in the United States. By 2006, these hybrids accounted for 24% of all subprime mortgage originations.[46]

Despite the potential abuse of ARMs and GPMs by mortgage lenders, realtors, and home owners, regulators didn't see the danger.

> The growth of subprime mortgage lending is one indication of the extent to which access to credit has increased for all households, including those with lower incomes. In 1994, fewer than 5 percent of mortgage originations were in the subprime market, but by 2005 about 20 percent of new mortgage loans were subprime. Indeed, the expansion of subprime lending has contributed importantly to the substantial increase in the overall use of mortgage credit. From 1995 to 2004, the share of households with mortgage debt increased 17 percent, and in the lowest income quintile, the share of households with mortgage debt rose 53 percent.
> —Ben Bernanke, speech at the Opportunity Finance Network's Annual Conference, Washington, DC, November 1, 2006

A wide range of topics is examined, including the GSEs' automated underwriting technology used throughout the industry, their many affordable lending partnerships and underwriting initiatives aimed at extending credit to underserved borrowers, their development of new targeted low down payment products, their entry into new markets such as the subprime market, and their attempts to reduce predatory lending. As that discussion emphasizes, the GSEs have the ability to bring increased efficiencies to a market and to attract mainstream lenders into markets.

—HUD, Final Rule at *Federal Register*, November 2, 2004

Lenders also widened the pool of potential buyers by reducing lending standards. Writing a standard loan involves checking and verifying the borrower's income, assets, employment, and credit score. Low-documentation borrowing skips one or more of these checks.

Low-documentation prime and subprime loans have existed for years, but they got more popular in the decade leading up to the financial crisis.[47] Some of the worst of these loans were known as NINJAs (No Income, No Job, and No Assets).

Low-documentation loans also made fraud easier. Fraud was a result, not a cause, of the housing bubble. In 2006, a total of $30 billion in mortgage originations, or about 4% of all mortgage originations, had some sort of fraud attached to them. In the same year, 37,457 suspicious activity reports (SAR) were filed about mortgages. Identity fraud was relatively common. Other fraud involved real estate agents and mortgage lenders who fictionalized loan applications just to make a sale and get commissions. The greedy home owners weren't concerned as long as they also got what they wanted: a home they couldn't afford.

One of the worst examples happened in Tampa, Florida, in the middle of the decade. Orson Benn, of Argent Mortgage Company, looked for elderly home owners and suggested that they make home improvements. He then used their personal information to apply for loans in their names. Argent prepared fraudulent documents, including W-2 forms, took out equity loans in the home owner's name, and pocketed the money. The elderly home owners never saw a dime. These crimes accounted for only 130 home loans for a total of $13 million; the majority of perpetrators have been convicted.

Property fraud also increased during the housing bubble. After the bubble popped, some appraisers intentionally misrepresented a home's fair price so an investor could buy it from a bank at a low price, then quickly sell it at a higher price later for a quick profit. In 2010, property fraud grew by 262%.

If banks and mortgage lenders had not devised these methods to encourage housing demand, housing prices would have either stagnated or returned to a more normal level before much damage had been done. Greed, however, pushed the bubble higher.

Home Owners

As home prices rose, many existing home owners took out second mortgages, called home equity loans, to pay for consumer goods. About 5% pulled out cash to buy a new vehicle. Another 40% borrowed to make tax payments, buy clothing, buy gifts, or pay for living expenses. In 2005 alone, home owners extracted $750 billion from their homes, spending two-thirds of it on personal consumption, home improvements, and credit card debt.[48]

Later, when housing prices dropped, these borrowers were stuck with loans they could not afford. There's a saying in trading: Until you realize a gain, you haven't made it. Borrowing money on a home's paper value doesn't mean you really have the money.

Some home owners took zero-down mortgages, borrowing a home's full value. That is equivalent to a leverage ratio of infinity. Many buyers purchased short-term investment properties, hoping to flip them for profit in a speculative market. In 2005, 2006, and 2007, 28%, 22%, and 22% of home purchasers bought investment properties. In 2005, 30% of existing home owners took out home equity loans to buy second properties. If worse came to worst, they could walk away from their properties. After all, with nothing down, what did it matter?

Profits and Politicians

As discussed earlier, Freddie and Fannie transfer risk from mortgage originators to investors. Throughout the bubble they continued securitizing mortgages and kept their own mortgage portfolios.

Both felt political pressure to support lower-income housing, an important part of both organizations' charters.[49]

Freddie and Fannie's push in this direction was so extreme that they even enlisted churches to initiate faith-based efforts to help low-income minorities buy a home.[50]

Politicians care about being reelected and oftentimes either neglect or do not understand the economic implications of their actions.[51]

The government found that housing was the major source of growth for the U.S. economy. In a congressional hearing in November 2002, Greenspan stated that the low interest-rate policy had stimulated the economy with low mortgage rates and " ... mortgage markets have also been a powerful stabilizing force over the past two years of economic distress . . . " Anything that might hamper growth would not have been popular with either Republicans or Democrats. They were thinking short-term, not long-term.

In 1995, Bill Clinton announced an initiative to boost home ownership from 65% to 67% by 2000 as well as raising the affordable housing goals. He argued, "We have to do a lot better." The expanded home ownership continued under George Bush, who introduced a zero-down-payment initiative that would reduce the 3% down payment requirement for certain types of FHA-insured mortgages.[52]

In 2004, Congressman Michael Oxley, chairman of the House Financial Services Committee, introduced a bill to regulate Freddie and Fannie, but it was a very weak bill. Congressman Jim Leach warned that the two companies were changing "from being agencies of the public at large to money machines for the stockholding few." Arguing against him was Massachusetts Senator Barney Frank, saying that they were in the business of lowering the price of mortgage loans.[53]

Fannie and Freddie, with profits to protect, spent lots of money on lobbying and political campaigns. From 1998 to 2007, Freddie and Fannie spent a combined $15 million lobbying Congress. Freddie donated nearly $9 million to candidates and committees during the same period. In 2000 alone, Fannie Mae gave $2.4 million in campaign donations, including $1.1 million in now-banned "soft money" checks delivered in $100,000 and $50,000 chunks to party committees. Fannie and Freddie also developed reputations for playing hardball with their opponents, threatening to withhold foundation money from local housing programs and labeling their critics as enemies of poor home owners.

In June 2003, an independent audit of the firm's accounting found that Freddie had manipulated its earnings in order to reduce reported volatility. One of Freddie's managers even tried to obstruct the investigation.

This highlighted another problem. The Office of Federal Housing Enterprise Oversight (OFHEO), the two institutions' regulator, failed to see problems—not surprisingly, as the organization was formed to be relatively weak. Established by the Federal Housing Enterprises Financial Safety and Soundness Act of 1992, it was charged with ensuring Fannie and Freddie's capital adequacy and financial safety and soundness.

The Office of Federal Housing Enterprise Oversight (OFHEO) needed Congressional approval for its budget. That gave lobbyists an opening. In a 2006 report OFHEO wrote, "Fannie Mae's lobbyists worked to insure that [the] agency was poorly funded and its budget remained subject to approval in the annual appropriations process . . . The goal of senior management was straightforward: to force OFHEO to rely on [Fannie] for information and expertise to the degree that Fannie Mae would essentially regulate itself."[54]

The Fannie Mae accounting scandal closely followed the one at Freddie Mac.[55] Fannie had booked certain tax credits to lower its annual corporate federal tax. Rather than pay a 35% corporate tax rate in 2003, they inappropriately reduced it to something near 26%. It's grimly comical that, after this attempt at tax evasion, the U.S. taxpayer absorbed all their losses.[56] Some criticized Freddie and Fannie as being places that socialized the risk, while privatizing the profit.[57]

Fannie Mae CEO Franklin Raines stood by the firm's accounting practices. An SEC investigation found that Fannie was wrong. Freddie Mac paid a then-record $125 million civil fine in 2003 in a settlement with the Office of Federal Housing Enterprise Oversight, which blamed management misconduct for the faulty accounting. Fannie Mae was fined $400 million in May 2006 in a settlement with OFHEO and the SEC, one of the largest civil penalties ever in an accounting fraud case.

Taxpayers absorbed the GSEs losses, but they received none of Fannie and Freddie's profits. From 1999 to 2006, Freddie generated a total $31 billion for its shareholders; Fannie generated $42 billion for its shareholders during those years. Goldman Sachs generated $33 billion over the same period.

After 2004, as the number of subprime mortgages grew, Freddie and Fannie's market share slipped because they could not directly purchase subprime loans.[58] Table 10.1 shows the total share of residential mortgages owned or securitized by Freddie and Fannie, which declined from 46% in 2003 to 39% in 2006.

At the same time, Wall Street began securitizing sketchier mortgages. Interest rates on traditional instruments such as Treasuries were declining, so investment banks sought higher yields in the mortgage market.

As a result, investment banks got a double exposure to the housing market. They had direct exposure through mortgage securitization, outright mortgage holdings, and CDOs and other mortgage derivatives. They had indirect exposure through Fannie and Freddie's bonds.

In 2004, HUD increased the main affordable-housing goal over the next four years, from 50 percent to 56 percent of the GSE's total mortgage purchases. John C. Weicher, then an assistant HUD secretary, said the institutions lagged behind even the private market and "must do more." The regulatory bodies said that Fannie and Freddie could buy securities backed by subprime mortgages from the Wall Street firms that securitized them. Doing so, the regulators said, would help them fulfill their mandate to support lower-income housing.

In 2003, Fannie and Freddie bought $69 billion in subprime securities, or 33% of the total market. In 2004, they purchased $144 billion—41% of the market. In 2005, they bought $139 billion, or 31% of the market. In 2006, they cut back to $110 billion, or 29%, and in 2007, bought a staggering 83% of the total market.[59] Generally, Freddie purchased more than Fannie and relied more heavily on these securities to meet its goals. Sharon McHale, a spokeswoman for Freddie Mac, said that "The market knew we needed those loans . . . [The higher goals] forced us to go into that market to serve the targeted populations that HUD wanted us to serve."

William C. Apgar Jr., who was an assistant HUD secretary under Clinton, later said he regretted letting the companies count subprime securities as affordable housing.

Freddie and Fannie's progress through the mortgage market is clearly seen in Table 10.1. In 1990, they owned or had securitized 26% of the entire mortgage market. That rose to 41% by the end of 2007.

At the end of 2007, the two agencies had more than $3.5 trillion in guaranteed securitized mortgage obligations and directly owned $1.45 trillion in mortgage securities, hedging interest rates internally by using derivatives. The two agencies had a capital base of $71 billion[60] and were exposed to $4.949 trillion in credit-based risk. If the default rate on home mortgages rose, Fannie and Freddie and many banks, central banks, and other investors were going to lose a lot of money. They might even go bankrupt without a bailout.

The greed of politicians and managers helped fuel the expansion of this massive hedge fund.

The Media and Regulators

Certain media elements were the next groups in the circle of greed. Stockbroker television shows such as *Mad Money, Fast Money*, and other programs were designed to keep investors riding the stock market wave, but took no responsibility for their ideas' performance. As the bubble moved on, shows advertised the benefits of widespread home ownership. Shows such as *Flip This House* made home buying and selling seem like a new video game.

Regulators were asleep at the wheel. To prevent the crisis, the Federal Reserve would have had to prevent originators from issuing low-document, low-FICO-score, ARM, and zero-down-payment loans. Without subprime loans, the crisis would never have happened. A very strict version of this might have permitted only fixed-rate mortgages with 20% down payments.

Regulators had no incentive to halt the economy's gravy train and wanted to avoid any suggestion that their policies were discriminatory. In 2005, the Fed's examiners conducted a confidential study that revealed a rapid increase in the volume of very risky loans. In 1998, Brooksley Born, former chairperson of the Commodity Futures Trading Commission CFTC, wanted the CFTC to reexamine its regulation of OTC derivatives. She received resistance.

> We have grave concerns about this action and its possible consequences… We are concerned about reports that the CFTC's action may increase the legal uncertainty concerning certain types of OTC derivatives.
> —Robert Rubin, Treasury Secretary, Alan Greenspan, Chairman of the Fed, and Arthur Levitt, Chairman of the SEC, May 7, 1998

After LTCM's collapse in 2000, President Bill Clinton signed the Commodity Futures Modernization Act (CFMA) into law. It eliminated the SEC and CFTC's oversight of the OTC derivative market. It is difficult to determine the consequences of this decision. It may have been the reason AIG Financial Products became so heavily involved in credit default swap transactions. AIG sold CDS that effectively insured every mortgage pool against defaults. Unlike traditional insurance contracts, the CDS didn't force AIG to set aside a large amount of capital against potential future losses, nor did the company have to post collateral. AIG's CDS protection let other banks continue betting on the housing market. AIG's position in credit default swaps rose to $500 billion. The entire market jumped from $6.4 trillion in 2004 to $58 trillion by 2007.

In 2005, the Bankruptcy Abuse Prevention and Consumer Protection Act extended collateral rights in repo transactions to include securities other than GSE debt or Treasuries, if the counterparty went bankrupt. This may have influenced the increased use of less reliable collateral (such as CDOs) in repo transactions, and made the banks' overnight borrowing market much more susceptible to a crowd's run on liquidity. Treasuries were quite liquid and had reliable pricing, but CDOs had less transparent pricing. If pricing became unreliable or untrustworthy, banks might have difficulty rolling over their collateralized borrowing.

There were many other regulation oversights, but these were probably less important. The Gramm-Leach-Bliley Act of 1999 overturned Glass-Steagal and allowed commercial banks with deposits to also act as investment banks and security issuers. There has been speculation that this act was passed to allow Citibank and Traveler's group merger, which ultimately led to a Citibank bailout when its bets went bad.

Grade Inflation

> I had no idea. I'd never been at Moody's, I don't know where they are located.
> [I invested in Moody's because they were a] natural monopoly. [This gave it]
> incredible [pricing power] the single-most important decision in evaluating
> a business is pricing power.
> —Warren Buffett's response when the FCIC asked him whether he
> was satisfied with internal controls at Moody's in 2010, CEO of Berkshire
> Hathaway (20% owner of Moody's). (FCIC 2010).

The rating agencies had their own roles to play in the subprime crisis. As
of 2003, there were only four nationally recognized statistical rating organizations (NRSROs). They were Moody's Investors Service, Inc.; Fitch, Inc.;
Standard & Poor's; and Dominion Bond Rating Service Limited.

Credit ratings help investors determine how likely it is that a bond will be
repaid. The rating agencies use letters to denote this, with higher letter grades
indicating better credit quality. Grades vary from firm to firm; the highest are
typically AAA and AA, followed by A, BBB, and so on. Rating agencies grade
most new debt, including MBS, corporate bonds, CDO, and many other
securities.

In 1936 bank regulators decided that banks should only invest in assets
with an "investment grade" rating (BBB or better) from credit agencies. The
rule's intention was good. Unfortunately, banks relied on agency ratings and
got sloppy about their own due diligence.[61]

Soon after this decision was made, little-known economist Malchior Palyi
wrote an article strongly criticizing the new regulation. He believed that rating
agencies were not transparent and that even well-rated firms would fail often
by assigning securities the wrong grades. Palyi thought regulation should limit
the percentage of medium- to long-term risky securities a bank could hold,
rather than rely on a questionable rating system with incentive and reliability
problems.

> Perhaps the most astonishing single result is that 70% of the volume of
> railroad bonds which defaulted in 1924 were rated BBB or better in the
> same year. Of course, 1924 was a recession year, hard on railway finance;
> but the interesting fact is that a minor recession is sufficient to cause an
> enormous percentage of error in the rating agency's foresight.
>
> Accordingly, the responsible agencies advise the customer not to rely
> upon the ratings alone but to use them together with the text of the manual
> and even to buy special investment advisory services which they are ready
> to supply. The candid observer cannot help wondering whether it would

not be a still more responsible attitude to stop the publication of ratings altogether in the best interest of all concerned.

It is therefore intelligible that the rating manuals emphatically refuse to guarantee their statements; but it is incongruous that ratings which cannot be guaranteed as to accuracy of the underlying material are officially made the guide for bank investments—the basis for the security of deposits.

—Malchior Palyi, January 1938

Eventually state insurance regulators issued similar guidelines for insurance company investments. In 1975 the SEC said broker-dealers could use debt ratings in calculating their capital requirements.

In the 1970s, the rating agencies switched from an "investor-pays" model to a "issuer-pays" model.[62] In the old system, an investor paid a rating agency to give a rating, much as a potential buyer pays a house inspector to report on a home. In the new system, any company that issued a new bond paid the rating agencies to rate that bond.

This had a huge potential for *conflict of interest*. When the investor paid the rating agency, a rating's accuracy and predictive power were paramount. If anything, rating agencies were biased toward more conservative ratings. When the issuer became the income source, the temptation was to please the issuer with a slightly more positive rating, but without damaging agency credibility or accuracy—not too much, anyway.

For many years, the rating agencies didn't create many problems, perhaps because many investors didn't pay much attention to them. After the Internet bubble collapsed in 2000, the market saw a series of accounting frauds perpetrated by major corporations, including Enron. Major rating agencies had rated Enron bonds as AAA up to five days before the company declared bankruptcy. Rating agencies also missed WorldCom's problems. On the morning of Lehman's bankruptcy, agencies had rated Lehman's commercial paper as investment grade. Many people knew that the ratings agencies were not quick to respond to sudden developments. Even so, many institutions still based investment policy on these ratings.

. . . I think those raters were a bunch of half-assed, dishonest villains who would do anything for a fast buck. I just don't believe they were that stupid. And anyway, I believe a plea of "stupid" is probably the saddest of all defenses.

—Lawrence McDonald, former Vice President at Lehman Brothers
(McDonald and Robinson 2009)

Then came CDOs, complex new instruments that were packaged by investment banks with help from ratings agencies around CDO payment structure. That increased the potential conflict of interest.

In general, rating agencies had nearly limitless business from thousands of corporate bond and equity issuers. There weren't so many CDOs, however, so rating agencies had to compete harder for that business. This, too, may have meant sacrificing some objectivity and accuracy. It was in everyone's interest to focus on short-term profits.[63]

Moody's revenues from structured products, which included mortgage-backed securities and CDOs, grew from $199 million in 2000 (33% of total revenues) to $887 million in 2006 (44% of total revenues).[64] Presumably other rating agencies' profits rose as well, but their numbers are not public. Fitch and Dominion are private companies and S&P is owned by McGraw-Hill.

Even the rating agencies seemed to think that competition for CDO business was unproductive. In a document released in 2003, the SEC says that Fitch complained that S&P and Moody's were attempting to squeeze it out of certain structured finance markets by "notching"—lowering ratings or refusing to rate securities issued by certain asset pools (such as collateralized debt obligations), unless a substantial portion of the pooled assets were also rated by them.[65]

> The main problem was . . . that the firm became so focused, particularly the structured area, on revenues, on market share, and the ambitions of Brian Clarkson [former president of Moody's], that they looked the other way, traded the firm's reputation for short-term profits.
>
> —Jerome Fons, former Managing Director of Moody's
> (FCIC 2010)

> When I joined Moody's in late 1997, an analyst's worst fear was that he would contribute to the assignment of a rating that was wrong, damage Moody's reputation for getting the answer right and lose his job as a result. When I left Moody's [in 2007], an analyst's worst fear was that he would do something that would allow him to be singled out for jeopardizing Moody's market share, for impairing Moody's revenue or for damaging Moody's relationships with its clients and lose his job as a result.
>
> —Mark Froeba, former Senior Vice President of Moody's CDO
> Group, Testimony to FCIC, June 2, 2010

In addition to this, the rating agencies weren't using good models. This was partly because the organization didn't offer enticing salaries to hire experienced employees.[66] Moody's didn't develop a model to adequately deal with the layered risks in subprime mortgages until after 2006, when they had already rated thousands of subprime mortgages. In CDOs, agency models did not consider correlations between the underlying collaterals. Moody's didn't have a good model on which to estimate correlations between mortgage-backed securities, so they made them up.[67] Making up correlations was bad enough, but had Moody's learned from the LTCM collapse, it might have at least chosen correlations of 1. That would have led to more conservative ratings.

These models had disastrous results. Starting in October 2007 and proceeding into 2008, rating agencies began downgrading most mortgage products. Moody's downgraded 83% of all the 2006 AAA mortgage products it had rated, as well as all its BBB-rated securities.[68]

The agencies downgraded nearly all the securities issued in the second half of 2007, both AAA and BBB. Of all the securities that were initially investment grade (BBB or higher), 76% of those issued in 2006 were downgraded to junk and 89% of those issued in 2007 were downgraded to junk.

Commercial Banks

Commercial banks were leveraged and writing mortgages, just like Freddie and Fannie.[69] Many banks either held mortgages on their balance sheets or sold them to securitizers such as Freddie, Fannie, or investment banks.[70]

Some banks had more to lose from a collapsing housing market. More leverage, more subprime or low-quality mortgages, more loans kept internally instead of securitized and sold, and more loans in bubble states such as California and Florida all increased a bank's exposure. Banks that failed to adjust their risk models for overvaluation were most at risk.

Many banks had financial problems in the wake of the subprime-lending crisis. For some 380 institutions, these financial problems were fatal. From January 2008 to June 30, 2011, 380 U.S. banks failed, costing a total $83 billion. These banks held median deposits of $233 million and cost the FDIC insurance fund a median $76 million.

Washington Mutual (WaMU), with more than $188 billion in customer deposits, was one of the largest failures. J.P. Morgan absorbed WaMU, with help from the FDIC. IndyMac's failure on July 11, 2008 was also large, with a total $19 billion in customer deposits. These banks had leverage ratios of 13 and 24, respectively, at the end of 2007.

Washington Mutual had a large real estate market exposure, including $118 billion in single-family loans. A more detailed look reveals that these loans included $53 billion in option ARMS and $16 billion in subprime mortgage loans, $53 billion in home equity lines of credit, and $11 billion in credit card receivables.[71]

The bank had 2,239 retail branch offices in 15 states and 43,198 employees. In late 2006, it had begun trying to modify its business strategy to deal with a housing market that was beginning to decline, but it was not enough. Through June 30, 2008, WaMU recorded net losses of $6.1 billion and warned that it might incur a further $19 billion in losses on single-family mortgages as the housing market deteriorated further.

A run on the bank started in September. From September 15, 2008, to September 25, 2008, depositors withdrew a total $16.7 billion, making it difficult for the bank to retain necessary cash reserves. The office of thrift supervision (OTS) intercepted the bank and sold it to J.P. Morgan.[72]

As one of the country's largest mortgage originators, IndyMac also had a heavy housing market exposure. The FDIC took it over and sold it to IMB Hold Co. on December 31, 2008 for $13.9 billion. The FDIC also sued IndyMac's former CEO, Michael Perry, for excessively creating mortgages in an illiquid and unstable market.

Freddie and Fannie's Foreclosure

> We have no plans to insert money into either of those two institutions, [the earnings results were] not a surprise.
> —Hank Paulson, Treasury Secretary, August 10, 2008

The real estate market's peak was around June 2006 (see Figure 10.4). The average price of homes fell by 33% in the top 10 U.S. metropolitan areas. Default rates spiked. The market had worried over Freddie and Fannie Mae's ability to hedge the interest-rate risk in their own portfolio. That certainly suffered. Even worse, however, was the risk that no one really considered: the possibility of a massive drop in overvalued home prices and a huge number of defaults, causing Freddie and Fannie to lose nearly all their capital. Freddie and Fannie's share prices declined from $57.01 and $48.10, respectively, at the end of June 2006 to 73 cents and 88 cents, respectively, by the close of business on September 8, 2008.

Share prices dropped because the market anticipated that, with falling housing prices, rising defaults, and significant leverage, these firms would continue to lose money.[73]

At the end of 2007, total shareholder equity in Freddie and Fannie was $26.7 billion and $44.0 billion respectively. In 2008, 2009, and 2010 the two firms' losses were −$51 billion, −$26 billion, and −$20 billion for Freddie and −$60 billion, −$74 billion, and −$22 billion for Fannie. In 2011, Freddie lost $12 billion and Fannie, $26 billion.[74]

On September 7, 2008, the Federal Housing Finance Agency (FHFA) took the institutions into conservatorship.[75] Preferred shares owned by the U.S. government massively diluted common equity.

As of September 2011, the Treasury department has spent a total of $151 billion in taxpayer money to cover losses on Freddie and Fannie's soured mortgages.[76]

Most of Freddie and Fannie's losses came from a collapsing housing bubble, during which they had massive exposure to mortgages originated near the market's peak in 2006 and 2007 or written to subprime borrowers. Their exposure to interest-rate-only loans, option ARM mortgages, mortgages to buyers with low FICO scores, loans with high loan-to-value ratios, and loans in Nevada and Arizona hurt them badly.[77] Just as the crowd helped build the real estate bubble quickly, it moved fast to deflate the bubble, taking Freddie Mac and Fannie Mae along in the process.

Ginnie Mae represented a very small sliver of the mortgage market when the financial crisis began in 2008. It was already government owned, but did not suffer losses during the crisis.[78]

Why Save Freddie and Fannie?

The government saved Freddie and Fannie for lots of reasons.

Investors from hedge funds to central banks bought Fannie and Freddie's securities with the belief that the U.S. government would stand behind them. Central banks all over the world, including China, held Fannie and Freddie's debt, as did large portfolio management shops such as PIMCO. Hedge funds, commercial banks, investment banks, and mutual fund companies owned Freddie and Fannie's paper.

Freddie Mac and Fannie Mae's failure would have meant a huge loss to U.S. and foreign banks, and to central banks around the world. The U.S. couldn't afford to upset China, as China finances most of the U.S. trade deficit by investing in U.S. Treasuries and agency debt. In 2010, the Chinese and Russian central banks owned more than $500 billion in GSE securities; U.S. banks owned over $1 trillion.[79]

Freddie and Fannie's collapse would have hit the U.S. housing market like an atomic bomb. With Freddie and Fannie doing most of the mortgage origination, the housing market collapsing, and banks already feeling the stress, the GSE's failure might have completely frozen the home-lending markets.

Did Anyone Know?

> We need a strong, world-class regulatory agency to oversee the prudential operations of the GSEs and the safety and soundness of their financial activities consistent with maintaining healthy national markets for housing finance.
> —John Snow, Treasury Secretary, September 10, 2003

Some people did foresee potential problems at the GSEs.[80]

As early as March 22, 2000, Gary Gensler, undersecretary of the Treasury, presented a bill to regulate the GSEs to the House Subcommittee on Capital Markets, Securities, and Government Sponsored Enterprises. He proposed many changes to the GSE's existing set of rules. He concluded his proposal by saying, "Mr. Chairman, the economy and the financial markets are strong. With no particular problems on the horizon, this is an ideal time to review the supervision and regulation of the GSEs." In 2002, Lawrence White of NYU was interviewed.[81]

> This means if housing prices crash or either company stumbles, the taxpayers could be on the hook for hundreds of billions. It's as if the public had cosigned Fannie and Freddie's debt... "
> —Lawrence White, NYU professor, August 2002

Alan Greenspan, who had promoted the low interest rates that helped cause the housing boom, may have offered the most direct discussion of the threats posed by Freddie and Fannie. In February 2005, he testified to the House Financial Services Committee and argued against Freddie and Fannie's excessive portfolios.

> If [Fannie and Freddie] continue to grow, continue to have the low capital that they have, continue to engage in the dynamic hedging of their portfolios, which they need to do for interest rate risk aversion, they potentially create ever-growing potential systemic risk down the road... One way the

Congress could contain the size of these balance sheets is to alter the composition of Fannie and Freddie's mortgage financing by limiting the dollar amount of their debt relative to the dollar amount of mortgages securitized and held by other investors.

—Alan Greenspan, Testimony to the House Financial Services
Committee, February 17, 2005

He repeated his concerns again before Congress.

The apparent froth in housing markets appears to have interacted with evolving practices in mortgage markets. The increase in the prevalence of interest-only loans and the introduction of more-exotic forms of adjustable-rate mortgages are developments of particular concern. To be sure, these financing vehicles have their appropriate uses. But some households may be employing these instruments to purchase homes that would otherwise be unaffordable, and consequently their use could be adding to pressures in the housing market. Moreover, these contracts may leave some mortgagors vulnerable to adverse events. It is important that lenders fully appreciate the risk that some households may have trouble meeting monthly payments as interest rates and the macroeconomic climate change.

—Alan Greenspan, Testimony at the Federal Reserve Board's
semiannual Monetary Policy Report to the Congress before the Committee
on Financial Services, U.S. House of Representatives, July 20, 2005

In 2005, Paul McCulley of PIMCO became worried about the housing situation and sent analysts to investigate across the country. They found that underwriting standards had deteriorated and PIMCO adjusted its portfolios accordingly. The Fed was warned in 2006 that in several states loan standards had declined, but did very little to fix the problem.[82]

Freddie and Fannie argued that large portfolios added liquidity to the secondary mortgage market and that buying mortgages reduced borrowers' interest rates.[83]

Despite these defenses, researchers found no link between the size of GSE portfolios and mortgage rates. Half the GSE's market capitalization was due to an implicit taxpayer subsidy.[84]

Fannie and Freddie, those taxpayer-subsidized arbitrage hedge funds, went into conservatorship under relatively calm market circumstances, despite the huge bills they sent taxpayers. Since 2008, the two organizations have cost taxpayers around $151 billion. The final bill could be anywhere between $220 billion and $311 billion (See Box 10.2).[85] A circle of greed, from homebuyers to hedge funds, took levered long positions on real estate, creating the greatest housing bubble in U.S. history. The bubble's collapse helped deflate them all.

Just one week later, the unthinkable happened: Lehman Brothers went bankrupt. The financial crisis was about to go into overdrive.

Box 10.2 Summary of How Freddie and Fannie Got into Trouble

1. Interest rates were lowered by Fed and world economy.
2. Owners get enticed to buy more homes.
3. Real estate agents and mortgage brokers find clever ways to make expensive homes look cheaper.
4. Home owners continue to buy, often under odd or untenable terms.
5. Banks and Freddie and Fannie keep securitizing loans, even risky loans. Freddie and Fannie don't really worry about credit risk, since housing prices "never go down."
6. Credit agencies rate mortgage loans higher than they should be because housing prices rarely decline and because of conflicts of interest.
7. Overvalued housing prices finally begin to lose demand and prices collapse. Everyone runs for the exits.
8. Housing prices continue to collapse in self-fulfilling run.
9. Freddie and Fannie have huge losses from credit risk and some from interest-rate risk.
10. Losses greater than equity. Bankruptcy time or as Uncle Sam calls it: Conservatorship.

CHAPTER 11

The Lehman Bankruptcy

There's no doubt that things feel better today, by a lot, than they did in March . . . the worst is likely to be behind us . . .
—Hank Paulson, Treasury Secretary, May 6, 2008

Seven days after the government rescued Freddie Mac and Fannie Mae, Lehman Brothers declared bankruptcy. Their failure made commercial paper markets falter, making it difficult for companies to borrow short-term funds. It caused a run on money market funds, created an imbalance in the bond and swap markets, and depressed the stock market.

Lehman failed because of its large real estate exposure and because of a market that didn't trust its solvency, leading to a run on the bank and guaranteeing its failure. The government did nothing to rescue Lehman.

To understand Lehman's failure and its place in the subprime debt crisis, it's important to also understand the intricate details of the investment banking business, as well as major investment banks' leverage and real estate exposures.

The Wall Street Club

Investment banks participated in the mortgage market to varying degrees and with varying amounts of leverage. All the major investment banks operating in the United States at the end of 2007 were in the mortgage market: Goldman Sachs, Lehman Brothers, Bear Stearns, J.P. Morgan, Deutsche Bank, Citibank, UBS, Morgan Stanley, and Merrill Lynch.

191

FIGURE 11.1   The Profits of Major Investment Banks and Federal Agencies

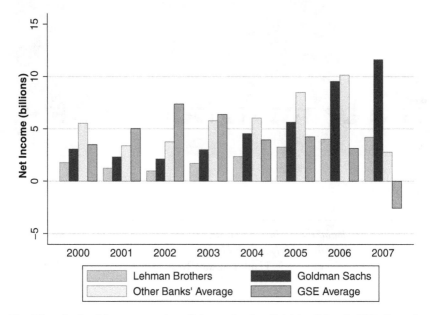

Note: The other banks' average consists of Morgan Stanley, Citi, Merrill Lynch, UBS, Deutsche Bank, Bear Stearns, and J.P. Morgan. GSE Average is the average profits of Freddie Mac and Fannie Mae.

Many of these banks also enjoyed consistently high profits from 2000 to 2007 (see Figure 11.1), in part because of their mortgage exposure. In 2007, Lehman Brothers profits, Goldman Sachs profits, the profit average of the seven other banks, and Freddie and Fannie's average profit were $4.1 billion, $11.6 billion, $2.8 billion, and −$2.6 billion.

Some investment banks, including Lehman Brothers, were big mortgage securitizers. Bear Stearns and Goldman Sachs issued lots of CMOs and other derivatives based on underlying mortgages.

All the banks had high leverage ratios, though their ratios were generally smaller than those of Freddie and Fannie (see Figure 11.2). Freddie and Fannie's leverage was computed two ways. The first method measured leverage as total assets divided by total equity. The second measure includes off-balance-sheet mortgage pass-throughs that contained credit risk exposure.

Freddie and Fannie had the highest leverage ratios in the mortgage business. Freddie's leverage at the end of 2007 was 81 and Fannie's leverage was 68, both by the more comprehensive second measure.

FIGURE 11.2   The Leverage of Major Investment Banks and Federal Agencies

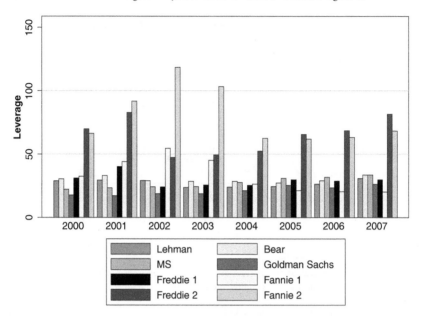

Note: Leverage is defined as the firm's total assets divided by total equity. The second measure for Freddie and Fannie adds off-balance-sheet mortgages to their total assets to compute leverage.

The banks were also very levered. At the end of 2007, the most-levered U.S. investment bank was Bear Stearns, at 34. The second highest was Morgan Stanley at 33, then Merrill Lynch at 32, Lehman Brothers at 31, Goldman Sachs at 26, Citibank at 19, and J.P. Morgan at 12, the lowest of the bunch. Some foreign investment banks had higher leverage ratios than U.S. investment banks, including Deutsche Bank at 46 and Barclays at 35.

Citibank and J.P. Morgan had lower leverage ratios, partly due to the large amount of commercial banking in their business.[1] High leverage meant high profits, but also steep losses if things went bad. Both leverage and the riskiness of the underlying investments determine overall danger.

Why Was Lehman Next?

Lehman Brothers and its investment bank peers faced similar challenges. Differences were in the degree of leverage, commercial and residential real estate exposure, and the amount of short-term financing each used to run its business.

TABLE 11.1 Exposure of Major Investment Banks to Real Estate (billions of dollars)

	Lehman[b,c]	Merrill[g,h,i]	Goldman[d]	Morgan[e,f]
Residential Mortgages	17.2	39.6	12.7	11.4
Commercial Mortgages	20.9	15.8	14.6	13.9
Other Real Estate/Mortgage	6.5	0.0	1.4	0.7
Potential Off-Balance-Sheet Exposure	11.7	0.0	0.9	0.0
Mortgage Trading Exposures[a]	0.0	0.0	0.0	0.0
Total Potential Exposure	56.3	55.4	29.5	25.9
Potential Exposure/Shareholder Equity	2.0	1.4	0.6	0.7
Other ABS	4.6	0.0	1.6	0.0
Leveraged Finance	7.1	55.6	13.0	14.6

Note: Getting the precise real estate exposures of these banks is extremely difficult due to the lack of transparency in the financial statements and the use of derivatives and other instruments used to hedge their outright exposure.
[a] Mortgage Trading Exposures are included in Other Real Estate/Mortgage numbers taken from quarterly statements.
[b] Lehman 3rd quarter 2008 information is attained from a press release prior to the release of Merrill, Goldman, and Morgan 10-Q releases.
[c] Lehman residential mortgage includes $4 billion potential sell off.
[d] Goldman's Residential Mortgage is calculated from page 75 of the Q3-2008 and includes $5.1 billion indicated in Footnote 1.
[e] Morgan's Residential and Commercial Mortgages include VIE's (consolidated and nonconsolidated).
[f] Morgan's Other Real Estate/Mortgage is Credit/Real Estate.
[g] Merrill's Residential Mortgages includes prime and other residential mortgage. See page 89 of the 3rd quarter 2008 10-Q.
[h] Merrill's Total Commercial real estate includes First Republic Bank. See page 94 of the 2008 3rd quarter 10-Q.
[i] Merrill's Leveraged Finance includes all derivatives contracts consolidated balance sheet.
Source: Company financial statements.

All the investment banks had housing market exposure through outright ownership, mortgage securities, CDOs, or other derivatives. To understand investment banks' risk, it is useful to examine their real estate exposure in the horrifying year of 2008. Table 11.1 shows the exposure to real estate for some selected major investment banks at the end of the third quarter of 2008.

Lehman and Merrill had the largest outright real estate exposure, with totals of $56.3 billion and $55.4 billion respectively. Goldman Sachs and Morgan Stanley had substantially less.[2]

Real estate represented a high percentage of banks' equity capital. Lehman had 200 percent of its equity capital in real estate, Merrill 140 percent, Goldman 60 percent, and Morgan 70 percent.

Merrill Lynch had a large exposure to leverage financing, which also did horribly during the crisis. Lehman and Merrill were the smallest banks by asset size.

A basic analysis of leverage and real estate exposure would conclude that either Merrill or Lehman would be the next firm to fail.

Not only did Lehman Brothers have residential real estate exposure, it also had a large commercial real estate exposure. Residential real estate had collapsed quite a bit by September 2008, and investment banks were seeing losses. From the peak to the September low, prices in the 10 largest metropolitan areas had dropped by 22%. Miami prices were down by 34%; Los Angeles prices had dropped by 31%.

Commercial real estate, on the other hand, had not really declined much by September 2008 (see Figure 11.3). The peak of commercial real estate prices was February 2008. From February 2008 to September 2008, they had declined by 9.1%.

The markets weren't much bothered by that small drop, but they were concerned about potential losses to Lehman's commercial real estate

FIGURE 11.3   The Moody's/REAL Commercial Real Estate Index

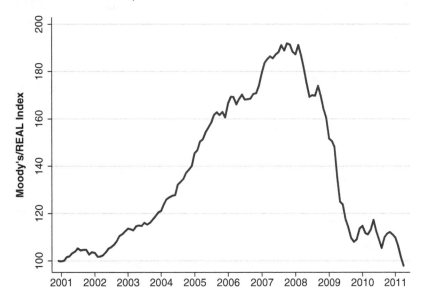

portfolio if numbers went lower. It turned out that they were right to worry. From September 2008 to April 2011, commercial real estate declined by another 39.7%.

The real estate market collapse, uncertainty about future real estate values, uncertainty about banks' health and financial statements, and the crowd's focus on safety all led to a system collapse. Lehman Brothers' story is one that could have happened to any investment bank during the 2008 crisis.

Business Exposure

> Never tell anyone on Wall Street your problems, old buddy. Ninety percent of those you tell don't care, and the other ten percent are glad you have them.
>
> —Lawrence McCarthy, Managing Director of Lehman Brothers
> (McDonald and Robinson 2009)

Of all the Wall Street banks, Lehman had the longest-reigning CEO, Richard Fuld. He had worked at Lehman Brothers since he was an intern in 1966. He rose through the ranks in large part because of his work ethic, which earned him the nickname "Gorilla." He witnessed the firm dissolve into Shearson/American Express when the latter acquired it in 1984. He was still there for the Lehman Brothers spin-off in 1994, which made Fuld the CEO. Since then, Lehman Brothers' assets had grown at an annual pace of 16%, from $110 billion in 1994 to $691 billion by the end of 2007. The firm's net income grew at an annualized pace of 38% over the same period.

To understand why Lehman was so vulnerable in 2008, it is important to understand the company's underlying business exposure.[3]

Most of Lehman's revenues came from its capital markets division (see Table 11.2). Net revenues in this division were equally split between equity and fixed income.[4] Within this area Lehman was highly levered, so some of its revenues came from borrowing money at the short end of the market and investing it in the longer end. Interest and dividends from investing, less interest paid on borrowing, netted the firm about $2 billion. The proprietary trading group made about $8 billion, and commissions made about $2 billion. The firm got 69% of its capital markets net revenues from proprietary trading.

From 2006 to 2007, Lehman's equity net revenues grew. Its fixed-income net revenues fell by 29%, though they were still large and positive. Most of the losses in fixed income came from residential and commercial mortgage positions. Total losses related to real estate were $5.9 billion, but the firm's

TABLE 11.2 Percentage of Profits from Various Divisions in 2007

Division	Lehman
Capital Markets	64%
Investment Banking	20%
Client Services	16%

Sources: Company annual and quarterly statements and author's own calculations.

hedging positions, which limited its real estate exposure, reduced net losses to $2.2 billion for 2007.

The hedging information was the first sign that the collapsing housing market could take a large toll on Lehman Brothers. It also showed that Lehman Brothers' managers were aware of their risks in the real estate market.

In October 2007, Richard Fuld told a *New York Times* reporter that the hedging positions were taken in order to "... protect mother, the lightship... The risk committee's view is not to take a proprietary position... that's just not our gear. Our gear is how to protect the balance sheet." It may have also been that Fuld was out of touch with the firm's real risks. His right-hand man, president and CEO Joseph Gregory, spent more time concerned with diversity, rather than with excellence and prudence. He organized company meetings where he said "Inclusion! That must be our aim!"[5] Were leaders caught up in another social trend, rather than focusing on the business at hand? According to a Lehman employee, Gregory implied that bonuses would depend on serving his diversity causes. Was this the role of a president of an investment bank? In 2007, Gregory hired Erin Callan to be Lehman's CFO during arguably the most important period of Lehman's history. According to Lehman's Lawrence McDonald, she did not have the experience for the role. Alex Kirk went to Gregory and told him that these hires made no sense.

> We're heading into rough seas, and you don't have the talent in the right places. You have the wrong commanders, the wrong helmsmen, the wrong lookouts. You're doing every damn thing wrong...
> —Alex Kirk, COO of Fixed Income at Lehman Brothers, in McDonald and Robinson (2009)

Lehman's investment banking and client services divisions also made substantial profits in 2007. The client services division made the bulk of its net revenues from asset management, with proprietary positions and commissions taking the next largest roles. The profit division between private client management and asset management was about equal. At the end of 2007, Lehman Brothers managed $225 billion in investment portfolios for other institutions and individuals.

From 2005 to 2007, the three divisions' profits were steady and growing, as shown in Table 11.3.

Most of our understanding of Lehman's positions and vulnerability at the beginning of 2008 comes from examining its balance sheet.[6]

Investment banks, with their exposure to short- and long-term risks and proprietary hedging strategies, have particularly complex financial statements. The financial markets began a run on Lehman Brothers in part because it was so hard to figure out Lehman's real risks by reading its financial statements. Lehman's mortgage group might have a huge exposure to a loan portfolio, but the fixed-income derivative group might short mortgages through a CMO, making the company's overall loan exposure difficult to determine. Lacking evidence to the contrary, the market assumed the worst.

At the end of 2007, Lehman's assets stood at $691 billion, up from the 2006 value of $503 billion. Of that amount, $301 billion was in collateralized lending agreements (CLA).

Lehman had three sorts of CLA. Reverse repo agreements totaled $163 billion.[7] In every repo transaction, one party does a repo, borrowing and posting collateral, and the other party does a reverse repo, loaning money and accepting collateral. These contracts are an efficient way for banks to borrow and lend money.

A repo and a reverse repo might go like this. A hedge fund gives a $100,000 U.S. Treasury bond to Lehman; Lehman loans the hedge fund $100,000.[8] The balance sheet shows new assets of $100,000 and new liabilities of $100,000.

Lehman's second CLA involved borrowing and lending securities. These transactions totaled $139 billion. This CLA was bound to confuse anyone reading Lehman's balance sheet, as a borrowed asset is both an asset—they have it—and a liability, in that they must return it.

The third CLA represented other secured borrowings, which comprised a minimal portion of the CLA.

Lehman and other investment banks insisted that these CLA transactions should not count as relevant assets. They constructed a net asset calculation of total assets minus the CLAs. Lehman also subtracted some other assets, such as cash kept for regulatory purposes and goodwill from total assets, to obtain a

TABLE 11.3 Profits of Lehman Brothers Divisions from 2005 to 2008 (millions of dollars)

Year	2008:Q3	2008:Q2	2008:Q1	2007	2006	2005
Capital Markets						
Net revenues	−4,148	−2,374	1,672	12,257	12,006	9,807
Costs	NA	2,135	1,436	8,058	7,286	6,235
Income before taxes	NA	−4,509	236	4,199	4,720	3,572
Investment Banking						
Net revenues	611	858	867	3,903	3,160	2,894
Costs	NA	665	685	2,880	2,500	2,039
Income before taxes	NA	193	182	1,023	660	855
Investment Management						
Net revenues	634	848	968	3,097	2,417	1,929
Costs	NA	619	723	2,306	1,892	1,527
Income before taxes	NA	229	245	791	525	402
Entire Firm						
Net revenues	−2,903	−668	3,507	19,257	17,583	14,630
Costs	2,921	3,419	2,844	13,244	11,678	9,801
Income before taxes	−5,824	−4,087	663	6,013	5,905	4,829
Taxes	−1,897	−1,313	174	1,821	1,945	1,569
Net Income	−3,927	−2,774	489	4,192	3,960	3,260

Source: Lehman Brothers' annual and quarterly statements.

final total of $373 billion in net assets at the end of 2007. Some of these assets represented the buildings and machines Lehman owned, payments owed from other banks, and cash. Subtract these and Lehman's total net invested assets were $313 billion. Figure 11.4 shows the distribution of Lehman's investments at the end of 2007.

FIGURE 11.4   Distribution of Lehman's investments in November 2007

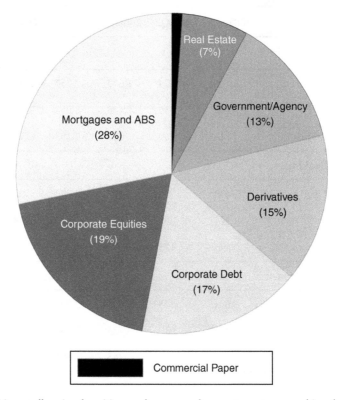

Note: This uses all notional positions and not net real estate exposure, as used in other tables.

At the end of 2007, Lehman's total real estate exposure was massive: $111 billion, or 35% of its invested assets. (This figure combines mortgage- and asset-backed securities with real estate.) Table 11.4 lists the mortgage types that Lehman held directly. Lehman's net real estate exposure was lower, at $89 billion.[9]

At the end of 2007, not only did Lehman own mortgage-backed securities worth a total of $29 billion, but it also owned actual real estate loans (through Lehman Bank) worth a total $46 billion. The firm also directly owned commercial real estate to the tune of $22 billion.[10]

Although not shown in the table, $5.3 billion of this residential mortgage portfolio was in illiquid subprime residential mortgages. For 99% of the mortgage securities, there was no traded market with daily quotes. Twenty-eight percent of the assets were so illiquid that the prices used to value them

TABLE 11.4 Lehman's Mortgage Portfolio November 2006–Second Quarter 2008 (millions of dollars)

	2008:Q3	2008:Q2	2008:Q1	2007	2006
Residential & ABS[a]					
Whole loans	.	8,250	11,913	19,587	18,749
Securities	.	14,986	18,179	16,488	7,923
Servicing	.	1,666	1,660	1,183	829
Other	.			86	16
	17,200	24,902	31,752	37,344	27,517
Commercial Real Estate					
Whole loans	.	19,862	24,881	26,200	22,426
Securities	.	9,528	11,229	12,180	1,948
Other	.			558	351
	32,600	29,390	36,110	38,938	24,725
Other ABS	4,600	6,482	6,553		
Total Mortgage & ABS	54,400	60,774	74,415	76,282	52,242
Real Estate Held[b]	.	20,664	22,562	21,917	9,400
	.	(10,400)	(12,900)	(12,800)	(5,900)
Net Real Estate Exposure	**54,400**	**71,174**	**87,315**	**89,082**	**58,142**

[a] Before the 2008 quarterly statements, ABS securities were included with the residential real estate loans.
[b] Lehman Brothers reported its total real estate held for sale, but argued that a significant portion of that was financed with nonrecourse lending. The number in parenthesis represented the true exposure to that real estate. For 2008:Q3 Lehman reported only some numbers, hence the missing values. For instance, Lehman did not report Real Estate Held for Sale, but this combined with Commercial real estate was reduced to $32.6 billion from $39.8 billion, so the total real estate exposure is accurate. One could also reduce the total real estate exposure by another $4 billion from residential loans that Lehman was in the process of transferring.
Source: Company annual and quarterly statements.

were Lehman Brothers' best estimates.[11] The difficult-to-value securities were pledged as collateral to finance Lehman's business activity. Just as with Bear, if these securities' value became suspect, other banks might stop lending to Lehman.

Lehman Brothers was also a major mortgage securitizer. Its total securitizing business, mainly involving residential mortgages, was worth $125 billion in 2007. That's a large amount of securitization, but in a business that was common for investment banks, it was not a direct risk to the firm, because Lehman didn't hold these mortgages as assets.

Lehman did retain many loans, however, and directly owned substantial real estate. That made Lehman Brothers look more like a commercial bank mortgage lender and real estate company than a securities firm. Lehman had departed from its core business and was gambling on real estate.[12] This part of Lehman's portfolio would become the major reason the firm couldn't save itself without government assistance.

The rest of Lehman's exposure was more typical of investment banks. Its portfolio had a 13% ($41 billion) exposure to government bonds and agency securities. The portfolio had a 19% exposure ($59 billion) to corporate equities, including investments in stocks and other stocklike exposure. The portfolio also had a 1% exposure ($4 billion) to commercial paper and money market instruments.

Lehman's portfolio had a 17% ($54 billion) exposure to corporate debt securities, including somewhat risky high-yield debt obligations used to finance leveraged buyout deals. In total, 28% of Lehman's business was exposed to real estate.[13]

> We were somehow out there buying wildly overpriced skyscrapers with distant views of the friggin' Eiffel Tower, still buying hedge funds. And we were still up to our ears in apartments—we probably owned more than two hundred thousand of them worldwide.
> —Lawrence McDonald, Vice President at Lehman Brothers, in McDonald and Robinson (2009)

A Chronology of the Gorilla's Death

At the annual Lehman Brothers meeting at the Museum of Modern Art in early 2006, Richard Fuld told his colleagues, "We are at war . . . ." Lehman Brothers' growth was impressive, with the firm's size catching up to larger investment banks such as Goldman Sachs and Morgan Stanley. Still, Lehman was the baby monkey on the block.[14]

Double Down in Real Estate

Hoping to gain even more ground on the bigger investment banks, the company went after the mortgage and housing boom. It increased its mortgage exposure from $52 billion at the end of 2006 to $76 billion at the end of 2007 (see Table 11.4). Over the same period, their outright real estate holdings grew from $9 billion to $22 billion.

The peak of the U.S. housing market was around April 2006. Despite this, Lehman continued to securitize mortgages, buy mortgages, write mortgages,[15] and buy real estate. In fact, this was part of a countercyclical strategy. By increasing real estate exposure as the market collapsed, Lehman hoped to snap up bargains.

Neither Lehman nor almost anyone else realized how bad the real estate situation would become. From November 2006 to November 2007, national real estate prices dropped by about 8% and Lehman's real estate exposure increased dramatically. They were "doubling down."[16]

Over this same period, Lehman's total and net assets increased by 37% and 39% respectively.[17] The firm's leverage grew from 24 at the end of 2005 to 31 at the end of 2007.

Most of this expansion was part of Lehman's strategy shift from the "moving" business to the "storage" business. The moving business involved originating assets primarily for securitization or syndication and distribution, as happened when Lehman originated mortgages and then sold a pool to other investors. This is a rather low-risk business, because it passes on its risk to investors. The storage business involved keeping mortgages and other assets on Lehman's balance sheet as direct bets on these markets.

Storage was riskier, and not part of a typical investment bank's main functions. Lehman emphasized storage in part because the firm had trouble selling off some of its securitized loans, so it had to keep them. Lehman also knew why Freddie and Fannie kept more mortgages in-house: If things stay the same, the bank makes more money. Lehman Brothers wanted a bigger table on the circle of greed, even if it meant straying from their core business.

In addition to increasing its mortgage market involvement, Lehman Brothers was growing its presence in the leveraged loan market, supplying financing to companies that wanted to use debt to buy other firms. The business of financing large private equity deals was exploding in the middle of the decade, and Lehman wanted to be part of it.

Lehman was involved in this business in two ways. It gave private equity companies loans with which to finance their takeovers of other companies. Or Lehman might actually take a stake in a buyout. The firm's lending commitments to both high-grade and high-yield deals went from $19 billion at the end of 2005 to $38 billion at the end of 2007. Management believed this expansion would improve Lehman's relationships and reputation.[18] From December 2006 to June 2007, Lehman participated in more than 11 leveraged buyout deals, each exceeding $5 billion.

This expanded growth strategy also included buying Archstone in May 2007. Archstone was a real estate investment trust (REIT), a company that directly purchased and managed condos and other real estate.

Senior management and the board of directors were on board with this business direction. Even so, not everybody at Lehman was persuaded that the firm's expansion into the leveraged lending markets was in Lehman's best interest.

In February 2007, Michael Gelband, head of the fixed-income division (FID), began to worry about heavy real estate market exposure. He had been at Lehman more than 24 years, and was one of the best and bravest traders in Treasuries and mortgages that Lehman had ever seen.[19] Joseph Gregory, Lehman's president and COO, invited Gelband to lunch in that same month. Gregory insisted that Gelband become more aggressive with risk.[20]

By April 2007, the firm's overall leveraged loan commitments were large and controversial within the firm. Alex Kirk, who was head of Lehman's credit business, and Gelband were concerned about Lehman's overall exposure. In April 2007, Kirk e-mailed Gelband:

> As a heads up our risk of mandated commits is up to 6mm a bp triple our previous high. Also the commits are coming in fast and furious I expect us to be well north of 30B this quarter. This is also unprecedented. In addition we are now seeing commitments that have crossed the risk tolerance so we may need your help with the bank in saying no to some key clients.
> —Alex Kirk, Head of Credit Business, e-mail to Michael Gelband,
> April 20, 2007 (Valukas 2010)

Soon after that, Lehman fired Gelband.[21] Lawrence McCarthy, another important part of fixed-income trading, left shortly thereafter. In his exit interview with human resources, he told them how out of touch Dick Fuld was with the company. He hadn't visited the fixed-income trading desk even once while McCarthy worked there.

Rumors suggested that Gelband was asked to leave because he did not cooperate with the company's newly aggressive growth strategy. In fact, shortly after Gelband's firing, Eric Felder wrote:

> We need everyone to be shooting beyond high. Gelband is gone because he didn't. I know roger will make us try for 2 b at some point. I actually think we are supposed to get rid of budgets. They do nothing but constrain. Also have plenty of room to take the risk up. We won't get any resources if we don't think really big.
> —Eric Felder, Co-Head of Lehman's Fixed-Income Division, e-mail to Thomas Corcoran, May 25, 2007 (Valukas 2010)

Roger Nagioff replaced Gelband as head of fixed income on May 2, 2007. He immediately advised a more moderate approach to the firm's leveraged loan business. On May 31, 2007, he met with Fuld and told him that Lehman was too big in the leveraged lending business and could lose a lot of money in *tail risk*. Tail risk is the possibility of a huge negative event.

Nagioff showed Fuld the numbers, which reflected a possible $3.2 billion loss under a stress scenario computed specifically for their meeting. According to Nagioff, he told Fuld that Lehman needed to reduce its forward commitments from $36 billion to $20 billion, impose rules on the amount of leverage in the deals, and develop a framework for limiting and evaluating this business. Fuld was surprised and concerned by the tail risk in the leveraged loan positions and authorized Nagioff to present his analysis to the Executive Committee and get authorization to move forward with a plan to limit the firm's leveraged loan exposure.

On June 28, 2007, Fuld, Gregory, and McGee authorized Nagioff to conduct a cross-firm initiative to reduce commitments to $20 billion by the end of 2007. In the time since the initial conversation, unfortunately, Lehman had made another $25.4 billion in loan commitments, raising its total loan exposure to $35.8 billion.[22]

Lehman's Global Real Estate Group (GREG), headed by Mark Walsh, conducted most of those deals, some of which are listed in Table 11.5.

Lehman would have been better off if it had stopped the money machine immediately after Fuld and Nagioff's meeting. The period from May to August 2007 began to show signs of a larger problem in the financial markets. The financial crisis that had previously been contained to the subprime residential mortgage market began to spread to other markets, including the commercial real estate and credit markets, where Lehman was particularly active. These concerns escalated in June and July 2007, when two Bear Stearns hedge funds

TABLE 11.5   Some of the Real Estate Deals by Lehman's Global Real Estate Group

Date	Deals
May 2007	$2.0 billion Lehman financing to Broadway Partners to acquire a subportfolio of Beacon Capital Strategic Partners III, LP.
	$1.3 billion Lehman financing to Broadway Real Estate Partners to acquire 237 Park Avenue
June 2007	$1.2 billion Lehman financing to Apollo Investment Corp. for a private stake of Innkeepers USA Trust
	$1.1 billion Lehman financing to Thomas Properties Group to acquire the EOP Austin portfolio
	$1.7 billion Lehman financing for the acquisition of Northern Rock's commercial real estate portfolio
July 2007	$1.5 billion Lehman financing to ProLogis to acquire the Dermody industrial portfolio
	$2.9 billion Lehman financing for the acquisition of the Coeur Defense office building
August 2007	$1.0 billion Lehman financing for the acquisition of Northern Rock's commercial real estate portfolio
October 2007	$1.5 billion Lehman financing to Blackstone for its acquisition of Hilton Hotels
	$5.4 billion Lehman financing for the acquisition of the Archstone Smith Trust

imploded, leading to panic in the credit markets and more general concerns that the subprime crisis would spill into the broader economy.

On October 5, 2007, the Archstone deal closed. Lehman joined a few other companies in purchasing this real estate company for $22.2 billion. Despite the internal worries, Lehman never considered walking away from the deal, in part because Lehman was able to sell approximately $2.09 billion in Archstone debt to Freddie Mac and another $7.1 billion of Archstone debt to Fannie Mae.

During the same time period, however, Lehman and its partners were able to sell only $710 million of the deal's $4.6 billion in bridge equity. That left Lehman and its partners with a lot of real estate debt. As of October 12,

2007, Lehman's exposure to the deal was about $6 billion dollars. Of that, $2.39 billion was in the riskiest equity portions of the deal: permanent equity and bridge equity.[23]

During the same period, Lehman's capital ratio deteriorated from 18.2% in early 2006 to 10.5% in August 2007. From August to November 2007, Lehman posted the lowest total capital ratio in the industry.

Personnel changes underlined the difficulties. On December 1, 2007, Madelyn Antoncic, Lehman's global head of risk management, was replaced by the firm's chief financial officer, Chris O'Meara. In January 2008, Nagioff decided to resign as head of fixed income for personal reasons. Alex Kirk, since October 2007 the co-chief operating officer of fixed income, also left Lehman.

As Lehman Brothers headed into 2008, its GREG report about world real estate markets was cautionary (see Table 11.6).

Mildly Seeking Capital

> No one will, 10 years from now, write the story that this crisis was about Lehman Brothers going down.
> —Hank Paulson, Treasury Secretary, October 21, 2008

Lehman's senior management realized that it might be wise to protect their company in case the environment deteriorated further. Managers had many chances to find potential buyers for their company, but didn't realize how desperate their situation really was.

On January 9, 2008, the Kuwait Investment Authority (KIA) approached Lehman about acquiring shares at a discount to the current market price. On January 11, 2008, Lehman's CEO of Europe and Asia Jeremy M. Isaacs told KIA that Lehman would be a "reluctant seller" at $65 per share, a 12% premium over the $58.15 closing price on January 11, 2008. Lehman expressed enthusiasm about developing a broader partnership with KIA, but showed no interest in selling shares without receiving a significant premium.

On January 31, 2008, the Korean Development Bank (KDB) expressed interest in investing in Lehman, proposing a $2 billion to $3 billion private-equity investment for a minority share of Lehman. Lehman was pleased to have KDB buy its stock on the open market, but it wasn't looking to raise capital or dilute its ownership through a discounted private placement.

By February 7, 2008, Lehman shifted course and issued a prospectus for a $1.59 billion preferred stock offering. Unfortunately, the best time had passed.

TABLE 11.6 Lehman Brothers' Global Real Estate Report in January 2008

Comments

1. The capital markets meltdown continued into the first quarter. CMBS spreads have widened to all-time highs and investors have been staying on the sidelines.

2. CMBS delinquencies are still at historic lows, but real estate is usually a lagging indicator.

3. Many of our bank loans and PTG positions are directly related to the residential housing sector, which is extremely troubled.

4. In general, the collateral performance of our whole loan positions has not been an issue, but the spread widening at all the debt tranches has led to lower values.

5. The inability to hedge our floating rate book and the mezz classes of our fixed-rate loans has continued to result in losses.

6. The markdowns effected in January are the best estimates by the business and product control at this time.

7. As part of its ongoing methodology, the Global Real Estate Group (GREG) performed a valuation review of their entire portfolio. The review took into consideration the continuing widening of credit spreads, continued sluggishness in the residential market, and lack of liquidity in the marketplace.

8. The Real Estate Product Control group has reviewed the mark adjustments and agrees with these adjustments.

9. The review resulted in a total markdown of $665 mn (approx. $505 mn in the United States, and $160 mn in Europe).

Bear Stearns' collapse came on March 16, 2008, shocking the financial world. If it could happen to Bear Stearns, the market reasoned, it could happen to Lehman Brothers. On Friday, March 14, 2008, Lehman's stock closed at $39.26. The next Monday, it dropped all the way to $21 and then rose to close at $31.75. The next day, March 18, it closed up, at $46.49. In just two days, the market went from thinking that Lehman would be next to thinking that Lehman was better than it was before Bear collapsed.

These price movements were a very obvious indication that market participants did not know very much. They were very uncertain about banks' overall condition, how much real estate exposure each bank really had, and how much more real estate prices would drop in the future.[24]

Later in March 2008, government officers came to monitor Lehman at its New York headquarters. Teams came from the SEC and the Federal Reserve Bank of New York (FRBNY), and focused primarily on monitoring bank liquidity.[25]

With the pressure on, Lehman's managers thought a capital increase might help them ride out a larger storm. They considered several options.

Lehman had two ways to reduce its leverage. It could sell assets, to reduce the numerator in the net leverage formula, or raise equity, increasing the denominator in the net leverage equation.

During the first quarter of 2008, Fuld decided that Lehman would not raise equity unless it could do so at a premium. Many of Lehman's competitors used strategic transactions to raise equity in late 2007 and early 2008. Lehman did not want to signal weakness by raising equity at a discount. Unlike its peers, it hadn't yet suffered losses that might have made capital a more urgent need. Or maybe Fuld was greedy. Lehman was also late in selling assets, only really beginning in the second quarter of 2008.

On March 20, 2008, reporter Jesse Eisinger published a negative article titled "The Debt Shuffle" about Lehman Brothers in Portfolio.com. The article questioned the firm's small write-downs from its first-quarter financial results. This article bothered Lehman's management because it suggested that the bank wasn't entirely trustworthy. The investment banking business requires trust and confidence, especially because most financing is short term. If the markets begin to distrust an investment bank, the firm will likely fail, even if it is completely solvent.

The market was losing confidence in Lehman's valuations, too, as seen in the collateral demands Lehman heard from its clearing banks. Management began a serious search for solutions.

They considered raising capital through an equity offering, or finding a strategic buyer at the right price. Lehman approached Warren Buffett, CEO of Berkshire Hathaway. On March 28, 2008, Fuld spoke to Buffett about a potential $3.5 billion private investment in convertible preferred stock with a conversion price of $54 per share. Lehman's stock price at the close of that day was $37.87.

In an interview on September 22, 2009, Buffett said that two things about the offer had concerned him.[26] First, Buffett wanted Lehman executives to buy under the same terms as Buffett. Fuld explained that he was reluctant to require a significant buy-in from Lehman executives, because they already received much of their compensation in stock. Buffett considered Fuld's statement a warning sign that Lehman executives were unwilling to participate significantly.

Second, Buffett didn't like Fuld's complaints about short sellers. Buffett thought that blaming short sellers was a sign that Fuld wouldn't admit to Lehman's own problems.

A subsequent conversation revealed that Paulson would have liked Buffett to invest in Lehman, but wasn't willing to offer the same sort of government guarantee that J.P. Morgan got when it took over Bear Stearns.

Buffett spent the rest of Friday, March 28, reviewing Lehman's 10-K and noting problems with some of Lehman's assets. Buffett's concerns centered around Lehman's real estate and high-yield investments, lending-related commitments, derivatives and related credit-market risk, level-three assets, and securitization activity.

Buffett is a famously acute investor, but even he probably didn't learn much that was new from Lehman's financial statements. His decision not to invest was based in part on fear. The real estate market was crumbling and Buffett didn't want an unknown real estate exposure, even as part of an otherwise good deal.[27]

On March 15, 2008, the sovereign wealth fund ICD approached Lehman about buying equity. Lehman wasn't interested in raising equity capital at that time. ICD responded that, if and when Lehman considered raising capital, ICD should be Lehman's "first call in the Middle East."[28]

In March 2008, Fuld appointed McDade "balance sheet czar" and instructed him to sell assets and take other actions to reduce the size of Lehman's balance sheet. This involved selling some of the firm's real estate exposure. From the end of the first quarter to the end of the second quarter of 2008, the firm's commercial-mortgage assets shrank from $36 billion to $29 billion. Total residential and commercial mortgage products went from $74 billion to $61 billion. Actual real estate held for sale decreased to $21 billion ($10 billion net).[29]

At the March 31, 2008, board of directors meeting, Fuld mentioned his discussions with Buffett. On the same day he told Buffett that Lehman could not accept his terms. Instead, the board approved a $4 billion public preferred stock offering. On April 4, Lehman completed that offering.

This went relatively unappreciated in the marketplace. More rumors began spreading about Lehman Brothers. On April 8, 2008, Greenlight Capital's David Einhorn, who had shorted Lehman Brothers stock, began to pitch his own position. At Grant's Spring Investment Conference, Einhorn said:[30]

> There is good reason to question Lehman's fair value calculations...
> Lehman could have taken many billions more in write-downs than it did.
> Lehman has large exposure to commercial real estate...Lehman does not

provide enough transparency for us to even hazard a guess as to how they have accounted for these items...I suspect that greater transparency on these valuations would not inspire market confidence.

—David Einhorn, President of Greenlight Capital, Public Speech,
April 8, 2008[31]

In April 2008, S&P lowered its corporate credit rating for Archstone from BB- to B, changed its outlook to "negative," and then stopped issuing ratings for this enterprise. On April 11, 2008, Fuld had a very positive dinner with Paulson. He sent an e-mail from his Blackberry:

Just finished the Paulson dinner...we have huge brand with treasury... loved our capital base...all in all worthwhile.

—Richard Fuld, CEO of Lehman Brothers, April 11, 2008
(Sorkin 2010)

On April 30, 2008, Lehman issued $1 billion in 10-year senior notes. On May 2, 2008, Lehman issued another $2 billion in 30-year subordinated notes and $2.5 billion in 10-year senior notes.

In late May 2008, Lehman began investment talks with a Korean bank consortium. By early June, the consortium and Lehman circulated a draft term sheet. But Lehman did not complete a deal with the consortium; instead, Lehman raised capital from other sources.

On June 6, 2008, Lehman's management presented a stock offering totaling $6 billion to the Lehman's Board of Directors.

On June 9, 2008, Lehman Brothers reported a second quarter revenue loss of −$4.087 billion and net income loss of −$2.774 billion due to tax carryovers. The losses stemmed from Lehman's decision to write down the value of its commercial real estate portfolio and from less liquid aspects of its residential mortgage origination business, which lost −$2.374 billion for the firm's capital markets division. The investment banking and client services divisions were still producing positive net profits of $193 million and $229 million respectively (see Table 11.3).

The market reacted to this by trading Lehman's stock down from $29.48 per share on June 9 to $27.50 on June 10. The board approved the offering proposal and on June 12, 2008, Lehman sold 2 million shares of convertible preferred stock for $2 billion. That same day, Lehman sold 143 million shares of common stock for $4 billion ($28 per share), completing the $6 billion offering.

The firm also changed leadership on June 12. Fuld replaced President and COO Joseph Gregory with Herbert McDade, who had been in charge of Lehman's equity unit. Fuld and Gregory were old friends, and Fuld described this decision as "one of the most difficult decisions he and I had to make together."

The U.S. government applauded Lehman on its efforts to raise capital. Treasury Undersecretary Robert Steel publicly stated that Lehman was "addressing the issues" by raising this extra capital.

By mid-June 2008, Lehman was still looking for a buyer or other substantial source of additional capital. Unfortunately, the Korean consortium had dropped out, leaving only KDB as a potential investor.

Fuld began considering spinning off Lehman's commercial real estate assets. In that scenario, Lehman Brothers would split itself into two companies. One would handle the investment banking, asset management, and trading business; the other would contain the firm's commercial real estate holdings. Lehman would then sell the second unit to an investor and be left with what could be called "clean" Lehman Brothers, or "core" Lehman Brothers. Fuld also thought about selling Lehman's very profitable investment management division to raise additional cash for the core business. These were interesting ideas, but they never developed, in part because it was difficult to value the firm's commercial real estate.

Lehman had raised additional capital, but the market still thought of it as standing on shaky ground. On June 13, 2008, Vice Chairman of the Federal Reserve Donald Kohn told Ben Bernanke that institutional investors believed that there was no question of whether Lehman would fail, but only of when the failure would occur.

Lehman continued its search for potential partners or purchasers. In mid-July, KDB proposed buying a controlling share in Lehman through a $5 to $6 billion tender offer. Around July 28 senior Lehman executives, including Fuld, McDade, McGee, Bhattal, and Cho met in Hong Kong with KDB Governor Euoo Sung Min and other KDB executives.[32]

On August 6, 2008, after KDB commenced due diligence, the suitor lost interest in the tender offer and joint venture. KDB was concerned that Lehman had not taken sufficient write-downs on its commercial real estate positions and residential mortgage assets. KDB also expected that further write-downs would be necessary as real estate markets deteriorated.[33]

At the August 6, 2008, Lehman Board meeting, Fuld reported that KDB was interested only if Lehman spun off its commercial real estate. In mid-July 2008, Lehman also began merger talks with Bank of America.

By the end of August, Lehman still had no deal with any other firm. Lehman had considered a modified KDB proposal and rejected it. The firm also failed to reach an agreement on two potential offers from MetLife and the Investment Corporation of Dubai (ICD). Lehman executives faced a stark choice: take a large discount on the current stock price or spin off the real estate exposure. Managers hoped to accomplish the latter by the first quarter of 2009.

As the summer drew to a close, the market grew more and more fragile. At the beginning of August, Lehman's share price was $18.65. It dropped by another 14% to $16.13 by the start of September. Despite real estate worries and the market's perception that Lehman would fail, the first two quarters of its 2008 financial statements looked surprisingly decent. Nevertheless, Lehman kept pursuing partners.

On September 4, 2008, ICD made two proposals to Lehman. Under the first proposal, ICD would pay between $3.25 billion and $4 billion for 50.1% of Neuberger Berman, the private wealth management arm of Lehman's investment management division. There is no evidence that Lehman ever responded to this proposal. ICD's next proposed a $3.25 billion investment in Lehman preferred convertible shares after the firm spun off its commercial real estate positions. The offer was conditioned on Lehman raising an additional $3.25 billion in capital from other investors, and required protection for ICD against up to $2 billion in Lehman's write-downs over the next year.

On September 7, 2008, market trust declined even more when the government took over Freddie and Fannie. It made the run on Lehman even more likely.

On September 9, a Korean government official announced that KDB's talks with Lehman had ended. The market took the news poorly, and Lehman's stock price dropped by 45% to $7.79.[34]

Later on September 9, 2008, after the KDB announcement, many of Lehman's hedge fund clients pulled out. Short-term creditors cut the firm's lines of credit, and the cost of insuring Lehman's debt surged by almost 200 basis points. On the same day, Lehman executed an amended guarantee, at J.P. Morgan's insistence. J.P. Morgan and Citi were Lehman's main short-term lenders. By modifying agreements and asking for more collateral, these creditors had a tremendous effect on Lehman's liquidity.

The Final Days

On September 10, 2008, internal management announced third-quarter financial results earlier than normal, hoping to calm the market.[35] At the same time, Moody's and other rating agencies placed Lehman on negative watch for a possible downgrade.

Just like LTCM's Meriwether, who sent his famous investor letter, Lehman sped up its earnings announcement to underline its transparency and show the market that things were much better than generally believed. Lehman reported that its liquidity pool—the assets used to run the business—was at $42 billion. The firm's tier 1 capital ratio had improved to 11%, a very high number for a bank. Lehman reduced its residential mortgage exposure by 47%, reduced its commercial real estate exposure by 18%, and reduced its high-yield acquisition finance exposure by 38%. Lehman reduced its leverage to 21 (total assets) and 11 (net assets). The firm said that it expected to spin off the real estate division in early 2009, and intended to sell a significant portion of its asset-management business.

Lehman had additional write-offs in the mortgage business, giving its capital markets division negative revenues of $4.15 billion. The investment banking and client services areas made significant profits.

The firm's total third-quarter loss was −$3.93 billion. Lehman's common equity was $15.27 billion and the total shareholder's equity (including preferred shares) was $27.36 billion.

This was all good news, but the market didn't trust Lehman and weren't convinced that Lehman had appropriately valued its real estate holdings. They doubted the numbers. The market harkened back to October 2007, when Merrill Lynch reported its net CDO exposures but wouldn't reveal its gross exposures, which were almost four times higher. Few traders had much trust in banks or the banking system. The trust in the banking system was weak. The market also didn't like the fact that Lehman still owned SpinCo, its separate business in commercial real estate assets, and didn't yet know how to get rid of it.

The day after the release, the market lost even more confidence, focusing only on the quarterly loss of −$3.93 billion and ignoring the positive information. They thought further deterioration in the real estate market would cause future losses. Even though Lehman had $15.27 billion in common equity—too much to evaporate even if the portfolio did decline—the markets had little trust to spare for any bank. The stock price fell another 42%, going from $7.25 to $4.22 by the close of business on September 11, 2008.

On September 11, 2008, J.P. Morgan demanded an additional $5 billion in collateral from Lehman. That same day, Lehman's management told the board that "liquidity is forecasted to decrease to $30 billion today as a result of providing collateral." The legal team that examined Lehman's bankruptcy determined that these collateral demands ultimately pushed Lehman into failure.

J.P. Morgan may have demanded extra collateral in reaction to privileged information it got from KDB. KDB signed confidentiality agreements around its negotiations with Lehman. Yet throughout August and September, KDB officials made public statements about the status of these negotiations, violating confidentiality agreements. J.P. Morgan had even more access to KDB through discussions between Steven Lim, J.P. Morgan's senior country officer and managing director, and Min Euoo Sung, KDB chairman. KDB was communicating with J.P. Morgan because it wanted Morgan to help finance the Lehman deal. On September 5, 2008, Lim e-mailed Morgan CEO Jamie Dimon, Black, and other J.P. Morgan executives stating that he did not believe KDB would get a deal done by Lehman's September 10, 2008, deadline. That same day, J.P. Morgan decided it needed additional collateral from Lehman.[36]

By September 12, two days after Lehman publicly reported liquidity of $41 billion, the pool had just a little more than $2 billion in readily monetizable assets. Lehman's liquidity pool disappeared very quickly, in part because it was never really there in the first place. In May 2008, Lehman's liquidity position was strong at $45 billion. During the summer of 2008, clearing agents such as J.P. Morgan and Citibank requested more capital for "comfort," and to protect themselves against Lehman's possible collapse. Lehman gave these banks additional collateral. On June 12, it posted $2 billion with Citi; it posted $5.7 billion with J.P. Morgan on June 19. Lehman Brothers counted these additional collateral postings as part of its liquidity pool, even though the funds may not have been accessible. The public didn't know it at the time, but on September 12, 2008, Lehman's liquidity pool stood at $32.5 billion, with only $2.4 billion readily convertible into cash.

Through the summer and into September 2008, Lehman saw Morgan's additional collateral demands, other demands for extra collateral, hedge funds pulling money, and short-term creditors cutting lending lines. Lehman could not survive—not because of its actual condition, but because so many believed that Lehman was done. It was as Mattone had said to Meriwether: "You're finished."

Over the weekend of September 12, Treasury Secretary Paulson, FRBNY President Timothy F. Geithner, SEC Chairman Christopher Cox, and the chief executives of leading financial institutions met to either facilitate Lehman's purchase or to mitigate the consequences of its failure.[37]

Several potential buyers were available, including Bank of America, which Fuld had first approached several months earlier. Bank of America (BofA) was willing to make the deal, but only if they received some form of government assistance, as J.P. Morgan had received when buying Bear Stearns.[38]

Ken Lewis, Bank of America's CEO, was worried about the $66 billion hole in Lehman's asset valuation. Lewis didn't think the assets were completely worthless; BofA didn't want those $66 billion in assets at any price. It wanted them off the books. Blankfein and Dimon were not as worried about Lehman, telling Paulson that a Lehman bankruptcy wouldn't be that bad. Geithner asked all the participants for their net Lehman exposure; at one point he said to the group, "I'm going to come back in two hours; you guys better figure out a solution and get this thing done."[39] A team from Lehman was at the meetings, but without Fuld, as Paulson did not want Fuld there.[40]

On the afternoon of Saturday, September 13, BofA began talks with Merrill Lynch, and on September 15, 2008, announced a deal to buy Merrill Lynch at $29 per share, a significant premium over Merrill's last traded stock price of $17.05.[41] Merrill's mortgage exposure was similar to Lehman's, yet Lewis was happy about the deal.

This turned out later to be a very bad deal for Bank of America.[42]

With BofA gone, the last suitor with any hope of purchasing Lehman was Barclays, the British bank. On September 11, 2008—before the weekend meetings—John Varley, Barclay's group chief executive, informed the Financial Services Authority (FSA), the United Kingdom's bank regulator, that the Barclays board would meet that day to consider whether Barclays should approach Lehman about a possible deal. Varley believed the Lehman deal would occur if three conditions were met. They would need a high degree of confidence that a deal could be completed "with the necessary support of the Federal Reserve," liquidity support from the Federal Reserve, and a discount on Lehman's net asset values.[43]

There was no time for shareholder approval, so a Barclays deal would have had to take place without it. For that to happen, the UK's FSA must waive the shareholder approval requirement. The FSA concluded that, because no precedent existed, granting a waiver would "represent a compromise of one of the fundamental principles of the FSA's Listing Regime."[44]

By early September 14, Barclays and Lehman had a deal that would save Lehman from collapse. Later that day, the deal fell apart when the FSA refused to waive UK shareholder-approval requirements.

Lehman no longer had sufficient liquidity to fund its daily operations. It faced a cash shortage of $4.5 billion on September 15, 2008. At 1:45 A.M. that day, Lehman Brothers filed for Chapter 11 bankruptcy protection.

A Classic Run on the Bank

> Smart risk management is never putting yourself in a position where you
> can't live to fight another day.
> —Richard Fuld, CEO of Lehman Brothers, April 24, 2008
> (in *The Economist*)

In the 1930s, when the financial system collapsed, many people went to the
bank to withdraw their money because they were scared that banks would go
bankrupt and they would lose all their savings if they didn't get there before
other depositors.

Banks keep a fraction of their deposits and lend the rest out, so they
don't have enough liquidity to give everyone their money on the same day. If
depositors incorrectly think that a bank is in trouble, their deposit withdrawals
will create a *bank run* and push even a very healthy bank toward failure.[45]

On March 6, 1933, U.S. President Franklin D. Roosevelt called for a
"bank holiday" and closed every bank in the country. They remained closed
until Department of the Treasury officials could inspect each institution's
ledgers. Banks in viable financial condition were primed with Treasury money
and permitted to do business again. Those in marginal condition were kept
closed until they could be restored to soundness. Numerous banks that had
been poorly run remained closed forever. This was one way to stop the endless
cycle of banking system destruction.

The Federal Deposit Insurance Corporation (FDIC) was one regulatory
response to the bank runs of the 1930s. Established in the Banking Act of
1933, it insured bank deposits so that depositors would not worry about
losing their savings to bank failures.[46] Investment banks do not have this
guarantee on their customer deposits.

Bear Stearns and Lehman Brothers both failed after classic runs on the
bank. But these weren't ordinary people withdrawing their deposits. Institutions withdrew their credit, loans, and assets from Lehman Brothers.

Lehman's mortgage securities had unknown values, so analysts and other
market participants repeatedly questioned whether Lehman had written down
enough of the losses. To value many mortgage-backed securities, companies
made their best estimates—a process potentially vulnerable to manipulation.
Even with honest estimates, market participants might worry that these securities were subject to greater losses if real estate prices collapsed further. This
created a situation where the market began to distrust companies' financial
statements. Given the economic environment, it was more prudent for them
to begin assuming the worst.[47]

Lehman funded itself through the short-term repo markets, borrowing hundreds of billions of dollars in operating capital from counterparties each day.[48]

This is not unusual for investment banks. Confidence is a crucial component of these loans. The moment that repo counterparties lost confidence in Lehman and declined to roll over its daily funding, Lehman couldn't continue to operate. The same was true for other investment banks. It's no coincidence that no major investment bank exists any longer. The remaining two investment banks, Goldman Sachs and Morgan Stanley, converted themselves to *bank holding companies*. The change let these banks become part of the Federal Reserve system with certain privileges, including the right to borrow from the Federal Reserve.

Lehman's balance sheet at the end of the third quarter showed $15 billion in common equity and $27 billion in total shareholder equity. If appropriate write-downs had been taken to date, a rough calculation shows another 28% decline in portfolio values was necessary to erode common equity, and a 50% decline was necessary to erode total equity.[49]

In the remainder of September 2008, residential housing prices in major metropolitan areas declined 11%, reaching their lowest point.[50] Commercial real estate prices dropped even more. From September to their worst point (February 2011), they dropped by 43%. By August 2011 they were down 35% from their high. Lehman's numbers suggest they would have survived these drops, though no one knew this at the time. Solvency is complicated when market crowds are running on your bank. Asked if Lehman was solvent right before the failure, J.P. Morgan's Barry Zubrow said, "from a pure accounting standpoint, it was solvent." Jamie Dimon was less sure.

> What does solvency mean? The answer is, I don't know. I still could not answer that question . . .
> —Jamie Dimon, CEO of J.P. Morgan, October 20, 2010, in FCIC
> (2010)

The legal examination of Lehman Brothers found " . . . insufficient evidence to support a finding that Lehman's valuations of its residential whole loans [RWL], RMBS, CDO or derivative positions were unreasonable during the second and third quarters of 2008." They also found that there was insufficient evidence to conclude that Lehman's valuations of its commercial real estate portfolio were unreasonable as of the second and third quarters of 2008.

Lehman failed because it was unable to retain the confidence of its lenders and counterparties and because it did not have sufficient liquidity to meet its current obligations. Lehman was unable to maintain confidence because a series of business decisions had left it with heavy concentrations of illiquid assets with deteriorating values such as residential and commercial real estate. Confidence was further eroded when it became public that attempts to form strategic partnerships to bolster its stability had failed.

—The Examiner Report (Valukas 2010)

Lehman's failure could have been prevented in many ways, most directly by Federal Reserve backing for any deal similar to the one involving Bear Stearns. That didn't happen. Suddenly 28,560 employees did not know what their future held and the financial markets went into chaos.

Why Let Lehman Fail?

Why did Paulson, Bernanke, and Geithner let Lehman fail? Many companies had been saved in the past: Chrysler in 1979, savings and loans in the late 1980s, General Motors, Bear Stearns in 2008, and many more.

There are a host of hypotheses, including the possibility of pressure from the growing public sentiment that Wall Street didn't deserve a bailout. The public—and perhaps some regulators—didn't consider how one part of the financial system affects the others.

Ironically enough, Ben Bernanke gave one of the best analogies of this concept, even though he learned it a bit too late.[51] His analogy goes like this. Suppose you live in a neighborhood where there is one guy who smokes a lot in his house. He's very careless. One day, his entire house is on fire because of a cigarette he left burning in his bed. The natural reaction is to say "Screw him. He deserves his house to go down!" And maybe that's right, but suppose that all the houses in the neighborhood are made of wood and are close to each other. Then it would be in the town's collective interest to get together and put the fire out, even if he acted irresponsibly.

Though the Fed is supposed to function independently of public opinion, Philip Angelides, chairman of the Financial Crisis Inquiry Commission, noted that "political consideration" may have been a reason that U.S. officials did not do more to rescue Lehman Brothers. He cited e-mails from Federal Reserve officials that said a rescue would look bad in the press.[52] The former head of the Bank for International Settlements (BIS) described the decision to allow Lehman Brothers to fail:

On Lehman, I think at the time it happened, the politics of saving Lehman were highly problematic. Large numbers of members of Congress, from both sides, as well as the general public, were strongly against, and most believed strongly that the balance of advantage was to let it go. This was partly a concern about moral hazard, partly public anger with banks, and partly a belief that the consequences would not be all that bad. It would have been very hard for the U.S. government and Federal Reserve to go against all this and save Lehman. There is also the argument, strongly advanced now by Paulson, that there was no legal basis for saving it. On this, I'm not so sure, though I understand why they make the argument. If they had really wanted to save Lehman, I don't see why they couldn't have offered Barclays the same sort of deal J.P. Morgan got when it stepped in to take over Bear Stearns. Incidentally, I don't believe the story that there was some kind of animus between Fuld and Paulson that made the latter less willing to save Lehman. Nor do I believe that AIG was rescued to help out Goldman.

—Sir Andrew Crockett interview, President of J.P. Morgan
International, former CEO of the BIS, October 31, 2010

Another possibility is that Paulson had no reason to care for Lehman Brothers. Paulson was a former Goldman Sachs CEO and Lehman Brothers was a smaller rival. Paulson claims that he repeatedly told Fuld that the government would do nothing for Lehman Brothers. Fuld does not recall any such warning.

Fuld had suggested re-creating Lehman Brothers as a bank holding company. This was denied. In fact, Geithner told the legal examination team that he considered Lehman's proposals to convert to a bank holding company "gimmicky."

But Goldman Sachs and Morgan Stanley converted to bank holding companies just six days after the Lehman bankruptcy. Did Paulson treat Goldman differently than Lehman out of ignorance, preference, public pressure, or something else?[53]

Another possibility is that the government authorities could do nothing for Lehman Brothers. The general counsel of the Federal Reserve argued that

[We did not bail out Lehman Brothers because] I do not think we had the authority to do so, and, even if we did, we did not think Lehman could repay the government.

—Scott Alvarez, General Counsel of the Federal Reserve, interview
with the *Washington Post* (September 2, 2010)

This is hardly plausible. First, they did something for Bear Stearns in March 2008. And within days of the Lehman collapse, authorities let Goldman Sachs and Morgan Stanley convert to bank holding companies, which Fuld had requested earlier. They gave AIG $85 billion one day later. They then approved the Federal bailout package, giving banks access to a total $750 billion. Bernanke later testified at a Senate hearing on December 3, 2009, that the Fed "should have done more" for Lehman Brothers. Merrill Lynch's John Thain talked about the weekend meetings regarding Lehman Brothers:

> There was criticism of bailing out Wall Street. It was a combination of political unwillingness to bail out Wall Street and a belief that there needed to be a reinforcement of moral hazard. There was never a discussion about the legal ability of the Fed to do this.
> —John Thain, CEO of Merrill Lynch, in FCIC (2010)

We will never know exactly what factors were most important in deciding to let Lehman fail. I think Bernanke, Paulson, and Geithner made a mistake by letting Lehman fall. Had the Fed forgotten the lesson of LTCM just 10 years earlier? Richard Fuld describes it most accurately in public testimonies:

> Until the day they put me into the ground I will wonder [why they allowed Lehman to fail, but not AIG, Morgan Stanley, or Goldman Sachs.]
> —Richard Fuld, House Committee Testimony, October 6, 2008

In the end, Lehman was forced into bankruptcy not because it neglected to act responsibly or seek solutions to the crisis, but because of a decision, based on flawed information, not to provide Lehman with the support given to each of its competitors and other nonfinancial firms in the ensuing days . . . Notably, on that same Sunday, the Fed expanded for investment banks the types of collateral that would qualify for borrowings from its Primary Dealer Credit Facility. Only Lehman was denied that expanded access. I submit, that had Lehman been granted that same access as its competitors, even as late as that Sunday evening, Lehman would have had time for at least an orderly wind down or for an acquisition which would have alleviated the crisis that ensued.
> —Richard Fuld, Testimony to Financial Crisis Inquiry Commission,
> September 1, 2010

Who Was at Fault?

> I, like a number of other people, thought that the mortgage crisis was
> contained to residential mortgages, and I was wrong.
> —Richard Fuld, House Committee Testimony, October 6, 2008

Our first reaction might be to blame Lehman for its own failure—but other
parties contributed to their death. Guilt properly belongs to four parties:
Lehman Brothers, the U.S. government, the counterparties, and market
structure.

Lehman Brothers

There are four areas in which Lehman Brothers sealed its own fate. The firm
had too much real estate exposure. It had tricky accounting practices, such as
Repo 105. Its risk management practices didn't properly account for the firm's
real estate risk. Finally, Lehman couldn't compromise early and raise enough
capital in the wake of market uncertainty.

Lehman Brothers had a large concentration of real estate sector investments. Its real estate exposure was between $87 and $111 billion, or 28%
to 35% of invested assets, including owning a bank that directly issued residential mortgages. This huge exposure made Lehman look more like a real
estate company than an investment bank. Merrill Lynch and Lehman Brothers
had substantially more exposure to real estate than did Goldman or Morgan
(see Table 11.1).

Lehman and other investment banks produced opaque financial statements. The lack of transparency in bank positions only increased the market's
distrust. It wasn't easy for market participants to interpret investment losses
and guess what losses were to come. Any hint that a bank wasn't forthright in
its financial statements led to a run on that bank. Lehman Brothers was the
most transparent about its real estate exposure, however it was also smaller,
more levered, and had more real estate exposure.[54]

Lehman's management used clever accounting tricks to make the bank's
leverage look lower than it was.[55] This trick was most commonly called Repo
105, named after the security that Lehman used to reduce its balance sheet
exposure. In a repo transaction, a bank gives a security to another bank and
then receives a short-term loan, which can then be used to invest or pay off
other obligations. Normally, these transactions are recorded on the balance
sheet, thus they make the bank's leverage larger.

One measure of leverage is total assets divided by total shareholder equity. A Repo 105 transaction, which is entirely legal, let Lehman give a counterparty a security with a value of $105,000 and receive in return just $100,000 or less. (The name Repo 105 comes from the fact that the security was worth 105% or more of the cash.) U.S. accounting rules let firms treat these transactions as a security sale, not financing. Substituting a sale for a loan made Lehman's leverage appear smaller.

This was legal but it was also deceptive. According to internal e-mail records at Lehman Brothers, the only purpose of Repo 105 was "to reduce balance sheet at the quarter-end." The company managers suggested that rather than sell assets at a loss, more Repo 105 transactions could help reduce the firm's leverage. Repo 105 practices had been used before 2008 and the firm's auditors, Ernst & Young, knew about this practice.

During the first and second quarters of 2008, Lehman Brothers used the practice to remove more than $50 billion in assets from its net asset balance sheet. This only slightly reduced the firm's net leverage ratio. In the first quarter of 2008, Lehman did $49.1 billion in Repo 105, reducing net leverage from 17.4 to 15.5. In the second quarter of 2008, the firm did $50.4 billion worth of Repo 105, reducing net leverage from 13.98 to 12.18.

[It was an accounting gimmick] . . . I am very aware . . . another drug we R on.
—E-mail from Bart McDade, President and COO of Lehman
Brothers, April 3, 2008 (Valukas 2010)

Lehman Brothers had poor risk management. The firm had concentration limits on its principal and proprietary investments, which restricted the total amount the firm could invest in any one trade. These limits helped insure investment diversification and limited the potential counterparty risk of any single investment. During the rush for profits, they violated this single investment concentration limit on 37 leveraged deals.[56]

Lehman did not include either its commercial real estate investments or its private equity investments in firm stress tests.[57] Although Lehman produced these stress tests on a monthly basis and presented them to the management, Board of Directors,[58] and regulators, the tests didn't include some of the major risks to which the firm was exposed.

Lehman Brothers raised its appetite for risk. Between December 2006 and December 2007, Lehman raised its firmwide risk appetite limit three times, going from $2.3 to $4.0 billion.

Between May and August 2007, Lehman omitted some of its largest risks from its risk usage calculation. The primary omitted risk was a $2.3 billion bridge equity position in the Archstone-Smith Real Estate Investment Trust real estate transaction, an extraordinarily large and risky commitment. Had Lehman's management included that risk in its usage calculation, it would have been immediately apparent that Lehman was over its risk limits.

At various points in 2006 and 2007, Lehman's risk managers considered whether to include private equity investments in Lehman's stress testing. An internal audit advised that Lehman "address the main risks in the firm's portfolio," including "illiquidity" and "concentration risk." But Lehman did not take significant steps to include private equity positions in stress testing until 2008, even though these investments became an increasingly large portion of Lehman's risk profile.

There was some movement inside Lehman Brothers to reduce firm risk, but this did not prevail.[59] Even more troubling was the risk committee's meeting schedule—just twice per year—and the fact that Fuld controlled it.

Like most other market participants, Lehman employed VaR calculations that used a short history and ignored valuation.[60]

During 2007 and 2008, Lehman Brothers had tried and sometimes succeeded in raising new capital, and had pursued potential buyers. The firm should have begun raising capital sooner. It failed to realize its dire predicament in time to take a deal at a reduced stock price, which would have been better than no deal at all.

Of course, it's easy to say this in hindsight. Many other banks had begun raising capital only a little earlier, partly because their troubles began earlier than did those of Lehman Brothers.[61]

It is difficult to know whether Lehman's management was right in not selling or raising capital at a discount. In hindsight, of course, it looks like a mistake. Without government action, some other investment banks may have failed, too.

The Counterparties

Once market participants know or believe an institution is in trouble, the crowd's behavior reinforces itself. When rumors of Lehman's trouble got out, the rating agencies downgraded Lehman Brothers. At the same time counterparties raised capital requirements for doing business with Lehman. The brokerage business is very sensitive to capital requirements. Most investment banks borrow money daily on a short-term basis to conduct their business. At the end of 2007, Lehman Brothers had $181 billion of repo transactions.

Counterparties asked Lehman to supply greater collateral for every dollar of borrowing, increasing the capital Lehman needed to run its operations. J.P. Morgan acted as Lehman's principal clearing bank. From the middle to the end of 2008, J.P. Morgan raised Lehman's collateral requirements, putting more stress on the bank. Morgan's collateral call contributed to the liquidity problems that hastened Lehman's bankruptcy.[62] Other counterparties, including Citigroup and HSBC, also raised collateral requirements.

The Government and Market Structure

The U.S. government could have done several things to prevent Lehman's bankruptcy, things they eventually did for AIG, Goldman Sachs, and Morgan Stanley. It is still unclear how that decision was made.

The market structure of banking and investment banking also was to blame. The banking system is riddled with pro-systemic triggers and has virtually no automatic stabilizers. An investment bank's business is based on short-term borrowing and long-term investments. If market confidence in these banks drops due to a systemic problem with the invested assets, customers withdraw money, counterparties raise collateral demands, and rating agencies downgrade the banks. This continues until the bank declares bankruptcy. This is a problem with the financial system. A break in confidence will break the bank.

The Legal Opinion on the Lehman Bankruptcy

The law firm that investigated the Lehman bankruptcy considered whether there were *colorful claims* against some of the parties involved in Lehman's failure.[63]

They concluded that:

1. *No claims against Lehman's business and risk management. Even though some of their decisions can be questioned in retrospect.*
2. *No claims against Lehman's valuation of the business for solvency analysis. Even though they found these may have been unreasonable.*
3. *No claims against Lehman's management for failing to find a way to survive. The evidence supported Lehman's attempt to find ways to not go bankrupt.*
4. *No claims against the way Lehman's management interacted and informed government agencies in the period prior to their collapse. Lehman seems to have made significant attempts to keep the Fed and other agencies informed accurately about the ongoings at Lehman Brothers.*

5. *Claims against Lehman executives, Richard Fuld, Chris O'Meara, Erin Callan,
   Ian Lowitt, and against the auditor, Ernst & Young, for failing to adequately
   disclose the practice of Repo 105.*
6. *Claims against J.P. Morgan and CitiBank due to their modifications of guarantee agreements and demands for extra collateral from Lehman Brothers in the
   final days of Lehman's existence. They found these demands directly impacted
   Lehman's liquidity pool and were central in the collapse of Lehman Brothers.*

Who Would Have Been Next?

Once Lehman Brothers failed, the stock prices of remaining investment
banks immediately began collapsing (see Figure 11.5). From September 15 to
September 18, Goldman Sachs fell 30% and Morgan Stanley fell 39%.

By September 15, 2008, the residential real estate market had fallen a
total of 23% from its peak. The commercial real estate market had fallen by
9.1% from its peak. Lehman's collapse added more doubt and imbalance to
the market.[64] Without a break in the frenzy, more banks would fail. Based
on leverage and real estate exposure, Morgan Stanley would have been next,
closely followed by Goldman Sachs.

FIGURE 11.5   The Market Value of Major Investment Banks. Normalized to 100 on
January 2, 2008

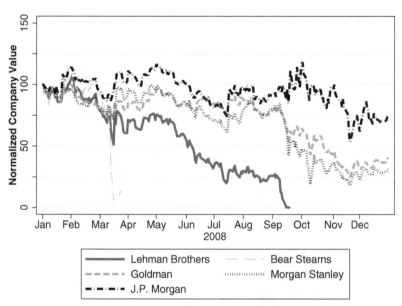

Goldman Sachs was so worried about its survival that Goldman CEO Lloyd Blankfein called Jamie Dimon and asked his firm to stop crushing Goldman's reputation. Dimon responded by sending an internal e-mail to J.P. Morgan employees cautioning them to not approach Goldman clients in a predatory way.[65] Blankfein called Citibank CEO Vikram Pandit and mentioned the possibility of a merger. The Treasury asked Dimon to consider buying Morgan Stanley and Dimon began reluctantly looking at this deal.[66] The banking world was in chaos. The crowds were running and no firm was safe.

The Spoils of Having Friends in High Places

Paulson, Bernanke, and Geithner ignored Fuld's requests to become a bank holding company; they let Goldman Sachs and Morgan Stanley become bank holding companies six days after the Lehman Brothers bankruptcy on September 21, 2008. Maybe it was helpful to have allies in Washington. Or maybe it was just their luck to have less housing exposure and sit further along the domino chain of failing banks than did Bear and Lehman.

A bank holding company is a corporation with a controlling interest in one or more banks. During the financial crisis, there were many positives to becoming a bank holding company. By becoming one, an investment bank became part of the Federal Reserve banking system. That gave them extra protection, including federal deposit insurance, access to loans from the Fed discount window, and an array of new Fed lending facilities designed to let banks borrow as much money as they needed to survive.

A day after Lehman collapsed, the U.S. government gave an emergency loan to American International Group (AIG), one of the world's largest insurance companies. The Fed lent AIG up to $85 billion and the government took an effective 80% ownership stake in the insurance company. AIG was ostensibly an insurance company, but its business more closely resembled a giant hedge fund.

In 2008, AIG had four major lines of business: general insurance ($122 billion, or 16%), life insurance and retirement services ($440 billion, or 56%), financial services ($166 billion, or 21%), and asset management ($53 billion, or 7%).[67]

AIG lost money in every quarter of 2008. By the end of September it had lost a total of $48 billion before taxes and $38 billion after taxes. The biggest losses came from the life insurance and financial services divisions. Within the life insurance division, some of the losses came from declines in the value of invested assets. A large part of AIG's losses came from its repo market activities. AIG used insurance division investments—bonds or other collateral—and repo'd it with other banks in exchange for cash. The company used the cash to buy subprime and other residential mortgage-backed securities, which lost $16 billion by the third quarter of 2008 as the mortgage securities' value declined. Many counterparties wanted either more collateral or their cash back, but AIG was stuck holding illiquid mortgage paper.[68]

The AIG financial products group was a levered hedge fund with a one-way bet on the mortgage market. About $21 billion of the division's losses came from its involvement in senior credit default swap portfolios (CDS). AIG lost even more during the rest of 2008 and in 2009. It had written CDSs on mortgage-backed securities, company debt, and CDOs. AIG insured mortgages, promising to make clients whole if the mortgage market collapsed.

Insurance helped the market continue issuing CDOs and other mortgage securities. Many banks used insurance contracts to reduce their required regulatory capital, because insurance made the mortgages they owned less risky. When the mortgages collapsed, AIG had huge liabilities to pay off very quickly. AIG's counterparties made collateral calls as the mortgage market collapsed. Ultimately, AIG's losses were so great that it could not make these margin calls.

By the end of 2007, AIG had written CDSs on a notional amount of $533 billion. They made no other provisions for losses because they believed these AAA-rated CDOs and related securities would not suffer losses.

> It is hard for us, without being flippant, to even see a scenario within any kind of realm or reason that would see us losing $1 in any of those transactions.
> —Joseph Cassano, Head of AIG Derivatives, Second Quarter
> Conference Call, August 9, 2007 (FCIC 2010)

Just like everyone else, AIG ignored the mortgage asset's true correlations, used historical data, and ignored the growing housing market valuation bubble. Amazingly, they lacked an internal risk model to value the CDOs on which they had written protection. They were at the mercy of counterparties' CDO valuations. AIG did not post initial margin on the CDOs, but they agreed to post collateral or variance margin if the underlying CDOs deteriorated or the rating agencies downgraded AIG.

This was not traditional insurance (see Box 11.1). AIG had no way to really hedge these credit guarantees. The entire real estate market was overvalued. A collapse in one mortgage pool meant a collapse for all of them. AIG wasn't offering insurance. It was offering a one-way directional bet on real estate by essentially writing put options on the real estate market.

As the mortgage market collapsed, AIG received margin calls on the CDSs. As of August 14, 2008, the firm had lost about $27 billion on these instruments mark-to-market, and had posted a total of $16.5 billion in collateral. It would need more collateral. On September 12, 2008, AIG executives told the New York Fed it was "facing serious liquidity issues that threaten[ed] its viability."[69]

Box 11.1 The Basics of Insurance

The standard insurance problem works like this. Take an almost truly exogenous event, such as the probability of being struck by lightning. Now imagine that the probability of this happening to any one person is $p = 0.001$ (a 1 in 1,000 event). The probability of person B being struck by lightning is independent of person A's probability, especially if these people are geographically spread out. Suppose the victim incurs $1,000 in medical expense. Assume an insurance company insures $n = 1,000$ people with this risk. In a world with no administrative costs, we can find the expected payout using the binomial distribution. The expected number of incidents in a given year is given by np or $0.001 \cdot 1,000 = 1$. The insurance company can reasonably expect only one victim in its client pool. The company's expected payout is $1,000 per year. The insurance company could charge each individual more than $1.00 per year for the insurance and on average would run a sound operation. The insurance company could be very cautious and charge each client $3.00 per year, which would securely maintain funds even in worse-case scenarios.

It's important that the probability of any one person being struck by lightning is independent of the probability that any other person will be struck by lightning. If the correlation were perfect, insurance would not be feasible, as each premium would be close to $1,000.

In recent years, insurance companies such as AIG began offering insurance on events that were truly not independent. In fact, these events became very highly correlated. Offering credit default swap (CDS) protection to companies that held risky corporate debt seemed like insurance, because it insured against the default of a company's bond. But the defaults were not independent. If the economy went into a recession, or if every bank was invested in similar assets, such as houses, then one company's default meant that all the others would likely default as well. To alter this simple model for high correlation among

(continued)

(*Continued*)

defalters, increase the p. Suppose the insurance company assumed a correlation of 0 (independent), but instead the real correlation was more like 0.90. The actual p might be more like 0.6. The company would collect $3,000 in premiums but have an expected payout of $600,000, leading to bankruptcy, acquisition, or a government bailout.

Goldman Sachs, which wanted to protect its mortgage exposure, was one of AIG's top CDS customers.

In testimony after the AIG bailout, Goldman Sachs' executives argued that they didn't need the government help and were doing fine.[70] Yet after Lehman's collapse, Goldman's stock price dropped to $52 per share on November 20, 2008 (a drop of 72% from one year earlier). Morgan Stanley didn't fare much better. Its stock price collapsed to $9.2 on the same day, for a total yearly drop of 82%. These big banks ultimately converted to bank holding companies; they needed Mother Fed to survive.

Between September 15, 2008, and May 12, 2009, Goldman Sachs borrowed 85 times for a total of $589 billion from the Primary Dealer Credit Facility (PDCF). The highest daily borrowing was on October 15, 2008, when it borrowed $18 billion. Morgan Stanley borrowed a total of 212 times for a total of $1,913 billion. The heaviest day was September 26, 2008, when it borrowed $47.6 billion. The British bank Barclays[71] that didn't rescue Lehman borrowed 73 times for a total of $408 billion. Its largest day was September 18, 2008, when it borrowed $47.9 billion. During this period, Barclays bought many of Lehman's scraps at fire sale prices.[72]

Goldman Sachs and Morgan Stanley also borrowed heavily from the Term Securities Lending Facility (TSLF). Between March 2008 and May 12, 2009, Goldman Sachs tapped this facility a total 53 times for $193 billion, while Morgan tapped it 34 times for $101 billion.

Hedge funds, foreign commercial banks, J.P. Morgan, Bank of America, Merrill Lynch, Citigroup, and other banks also borrowed billions. The group borrowed a total of $9 trillion ($8,951 billion) from the PDCF. Goldman Sachs represented 7% of that borrowing; Morgan Stanley represented 21%.

With some of their competition out of the way and the Fed funding their own survival, Goldman Sachs and Morgan Stanley saw their profits balloon. In 2009, Goldman Sachs had the highest profits in their history: a whopping $13.39 billion after taxes. The proprietary trading and investment division generated $17.3 billion of these profits. By the third quarter of 2010, Goldman Sachs reported profits of $5.967 billion. Of that, $8.6 billion came from the proprietary trading and investment division.

Morgan Stanley did not do as well as Goldman Sachs in 2009, partly because it was still writing off bad real estate investments and trying to survive. Morgan earned $1.3 billion in profits. Real estate portfolio losses of −$1.05 billion reduced the tax the firm paid.[73] However, 2010 turned out to be a banner year for Morgan Stanley. With Lehman Brothers out of the way, the firm's asset management and commissions profits were $4.6 billion.

Lehman's funeral took place on the morning of September 15, 2008. The uncertainty and chaos in the marketplace would only get worse.

CHAPTER 12

The Absurdity of Imbalance

Next to love, balance is the most important thing.

—John Wooden

When Lehman Brothers went into bankruptcy, the first sign of trouble happened in a money market fund called the Reserve Primary Fund (RPF). With $65 billion in assets, the RPF was one of the largest money market funds in the United States. Money market funds are a short-term savings vehicle and are considered extremely safe, because they invest in short-term, safe assets.

One of RPF's investments was in Lehman Brothers commercial paper, which companies issue for short-term financing. When Lehman Brothers went bankrupt, the RPF lost $785 million from its Lehman exposure. The fund "broke the buck," meaning its net asset value was less than $1 a share. It was losing money, which is nearly unheard of in a short-term, almost riskless investment.

Investors began to panic. The RPF had a total of $39 billion in withdrawals, and other crowds withdrew money from other money market funds, pulling a total of $172 billion from a $3.45 trillion market.

The market stopped trusting commercial paper. Commercial paper yields shot up, going from 10 basis points over the Federal Funds rate to 150 basis points over the Fed Funds rate in just two days. Large U.S. companies fund themselves through the commercial paper market, and the yield spike made it too costly for them to finance their activities. The Federal Reserve moved quickly and launched new programs to help resolve the mess that they had created by letting Lehman fail.[1]

The price of short-term lending between banks also soared as trust between banks weakened. Before Lehman's bankruptcy, the three-month LIBOR traded around 1% over a three-month U.S. Treasury bill. By the close of September 16, it was trading at 2.03%, and by October 10, 2008, it was trading at 4.57% above U.S. Treasuries (see Figure 12.1).

> We could have survived it in my opinion, but it would have been terrible. I would have stopped lending, marketing, investing . . . and probably laid off 20,000 people. And I would have done it in three weeks. You get companies starting to take actions like that, that's what a Great Depression is.
>
> —Jamie Dimon, CEO of J.P. Morgan (FCIC 2010)

Lehman was a major prime broker. All the hedge funds with prime brokerage accounts at Lehman had to scramble, causing further market turmoil by selling stocks and other securities. The bankruptcy affected 8,000 subsidiaries with $600 billion in assets and liabilities, more than 100,000

FIGURE 12.1 Spread of LIBOR over U.S. Treasuries

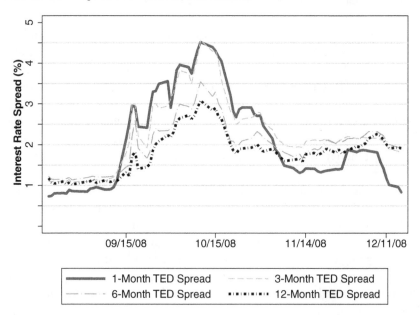

Sources: FRED and Bloomberg.

creditors, and 26,000 employees. Creditors filed more than 66,000 claims against Lehman Brothers. It was the most complex bankruptcy case ever filed in the United States.

The period saw staggering job loss in the financial industry alone. A total of 711,000 jobs disappeared from 2007 to 2009, not counting the other jobs linked to the financial sector.

The Lehman bankruptcy affected everyone. One of the more obscure absurdities occurred in the long-term lending markets. This absurdity hurt lending markets and destroyed a large class of hedge fund intermediaries.

Markets depend on valuation and the actions of market participants. Any disturbance in the natural course of supply and demand can dramatically alter market prices, sometimes pushing them far from what might be considered reasonable.

Each marketplace participant has a usual, specific role. Generally speaking, fixed-income relative-value hedge funds act as financial intermediaries for medium- and longer-term demand and supply imbalances. When most market participants crave short-term liquidity at the expense of long-term yield, for instance, these hedge funds will sell short-term bonds and buy longer-term bonds (or bond-equivalent instruments). The hedge funds are long the yield curve in order to satiate the supply-demand imbalance. The spread usually compensates them for the risk of this activity, because they absorb an imbalance that other participants aren't willing to bear.

In this respect, many of these hedge funds complement the dealers' function.[2]

Dealers, including Lehman Brothers, Bear Stearns, Goldman Sachs, and Morgan Stanley, perform similar market functions. They stand ready to buy when the market is rushing to sell and stand ready to sell when the market is ready to buy.

There is a symbiotic relationship between these hedge funds and the dealer community. Some hedge funds actually augment dealers' risk capacity. These hedge funds also create leverage by borrowing from broker-dealers through repo agreements and other mechanisms.

Lehman was a massive financial intermediary. It absorbed supply and demand imbalances and offered revolving financing to a whole host of institutions, including relative-value hedge funds. Before Lehman went bankrupt in September 2008, no large OTC-intermediary had ever been allowed to fail in a disorderly fashion. Even when Drexel collapsed in the late 1980s and Refco failed in 2005, regulators preserved their trading books to unwind or transfer positions to another institution.[3]

Lehman was involved in all sorts of dealer trading, including commodities, real estate, equities, and fixed income. Many of its positions were OTC deals, rather than exchange-cleared deals. This created a web of interdependencies, as with LTCM in 1998. Because Lehman was relatively more involved in fixed-income trading and was generally known as one of the world's premier fixed-income intermediaries, its bankruptcy had the potential to disrupt fixed-income markets.

The International Swaps and Derivatives Association (ISDA) stipulates that counterparties have the option to terminate positions with a bankrupt firm at the closing prices on the day of the bankruptcy filing. Counterparties could do this by simply sending Lehman a fax on September 15, 2008.

The Long-Dated Swap Imbalance

Lehman was in the intermediary business.[4]

To illustrate the damage that Lehman's bankruptcy did to the financial system, assume that all of Lehman's exposure was from market making, giving the firm only counterparty risks from its large OTC book. Then consider one part of Lehman's book: 30-year interest-rate swaps (IRS).

An interest-rate swap is an agreement between two parties to exchange a series of cash flows over a defined number of years. In a typical IRS, one party pays a fixed interest rate for the entire period and the other party pays a floating rate, which depends on prevailing interest rates at the time of payment. Payments are usually made every six months, although they can be made at any interval.

Investors tend to invest in their *preferred habitats*—the places that make the most sense for their businesses. Pension funds are the most likely *receivers* on a 30-year IRS. Generally, pension funds promise to pay retirees some guaranteed amount in the distant future. The present discounted value of this liability is very sensitive to interest-rate changes.[5] The pension plan has assets, which need to match the liabilities so that the pension will be *fully funded* and be able to meet its liabilities. To measure this, consider the Surplus $= A - L$, where A represents the assets' present discounted value and L represents the liabilities' present discounted value. If these are equal, the pension fund has exactly enough assets to pay off its liabilities.

Over time, interest rates may change, altering the present discounted value of the liabilities by a significant amount, given their long duration.[6] To minimize the risks from interest rate changes, a pension fund should invest assets such that its interest rate exposure is equal to that of its liabilities. One way to do this is to match the assets' durations to those of the liabilities.

This is why pension funds are natural receivers for the fixed-rate leg of an IRS. The investor that receives the fixed part of an IRS is long duration, while the floating rate's receiver is short duration. Pension funds would have entered into an IRS with Lehman Brothers to receive fixed.

Lehman, being an intermediary, did not want to hold this risk. Market makers provide a service by buying or selling, but they don't want to keep the risk they incur. On this IRS, Lehman was short duration. To offset the trade and stay neutral, Lehman would enter contracts with other institutions—natural payers for the IRS's fixed rate.

Natural fixed-rate payers included sovereign debt management offices and hedge funds. These institutions used IRS to balance the durations of their debt portfolios.

For an example, consider Italy. Figure 12.2 shows the Italian government yield curve and the Italian Euro swap curve. In 2004 and for long maturities, Italy's debt curve had higher yields than did its swap curve.

A smart Italian Treasury official might issue five-year Italian bonds. But the bonds won't have a sufficiently large negative duration.[7] Governments often issue longer-date bonds, such as 30-year bonds. Instead, the Italian Treasury

FIGURE 12.2   The Italian Swap and Government Zero Curve on February 20, 2007

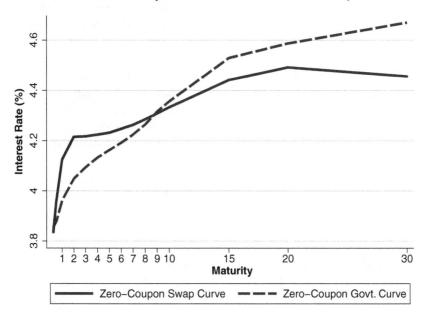

FIGURE 12.3   A Typical Swap Situation with Lehman Brothers

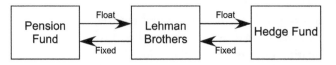

could pay a fixed rate on the 30-year swaps, at a cheaper cost than that of similar maturity Italian government bonds and extend negative duration to the desired level. This could also be true for other sovereigns.

Hedge funds, especially fixed-income hedge funds, use these swaps to alter portfolio duration. Paying a fixed rate on an IRS is equivalent to being short duration, so a hedge fund uses swaps to reduce portfolio duration in the presence of other fixed-income instruments.

Figure 12.3 depicts Lehman's basic intermediary function.

Now that we understand the natural habitats of different market participants in these trades, we can analyze what happened on September 15, 2008. Lehman announced bankruptcy and the ISDA allowed swap counterparties to terminate their positions. What moves do various investors make?

A pension fund could close its position with Lehman or keep it open. Suppose it keeps the position with Lehman. Because of the crisis and recession, 2008 had a declining interest rate environment. The pension fund would receive cash payments at regular intervals from Lehman going forward. But Lehman was bankrupt, so it would likely take years to receive those payments, if the fund ever received them at all. Keeping the contracts open did not make sense. Pension funds and fixed receivers with Lehman terminated these positions.

Once the pension funds closed their positions with Lehman, they would be exposed to an asset-liability mismatch. They would be extremely short duration in an environment where interest rates were expected to decline. This would be devastating for managing their liabilities, which would increase over their assets. They replaced all the swaps they had with Lehman with other counterparties.

What about hedge funds and parties paying fixed rates to Lehman? If interest rates rose, they would have the same problem collecting payments from Lehman. If interest rates went down, Lehman would come after them for money. There was no upside—and substantial potential downside—to keeping the contracts with Lehman, so they also closed their Lehman contracts. (This could be done without market impact, as no trades were necessary.)

Once they terminated their contracts with Lehman, these hedge funds wouldn't necessarily rush to replace their fixed-rate paying swaps. Many thought interest rates would come down, so being a fixed-rate payer was not wise. Many hedge funds waited for the uncertainty to resolve itself before reestablishing positions.

That created an imbalance of supply and demand. The demand for receiving long-dated swaps was very high, but the supply of investors willing to pay on long-dated swaps was very low. This imbalance had two unprecedented results.

First, the swap yield relative to the Treasury narrowed and became more expensive. The U.S. dollar swap curve nearly always trades at a higher interest rate than U.S. Treasury debt, because the swap rate depends on loans between banks, and banks are considered riskier than the U.S. government. After the Lehman collapse, the one-year swap spread stayed positive, the 10-year became slightly negative and hovered around zero, but the 30-year spread went significantly negative (see Figure 12.4).

These rates implied that 30-year interbank loans were safer than government loans. This same phenomenon also occurred in other countries (see Table 12.1). This seems insane, but it was the dominant effect created by the supply and demand imbalance.

FIGURE 12.4   The U.S. Swap Spread

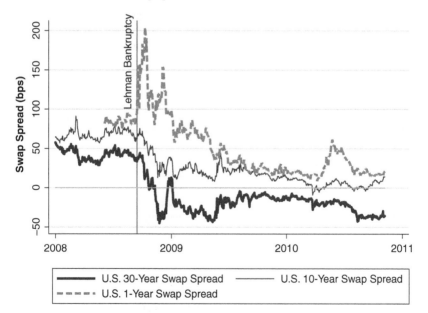

Source: Bloomberg.

TABLE 12.1   Historical Average Swap Spreads

	Average Daily Spread		
	Before Lehman	After Lehman I	After Lehman II
United States			
1-Year	55.392	124.021	43.599
10-Year	58.924	43.468	16.352
30-Year	54.821	0.692	−19.606
United Kingdom			
1-Year	45.901	138.544	63.386
10-Year	48.747	35.729	17.394
30-Year	49.213	−29.319	−30.154
Japan			
1-Year	13.105	39.830	35.453
10-Year	15.793	4.061	4.014
30-Year	6.947	−24.756	−10.377
Italy			
10-Year	−2.378	−39.427	−86.276
30-Year	−10.980	−105.976	−143.559
Germany			
1-Year	19.525	133.163	72.410
10-Year	28.766	64.074	31.425
30-Year	20.278	−6.413	−9.329

Note: Before Lehman was measured from January 2, 1995, to September 1, 2008. After Lehman I was measured from September 15, 2008, to December 31, 2008. After Lehman II was measured from September 15, 2008, to March 24, 2011.

Source: Generic swap and government curves from Bloomberg measured in basis points.

Hedge funds that had provided capital by paying swaps to pension funds drowned in the sea of absurdity. Relative-value hedge funds that provided market liquidity by being long the 30-year spread got crushed. Many did not survive, which made the overall situation even worse.

Second, spreads widen in many financial crises, including the LTCM and Russian crises, as firms take up a flight to quality. This time it did not happen. The Lehman bankruptcy caused a very unusual imbalance between swaps and government bonds.[8]

The Repo Imbalance

One of the functions of a hedge fund or arbitrageur is to buy cheap securities and sell expensive securities. Of course, everyone tries to do that in the money management business.

There are reasons that market participants create cheap and expensive securities. Behavioral biases might cause them to invest in ways that create opportunities for others. Or perhaps institutional constraints create market disequilibrium and let investors without these institutional constraints profit from it.[9]

When a majority of institutions sell a particular bond rather than another very similar bond, the sold bond becomes cheaper versus the other bond. For example, if the major money in the corporate 10-year bond space is pension fund money, and most pension funds won't buy debt rated below AAA, this might create a natural opportunity in debt rated below AAA.[10] A relative-value hedge fund might benefit by purchasing cheap bonds and selling expensive ones. As long as just a small fraction of market dollars chase these strategies, these funds will make risk-adjusted profits over time.

Lehman was one of the most active brokers in the global fixed-income repo business. It generally acted as a true broker, or intermediary. A typical transaction might look like this.

A hedge fund buys a cheap bond and repo's it to Lehman. Lehman gives the bond to a second-tier bank in exchange for a securitized loan, which goes back to the hedge fund. Both the bond and the funds pass through Lehman, which serves as the intermediary.

Lehman also acted as the intermediary in reverse repo trades. In this case, a long-only bond manager, treasury department, or central bank lent a bond to Lehman. These were usually expensive bonds, such as on-the-run bonds, that the long-only portfolio manager would lend out to earn a little extra

FIGURE 12.5   Example of Lehman Repo Book with Relative-Value Hedge Funds

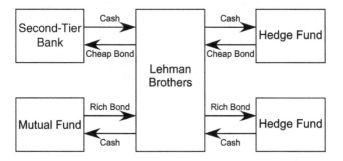

on the portfolio. Financing at repo and lending at LIBOR would give the long-only manager this extra spread.

On the trade's other side was the hedge fund, which engaged in a reverse repo by giving Lehman cash in exchange for the expensive bond. Then the hedge fund sold the bond in the marketplace. The transaction made the hedge fund long cheap bonds and short expensive bonds. Figure 12.5 depicts this situation.

Lehman's bankruptcy wreaked chaos and imbalance in the repo marketplace. To understand how, start with the cheap bond side. At Lehman's bankruptcy, its counterparties had the option of terminating repo or reverse repo contracts. Virtually all parties had an incentive to do so, because keeping the contract was too risky and might have involved spending years in bankruptcy court, hoping to be paid.

The second-tier bank would close the contract. The bank was left holding a cheap bond, but really wanted cash. So the bank would sell this cheap bond, making the bond even cheaper. The hedge fund on the other side was left holding cash. Given the turbulent markets, hedge funds might have wanted to reduce risk, and cheap bonds were losing value in the face of selloffs. The hedge fund might have kept the cash.

A mutual fund would be left with cash and thus the wrong exposure in its fixed-income portfolio. To balance that exposure, the mutual fund would immediately replace the expensive bond. The purchase made the bond even more expensive. The hedge fund on the other side had originally borrowed the rich bond in order to sell it. That hedge fund would be net neutral and take no action.

That's how these two imbalances made expensive bonds more expensive and cheap bonds even cheaper. This was not a big problem for the overall markets, but it caused severe trouble for a group of relative-value hedge funds.

These funds (and other intermediaries) suffered large losses because they were generally short expensive bonds and long cheap bonds.

Box 12.1. Buy Cheap and Sell Expensive

How does an intermediary hedge fund find a cheap bond to buy and an expensive bond to sell? One way is to look at the swap curve and the government bond curve of yields plotted versus maturity. Draw a curve through the points. The curve is relatively smooth until it reaches the 10-year maturity.

After this point, the curve shows a jump in yields. This is because most of these securities—with maturities around 11, 12, or 13 years—are really old 30-year government bonds. The U.S. government auctions the 10-year and 30-year bonds, but no maturities in between. Old 30-year bonds have higher coupons because interest rates were higher 20 years ago. They are very illiquid, largely because the pension funds and other institutions that buy them don't typically sell them. Because they're not very liquid, these bonds offer a more attractive yield. These are cheap bonds.

Mutual fund managers, on the other hand, usually own Treasuries with maturities of fewer than 10 years. More people purchase securities with maturities of fewer than 10 years than purchase securities with maturities of more than 10 years. But a twelve-year-old, off-the-run bond might have the same duration risk as a relatively new eight- or nine-year bond. A hedge fund might go long the twelve-year bond and short the nine-year bond, making a yield pickup of 12 basis points with a portfolio that has most risk shut down to 0. Of course, there is a shadow risk in this trade: liquidity risk.

The 228 Wasted Resources and the Global Run on Banks

On September 29, 2008, the House failed to vote for the Troubled Asset Relief Program (TARP) and the global run on banks began.[11] Banks and dealers began cutting their risks, which included reducing their balance sheets. Many investment banks had positions that were similar to those of the relative-value hedge funds. Both groups were long cheap assets and short expensive assets. As banks began cutting their positions, they sold cheap assets and bought back expensive assets, in order to reduce their leverage and trim their balance sheets. These actions significantly affected the relative-value hedge funds that had similar positions. Their positions began losing money.

Banks began cutting their balance sheets in other ways. They reduced financing to hedge funds and other counterparties. Hedge funds and other investors that did not have contingent lending agreements had to reduce their own net exposures, again by selling cheap assets and buying back expensive assets. This increased the huge market imbalance.

As this feedback loop continued, relative-value hedge funds and other market intermediaries continued reducing risk in a downward spiral that generated further imbalance and large losses for all involved.

Lehman's failure affected all lending markets, corporate borrowing, relative-value hedge funds, and even quantitative hedge funds. When Barclays took control of Lehman Brothers after the bankruptcy, its lack of knowledge led to actions that had dire consequences for some counterparties.

One very well-known quant hedge fund at Goldman Sachs had used Lehman as a prime broker. They had derivative trades with Lehman. When the bankruptcy hit, this quant fund didn't even know what its positions were, including swap trades and equity futures. According to someone at this hedge fund, Barclays ordered Lehman to liquidate its futures positions, and by mistake they liquidated customer positions. The hedge fund called Barclays the next morning and asked what Barclays had done with its position. "Get in line with all the creditors and sue us," Barclays reportedly replied. The hedge fund had to quickly redo all its positions, causing more marketplace chaos.[12]

We found out the hard way that you can't let a major market intermediary unexpectedly fail. For those who wondered what would have happened had LTCM failed in 1998, Lehman Brothers was the answer. Its failure caused absolute chaos in both the short and long ends of the markets.

We also learned that, because of the symbiotic relationship between hedge funds and dealers, it is not clear that hedge funds can provide intermediation services when the market needs them most. A large OTC dealer's bankruptcy is not the same as that of a broker-dealer operating in markets that trade through exchanges.

When Lehman failed, the market realized that government officials were making it up as they went along. So were banking regulators. Why didn't anyone in Basel smell disaster approaching?

CHAPTER 13

Asleep in Basel

> *You will never understand bureaucracies until you understand that for bureaucrats procedure is everything and outcomes are nothing.*
>
> —Thomas Sowell

It was a cool day in Mooslargue, France, in 1999, where I stood at the first tee of La Largue golf course, the private course near Basel where members of the Bank for International Settlements (BIS) played. It was a day of golf for Fed Chairman Alan Greenspan and Bank for International Settlements (BIS) head Andrew Crockett. Angus Butler, head of central bank sales, and I were invited, too. Greenspan was very old, and I was surprised at how well he hit the ball on the driving range. Crockett, a native Scot, was a very respectable golfer, as was Butler.

Greenspan aimed his ball down the left side of the fairway. On the first hole at La Largue, there is a large pond to the right of the fairway. His swing was brisk, but some sidespin sent it slicing into the lake. Splash! Someone yelled, "Your ball went into the water." Greenspan just nodded his head and in a New York accent said, "You don't say."

Greenspan, who had been considered a financial-markets god, was human. We could slice a ball into the water, and so could he. The same logic applies to all regulators. They don't always have the right rules, and they can't always keep up with private-sector innovations.

The Bank for International Settlements (BIS) is in Basel, Switzerland. One of its two main offices is in front of the Bahnhof and houses the monetary and economics department (MED). This is where economists do research for central banks and the global economy. They also host monthly meetings of central bank governors from around the world. This is also the home of a curious little group known as the Basel Committee.

About a block down Aeschengrabbe Strasse is the former UBS building, which became a BIS office in 1999. This office hosts BIS trading and banking operations, routing hundreds of billions of central bank reserves through the markets every day.

It's the Basel Committee that had the most to do with the banking crisis, because it set standards for banks across the world.[1] The committee meets four times per year. The BIS provides its secretariat and expert advisor subcommittees.

The committee has no formal supranational supervisory authority and its rules have no legal force. They are regulatory guidelines only. In practice, however, its recommendations have the force of rules and are generally followed.

To understand the Basel Committee, one must understand BIS dynamics. The BIS is very conservative, a trait that other regulators share. Its staff members are typically good politicians, though not always especially innovative or financially keen. The BIS doesn't generally appreciate creative or critical thinking, and this weaves into the Basel Committee's proposals for regulation.[2]

The committee is best known for its international standards on capital adequacy for banks and core principles for effective banking supervision. It expressed these ideas in three major documents about banking supervision: Basel I, II, and III.

Basel I

Basel I was published in 1988. It focuses on bank *credit risk*, thought to be the major risk that banks face. Basel I proposed adequate capital ratio guidelines for banks. By proposing a minimum capital adequacy ratio (CAR), the committee hoped to prevent the banking crises that might follow excessive risk. It also hoped to create a global banking standard that would limit geographical bank arbitrage and create a level playing field.

The Concept

The CAR has two components: a firm's weighted risk assets and its capital.[3] The formula divides capital by risk-weighted assets. The higher the capital ratio, the lower the bank's leverage and the greater its security. More capital

TABLE 13.1 Basel I Risk Weightings for On-Balance-Sheet Items

Weight (%)	Type of Asset
0	Cash, Government Debt of OECD countries.
20	Claims on banks and the public sector of OECD countries.
50	Mortgage loans on residential real estate.
100	Claims on private sector, equity investments, subordinated loans, claims on government debt of non-OECD countries.

Note: The Basel I documents also include off-balance-sheet items. The conversion into loan-equivalent values and then into the corresponding risk weighting is more complicated and not included in this table. OECD is the group of 34 countries that make up the Organisation for Economic Co-operation and Development.
Source: BIS.

and fewer assets push ratios higher. Asset type also matters. Very liquid or relatively safe assets also push ratios higher. (See Table 13.1 for common risk weights.)

Banks with more capital relative to assets and more high-quality assets have higher CARs. Suppose a bank had $100 million in assets and $10 million in equity capital. If all the assets were secure U.S. Treasury bills, its CAR would be infinite. If the $100 million were invested in mortgage-backed securities, the bank's CAR would be 20%. U.S. Treasuries are extremely liquid, so they have no risk weight. Mortgages are more risky and thus have a higher weight.

The Basel Committee proposed 8% as a bank's minimum CAR.[4] Most regulatory agencies adopted these guidelines.

There are two ways to interpret the minimum capital ratio. First, a bank with more shareholder capital has more skin in the game, which explicitly limits its leverage. (Leverage and the capital adequacy ratio are inversely related.) Second, if a bank's assets and liabilities are marked to market, the firm's true shareholder equity is the difference between its assets and liabilities. A bank with more shareholder capital can bear more losses, because its assets are higher than its liabilities.

The Problems

There were several problems with Basel I as a risk-measuring mechanism for banks.

Basel I was mainly concerned with credit risk. OECD countries received a smaller risk weighting (a weighting of zero percent). Non-OECD countries were given a 100% risk weighting.

Market risk matters for predicting losses. Basel I didn't account for the possibility of two non-OECD countries, one with much higher bond volatility.[5]

Basel I considered risk weightings for different private loans as the same, even though different companies have substantially different risks.

Basel I didn't accurately consider loan and bond maturities in assessing risks. Its deductions were crude and imprecise. For example, longer maturity instruments are generally more risky than shorter maturity instruments, but Basel I doesn't account for this.

The guidelines didn't consider risk diversification. In Basel I, a pool of credit risks with well-diversified counterparty correlation has the same risk weight as one with heavily concentrated counterparties.

Basel I let banks engage in regulatory arbitrage. Many instruments' true measured risk was different than their assigned risk under the regulatory requirements, so banks might replace assets with lower true risk with assets carrying higher true risk. That gave a lower measured risk, according to the BIS ratio, but meant that banks could look healthier than they actually were.

Banking capital ratios can be very effective if assets and liabilities, and therefore equity capital, are measured accurately. If measurements are stale, then it's very difficult to know whether current capital ratios are compliant or not, or to know which banks are riskier than their peers.[6]

Why did regulators leave these errors in Basel I? The BIS emphasis on conservatism over creativity and accuracy is one reason. Regulators must compromise, and the rules aim to be simple, which can sacrifice accuracy.

Basel II

Seeing Basel I's limitations, the committee began modifying Basel I in the years after 1988. The main modification was a mechanism to account for market risks.[7]

The Concept

Market risk modifications were strongest for bonds. (The risk weightings were adjusted so that longer-duration bonds counted as higher risk.) The changes also included modifications to account for risk in equities, commodities, and foreign exchange rates, but these had much weaker criteria.[8]

Adjusted rules also let banks measure their own market risk internally with techniques such as VaR.[9]

The group released Basel II in June 2004.[10]

Basel II enhanced risk weightings to include an institution's rating as defined by nationally recognized rating agencies (Moody's, S&P, and Fitch). Higher-rated debt would receive a lower risk weighting than would lower-rated debt. For example, AAA-rated corporate bonds received a 20% risk weighting, versus a 100% risk weighting for bonds rated BBB + or lower.

In one of the most important changes related to the 2008 financial crisis, Basel II reduced the mortgage-loan risk weighting from 50% to 35%. Credit losses on mortgages had been historically low, and the committee was fooled by the history of real estate and mortgage prices, just like everyone else.

The new rules specified minimum haircuts for different types of collateral, including stocks. These haircuts reflected assets' general market risk.

Basel II let banks use internal models to assess market risk, which had already been part of the amendments to Basel I. This change established a new role for supervisory authorities, which would issue rules and procedures for banks that wanted to assess their own market risks.

Basel II also intended to make it easier for third parties to assess a bank's risk, while recognizing that this is a difficult goal. The new rules required banks to give market participants prompt, detailed disclosure of risks and capital, including asset size and composition, credit exposure distribution, risk measurement and control systems, accounting practices, and capital allocation criteria.

Finally, Basel II suggested that banks have capital requirements to account for operational risk: the risk of loss from inadequate or failed internal processes, people, and systems, or from external events.

The Problems

Basel II was better than Basel I. Most importantly, it fine-tuned the capital ratios for credit risk, considering differently rated debt.[11] The addition of market risks was conceptually very important, but its application may have brought too much comfort to banks and their investors.

Basel II also had its problems. Lowering mortgage weights encouraged banks to load up on more real estate and related investments.

Basel II's risk weightings didn't correlate entirely with the actual differential default rates of different type of bonds. For example, a typical B-rated bond's default rate might be 100 times higher than that of a typical BBB-rated bond, yet the difference in credit weights was just 150% versus 100%

(a difference of 1.5 times). This was an inconsistency and an opportunity for regulatory arbitrage.

Although Basel II considered how hard it is for outsiders to monitor banks' true risks, the standard reporting items it required were not sufficient to truly expose bank risks. This, in part, led to runs on banks that may have otherwise been healthy.

Basel II let banks use a VaR structure with simplified minimum requirements. These requirements let banks use different methodologies (short term instead of long term measurement periods, for instance). Most of all, the new rules let banks rely on a historical variance-covariance return matrix that might not reflect correlation's behavior in a crisis. This may have helped banks become too comfortable with their risk.

In 2000, Myron Scholes cautioned against VaR in Davos, Switzerland. He had witnessed firsthand the market craze in the LTCM debacle.

> Before the financial crisis in August 1998, most financial institutions were well within the guidelines for capital adequacy specified by the Bank for International Settlements (BIS) on standard measures such as VaR, leverage, or tier I or tier II capital. Then in August, investors rushed to more liquid securities. Over the last several years, regulators have encouraged financial entities to use portfolio theory to produce dynamic measures of risk. VaR, the product of portfolio theory, is used for short-run day-to-day profit and loss-risk exposures. Now is the time to encourage the BIS and other regulatory bodies to support studies on stress-test and concentration methodologies.
> —Myron Scholes (Scholes 2000)

When banks could use internal market risk models, they took on more risk. A 2003 Federal Deposit Insurance Corporation (FDIC) study found that the new requirements would probably reduce the capital levels of most American banks. Others believed that this might also favor large banks, which would have the in-house resources to do their own risk monitoring and might lower their capital ratios as a result. Political influence from the International Swaps and Derivatives Association (ISDA) may have influenced the Basel Committee when it decided against including provisions for regulating banks' trading books.[12]

Basel and the Financial Crisis

Financial regulation is inherently difficult, because private markets use progress and innovation as survival tactics. Capital markets and their participants typically find ways to follow the rules while also maximizing profits. If regulators propose capital rules that are incorrect but widely recognized, then individual banks will exploit this opportunity so they can borrow capital at artificially lower rates and invest at higher rates.

Basel I and II had major shortcomings, all of which exposed the financial system to danger in 2008.

Perhaps the most important problem was that Basel II lowered the mortgage risk weighting from 50% to 35%. This gave banks one more reason to load up on real estate exposure. Suppose a bank has $100 in assets, with $20 invested in Treasury bonds and $80 invested in residential MBS. It also has liabilities valued at $96 and therefore shareholder equity of $4. Its CAR would be 10% under the Basel I mortgage rules. Under the Basel II mortgage rules, its ratio would rise to 14%. If a bank wanted to keep a 10% capital ratio, it could now substitute MBS for Treasury securities. Even if this hypothetical bank placed 100% of its assets in mortgages, its capital ratio would still be 11.4%. By investing an additional 20% in mortgages, the bank would improve its capital adequacy ratio under Basel II as compared to Basel I, absent the investment.

This modified incentive to buy mortgages is one of the reasons that U.S. on-balance-sheet mortgages grew from 6% of GDP to 20% of GDP from 2004 to 2008. This occurred in other countries as well. The British government took over the lender Northern Rock on February 22, 2008, due to subprime mortgage troubles. In July 2007, the bank increased its dividend. CEO Adam Applegarth's reason? "Because we had just completed our Basel II two-and-a-half-year process and . . . it meant we had surplus capital and therefore that could be repatriated to shareholders through increasing the dividend."[13]

Banks exploited Basel II's reduced capital charges for AAA-securitized assets. Some loaded up on securitized AAA-rated mortgage tranches, which carried a 7% capital charge. From March 2004 to June 2007, these exposures grew enormously, more than they had in the previous 20 years.

The new rules' reliance on VaR as a market-risk measure allowed banks to understate risks. In economic crises, many instruments' correlations move close to one. Popular VaR measures didn't account for crowds, for interconnectedness, or for securities' underlying valuations.

Basel II's requirements for capital ratios and types were too low. It may have allowed implicit leverage that was too high because it required too little capital and had incorrect risk weightings.

The Basel accords bring procyclicality to the system. As more and more banks follow similar rules, they may behave similarly during booms and crises, further exacerbating the cycles. For example, if VaR models are widely used and based on recent historical volatility, they may encourage all participants to cut risk at exactly the same time.

After Basel II, in 2005, the Basel Committee examined the issue of CDOs and credit default swaps. The committee concluded that no undue concentrations were developing and that the monoline financial guarantors (such as AIG) knew what they were doing. Furthermore, they suggested that firms involved in CDOs should make sure they understand their risks.[14] The committee missed this one.[15]

In the future, the Basel Committee and other regulators must be more ambitious, not so much in the number of rules they create, but perhaps by substituting forward-thinking talent for risk-averse bureaucrats. Regulators need stronger incentives to attract top talent, talent that is motivated to keep up as the markets innovate around specific guidelines.

By reducing the risk weighting for mortgages and allowing banks a relatively high amount of leverage assisted by regulatory arbitrage, the Basel Committee encouraged banks to load up on mortgage-backed securities. That fueled the boom. When the mortgage market crashed and Lehman failed, the financial turbulence washed away the last intermediaries: the relative-value hedge funds. One of the casualties was JWMP, Meriwether's new hedge fund.

CHAPTER 14

The LTCM Spinoffs

> *... LTCM will emerge a stronger and better firm.*
>
> —John Meriwether

JWM Partners LLC

LTCM finally closed in December 1999. Its principals remained with the firm for a year, working with the fund's new owners to carefully close it down. The partners were stressed and demoralized, but many still found the energy to prepare for the next stage of their professional lives. The most notable new venture was JWM Partners LLC (JWMP), launched in December 1999. The initials in the firm's name were those of John W. Meriwether.

To raise new capital, LTCM's partners assured investors that the crisis had taught them a lot, and that the new funds would maintain lower leverage ratios than LTCM.[1]

John Meriwether had incubated his idea for a new fund for a while. After paying off original investors in April 1999, the partners began talking about starting a new fund. Some partners wanted a sense of personal redemption, others wanted to try again after learning LTCM's lessons, and a third group, including Meriwether, simply loved trading and saw terrific opportunities in arbitrage.

Hans Hufschmid was one of the few who did not join Meriwether in launching a new fund. He thought that the new firm "was always going to be a tainted firm," and that the "trading strategy was flawed." He saw a lot of the relative-value trades as basic mean-reversion trades.[2] LTCM traders thought about the economics of their trades, but Hufschmid still felt that statistics drove many trades. Traders, he believed, needed to think more about why something was cheap or expensive. He thought that the relative-value market was becoming too much like the foreign-exchange market, where models were less important and trader intuition was growing more important. Nevertheless, a group of core LTCM partners, including Dick Leahy, Larry Hilibrand, Victor Haghani, Arjun Krishnamachar, and Eric Rosenfeld joined Meriwether and began to raise capital for the new fund.

Raising money was very challenging. Eric Rosenfeld tells the story of visiting a very wealthy Brazilian family. He presented the new fund, talking about what the partners had learned and how they would manage risk better in JWMP. The father was skeptical, saying that he couldn't risk his savings with JWMP. The son claimed that JWMP's partners were so burned by the LTCM crisis that they would be afraid to take risks, so the fund would never perform very well.

Despite these struggles, the partners found a new group of about 70 investors. They started the fund with $250 million, of which less than $10 million came from the partners.

At the time, some criticized hedge funds, in particular JWMP, for having a "devious" scheme for starting a new fund and hanging the old investors out to dry. When hedge funds lose a significant amount of money, managers often close that fund and start a new one. Incentive fees, which are based on hedge fund performance and can be as much as 20% of raw returns, can only be awarded once a hedge fund reaches its calculated high-water mark.

A fund that drops by a large amount—perhaps 50% or more—will take many years to climb back to its original level (its high-water mark), so it won't be able to charge incentive fees. Managers, who are very interested in incentive fees, often close that fund and start a new one. It's almost a normal practice, which is probably not good for the overall hedge-fund community.

JWMP offered LTCM investors a chance to invest in JWMP with not just the old high-water mark, but double the high-water mark. That was potentially a very good deal. Suppose an original LTCM investor was left with $100 when LTCM closed at a high-water mark of $1,000. JWMP said that, for every new $50 invested, the high-water mark would be $1,000. Investors took JWMP up on the deal, putting in $30 million to $40 million, or about 7% of original investor assets.[3]

JWMP was significantly different from LTCM. LTCM saw itself as a financial technology company. It had planned to do other things in addition to managing money, including an asset-management partnership with an Italian bank.

LTCM helped a major Italian bank, Banco Nazionale del Lavoro (BNL), modernize and revolutionize its retail investment space. Project principals included Bob Merton, Myron Scholes, and Italian native Alberto Giovannini.[4] I was slated to be the junior guy on this project.

At the time, in 1998, the U.S. financial markets had begun using technological innovations, including eTRADE and other discount brokerages, to improve the investment landscape. Italy was far behind in this respect. The LTCM-Banco Nazionale del Lavoro partnership hoped to offer Italian investors a product suite that let them invest efficiently and cheaply while making full use of investment theory.

For example, suppose an investor had an occupation with heavy exposure to the construction industry. Finance theory tells us that ideally, this person should own a portfolio of stocks that has a lower proportion of construction stocks than the average investor's portfolio. When you consider the person's wage income, her true portfolio has a much larger exposure to construction than it should. One of the ways to improve this investor's overall diversification is to build a portfolio that has a lower than normal or even negative exposure to construction stocks. This was one of the many ideas that this joint collaboration would have achieved. It wasn't a hedge fund and it was very innovative. LTCM didn't see its hedge fund as the end product. Its goal was to apply quantitative and creative techniques to create an impressive financial company. Unfortunately, the hedge fund that would have provided the initial fuel to do this collapsed before it could be done.

> We were a couple of decades ahead of the market, designing solutions that now are being introduced for the first time: life-cycle savings and other innovations. Unfortunately, I don't think the bank in Italy really understood this and caused negotiations to drag on. They were after the high returns of the LTCM fund at a time when stock markets were yielding double digits. That was of course the wrong attitude. Management in the bank was fearful that this partnership would cause them to lose control. So there was a lot of resistance. Thirteen years later, asset management in Italy is still where it was then.
>
> —Alberto Giovannini interview, Senior Member of LTCM,
> October 20, 2011

LTCM invested a lot of resources in researching and developing technology. JWMP was less interested in technology and more focused on money management.

Beginning in December 1999, JWM Partners launched two funds. The Relative Value Opportunity fund was a bond fund in the LTCM tradition. This was JWMP's principal fund. The JWM Global Macro fund invested in broad global trends through currencies, commodities, stocks, and bonds. John Meriwether and Dick Leahy managed it from its May 2003 launch.

The relative-value fund had a 2% management fee and a 20% incentive fee.[5] The macro fund charged a 1.5% management fee and a 20% incentive fee. The global macro fund's after-fee performance from May 2003 through December 2007 was 6.70% with 9% volatility and a 0.40 Sharpe ratio.

The relative-value fund differed from LTCM mainly in risk management. The fund's risk management practice focused on the extreme possibility that strategy correlations could reach 1. LTCM had considered higher strategy correlations, but the new fund made decisions as if all strategies had a realistic potential of having correlations of 1. This was a more arduous stress test than any used at LTCM.

As a result, the new fund had a lower leverage ratio: 15:1, compared with LTCM's 25:1 leverage ratio. In each fund's first three years, LTCM had an average monthly return of 2.31% and a monthly volatility of 2.59%. JWMP had a 0.87% monthly return and a 1.28% monthly standard deviation. The new firm's risk was about half that of LTCM, and its returns were between a third and a half of its predecessor's. LTCM's Sharpe ratio was 2.54 during its first three years, much higher than JWMP's 1.63.

JWMP existed from December 1999 to April 2009. It performed reasonably well during its first eight years, which led up to the 2008 financial crisis. Before 2008, the fund's average annual return was 8.55%, with a standard deviation of 3.81%. The fund's Sharpe ratio was 1.33. In comparison, the S&P 500 had a Sharpe ratio of 0.00 over the same period. The fund's best monthly return was 3.64%; its worst monthly return was −2.99%.

Table 14.1 shows JWMP's performance and that of other well-known relative-value hedge funds and major asset classes, such as the S&P 500.

JWMP's raw returns didn't fare well against copycat funds.[6]

Its Sharpe and Sortino ratios put JWMP somewhere in the middle of this selection of relative-value funds.[7]

JWMP controlled its downside better than the other funds. Its worst monthly return was −2.99%, which is better than all but two of its peers (Parkcentral and Smith Breeden). A portfolio of relative-value hedge funds (HFR RV Index) has a much higher Sharpe ratio than all the selected relative-value funds.[8]

The JWMP fund provided a much better alternative to standard asset classes over this period. Its Sharpe ratio was nearly double that of the asset class with the highest Sharpe ratio in this table, showing that these other asset classes could not be leveraged to provide the same level of return as JWMP without having much more monthly risk. Even considering their leverage, these hedge funds did better than other asset classes.

With success came more assets. By 2007, JWMP managed roughly $3 billion in assets, most of it from fund-of-funds investors.

TABLE 14.1 The LTCM Spinoff and Copycat Returns

Hedge Funds	Average	S.D.	Sharpe	Sortino	$\hat{\alpha}$	Max	Min
December 1999–December 2007							
JWMP	8.55	3.81	1.33	0.53	4.15	3.64	−2.99
June 2000–December 2007							
JWMP	8.56	3.88	1.35	0.54	4.04	3.64	−2.99
PGAM	8.98	4.54	1.25	0.49	4.83	4.26	−3.16
Smith Breeden	12.64	5.23	1.73	0.80	6.22	4.89	−2.24
Parkcentral	11.11	4.53	1.68	0.80	6.97	7.98	−2.63
III	9.98	4.17	1.58	0.63	5.68	4.22	−3.45
Endeavor	8.53	4.86	1.08	0.43	6.74	3.94	−3.11
Common Indices							
S&P 500	2.14	13.50	−0.00	−0.00	−0.27	8.80	−10.87
10-Year Treasury	7.06	7.10	0.57	0.22	−2.45	4.34	−6.71
World Equity	4.41	13.24	0.16	0.06	−1.63	8.93	−10.98
World Bond	7.75	6.18	0.74	0.31	−0.97	5.65	−4.30
HFR RV Index	8.24	2.22	2.21	0.90	2.26	2.19	−0.84

Note: All hedge fund returns are net of fees. The average return is the geometric average annual return for the period. S.D. is the standard deviation of monthly returns over the period multiplied by $\sqrt{12}$. The Sharpe ratio is the fund or asset class's average monthly return minus the average monthly risk-free rate of return divided by the standard deviation of the hedge fund or asset class's monthly returns multiplied by $\sqrt{12}$. The Sortino ratio is the fund or asset class's average excess return divided by the semistandard deviation. The $\hat{\alpha}$ is the alpha estimate, which is based on a hedge-fund-appropriate risk-factor model and presented as an annualized percentage (Chincarini 2010). Max is the monthly maximum return and Min is the minimum monthly return.

Platinum Grove Asset Management

Former LTCM principals Myron Scholes and Chi-Fu Huang, along with three former LTCM employees, Ayman Hindy, Lawrence Ng, and Tong-Sheng Sun, left to start their own hedge fund. Platinum Grove Asset Management LLC (PGAM) was located in a beautiful office in Rye Brook, New York. Its dealing room was quiet and organized, unlike the typical trading-floor chaos. PGAM was primarily a fixed-income hedge fund. It used the same variety of fixed-income strategies that LTCM had favored.

Myron Scholes believed this new operation was more sound than LTCM had been, mainly because Scholes was running it.[9] PGAM also made some of the same risk-management changes that JWMP used.

Scholes and Huang saw LTCM's business as wholesale capital market intermediation over medium- to long-term horizons that had attractive returns and provided a needed service in the financial markets. Such a firm should avoid directional bets, profiting instead from temporary supply and demand imbalances.

PGAM worked to find imbalances, hedge away all unwanted or little-understood risk, and focus on the core risk that interested the firm. It used leverage to amplify returns, as most of its strategies had high Sharpe ratios and small absolute returns.

The LTCM disaster had pointed to a key problem with financial inter-mediation: It contained tail risks during financial crises, including the August 1998 Russian crises that sealed LTCM's fate. PGAM used about a quarter of the leverage that LTCM had used. Less leverage meant lower returns. PGAM's returns were also about a quarter of LTCM's returns before the 1998 crisis. Before 1998, LTCM's average annual return was 27.76%. Before 2008, PGAM's average annual return was 8.98% (see Table 14.1).

PGAM also considered risk in a variety of more conservative ways. After the consortium injected capital into LTCM in September 1998, Chi-Fu Huang and other LTCM partners redesigned the firm's risk-management system. PGAM expanded on the new version. Its principals realized that VaR did not measure risks in the fixed-income relative-value business very well. Most of the time, overall portfolio risk is very low, because of low correlation across strategies. But when financial institutions need to simultaneously cut risk and balance sheets, idiosyncratic risks become almost perfectly correlated. PGAM needed a way to measure this risk.

PGAM calculated a stress loss for every individual strategy, then assumed that in a crisis, all strategies would suffer that loss. In other words, they assumed a correlation of 1 between strategies. Individual strategies' stress losses were calculated as the maximum of the strategy's largest historical two-week movement or five times its historic biweekly standard deviation.[10] The look-back period was as long as possible. Some strategies had no data before 1998.

After stress testing individual strategies, managers chose how much stress they would accept for the fund as a whole. They chose 40% of capital. Assuming all strategies were perfectly correlated and all strategies reached their tail limit, the fund would lose 40% of its capital. PGAM considered this sufficient to protect the fund. They also examined historical and prospective scenario analyses, though these scenarios generally had less risk than the tail risk of perfectly correlated strategies.

PGAM's performance was very reasonable before the 2008 financial crisis (see Table 14.1). Its average annual return was 8.98% with an annualized volatility of 4.54%. Its Sharpe ratio was very high, at 1.25, but lower than JWMP's or LTCM's Sharpe ratio.

The Others

Not all of LTCM's former principals went to JWMP or PGAM. Gregory Hawkins and James McEntee went to Caxton Associates, a global macro hedge fund. After spending several years there, Hawkins moved to Citibank in February 2008, where he became the chief risk officer for global real estate and mortgages.[11] In his Citigroup role Hawkins deals with issues of investment strategy and valuation for a significant portion of Citigroup's balance sheet. He has been instrumental in evaluating proposals related to the financial crisis, considering their impact on Citigroup and on the financial sector generally.

Robert C. Merton left LTCM and continued his appointment as a professor of finance at Harvard Business School; he was also a senior advisor to J.P. Morgan. In 2010, he moved back to MIT as a professor at MIT's Sloan School of Management. He is also the resident scientist at Dimensional Fund Advisors, where he hopes to implement many of the individual retirement products that would have been part of LTCM's 1998 Italian project.

David Modest has had a string of jobs, including working as managing director at Morgan Stanley. At Morgan Stanley, he created and oversaw the capital structure arbitrage group and a long/short equity proprietary trading group, both of which focused on exploiting market-neutral trading opportunities across and within the fixed-income, credit, and equity markets. He was also extensively involved in enhancing Morgan Stanley's internal risk management capabilities and the firm's ability to provide state-of-the-art risk management. He teamed up with Mullins to form Azimuth Advisors, then became managing director at J.P. Morgan. In 2008, he left J.P. Morgan to join the Soros fund.

In March 2008, after unsuccessful attempts to raise money with Rosenfeld for Quantitative Alternatives, Robert Shustak re-joined Quantitative Financial Strategies (QFS) as president, where he oversees the firm's business operations. (He was COO from 1999 to 2002). QFS is the quantitative hedge fund run by Sanford Grossman.[12]

Hans Hufschmid, an LTCM partner who focused primarily on the foreign-exchange business in London and was part of LTCM's 12-person risk management committee, had a particularly interesting subsequent career. After a frustrating year spent unwinding LTCM, Hufschmid became less interested in managing money.

> By May of 1999, we had to substantially reduce the risk. The partners started talking about raising money for a new fund. I thought it was going to be a tainted firm. Always tainted. I think the trading strategy was flawed. Mean-reversion trades have issues. LTCM for the longest time would not ask the question about "Why is something so cheap?" If you can explain the underlying forces that drive this asset, you will have much better quality trades. People learned and after LTCM we focused more on underlying economics, rather than just statistical movements. Market intelligence in FX trading is very important. Relative-value fixed-income trading moved closer to FX markets toward the end of LTCM. The relative-value market was going to rely less on models going forward. I just didn't feel like doing this again. It was a pretty harsh experience and we lost a lot of money.
> —Hans Hufschmid interview, September 30, 2010

LTCM built an amazing back office to handle trillions of dollars in multiple counterparty positions, each marked to market daily. The system worked even during the 1998 crisis, when counterparties tried to avoid paying collateral. LTCM's system kept everything running smoothly and effectively during the turmoil. LTCM never missed a payment and never had a restatement.

Sometime in May 1999, Hufschmid went to New York and told John Meriwether that he wanted to leave LTCM. While he was there, three senior LTCM employees approached him with a business plan for a company that would offer other hedge funds middle- and back-office services by replicating LTCM's operations system.

Hufschmid and LTCM operational employees Jim Webb, Tom Deacon, and Ira Rosenblum agreed that, if they could get one client, they would start the firm. Sure enough, their first client was Paul Matthews of Endeavor, a relative-value hedge fund created by the former Salomon arbitrage guys in London.

Hufschmid became CEO of GlobalOp Financial Services in January 2000. The firm provides back-office and other administrative services for hedge funds, including handling derivatives trades. By 2010, the firm had about 190 clients, representing approximately 1,500 funds and $120 billion in assets under administration. It employs approximately 1,600 people in 10 offices on three continents, with locations including London, New York, the Cayman Islands, and Ireland.

Hufschmid still makes strategic decisions, but without the sometimes instant gratification that can come from trading. Many of his new strategic decisions take much longer to bear fruit. On the other hand, he avoids the sometimes irrational markets that can lead to bankruptcy. He's happy to know that "the company will be here even if I'm gone, which is not true with a hedge fund. A hedge fund really survives based on the few key people that run it."

Hufschmid learned an important lesson from his LTCM experience.

> It made me very suspicious of success. At LTCM, we had a very successful firm for most of its life. We never viewed the fund as a substantial risk. None of the partners would have thought it was possible that the fund could lose 80% to 90% of its value within a three-month span. My lesson was that you can never trust your success. I can't look back and point to a change in a specific decision or philosophy that could have changed the outcome. If we had had a different philosophy, we would never have had the success that preceded the failure. In general, one can try and address known problems; it's the risks that are not known that are dangerous.
> —Hans Hufschmid interview, September 30, 2010

William Krasker became a finance professor at NYU's Stern School of Business.

In 2002, David Mullins formed Azimuth Trust, a fund-of-funds firm, along with Steven Gluckstern, David Modest, and Wesley Williams. Mullins served as executive director and chief economist. In 2004, he also assumed part-time responsibilities as the chief economist at Vega Asset Management, a global macro and fixed-income relative-value hedge fund group that managed approximately $12 billion in assets when he joined in 2004. He no longer works for any of these firms.

The Copycat Funds

Just as in the days when everyone wanted a slice of LTCM's successful pie, other relative-value fixed-income funds joined JWMP and PGAM in seeking alpha. The most notable included Endeavor Fund, III Fund (pronounced triple I), Smith Breeden Mortgage Partners, and Parkcentral Global.[13] They all focused on strategies similar to those of LTCM, with Smith Breeden having a slightly higher interest in mortgage-backed securities.[14]

Parkcentral Global was managed out of Plano, Texas. The hedge fund originally started as a private fund for billionaire Ross Perot, then opened its doors to investors in January 2002. Like LTCM, this hedge fund mainly pursued fixed-income strategies, and also had a significant interest in credit derivatives. Steve Blasnik, Peter Karmin, Michael Presley, and Jason Pizer led the firm.

Typical trades involved trades on whether the yield curve would steepen or flatten, long Asian volatility, and AAA municipals versus swaps in the fixed-income space. In the equity space, this fund might be short correlation and long volatility; in the credit markets, it might be long idiosyncratic, short systemic risk, and long FX volatility. The fund made some interesting relative-value trades in the mortgage-backed securities market, usually between debt tranches.

The fund's leverage varied over time, but was around 16, divided between a long and a short portfolio. The fund's minimum investment was $5 million. It offered a two-year lockup, a 1.5% management fee, and a 20% incentive fee.

Salomon's former London arbitrage team, including Paul Matthews, Paolo Kind, George Polychronopoulos, and Domenico Veronese, ran Endeavor, which also used strategies similar to those of LTCM.

Tim Cunneen, Dan Dektar, Stan Kon, and Kent Fleming ran Smith Breeden Mortgage Partners from Durham, North Carolina. Smith Breeden Associates is the fund's parent firm; it specializes in fixed-income research and trading. Eugene Flood was the entire organization's CEO. He left Smith Breeden in March 2011 for TIAA-CREF.

Smith Breeden launched in 1998 and ran straight into the LTCM crisis, but it was small and new and only lost a little. In 2004, the fund targeted an annual volatility between 7% and 10%, with target returns of 5% to 10% over risk-free rates of return. The firm had about 66 people, 27 of them in investment management.

The fund focused on fixed-income strategies, but was more heavily involved in mortgage-related securities than was LTCM. Smith Breeden was generally long mortgages and other assets correlated with interest-rate swaps; it hedged interest rate risk with Treasuries and swaps.

In 2004 Dektar argued that the fund was built to perform well during unexpected marketplace stress, and had to be ready to take advantage of stressed situations. "We need to have dry powder to take advantage of those situations," he said.[15]

Clifford Viner, Warren Mosler, Michael Reger, Bill McCauley, Sanjiv Sharma, and Garth Friesen launched III from Boca Raton, Florida, in 1982.

By the beginning of 2008, JWMP's relative value fund had about $1.26 billion in assets under management, PGAM had about $5.5 billion, Endeavor had about $3 billion, Smith Breeden Mortgage had about $744 million, Parkcentral had about $2.5 billion, and III had $2 billion. Their assets grew over the years since the LTCM crisis, with very good performance and high Sharpe ratios. Their assets under management, however, would shrink rapidly when the markets encountered the 2008 financial atomic bombs; the failures of Bear Stearns and Lehman Brothers; and big, fast asset withdrawals from customers desperate for cash. The year of 2008 didn't just mark the death of the Bear and the Gorilla. It marked the end of the *Liar's Poker* crowd.

CHAPTER 15

The End of LTCM's Legacy

The first magic of love is our ignorance that it can ever end.

—Benjamin Disraeli

Even before the financial crisis began in 2008, there were signs that Meriwether's fort wasn't intact. In September 2005, long-time collaborator and firm co-founder Eric Rosenfeld left JWMP, partly because of burnout and partly to pursue other opportunities.[1]

Then came 2008's financial crisis. The housing market collapse, the collapse of Bear Stearns, Lehman Brothers, many commercial banks, and Freddie and Fannie badly disrupted capital markets. Funds in the business of providing leveraged liquidity were in the thick of the storm. JWMP was no exception.

The troubling signs began early in 2008. January and February are typically good for fixed-income relative-value funds, because banks window-dress their balance sheets near the fiscal year's end in November and December.[2] The housing crisis made 2008 an exception. JWMP started the year with its worst-ever monthly return: −4.14% in January 2008. February was even worse, at −5.25%. By the end of February, JWMP began to unwind some of its risk.

The Bear and the Gorilla Attack

Then came the institutional bank run on Bear Stearns in March 2008. Bear Stearns, a major prime broker and liquidity provider for hedge funds, was heading for bankruptcy. Dimon and J.P. Morgan bought it at the fire sale

265

price of $2 per share.[3] That month, JWMP lost 24.8% of its fund, a loss that was eight times more than its previous worst monthly loss. Even with a new, more conservative risk management system, the LTCM crew was getting pulverized again. John Meriwether wrote in the March investor newsletter:

> The recent deleveraging and liquidity difficulties continued and intensified during March. Many of our strategies felt like they were at the center of market "storms..." We moved aggressively throughout March to reduce risk and increase liquidity... leverage [has been] cut roughly in half since Jan 1, 2008... we chose to reduce strategies which we believed had more "tail" risk or those more likely to be influenced by credit pricing effects... We appreciate your patience and trust during these difficult market conditions.
> —John Meriwether, letter to investors, April 17, 2008

JWMP's RVOP fund began the month with $1,156 million in assets and finished the month with $865 million in assets, with no withdrawals in between. As rumors spread about Bear Stearns, JWMP suffered. The fund lost money every day from February 29, 2008, to March 17, 2008, from as little as $10.9 million on March 13 to as much as $97 million on March 17, the first trading day after J.P. Morgan bought Bear Stearns.

JWMP reduced fund leverage from 13.4 at the end of 2007 to 7 at the end of March. As the year continued, JWMP had lower leverage and was much more prudent in the face of market uncertainty. Eric Rosenfeld, who had left the firm, remembers attending an investor meeting where Meriwether mentioned that the opportunities were "incredible," but that broker-dealers were pulling credit lines. It was becoming hard to finance positions.

The Japanese fiscal year-end aggravated March losses. March was bad for banks, the market was illiquid, and the *box trade* crashed. In the box trade, a hedge fund bets that government bonds in the long part of the curve will grow more expensive versus the swaps, and that government bonds in the medium-term part of the curve will get cheaper versus the swaps.[4] Every relative-value hedge fund had this particular trade on in Japan that spring. There were two reasons for this.

First, the spread was trading at the far end of its range, with 20-year bonds looking cheap even from a statistical point of view. Second, as the Japanese fiscal year-end approached, life insurance companies were targeted duration buyers. They typically set quarterly targets. As interest rates declined away from their target, they backed away from buying, which typically made the 20-year bond cheaper. If interest rates rose above their target, they bought the 20-year bond, making it more expensive. If interest rates stayed low for a long time, they might be desperate enough to reduce their target. These actions created cycles in the spreads.

The trade was at the 20-year and the 7-year curve areas, combining a long 20-year swap spread trade with a short 7-year swap spread trade.[5]

This trade involves holding inventories over time. Bear Stearns's March collapse was unexpected. One of the hedge funds in this space panicked and began to close its box trade position. Rumor has it that this hedge fund was Endeavor, which lost about $725 million (25% of the fund) in March of 2008. By closing this position, Endeavor put pressure on every other box trade.

Figure 15.1 represents the Japanese 20-year swap spread minus the 7-year swap spread. When this spread increases, the long box trade makes money; when it declines, the long box trade loses money. At the beginning of 2008, the spread looked low relative to its history. PGAM was long this spread going into March 2008. In March 2008, the spread crashed from −14 basis points to −60 basis points. From 1996 to 2007, the daily spread typically moved 1.26 basis points. In March 2008 it moved six times that amount. The trade suffered, because Bear Stearns's failure created imbalances that prevented a mean reversion.

FIGURE 15.1   The Japanese Box Trade. The 20-Year OAS Spread Minus the 7-Year OAS Spread

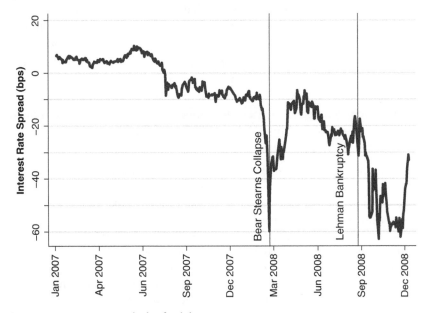

Source: Anonymous private hedge fund data.

JWMP and copycat funds, especially Endeavor, worked to reduce risk. That undoubtedly caused some spread movement. Bear Stearns's collapse, however, was the large catalyst. Losses were not limited to JWMP. In March alone, JWMP lost 24.8%, PGAM was down 11.43%, III was down 7.4%, and Endeavor was down a whopping 35%. Parkcentral and Smith Breeden were the only funds with positive returns: 5.29% and 2.48% respectively.

Chi-Fu Huang, CEO and CIO of PGAM, described the events:

> That Sunday evening, [March 16, 2008], when Bear Stearns was pur-
> chased, the box trade spread moved like crazy. I believe it's because another
> hedge fund exited the trade that night causing a massive movement in the
> spread . . . JWMP, PGAM, and Endeavor suffered a lot, PGAM was down
> about 15%. In April and May, the positions came back, but only PGAM
> made their money back, because other funds had cut risk significantly.
> —Chi-Fu Huang interview, September 10, 2010

April and May were quite good for relative-value arbitrage trades. Except for Endeavor, all the LTCM spinoff and copycat funds were up for these months to differing degrees, depending on how much they had reduced their risks. After that recovery, on June 1, 2008, PGAM substantially reduced its risk and its balance sheet.

Meriwether was optimistic, hoping that the worst was over. In August, he called Sir Andrew Crockett, president of J.P. Morgan International, who had recently returned from the annual Jackson Hole conference and Aspen Institute Roundtable.[6] Aspen conference speakers included former Salomon CEO and Citigroup vice chairman Sir Deryck Maughan, who at the time was a partner at KKR. His team had done extensive research on the banking system, which included visiting a large number of banks as well as government officials. He was gloomy about the banking system's solvency.

> There is little confidence in the balance sheets of many banks. The credibility
> of many management teams is severely eroded and public investors are shying
> away from the sector. Of the top 20 U.S. banks, only 4 would pass regulatory
> standards as being adequately capitalized. There isn't enough equity in the
> system, with the housing market collapse, too much leverage and weak
> underwriting standards. My personal view is that the banks do not have
> the luxury of waiting for the markets to settle down. Rather than hope for
> growth and stability, the authorities should prepare now for the failure of
> one or more major banks. The financial system probably needs somewhere
> between $250 billion and $400 billion of capital to survive, depending on

the depth of the recession. Public capital might well be required. We need to strap on our seat belts and prepare for a systemic crisis.

> —Extracts from Sir Deryck Maughan speech at Aspen, Partner at
> KKR (November 22, 2011 interview)

Maughan also quoted asset, leverage, and capital ratios for a number of institutions, including Fannie Mae, Lehman Brothers, Wachovia Bank, and Washington Mutual.

Crockett thought this meant that, of the 20 biggest financial institutions, 16 would fail or would require rescuing.[7] Crockett told Meriwether that most likely "bank troubles were only going to worsen." Meriwether cut risk further, thinking that JWMP might be facing its last days.

At the beginning of September, JWMP was down 26% for the year, III was down 6.38%, and Parkcentral was down 10.37%. Smith Breeden and PGAM had done better. Smith Breeden was down 3.81% and PGAM was down just 0.5%.

Lehman Brothers' bankruptcy announcement came on September 15, 2008. Bernanke neglected to review the importance of the LTCM rescue in 1998, as did Paulson and Geithner.[8] Lehman's failure had a devastating impact on relative-value arbitrage funds and the general markets. It gave LTCM spinoffs and copycats a knockout punch.[9]

> The risk management team had also run the portfolio against the market moves that occurred after the Russian default from August 17, 1998, through September 30, 1998, which had fatally damaged LTCM. The PGAM portfolio of September 2008 would have actually done relatively well during the type of market conditions that existed during the LTCM crisis. Indeed, the fixed income part of the portfolio would have made money. Then came the Lehman bankruptcy on September 15. We had moved almost all counterparty exposures away from Lehman as of June and hedged residual risks with more than sufficient CDS. The portfolio thus made money from the direct impact of the bankruptcy. Nevertheless, the indirect impacts from the disorderly unwind of Lehman's swap and repo business devastated fixed-income relative-value funds.
>
> —Chi-Fu Huang interview, October 20, 2010

In September and October, JWMP lost another 23%, PGAM lost 46%, Smith Breeden and Endeavor lost 19%, III lost a whopping 44%, and Parkcentral lost 36%. The firms had to cut deteriorating positions, which accounted for most of these losses, but the crowd's scramble to sell positions also meant large total transaction costs—10% to 15%. Almost any fund would have had trouble recovering from these losses. The writing was on the wall.

John Meriwether summarized the post-Lehman period:

> The Lehman bankruptcy and its results—the disorderly unwinding of security positions globally and the fear of trading with almost any counterparty—produced severely dislocated security prices. Market liquidity further declined, as evidenced by some of the largest bid-offer spreads we can recall. Financing government securities, RVOP's principal security holding, became noticeably more difficult for terms longer than 30 days. And these conditions have continued so far in October.
> —John Meriwether, letter to investors, October 16, 2008

> The difficult market conditions experienced in September continued in October. Governments around the globe attempted in various ways to counteract the dysfunctional market conditions. . . . We have continued to reduce risk, decrease leverage, and maintain liquidity. . . . October's performance resulted from hedged government bond positions. These positions, which we believed were cheap relative to other bonds issued by the same government, became much cheaper. We believe the liquidation of similar positions held by other leveraged investors was the principal factor responsible.
> —John Meriwether, letter to investors, November 17, 2008

JWMP lost money on trades across the board, including AAA commercial mortgage spread trades, agency spread trades, and differential swap spread trades. Meriwether reacted by reducing risk and leverage. By December, JWMP's leverage was down to 3.8 from 13.4 a year earlier. PGAM also lowered its leverage. LTCM partners knew just how bad market imbalances can be, even on very attractive positions, but some of the copycats had not yet learned this vital lesson. While JWMP and PGAM reduced risk, Parkcentral kept its risk level the same and Smith Breeden salivated at the amazing opportunities.

In October 2008, Daniel Dektar, chief investment officer at Smith Breeden, believed that "this is a multigenerational opportunity." Smith Breeden began using its "dry powder" to load up on bets during the market combustion.

Among other opportunities, Dektar pointed out Bank of America's AAA-rated commercial mortgage-backed securities, which normally traded at 20 to 30 basis points above Treasuries. In October it traded at 80 basis points above Treasuries; before the government bailout plan it had traded as high as 370 basis points above Treasuries.

Smith Breeden began buying low-risk, shorter-maturity subprime securities. Dektar believed these were great opportunities. "You get exposure to sectors where the babies are being thrown out with the bathwater," he said.[10]

November Rain

In a revolution, as in a novel, the most difficult part to invent is the end.
—Alexis de Tocqueville

After Lehman, the relative-value community's future did not look bright. As KKR CEO Henry Kravis put it on October 3, 2008, the "deleveraging process will take a long time to complete and this will be a long slow recession." As October ended, Parkcentral and Smith Breeden were relatively undamaged compared with JWMP, PGAM, III, and Endeavor.

In fact, the worst was still to come for hedge funds that had loaded up on opportunities. Parkcentral stopped reporting returns to hedge fund databases in October and Smith Breeden stopped reporting returns in November.

Ironically, the funds that lost early were fortunate. This caused them to cut back risk. Funds that didn't lose early became more aggressive or retained the same level of risk. These funds lost everything in November 2008 as spreads widened enormously.
—Anonymous trader at hedge fund interview, September 23, 2010

November's security price movements wiped out Parkcentral. Its losses accelerated after October and sped up again after November 12. As the markets continued to sour, Parkcentral's counterparties requested more and more margin. On November 18, the fund lost a total of $300 million. By November 20, it was unable to meet the large margin calls any longer. J.P. Morgan alone demanded $125.4 million, then froze Parkcentral's assets in its custody account.

Parkcentral told its brokerage and banking counterparties, "We are locked down." The hedge fund could not unwind or make any trades at all, because it couldn't settle trades with frozen accounts.[11] According to hedge fund director Roderick Forest, "By this time the company had exhausted its liquidity and its ability to trade was basically at an end."

On November 25, the fund announced that it was shutting down and selling remaining assets to satisfy creditors.

It had started the year with roughly $2.5 billion in assets and ended the year bankrupt and owing creditors $266 million, though legal claims were much higher. J.P. Morgan argued that it was owed at least $700 million.[12]

The Perot family was among the fund's largest investors, and also lost the most money: about $500 million.

A Parkcentral spokesman summarized its failure as an

> . . . unprecedented upheaval of the capital markets in general and the freezing of credit markets in particular.
> —Eddie Reeves, November 26, 2008 (Case 2008)

Smith Breeden also left the markets in a hearse. Details are not available, but rumor said that this fund lost everything in November.[13]

After Smith Breeden and Parkcentral collapsed, LTCM's surviving spinoffs were so damaged that they also began closing their operations. Long-time Meriwether partner and key idea generator Larry Hilibrand left JWMP in December 2008. His departing words: "I'm looking forward to a nice long break."

In February 2009, Endeavor closed its fund. In March 2009, III Fund Ltd. permitted investor redemptions after a three-month lockout period designed to allow fund restructuring. In a May 19, 2009, letter to investors, Meriwether wrote "we believe it is desirable to return capital to investors at this time." With JWMP closed, there was only one spinoff left: PGAM.

The 2008 financial crisis had been unkind to PGAM, which lost 54% of its fund value. PGAM started the year with about $5.5 billion in capital; by the end of 2009 it had only $400 million, with the remainder lost to the market and investor withdrawals.[14] At the end of 2009, PGAM's principals transferred ownership to the fund's senior employees, though they retained some economic interest. Myron Scholes and Chi-Fu Huang left, along with Hindy, Ng, and Sun.

Loyal, long-term investors helped keep PGAM afloat, even with its extreme losses. The fund had invested in managers who were willing to keep going even when LTCM alumni had had enough. PGAM had also invested significantly in technology and trading systemization, which let the firm reduce personnel and continue operating at a lower cost.

In a sense, PGAM and JWMP finally answered the big question: Would LTCM emerge a stronger and better firm, as Meriwether had said on that day in September 1998? The answer? Sort of. PGAM and JWMP had controlled risk better, avoided a government rescue, and had lower losses than those of some failed investment banks, commercial banks, and government-sponsored agencies. PGAM and JWMP also fared better than many other copycat funds. Table 15.1 and Figure 15.2 show 2008 returns for various relative-value hedge funds and major indices.

TABLE 15.1 The LTCM Spinoff and Copycat Returns during the Financial Crisis

Hedge Funds	Average	S.D.	Sharpe	Sortino	Max	Min
December 1999–April 2009						
JWMP	1.44	11.73	−0.06	−0.02	7.44	−24.80
January 2008–December 2008						
JWMP	−41.56	31.41	−1.56	−0.56	7.44	−24.80
PGAM	−50.51	42.28	−1.42	−0.50	8.83	−36.73
Smith Breeden[a]	−100	103.18	−1.33	−0.43	4.61	−100.00
Parkcentral[a]	−100	105.07	−1.57	−0.52	7.47	−100.00
III	−53.66	38.61	−1.75	−0.59	3.59	−37.21
Endeavor	−53.46	35.77	−1.91	−0.63	1.67	−34.86
Common Indices						
S&P 500	−37.00	21.02	−2.13	−0.83	4.87	−16.80
10-Year Treasury	19.24	11.03	1.51	0.81	9.02	−2.14
World Equity	−40.33	25.01	−1.96	−0.77	5.34	−19.37
World Bond	−7.54	9.50	−0.95	−0.39	3.58	−5.42
HFR RV Index	−18.01	9.71	−2.15	−0.77	1.38	−8.03

Note: Returns for all hedge funds are computed net of fees. The average return is the geometric average annual return over the period. S.D. is the standard deviation of monthly returns over the period multiplied by $\sqrt{12}$. The Sharpe ratio is the average monthly return of the hedge fund or asset class minus the average monthly risk-free rate of return divided by the standard deviation of monthly returns of the hedge fund or asset class multiplied by $\sqrt{12}$. The Sortino ratio is the average excess return of the hedge fund or asset class divided by the semistandard deviation.

[a] These funds closed in November of 2008 due to extreme losses. Parkcentral's losses in November were −100% for equity holders. Smith Breeden returns for November have not been verified but are assumed to have been −100%.

FIGURE 15.2   Net-of-Fee Performance of LTCM Spinoffs and Copycats. Cumulative
Value of Investment of $100 on December 1999

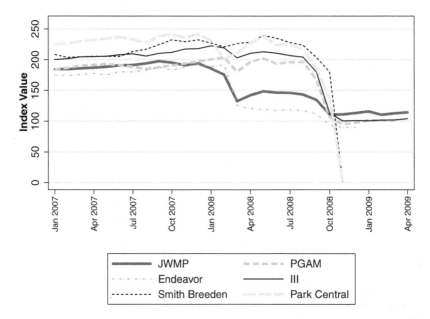

JWMP lost 41.56% in 2008, less than losses of −50% for PGAM, −54%
for Endeavor and III, and −100% for Smith Breeden and Parkcentral.[15]
JWMP performed slightly worse than U.S. stocks and world equity, but not
by much. Only an all-bond portfolio did significantly better. From its 1999
inception to JWMP's closing, the fund returned an annual 1.44% after fees.

The LTCM team did better the second time around, but no firm is
invulnerable to market shocks.

What Went Wrong?

> Risk management is a combination of quantitative and qualitative judg-
> ments, a mixture of science and art. The science part is easy; it's the art that's
> hard.
>   —Parkcentral Global Fund Quarter Review, first quarter 2008

JWMP and PGAM had learned from the LTCM crisis. Both funds lowered their risk and used more rigorous stress tests. But JWMP and PGAM
had levered positions in fixed-income markets, including mortgages, that deteriorated enormously and caused massive losses. Market insanity ruled the

day in 2008. As the real estate market collapsed, financial instruments' prices changed not according to market fundamentals, but according to the crowd's movements. The fixed-income markets took much larger shocks than in previous crises, including that of 1998. Market movements were approximately 2.5 times as large as in 1998, though this varied by sector.

Lehman's failure created a huge market imbalance. The prices of many financial securities moved in opposite directions from how they might normally react. Even positions that were positioned to profit from a market collapse did just the opposite.

As market anxiety grew, dealers and major investment banks wanted to look safer, so they began reducing counterparty risk. This caused even more imbalance in the financial markets.

Market Insanity

Parkcentral began 2008 with a leverage of 20.65, but had reduced it to 15.94 by the summer of 2008. Table 15.2 shows a summary of Parkcentral's trade positions before the devastating months of October and November.

These trades reflect some of Parkcentral's main strategies. Their largest exposures came from credit derivative trades, interest rate curve trades, and swap spread trades. They also bet on widening European swap spreads, which is typical during crises. But in 2008, the market behaved strangely after Lehman Brothers failed.

One of Parkcentral's biggest losses came from mortgage-backed securities, which were also the fund's largest risk exposure. In September, October, and November 2008, the commercial MBS market behaved oddly. The AAA spreads widened while subordinated spreads tightened. In 2008, the fund lost 19.5% just from trades that were long AAA CMBS and short junior tranches.[16] This did not make valuation sense. In a crisis, the safer securities should be the AAA-rated investments, not the subordinated securities.

> Hard to find a rational explanation of this. How does this happen? Someone is selling senior debt and has to? The hedge fund community has to cut the position and buy one end and sell the other end, causing the prices to diverge even more.
> —Steve Blasnick interview, Parkcentral principal, November 10, 2010

A trade Parkcentral made on credit default swaps (CDS) using the CDX showed the market's insanity. CDX indices represent the cost of insuring a basket of corporate bonds. The investment grade (IG) index reflects the underlying cost of insuring the debt of 125 major U.S. companies. This

TABLE 15.2 Parkcentral's Trade Positions as of September 30, 2008

Strategy	Description	Risk Weight
Fixed-Income		
Muni Tax Arbitrage	Bet that tax-exempt versus taxable spreads tighten.	11.09
Intra-Market Curve Trades	Bet that global interest rates curves steepen.	5.02
Japanese Yield Curve Trades	Bet that JPY swap curve steepens and curve volatility trades.	3.84
Swap Spread Trades	Bet that swap spread widens in GBP, KRW, CZK, and HUF.	2.38
MBS Trade	Bet that spread of mortgages over swaps would tighten.	1.31
Currency Basis Swap Trade	Bet that currency basis swaps would tighten.	0.85
Japanese Swap Spread Trade	Bet that JPY Swap spread widens.	0.63
Other Trades	A variety of other fixed-income trades.	5.18
Equity-Linked		
Long-Short Trades	Bet that A versus B share spread would tighten.	6.40
Volatility Trades	Bets about volatility and correlation of equities.	5.61
Risk Arbitrage	Bets about various takeovers, restructurings, etc.	0.23
Convertible Arb	Bets that are long convertible bonds and short stock.	0.07
Other Trades	Bets on relative value.	2.98

TABLE 15.2   (*Continued*)

Strategy	Description	Risk Weight
Systematic		
Quantitative Stock-Picking Trades	Bets that long stocks beat short stocks.	6.47
Quantitative Relative Value	Bets of long and short stocks across globe.	3.83
Quantitative Equity Volatility	Bets of long and short of volatility of stocks.	2.15
Credit and Commodity		
Credit Derivative Trades	Bets on relative value in CDS, equities, options, and bonds.	29.69
High-Yield Trades	Bets that capture attractive yield spreads—short spread.	6.53
FX and Commodity Trades	Bets on volatility and correlations.	5.74

Note: The risk weightings reflect the percentage of risk capital allocated to that particular trade or group of trades.
Source: Parkcentral.

basket included such companies as McDonalds, Bristol-Meyers, GE, IBM, Loews, and Southwest Airlines. CDX buyers make money when the cost of insuring corporate debt declines.

The CDS indicates the price of protecting a dollar's worth of debt issued by this basket of companies. The index is divided and traded in tranches: 0 to 3, 3 to 7, 7 to 10, 10 to 15, 15 to 30, and 30 to 100. If companies default on their debt, the 0 to 3 tranche takes the first losses, followed by the 3 to 7 tranche, and so on. The 125 companies' debt would have to drop by 30% before the 30 to 100 tranche suffered any losses.[17]

When a company defaults on its debt, the debt holders still usually recover a percentage of their original investment, called the recovery rate. These derivative contracts specify the recovery rate. Suppose the recovery rate is 40%. In a company default, the contract will pay back losses above 40% of the original debt value. For the 30 to 100 tranche to lose *any* money, 63% of the largest, best-known U.S. companies would have to default.[18]

FIGURE 15.3 The Percentage Increase in the Cost of Insuring the 30–100 Tranche versus the 3–30 Tranche (Base Period: November 5, 2007)

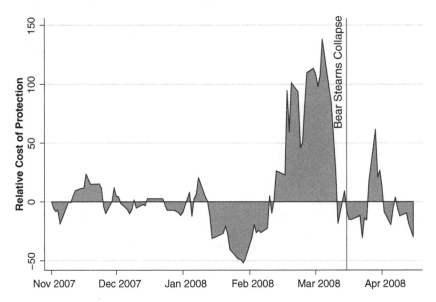

Parkcentral's trade involved selling insurance protection on the 30 to 100 tranche and buying protection on the 0 to 10 tranches. In theory, this trade is great in a crisis, because the lower tranches take the brunt of defaults. But in 2008, prices moved more in line with demand and supply than with rationality. In March, when Bear Stearns collapsed, credit default spreads rose on all tranches. Oddly, they rose the most on the 30 to 100 tranche.

The cost of protection in the 30 to 100 tranche minus the average cost of protection for the other tranches rose by more than 150%, which made no economic sense (see Figure 15.3).[19]

> We would write the protection and buy the lower end as a spread. I was surprised people would buy this from us, because if the event occurred where we would have to pay, it would mean that the world would be gone, how would you collect? You should not buy protection of a meteor hitting the earth or destroying the entire economy. Not an option you should buy. We wrote the 30 to 100 tranche and bought the whole index rather than the subparts, since it was easier and more liquid. We were cash-flow neutral. We would benefit from every default in the index, until the point at where 70% of the companies defaulted (that's 70% of the biggest, well-known companies in the United States). The market movements in 2008 tell a

different story. The market prices moved such that the market believed Armageddon was coming, not just a recession.
  —Steve Blasnik interview, Parkcentral principal, November 10, 2010

According to Blasnik, this happened because of a fundamental imbalance between buyers and sellers for these securities.

Why did it happen? It happened because of flows and who held what. So it was irrational. My understanding is that the super senior risk had been written by certain insurance companies and dedicated special purpose leverage vehicles. These instruments started sometime in 2007. They were off-balance-sheet conduit vehicles for banks. They were particularly used in Canada. They would create a vehicle that would raise $3 million cash in equity, borrow $97 million issuing commercial paper, then write $100 million of 30 to 100. That made sense, because it was rating-agency driven. The rating agency viewed that senior risk at AAA to the power of 10, thus an institution could lever it 33 to 1, because all that debt was considered so good. The debt issued for these vehicles that issued this short-term debt, would still get A1+ ratings. Money market funds would buy the short-term paper. The money market managers would blindly buy these without due diligence since they had the A+ rating. However, when market movements first occurred, there were margin calls, then rating agencies changed the ratings on the commercial paper, and then the spiral started. These organizations were very highly levered holders and thus very modest movements in spreads became very reinforcing.
  —Steve Blasnik interview, Parkcentral principal, November 10, 2010

A spread trade in the commercial mortgage-backed market also lost relative-value hedge funds a lot of money. On this trade, investors were short the spread between AAA-rated CMBS and A-rated CMBS.[20]

Parkcentral initiated this trade before 2008. At the end of December 2007, the AAA was trading at a yield of 5.27% and the A was trading at a yield of 8.75%, a spread difference of 3.48%.[21]

Parkcentral believed that the junior tranches had significant chance of impairment, but thought the AAA tranches would be fine. As one person at the firm described it, "We didn't think the world was going to go to zero and we would be living in caves."

Different hedge funds made this trade in different ways, but the overall idea remained the same. Both profits and losses were related to the trade's design. Hedge funds often enact a spread trade by attempting to offset any

TABLE 15.3   Approximate Returns for CMBS Securities and CMBX Indices

	AAA-Rated		A-Rated		BBB-Rated		
	BofA CMBS	CMBX	BofA CMBS	CMBX	BofA CMBS	CMBX	Hedge Fund 3-1 Position
September-08	−8.03	−0.09	−6.08	7.82	−4.27	11.53	−10.64
October-08	−12.71	−4.23	−30.93	−29.07	−28.83	−28.86	−3.02
November-08	−38.61	−27.57	−51.48	−37.70	−44.01	−35.38	−26.04

Note: Returns for the CMBX indices are actual returns for the month and given in percentage terms. The Bank of America CMBS returns are approximate, computed from the actual yields.
Source: Parkcentral, Bank of America, and Bloomberg.

directional risk. "A" yields are about three times more volatile than "AAA" yields, so it was reasonable to construct the trade with a 3-to-1 hedge ratio.

The trade was more heavily exposed to directional exposure on the AAA CMBS. It would have been difficult to short the lower-rated securities, so some hedge funds used CMBX-traded indices on the short side and Bank of America CMBS indices on the long side of the trade.

The strategy's returns, as well as individual returns for all instruments from September to November 2008, are shown in Table 15.3. The 3-1 position lost 11% in September, −3% in October, and a crushing −26% in November.[22] These losses are without leverage. With leverage, losses would have been more severe. The trade lost so much because of net-long AAA CMBS positions that lost −8%, −13%, and −39% respectively in those three months.

The position lost even more because hedging instruments (CMBX) didn't decline as much as the underlying Bank of America CMBS indices. In September, for example, the CMBX index for A and BBB was up 7.82% and 11.53%, respectively, while similarly rated Bank of America indices were down 6.08% and 4.27%, respectively.

The hedge funds hedged these trades for risk. In these months, however, the junior tranches (A and BBB) moved much less than usual. The funds knew the positions would come back, but didn't have the cash to meet their collateral payments and so went out of business.[23]

Parkcentral's CMBS trade made intuitive and logical sense before 2008, but in the end the hedge was wrong and the position lost money. The hedge failed for three reasons. First, the hedge was based on the theoretical relative movement of AAA and A. In the absurd, post-Lehman world of 2008, this was completely unrelated to the actual securities' movements.

Second, Parkcentral hedged with a new derivative contract, the CMBX, rather than with the same underlying instrument. There was no history to measure its risk, no detailed knowledge of which institutions held the security, and no way to know how its value would change in different economic circumstances.

Moreover, Parkcentral didn't realize that a peculiar set of investors held these securities. Most of the investors who held the A-rated and BBB-rated tranches had created the CDOs; banks and other institutions held the higher-rated securities. During the panic, the most leveraged players with exposure to AAA securities quickly sold them. The price movements were related to the crowds holding them and had less to do with economic fundamentals.

Third, as prices dropped, durations got smaller and smaller, especially for BBB-rated securities. The hedge was unbalanced. Rebalancing hedges during the malaise was difficult or impossible. No one was willing to trade. Parkcentral traders told investors, "Although we have taken and continue to take steps to reduce overall risk, extremely illiquid markets have made this expensive or impossible in many cases."

Bigger Shocks

JWMP and PGAM collapsed, despite everything traders had learned about risk control from the LTCM collapse. In 2008, market movements in the staple relative-value trades were two and a half times larger than those in 1998.[24] Many relative-value hedge funds finance themselves in the short-term market. Between August and October 1998, the financing rate, three-month LIBOR minus the Repo rate, went from 16.75 basis points to 46.5 basis points. In 2008, these rates went from 84 basis points to 407 basis points. In 2008, the movement was almost two times bigger.

Funds' credit trades also made enormous movements in 2008. Relative-value hedge funds tend to be short the mortgage spread. This was a devastating trade in 2008. For example, the yields on AAA-rated commercial real estate went from 5% to 13%. Yields on BBB-rated CMBS went from 13% to 84% (see Figure 15.4).

JWMP and PGAM built stronger risk management systems. Even with larger market movements, they didn't require a bailout of any kind. Once they suffered large losses, they could choose to continue or shut down.

PGAM took one-quarter of the risk that LTCM had shouldered. In 1998, LTCM lost 90%. In a logical world, PGAM might have lost about 22.5%

FIGURE 15.4   Commercial MBS Bond Interest Rates by Credit Rating

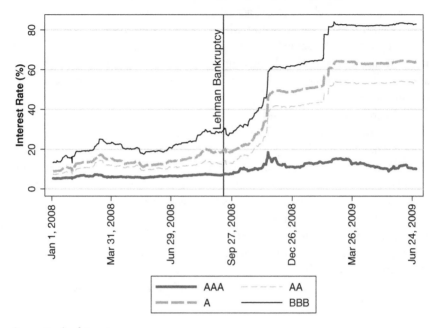

Source: Bank of America.

in 2008. Instead they lost about 50%, mainly in October and November 2008. At the beginning of September, they reduced their risk even further, to about 15% of LTCM's 2008 risk, so one might have predicted a 34% loss for PGAM in 2008 (0.15 times 0.90 times 2.5). The additional 15% came from the transaction costs of reducing positions. As they sold positions into an illiquid market with the crowd racing toward the exits, they paid dearly for execution.[25]

Market Imbalance

Market prices behaved irrationally after the Lehman collapse. Moreover, they didn't reflect the intuitive behavior that typically occurs during market crises.[26]

The behavior of longer-term swap spreads illustrates this. In most market crises, swap spreads widen as market participants seek a safe haven, reducing investment maturities and seeking government securities. Swap spreads at the long end widened during the Russian default and during the LTCM crisis in 1998. But in 2008, after the Lehman bankruptcy, these spreads narrowed so much that government bond yields traded above swap yields. The market treated government debt as riskier than bank debt in many countries. In the

FIGURE 15.5   Swap Spreads during LTCM Crisis and 2008 Crisis

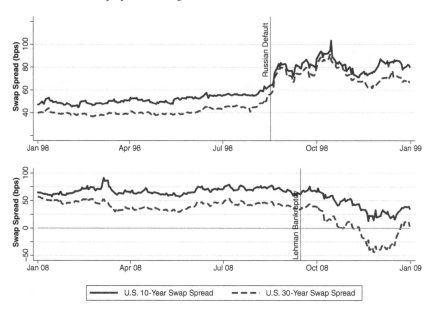

United States the 30-year swap spread moved from 40 basis points before the Lehman collapse to −40 basis points by the end of November 2008 (see Figure 15.5).

This trade cost III the bulk of its losses. It was long the asset swap spread in 10-, 20-, and 30-year U.S. Treasuries and UK Gilts. Further deleveraging meant substantial losses for this trade and for others in the same space.

> Had we owned the same trades in the 2-year maturity area of the curve, we would have been up 50%, but we owned these long swap spreads at the 10-, 20-, and 30-year maturity. Contrary to a typical flight-to-quality movement, the spreads moved in an unexpected negative direction.
> —Cliff Viner interview, CIO of III Fund, December 1, 2011

The butterfly trade is another staple for relative-value hedge funds, which could be long or short the position. PGAM, JWMP, and other funds had this trade on in 2008. They could implement it with government securities or swaps, but typically executed it with swaps. The trade is short the 30-year and 5-year areas of the yield curve and long the 10-year part of the curve. It's constructed to eliminate interest-rate risk (duration neutral) and eliminate curve-slope risk.

FIGURE 15.6   Butterfly Swap Yield

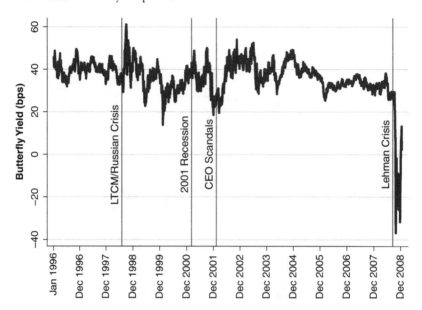

Source: Anonymous hedge fund.

This position lost quite a bit in 2008. PGAM (and others) had a large position in this trade across a variety of different currencies. For PGAM, this was a hedge position, designed to diversify its holdings. This trade should have done well in a crisis, when the yield curve typically steepens and the 10- to 30-year part of the curve steepens more than the 5- to 10-year area. When monetary authorities lower interest rates, natural long-term debt buyers such as pension funds shy away from the long end of the curve, and higher risk aversion means that investors shorten durations, moving away from longer-dated securities. That has helped this butterfly trade do well during crises over the past 20 years (see Figure 15.6).[27]

The trade did well in the LTCM crisis, during the 2001 recession, and after the Enron collapse and the 2002 crisis of confidence in CEOs.

After the Lehman Brothers bankruptcy, this trade moved against the hedge fund. From 1996 to 2007, the trade might typically move by 6 basis points on a given day. After Lehman's collapse, it moved by 20 basis points per day.

> In a crisis, we thought spreads would tend to widen at the long end of the curve between swaps and Treasuries. It turned out because of the failure of Lehman that some of the pension funds in Europe triggered a massive

movement from equities into swaps, due to fear or legal restrictions, the swap market looked like a AAA+ market and the curve inverted. You wouldn't think it would be inverted, the front-end was steep up to 10 years, but after 10 years it looked like the 30-year was safe. In every other crisis, spreads tended to go out across the yield curve.

—Myron Scholes interview, chairman of PGAM, July 9, 2011

Deleveraging

As 2008 began, JWMP had a portfolio filled with many of LTCM's staple trades. JWMP lost across the board in fixed-income positions, including mortgages, yield-curve trades, swap-curve trades, and many other standard fixed-income trades. Some of its largest losses occurred in the commercial mortgage market, the agency mortgage market, swap-spread trades, and with Japanese inflation-protected bonds. JWMP had built a short-spread trade in CMBS. When the spreads widened in 2008, this position lost a lot of money (see Figure 15.4).

One standard relative-value trade is short the spread between Treasuries and bonds issued by Freddie Mac and Fannie Mae. This trade was clobbered in both March and October 2008. At the beginning of January, the spread of agencies over Treasuries was 81 basis points. By March 6 it was 199 basis points. At the start of October, the spread was 135 basis points; by the end of October it was 175 basis points. Short positions on these trades in March and October cost the relative-value hedge funds dearly. To make matters even worse, spreads had looked extremely attractive at the beginning of October 2008, tempting hedge funds to increase their positions.

JWMP lost money on the swap-spread irregularity in the long end of the curve in most major countries. In 2008, these spreads moved in seemingly irrational ways.

JWMP also had a long position in Japanese inflation-protected bonds and a short position in the underlying Japanese government bonds. The hedge fund was banking on higher expected inflation in Japan. The difference between a regular bond's yield and that of an inflation-protected bond generally reflects the market's expectation for future inflation. If inflation expectations increase, the spread usually widens, benefiting JWMP.

During 2008's market malaise, Japan's bond market behaved as if investors expected a strong deflation. Yields on the 10-year inflation-protected securities traded at 4 basis points more than yields on regular Japanese bonds, the lowest difference since Japan introduced inflation-protected bonds in 2004. This movement opposed JWMP's trade and caused losses.

According to a trader at ABN in Tokyo, the spread's strange behavior was caused by "the big sell-off. . . by a few leverage accounts being forced to sell." The abnormality disappeared and JWMP recovered some of these losses in April and May, but the deleveraging process put stress on many hedge funds. Investment banks and other dealers needed to reduce their leverage in light of the mistrustful marketplace. Nontransparent financial statements made it very difficult for the market to know how much bank leverage was due to client positions and how much was due to proprietary positions. Banks cut risk by reducing financing for their smaller customers, including hedge funds. That made it difficult for JWMP to do Treasury repos with dealers.

JWMP and others were forced to close their financing arrangements, so they reduced positions further. This happened across the market. Banks deleveraged, hedge funds cut positions, the positions moved further out. That caused more losses and more deleveraging all around.

JWMP suffered in 2008 because of real estate exposure and fixed-income trades that went sour, behaving very differently than they typically do in crises. Massive deleveraging made things even worse.

Coup de Grace

Relative-value funds lost in a variety of trades: standard swap-spread trades, butterfly trades, and mortgage trades. Bad mortgage-related bets caused some losses, and the imbalances that followed Lehman's collapse caused markets to move in seemingly irrational ways. Trades moved by much larger magnitudes in 2008 than in 1998. Even with lower leverage and risk, losses were large.

The massive housing bubble's collapse affected everyone, including hedge funds. Some hedge funds took advantage of this opportunity and made billions shorting the housing market. Atypical yield curve movements that were more than double the size of those felt during the LTCM crisis destroyed many others, especially relative-value hedge funds. A flight to quality caused some yield-curve movements, but other moves seemed based on irrational investor behavior, as prices responded to the actions of the types of investors who held the positions. Marketplace crowds and unexpected events caught everyone by surprise. Many hedge funds closed or went bankrupt.

The hedge fund Citadel was one of the survivors. It had around $20 billion before the crisis. By April 2011, it had around $11 billion.

While our boldness has served us well, we are not blind to the lessons of 2008. We were overly confident that we could weather any financial storm.

Now, we are firmly grounded in the understanding that even the best-run firms . . . can face almost unimaginable market forces.
—Kenneth Griffin, letter to investors, December 2010
(Strasberg 2011)

In 2008, the S&P 500 returned −37%. The U.S. real estate index was down 43%, global equities were down 40%, and global bonds were down 8%. U.S. Treasury bonds went up 20%, and surviving hedge funds often did even better (see Table 15.4).[28]

TABLE 15.4 Annualized Returns of Hedge Fund Strategies and Major Indices

Hedge Funds	1994–2000	2000–2010	2008
Equity Hedge	22.50	5.83	−26.65
Event Driven	16.79	8.21	−21.82
Macro	12.32	7.68	4.83
Relative Value	11.13	7.65	−18.04
All Hedge Funds	15.79	6.75	−19.03
Common Indices			
S&P 500	23.55	0.41	−37.00
U.S. Treasury Bonds	5.59	6.69	20.23
U.S. Treasury Bills	5.00	2.50	1.24
U.S. Corporate Bonds	6.44	7.73	1.80
U.S. Real Estate	0.04	5.09	−43.43
World Equity	17.67	1.27	−40.33
Global World Bonds	5.77	5.70	−7.54

Note: Returns for all hedge funds are computed net of fees. The returns are the geometric average annual return over the period.

John Meriwether summed up 2008 eloquently:

Astonishing market events continue to transpire with unprecedented regularity.

—John Meriwether, September 12, 2008

For those who were paying attention, these astonishing events taught valuable lessons.

CHAPTER 16

New and Old Lessons from the Financial Crisis

Don't be too proud to take lessons. I'm not.

— Jack Nicklaus

Traders learned many lessons from the 2008 financial crisis, relearned some of LTCM's 1998 lessons, and forgot some lessons entirely.

Interconnectedness and Crowds

The LTCM crisis demonstrated how investors in certain markets are interconnected.[1] During the 2008 financial crisis we saw how important this phenomenon can become, especially when everyone rushes after the same investment. In 2008, this investment was real estate. Traders pursued it as one, then dropped it at the same time. Without natural buyers, overvalued prices collapsed. Market correlations change depending on crowds' behavior.

Haircuts on financial loans provided another example of market psychology. During the financial crisis, haircuts went up across the board, so capital became a problem for everyone. Haircut movements are procyclical. Before the crisis, Treasuries got a 0.25% haircut, AAA-rated CDOs got a 2% to 4% haircut, and prime mortgage-backed securities got a 2% to 4% haircut. During the crisis, the haircuts rose to 3%, 95%, and 10% to 20%, respectively.[2]

In August 2007, quantitative equity portfolio managers learned some valuable lessons about crowding.

A successful hedge fund must carefully manage its growth. As some quant funds became too big, they noticed that their size was affecting their trades. Smaller firms were more nimble and might even trade ahead of the large firms. A trader's size affects market prices, as does the quantity of similar traders in a space. Thus, traders must think of market prices as endogenous rather than exogenous, especially in saturated trading spaces.

By 2007, the market had more quantitative hedge funds than it used to, so the space was more crowded. Hedge funds running similar strategies in similar ways helped cause the 2007 quant crisis.

Large quant funds must be thoughtful in using well-known strategies. Most less-sophisticated players also use these strategies, making funds more correlated. The former co-head of one of the world's largest quantitative hedge funds commented on these lessons:

> With the benefit of hindsight, our firm and the industry was too big. There are subtle issues that arise when you are a big firm. We had some analytics to figure out the deterioration of Sharpe ratio due to more assets chasing the same strategy. Also, being the biggest boy on the block, people take shots at you, front-running you, etc. Quants implicitly tended to think that prices were exogenous. They think market impact was a few basis points, but the industry could actually influence its own pricing. In the future, we need to be more dynamic with the models. If we are going to take risk in factors that are susceptible to liquidity events or crowding, we should have a process to make it possible to identify early in the game that we might want to take risk down in those particular factors. We also didn't appreciate how overcrowded the space had become and how correlated it became. When putting a quant model together, you need to think about this correlation during the modeling process. We used some very simple factors that everyone knows like momentum, value (book-to-price), and some unique proprietary factors. We all thought we had some unique factors. We were always looking for unique factors. Take book-to-price. We would say we have a bunch of value factors, and a bunch of other factors. We know book-to-price is very naive and simple, and anybody who took investments 101 knows this variable. But if you look at the data, it still works and still has a small information ratio. It's not perfectly correlated and does have some marginal impact on the quant model. The optimizer would ask you to put this into the model. This is great for an academic or for a published paper; however, the more you throw in factors that are well known, the more you are becoming susceptible. The quant world consisted of big teams, like

BGI, AQR, GSAM, and the peripheral players. The peripheral players will usually have only the naive factors. As a big guy, if you use these, then you are more correlated with these other guys, and those guys are more likely to run for the gates or have a higher chance of getting the plug pulled on them. This is dangerous. Thus, you have to build models that are more cognizant of this. Finally, we learned that you must have procedures in place to raise cash quickly during crises.

—GSAM trader interview, November 8, 2010

Dependence on rating agencies also led to institutional crowding. When ratings guide most investors, those investors move together in chasing better-rated securities and abandoning those with weaker scores. Downgraded Greek debt is a good 2011 example. After the downgrade, the markets sold off and Greek yields rose. Reaction from institutions that now face lower capital ratios from holding Greek debt and serious problems in Greece helped cause the selloff, but ratings still create a focal point for crowds.

Financial models and investment philosophies must account for crowds and interconnected markets, both of which affect market prices regardless of inherent valuations. Bubbles sometimes form and capital allocation can become inefficient when crowds chase the same assets.

Leverage

After LTCM's crisis, it was clear that too much leverage can bring down a firm regardless of the soundness of its positions. In the years before 2008, excess leverage was everywhere, on Main Street and on Wall Street. Leverage is the main reason the bubble burst so violently. It began with the circle of greed. Home owners didn't just maximize credit card debt, they also took mortgage loans with 10% down (leverage of 10), 3% down (leverage of 33), and even 0% down (leverage of infinity). They sometimes walked away from overmortgaged homes, leaving the leverage with the loan's owner. Greedy home owners at every economic level overestimated leverage's benefits. A minimum standard of 20% down and fixed-rate mortgages only would have benefitted both home owners and investors in the long run.

Politicians disguised subsidies to lower-income people as quasi-affordable home loans. Taxpayers inherited this disguised leverage when Freddie Mac and Fannie Mae went into conservatorship.

Banks packaged and sold loans to other banks, investment banks, insurance companies, and hedge funds, again using leverage. Many failed or rescued institutions had high leverage and declining asset values. Without bank runs, some institutions might have survived, but leverage combined with mistrust can make any institution fail, even ones with sound positions.

Most financial systems, including the U.S. financial system, are designed to have leverage. Most commercial banks have between 6 and 15 times leverage; investment banks and hedge funds have anywhere from zero to 30 times leverage. If assets are impaired, damaged, or worth less, a small loss in asset value can cause insolvency.

Appropriate leverage levels depend on business type. Hedge fund positions are marked-to-market daily. Funds immediately recognize a temporary decline in asset-value, and either post to margin or default.

Other firms may not immediately recognize asset value dips and could potentially survive longer. Customers and counterparties prematurely concluded that Lehman was insolvent, based on market rumors and the firm's large commercial real estate exposure. Then their actions really did push Lehman into insolvency. The same was true for Bear. Eventually Goldman Sachs, Morgan Stanley, and even J.P. Morgan would have failed. Both their leverage and real estate exposure were too high.

Relative-value hedge funds learned to treat leverage carefully, especially after the crises of 1998 and 2008. No leverage means very small (and potentially less attractive) returns, but funds that eschew leverage can hold through any market imbalance until positions converge, which can take a long time. Some JWMP and PGAM principals, including Myron Scholes, suggested employing relative-value fixed-income strategies in an enhanced portfolio that uses no leverage. These strategies would produce very small returns, but add a bit to a portfolio's performance over its benchmark.

> My general belief is that you should not leverage these portfolios. Not the way we did it. We had a long-term focus, relative-value approach. The danger in a strategy like that, with any value strategy, is that you might not be able to hold positions until the divergences converge. If you don't have leverage, you can wait. You introduce the risk of being margined out at the bottom. It's the risk behind all large financial failures. We were leveraged in 1998 as well, but we made it through because the dislocation of markets was 3 or 4 times less than in 2008. It would be really helpful to understand who is invested in the securities that you are invested in. It would have helped us to know that these conduits in Canada that had 50 times leverage were out there. By type, by leverage, it's not so easy to figure out who owns it. It was hard to figure it out, but as spreads came to really low levels, you must ask yourself, who in the world is getting in?
>
> —Steve Blasnick interview, Parkcentral principal, July 19, 2011

Leverage is dangerous for a single firm, and for the entire economy when every player leverages the same asset. But leverage can also encourage innovation and national economic growth.

It may be that the tradeoff is more crises, but fundamentally a higher trend in economic growth. If that is the case, societies will ultimately have to make a choice on what is their desired tradeoff.[3]

In the 2008 crisis, the system's massive leverage was applied to a rather unproductive, conventional asset: housing. Housing was also immensely overvalued. When the bubble burst, it left no real growth behind and destroyed the illusion of progress.

Systemic Risk and Too Big to Fail

The issue of companies that are "too big to fail" has been brought up many times throughout history, including during the LTCM crisis. Larger firms might be harder to manage, less transparent, and treated differently than smaller firms on the assumption that they will be bailed out in case of trouble. If they fail, large firms cause equally large reverberations, because so many other market participants are connected to it.[4]

Firms can be too big to fail for many different reasons, including the amount of leverage they have, the interconnectedness of their space, and the web of financial system connections they provide. These large, interconnected institutions have their benefits. Large-scale operations can be more efficient, and it might be easier and quicker to bail out a few large institutions due to a global shock to restore stability, as opposed to many smaller ones with similar exposures.

Designing a system that's less vulnerable to market crises involves tradeoffs. A better system would make it harder for large institutions to exploit their "too big to fail" status while still allowing lenders of last resort. The current bankruptcy process for large financial institutions does not work well, as Lehman demonstrated. Any reform must recognize that the largest "too big too fail" institutions were government-sponsored agencies: Freddie Mac and Fannie Mae. The U.S. government encouraged them to get bigger and bigger.

The 2008 financial crisis underlined that speculative activities in one division of a large firm can not only disguise the company's risk, but also put the entire firm in danger of bankruptcy. Both Lehman and Bear had legitimate asset management, investment banking, and broker-dealer businesses, but their large, levered real estate bets cost them money. Eventually the market didn't trust the true value of their assets, leading to a run on their businesses and ultimately their failures.

Since the financial crisis, similar activities have destroyed other good firms, including MF Global and even Madoff Securities.[5]

Big firms enjoy economies of scale and are usually more diversified than smaller firms, but they take an inherent risk by mixing different lines of business, and particularly by mixing client businesses with capital management businesses. Maybe a broker-dealer should just be a broker-dealer, a bank should just be a bank, and an insurance provider should just be an insurance provider.[6]

Systemic risk is ultimately a bigger risk for the entire economy than are "too big to fail" firms. Systemic risk is the widespread failure of financial institutions, or frozen capital markets that impair both financial intermediation payment systems and lending to corporations and households. More generally, systemic risk is an event that leads to the widespread loss of significantly important, linked institutions associated with economic functioning.

The 2008 financial crisis had its roots in real estate exposure, which was the common link between banking institutions, including regular banks, investment banks, hedge funds, insurance companies, and government-sponsored enterprises. When real estate values dropped, this immediately generated a string of losses throughout the economic system, then led to further economic problems.

Society must identify appropriate ways to buffer systemic risk. Ideas include higher capital for institutions with higher risks, which would reduce their leverage. Alternatively, high-risk institutions might pay a type of insurance premium. The premium would go in a bailout fund, to be used in times of crises, much the same way that FDIC insurance works for banks. The FDIC system has worked incredibly well, even during the financial crisis.[7]

Economists and society must also begin to identify dangerous and benign links. For example, the bursting Internet bubble did relatively little damage to the financial system, perhaps because businesses within that bubble had less leverage than did the players in the housing bubble. Or perhaps fewer institutions and individuals were exposed to the Internet bubble than were exposed to the housing bubble.

Derivatives: The Good, the Bad, and the Ugly

The financial crisis imprinted the public with two persistent ideas: derivatives are bad, and financial professionals don't do anything useful.[8] It's easy to pin the blame on derivatives or financial instruments, but education—or a lack of it—is the real culprit. From mortgage purchasers to bank CEOs, housing bubble participants didn't fully understand their businesses, nor the full implications of their actions. Financial executives should have the skills to understand and evaluate complicated businesses and create management structures that transparently communicate risks.

Executives should also understand that derivatives are everywhere. Economist Robert Merton points out that even a simple bank loan involves hidden derivatives. Standard loans have a prepayment option, also known as an implicit put option. Home owners could default on a loan payment—another hidden put option in the loan contract. An ordinary loan's value is the value of a risk-free loan, minus a put option. If housing prices decline, the put option's value grows and the loan decreases in value, because the probability of default goes up. Interest-rate and housing-price volatility also increase the put option's value and decrease loan value. Bank managers must understand this.

> Senior management, board members, and regulators need to be better educated, not as quants, but in the very simple manner of understanding how to ask important questions about even a simple business. We need to produce much larger numbers of trained people in finance. Even if the world becomes more regulated, this will mean more education in finance, not less. One of the big lessons from the crisis is that we need more people in both the regulatory and private sector to be better trained. This is not to say they need to be rocket scientists. They need to know how risks and values should change. They need to understand when a report doesn't make sense. A rule to add a risk officer to report directly to the board per se won't do this. He will just tick a box and mistakes will go on as usual.
>
> —Robert Merton interview, Nobel prizewinner in economics,
> July 9, 2011

Large insurance companies' use of credit-default swaps is another example of misusing derivatives. AIG and other insurers sold credit protection on mortgage pools using a derivative known as the credit-default swap (CDS). Traditional insurance is based on pooling many independent risks, but AIG was insuring the interlinked housing market. Given the probability of losses, AIG should have put many reserves aside, but it did not.

With equities and other liquid securities, traders essentially vote on an asset's proper price every time they buy or short it, and the price eventually reflects these votes. The CDS market let traders buy mortgages and keep the housing bubble rolling, because they could hedge their risk with a major insurance company. Unfortunately, the insurance company didn't then hedge the risk in the marketplace. These derivatives may have helped create misleading votes for appropriate security prices, harming the market overall.

Some firms created derivatives on insurance contracts they couldn't realistically honor. For example, a company that insures the 30 to 100 tranches of debt issued by investment-grade companies is offering to pay for the losses when 60% of the best companies in the United States fail. In that case, it's unlikely that the insurer would be in financial shape to make these payments. Perhaps some systemwide, catastrophe insurance should be prohibited— derivatives that pay two seconds before a large meteor hits the Earth, for instance. These are not credible contracts.

Lehman's bankruptcy caused market imbalances for a variety of reasons. One of the principal reasons was that all its OTC derivative transactions were somewhat netted within Lehman Brothers, but not with individual counterparties. This was also the case for LTCM, and was one of the reasons regulators didn't let the firm fail. An orderly liquidation of Lehman Brothers may have been less distorting had there been an active clearinghouse or electronic tracking system for OTC derivatives, especially the most common ones. Such a system may also have alleviated some of the problems surrounding CDS contracts. This was an old lesson forgotten.[9]

Derivatives were originally intended to expand opportunities for sharing and transferring risk. In the lead-up to the financial crisis, some newly created derivatives had questionable usefulness. They seemed designed for pure speculation, serving the few and not the many. For example, how important were CDO-squared in transferring risk? Were they really necessary? These instruments were only available to very sophisticated money managers, not to the many home owners who might have wished to diversify or hedge some of their housing risk. What was the overall economic benefit when banks created special-purpose vehicles to leverage their investments at 20 to 1, just to enhance their returns? Unfortunately, there may not be an efficient way to discourage less useful derivatives.

The ways that different counterparties booked derivative profits showed the market's lack of education and transparency. Suppose Goldman Sachs booked a profit on an exotic derivative they sold to another investor for $100 million, but the other side did not book a loss of $100 million. One side didn't understand the transaction and had no business making the trade. Maybe counterparties should be more transparent with one another, sharing their mark-to-market information on OTC transactions to double-check accuracy.

Some of the insurance companies would sell insurance contracts against AA pools for just a few basis points. As soon as this insurance was bought by one bank at something like LIBOR + 2 basis points, they would then book a profit, because their risk had now been reduced to AAA status. How can it be the case that you buy insurance and you make a profit? Accounting profits went up dramatically. In a world of common sense, someone is stupid selling insurance at a low price and making money from it. It would be better if there were more communication on these sorts of things. There needs to be symmetry. When I was working at the CBOE, I remember traders selling options some days and then being so excited they took their wife out for dinner that night. It's the same idea. They hadn't made a real profit. They had sold an option and created a liability for themselves.

—Myron Scholes interview, July 9, 2011

Financial leaders and followers alike need more and better financial education. In the United States, growing affirmative action (aka diversity) in the workplace and schools, grade inflation, and meaningless degrees are all movements in the wrong direction. More financial education would help people understand their risks, from buying a home to managing a business. Better education could also help financial professionals make appropriate distinctions between helpful derivatives and those of questionable usefulness to society.

Conflicts of Interest

It is hard to quantify the role that conflicts of interest played in the 2008 financial crisis. Compared to greed and loose lending standards, conflicts of interest were relatively minor, but still worth understanding. The crisis involved a host of conflicts of interest, from rating agencies to realtors to bankers to politicians.

There were a variety of reasons that rating agencies gave poor-quality ratings, but conflicts of interest were a major cause.[10] Issuers paid rating agencies to rate new securities, so agencies had a strong incentive to give favorable ratings: to attract more business and make larger profits. An independent computer system or organization that randomly pairs a new security and a rating agency could create fewer conflicts of interest. An assignment system could also award business based on rating agency accuracy, which would realign incentives.

Rating agencies were not the only group with conflicts of interest. Investment banks built products with customers who planned to short the security, then sold that security to another group of customers without considering their fiduciary duty. After all, they made a commission on every deal.

Conflicts of interest may also have been built into compensation practices. Most compensation models reward short-term success, rather than long-term success. Mortgage lenders get commissions as soon as the loan is made, regardless of the loan's future performance. As a result, lenders try to write as many loans as possible. Our society has no generally acknowledged, perfect compensation system. Even so, a short-term bonus system focuses management, especially junior management, toward high-risk, high-return, short-term goals that may have negative long-term consequences. During the mortgage boom, an investment bank division might securitize a risky mortgage pool and sell it to other investors, a potentially difficult task that could earn that division a giant bonus. If the sale never happens, the firm is stuck with the mess. If a company tilts compensation toward longer-term company performance, securitizations might slow down or even halt as conditions grow riskier.

On the other hand, it would be wrong to penalize a worker for phenomenal work in one year that others later squandered. And some employees may prefer one type of compensation over another. It probably makes sense to tie compensation to both short- and long-term performance. Many corporations and banks already do this.

Much of Lehman Brothers' compensation was deferred. Fuld owned 10.8 million shares, which were worth $672 million as of January 1, 2008. He sold that position for $597,000 on September 15, 2008, losing almost all of the $672 million. Before that, he and other senior managers received bonuses and sold Lehman stock from 2000 to 2008; he did not lose these gains when Lehman collapsed. Fuld took home a pretax total of $541 million during this period. Other main senior managers took home another $492 million before Lehman's collapse. An optimal compensation scheme is not easy to design.[11]

Institutions that offer both client services and capital management also have a conflict of interest. It's tempting to use customer accounts as a source of information for trading before a customer's buy or sell order is executed (also known as front running, an illegal practice). Separating these two businesses could make sense. On the other hand, there may be economies of scale to housing both businesses internally.

Policy Lessons

In 2008, we learned that the government's inexperience with major crises may have worsened the situation. Regulatory agencies had a deep information deficit and proved unable to effectively identify the financial systems' key weaknesses and risk concentrations, then take preventive action.[12]

Under Alan Greenspan, the Federal Reserve kept interest rates low for far too long.[13] Low interest rates led to low mortgage rates and helped fuel the housing bubble.

Even worse, the Federal Reserve also failed to monitor the home lending market, which is under its jurisdiction. The Fed didn't stop the loose practices that gave rise to irresponsible mortgage standards and gave us mortgage loans with low documentation or no down payment, borrowers with insufficient funds, and exotic ARM and teaser mortgages. If the Fed had stepped in, there would never have been a housing bubble or the mess that followed. The Fed, perhaps due to inexperience, let home owners and their facilitators behave like massively levered hedge funds with government backstops.

Simple regulations could have prevented this. Mortgages could be fixed-rate only with a minimum down payment. This would keep many people from buying a home, but might be the right tradeoff between prudence and accessibility. Another regulation could impose larger penalties for walking away from a mortgage, though this would be slightly more complicated.

When the 2008 crisis was well underway, government officials had no clue what was happening and no idea how to handle it. A former CEO from one of the largest banks in the United States had alerted officials in both the Treasury and the Federal Reserve to the potential solvency problems of banks, but many said that they could not act preemptively. This former CEO reacted by saying the market was "overleveraged" and that everyone was in a state of "collective denial."[14]

Regulatory institutions, including the Fed, must prepare themselves in advance for meltdowns. The more prepared and consistent the policy response, the more tranquil markets will be. The government chose to let some firms fail, others not. There might have been many reasons for these choices, but perhaps the principal one was inexperience.

Lehman could have been handled better. It wasn't reassuring when Mr. Bernanke and Mr. Paulson went to the government with three pieces of paper to buy illiquid assets of banks with the view that the "world was coming to an end." This undermined confidence even more and may have been a catalyst for the system to collapse. Market participants said to themselves, "They must have much more information than I have, so I'm getting out of town." They got rid of any remaining confidence. It set up a chain wave of selling. Everyone in the financial world knows that it is impossible to buy illiquid assets in a short period of time, it takes a long time. Dodd-Frank is not pointing in the right direction as well. You can't fire everyone and have a government employee getting paid $18,000 per year liquidate the positions. This won't work.

—Robert Merton interview, Nobel prizewinner in economics,
July 9, 2011

Funds transfer quickly and easily today, thanks to advances in banking technology. Rumors move even more quickly, and counterparties, customers, and depositors can withdraw funds before they fully understand marketplace information. Major U.S. exchanges halt market trading in times of chaos so market participants can take time to understand the situation. Franklin D. Roosevelt declared a national bank holiday in 1933, and banks closed for several days to stop the massive run. Suddenly halting trading or restricting short selling could create a panic, so it's best to make emergency plans in advance, not on the fly. A series of rules specifying when to halt an expanded market range in the face of difficult-to-digest information may be helpful.

Innovation always outpaces regulation, so regulations must be adaptive and flexible. Regulating functions, not institutions, is one way to do this. Rather than state that a bank has these regulations and a mutual fund those regulations, regulations could apply to a market function, such as business transaction hedging.[15]

Despite all the controversy that accompanied bank bailouts, the crises of 1998 and 2008 showed that there is value in a lender of last resort. The lack of such a lender can make desperate situations even worse.

I think they should have saved Lehman Brothers. It was one of the world's most costly experiments. What did we learn from Lehman? What was it in the bankruptcy of Lehman that we should change for the future? I'm afraid that the rules that are being constructed are not the right rules. We don't want to fire people and have a government authority take over the institution. Elements of Dodd-Frank are throwing away history and starting over again. Instead, we should begin with current bankruptcy rules and fix them for an orderly liquidation of financial institutions. In terms of Lehman Brothers, we learned that finance can't handle two million contracts in one afternoon. It's a peak load pricing problem. Even a regular sandwich shop can't handle 1,000 people coming to the store on day 1. Everyone plans for some peaks, but not for the maximum peak. We need a system for orderly liquidation of the system and for people to have sufficient time to understand the new equilibrium. Some of the suggestions for reform may lead to a worse situation whereby participants will begin withdrawing early from an institution as they try to get out before the government jumps in and makes mistakes.

—Myron Scholes interview, Nobel prizewinner in economics,
July 9, 2011

Many people criticized bailouts for creating moral hazard, but it isn't clear that this was a problem. Many bank equity holders lost almost everything in the bailouts. In all cases, the government bailed out bond holders, who don't really manage an institution.[16]

Shareholders and managers run firms. The market needs rules that reduce moral hazard as much as possible before a lender of last resort gets involved. This is no easy task.

I presume the Fed understood the importance of the coordination for LTCM in 1998. In 2008, did they really understand that Lehman Brothers wasn't like an airline? The bankruptcy unleashed enormous amounts of risk into the system. Do you bail out shareholders? No. Maybe you bail out some creditors.

It was hard for people inside Lehman to understand the risk of Lehman, so it was that much harder for creditors.

Lehman's Dick Fuld lost $900 million and his reputation; what other incentives do you need for him? We are going to have to look for other methods to align incentives.

—Robert Merton interview, Nobel prizewinner in economics,
July 9, 2011

Risk Management

In normal times, risk management is relatively easy, but it's enormously complex in a crisis. VaR and other risk models don't consider connections within a trading space and ignore fundamental valuation. Risk models should explicitly consider other players' behavior as part of risk calculations. Risk models should also contain a valuation component. They should not be based solely on the statistical analysis of historical data or recent price movements. If a bond will pay $100 in 3 days with a nearly zero default probability and the price drops to 1 cent, the position's risk should be nearly zero, not higher. Similarly, an Internet stock that trades at a multiple that seems disconnected from growth expectations or fundamental values should have a risk much higher than the one implied by its historical standard deviation or beta. VaR and other risk measures are now somewhat pro-cyclical.

Stress tests also need improvement. Many stress tests are based on a trade's worst, relatively recent history—during the past 10 years, for instance. Better stress tests would incorporate valuation, crowding estimates, and crowd behavior assessments during both turbulent and calm market conditions.

In both theory and in practice, risk management should be driven by models that account for interconnections and fundamental value.

Risk management must also consider accounting. Before the 2008 crisis, many investment banks produced financial statements that were very difficult to understand. An intelligent reader couldn't see what real estate the bank owned, which real estate exposures were hedged, which were not, or the real estate's true value. With or without regulation, the private sector should push to make bank and other corporate financial statements less concerned with legal disclaimers and more focused on clarity and transparency. This would help investors judge risks more accurately and make rumor-based bank runs less likely.

Mark-to-market accounting is also pro-cyclical and susceptible to crowd behavior. Mark-to-market accounting values assets at today's price. When investors panic in a crowded space, there may be few (if any) buyers for a security. That pushes the mark-to-market price to a very low value, even when the price would be much higher without the investor panic. As with VaR measurements, the market would be better off with marks that consider fundamental value.

Some businesses go through predictable cycles. For these, a fair asset valuation might involve two sets of numbers: the mark-to-market value and the expected present discounted cash-flow value over a longer horizon.

In 2008, bank capital wasn't sufficient to withstand a major crisis, though most banks had the minimum Basel ratios. Different banks computed Basel ratios in different ways, so it was difficult to compare institutions. Banks also lacked sufficient liquidity cushions. There are still no standardized, reliable measures for liquidity risk. Banks need better liquidity risk measures, especially during times of crisis. These measures should explicitly consider other issues, including market interconnections.

Counterparty Interaction

> Every banker knows that if he has to prove that he is worthy of credit, however good may be his arguments, in fact his credit is gone.
> —Walter Bagehot

Banking is built on trust. Without government intervention, all the major investment banks, many large corporations, and many more commercial banks might have failed, not because of their actual solvency, but because of declining trust throughout the financial system.

Trust declined for many reasons: opaque financial statements, uncertain values in the real estate market, and uncertainty around policy decisions. As institutions stopped trusting each other, the entire banking system risked failure. Future emergency policy plans must include provisions to deal with cycles of mistrust.

Banks and hedge funds used Lehman as a counterparty in repo and reverse repo transactions. In a repo transaction, Lehman borrowed cash, gave collateral, and paid counterparties the repo rate. As Lehman became a riskier institution and default became more likely, Lehman counterparties had two choices. They could have closed their Lehman accounts, which would have accelerated Lehman's demise. They could also have bought insurance protection on Lehman's default, perhaps through a CDS. This second option would have been prohibitively expensive, because the CDS rate was much higher than the rate they were receiving on their financing. Eventually the best option was to close their business with Lehman.

In the future, collateralized financing arrangements should account for counterparties' real risks, perhaps by asking counterparties to pay a rate that's related to their business's risk: the Fed funds rate plus the CDS spread, for instance.

Market practice should also modify other arrangements to account for swaps' replacement value and to facilitate orderly counterparty changes. During the 2008 crisis, relative-value and other hedge funds were unable to meet margin calls on some of their swap and other OTC positions. In these situations, counterparties had few options, according to the International Swaps and Derivatives Association (ISDA).

Counterparties could offset swap positions with other counterparties. They could easily compute the loss in this circumstance: the difference between the new transaction's cost plus the capital loss on the closed position. Or they could keep the swap on their books and estimate the position's loss.

In bankruptcy court, counterparties often overestimate the value of their losses in both situations. This makes logical sense. In bankruptcy, ultimate recovery amounts are often unclear. By claiming a larger amount, a creditor might get a pro-rata payout that is in line with true losses.

Unfortunately, this behavior distorts losses and leads to inefficiencies. When Lehman went bust, most counterparties claimed more losses than they truly had. Some Lehman counterparties were fair, finding the swaps' replacement value and charging Lehman a reasonably accurate replacement cost. An improved system should have fair, orderly ways to deal with liquidations. The private market can make these changes; no regulator is required.

The quant crisis supplied another lesson about counterparty transactions. When Bear and Lehman failed, many counterparties faced unnecessary upheaval. Many hedge funds and counterparties that used Lehman as a broker or prime broker suffered when Lehman went bankrupt.

A well-known quant manager said, "Whenever we decided who to trade with, our decision was always based on who has the best price, not about credit or default issues, which we now realize are very important."[17]

> The Lehman bankruptcy affected everybody in lots of big ways. We learned how important liquidity management is for the quant business. We had always talked about counterparty risk, but after Lehman it is taken much more seriously. Now we are much more concerned with where our capital is.
> —Ken Kroner interview, Managing Director and
> Head of Global Market Strategies for Blackrock, October 29, 2010

Hedge Funds

Hedge funds were front and center in 1998, but were peripheral players in 2008, when many hedge funds performed better than other asset classes, but many hedge funds also went bankrupt or closed. Many hedge funds, particularly relative-value hedge funds, depend on intermediaries for funding. In a crisis, intermediaries also have problems, so financing becomes difficult. More research must focus on understanding the multitude of issues around short-term financing during crises.

Hedge fund gates also need research. Hedge funds are less liquid than many investment vehicles, because investors can withdraw only at specified intervals: sometimes as short as a month, sometimes as long as three years, as was the case for LTCM investors. During the financial crisis, investors wanted to withdraw their money from hedge funds at a screaming pace. Some were worried that the hedge fund would fail, some needed cash for other problematic positions, and some felt a circumstantial heightened risk aversion.

If every investor withdraws money, a hedge fund must sell sound, illiquid positions at a discount. That causes suffering for all investors. This is a key reason that LTCM locked investments in for three years: to avoid irrational runs that would damage all investors.

To prevent this, hedge funds have adopted *hedge fund gates*. A hedge fund gate lets the fund reduce redemption requests to a certain percentage of total assets during any redemption period. If a fund has a 15% gate and investors request redemptions that equal 20% of the fund's NAV, then the fund reduces all redemption requests until the total equals 15% of NAV.

This solves one problem but introduces another. In a crisis, it's better to withdraw money early, while the fund still has it. Some investors withdraw because they're afraid to be left out. This, of course, can fuel the equivalent of a bank run.

Some hedge funds designed innovative schemes to deal with this problem. At Parkcentral, they called this the "gating game." One fix says that if redemptions in a given period are less than the gate (15%, for example), all investors get their money. If redemptions are greater than 15%, the fund throws out all redemption requests and all investors can request a new withdrawal. The fund allows withdrawals, but in amounts proportional to an investor's capital balance in the fund. This isn't perfect, but could reduce the amount of gaming.

Suppose the fund had $100 million and five investors, one with $60 million and the other four with $10 million each. Two of the smaller investors want to withdraw their entire investment. That withdrawal would exceed 15% of the fund's value, so the fund would notify all investors. If all the investors wanted all their money, the large investor could withdraw $9 million and the smaller ones could withdraw $1.5 million each. Other large investors know how the system works, so this plan could remove investors' anxiety to withdraw so they're not left out.

Many hedge funds learned the value of dynamic risk hedging during the crises.

The biggest lesson from the quant crisis is the importance of dynamic risk budgeting. You must understand the overall market environment and adjust the internal risk of the portfolio. This includes modifying the factor weights based on the overall risk. For example, for the macro fund, we saw turmoil all over the markets. On Day 3 of the quant crisis, we all got together. The first days of the week, the problems were from credit markets. Thus, we asked everyone to think about what was the next domino to fall. We identified the next domino by Thursday morning. On Thursday evening, we began trading out of those exposures.

It was the right thing to do. We eliminated carry exposures and then eliminated most of the beta exposure. This is dynamic risk budgeting. Eliminate beta by selling S&P 500 futures rather than liquidating the positions.

The other important lesson is that of being able to communicate internally and externally during a crisis. The macro business communicated much better than the quant business. We reached out proactively and kept clients calm. It's really a lesson in business practice.

—Ken Kroner interview, Managing Director and
Head of Global Market Strategies for Blackrock, October 29, 2010

Many hedge funds deal with counterparties' whims during financial market crises. In particular, relative-value hedge funds depend on repo arrangements with counterparties to fund their trades. When funding became difficult, this posed problems for hedge funds. Since the 2008 crisis, some hedge funds, including III, have modified their trade structures to depend less critically on system interconnections. These hedge funds now structure their trades to rely very little on dealer financing. They have small repo books and use other sources of financing.

On the risk side, many relative-value hedge funds still use the same ideas and look for the same anomalies and convergences. However, they construct shorter duration structures with shorter convergence periods and use options to more precisely define their trades' risk characteristics. Rather than doing a plain swap spread trade, for instance, they try to structure some parts of the trade with option positions.

Separating and managing risks is not as straightforward as financial theorists believed before 2008.

The financial crisis of 2008, in some ways, threw out 30 years of financial theory. The big innovation in finance was to separate alpha from beta. One should stay away from risks one doesn't understand and focus on the value-added, or alpha. Focus on alpha and leverage to restore equilibrium in markets. Any hedge fund that did this in 2008 went bankrupt. It doesn't work.

—Chi-Fu Huang interview, October 23, 2010

The Importance of Arbitrage

The real estate bubble primarily caused the 2008 financial crisis. Once again we learned that markets can be irrational and that sustaining a bubble may be in everyone's interest. Arbitrageurs were rare during the housing bubble, so prices had just one way to go: up. In part, arbitrageurs were scarce because it was difficult to short the housing market, and potentially too risky to bet against a massive bubble with lots of dollars behind it.

During the crisis, many relative-value hedge funds, broker-dealers, and other hedge funds that were supposed to bring market efficiency went bankrupt or were forced to close their positions. The market needs entities that can provide continuous liquidity when other sources dry up. Hedge funds may provide some liquidity, which is possible precisely because they are unregulated, but the market may need a backup liquidity source. We need to think about finding or inventing that type of institution.

> Why is a hedge fund a good intermediary? If you're going to do intermediation and you must play by the same rules, you can't do it. If all Japanese banks have the same rules, then they can't help each other. So you need an entity that doesn't have to follow the same rules. Thus, a hedge fund might be the optimal vehicle, because it's lightly regulated. If you have to be the other side of trades with institutional rigidities, then you must be lightly regulated. That's why regulating hedge funds like banks doesn't make sense. What entity will perform this financial function? In 2008, the financial swap spread went negative, that gives you an example of what happens when intermediation disappears. Hedge funds and trading desks couldn't get financing and credit standards tightened up. There was an imbalance in primary users. Hedge funds take risks because they get paid for it. They are not necessarily smarter than others. Someone who trades cocoa wouldn't necessarily think that they know more than Hershey or that by trading oil that they know more than oil companies. One must understand the actual business. What is the comparative advantage?
> —Robert Merton, Nobel prizewinner in economics, July 9, 2011

The society at large benefits greatly from financial activities. In normal times:

- Market makers, such as Lehman Brothers, Goldman Sachs, and others, buy or sell securities on demand. By taking these risks, they offer the markets lower transaction costs, better execution, and more reliable prices.
- Derivatives help Main Street companies run their businesses more reliably. A bank makes mortgage loans and implicitly takes on interest-rate risk. The bank may transfer this risk through interest-rate swaps or other derivatives. That lets banks make more loans and leads to lower mortgage rates.
- Investment banks and other banks help transfer risk, which creates opportunities that would not otherwise arise. Venture capital, public offerings, and debt issues all rely on risk transfer for society's benefit.
- Investments involve real and financial risks. In many contexts, insurance can reduce those risks.

The 1998 and 2008 financial crises demonstrated what happens when financial institutions do not provide these services, either because of a crisis or because they abused the system they were serving. Some of the financial system's glitches reappeared just two years later, during the Flash Crash.

Box 16.1   New and Old Lessons from the Crisis

1. Risk management demands an understanding of investment spaces' interconnections and crowding.
2. The financial system used too much leverage.
3. The size and composition of a firm's activities can help create a system that's vulnerable to systemic risk.
4. Some derivatives add little societal value, but have the potential for great costs.
5. Many participants in the housing bubble's circle of greed had conflicts of interests.
6. Policy makers were ill prepared for financial emergencies and took actions that may have exacerbated the crisis. Later on, however, the Fed established some useful stabilization policies.
7. Improved risk-management systems must account for interconnections, crowds, and liquidity risk.
8. Counterparty arrangements are currently subject to crowd behavior during crises. Improved counterparty arrangements should address this vulnerability.
9. Hedge funds did not cause the crisis, but the crisis damaged them. They could not provide intermediary functions when they were most needed.
10. The current financial system does not provide liquidity when it is most needed.

PART III

The Aftermath

Insanity is doing the same thing over and over again but expecting different results.

—Anonymous

After the 2008 financial crisis, a few crowded spaces remained. On May 6, 2010, the U.S. equity market—one of the most liquid markets in the world—crashed for a few minutes when crowded market makers disappeared all at once.

Banks all across the world had been loading up on Greek debt for years, attracted to the slightly more attractive yield it offered over German Bunds. Banks felt the small extra return was worth the risk, because in the end, the Europeans would bail out Greece.

In 2009, the Greeks suddenly announced that they had lied about their finances. Banks across Europe found themselves in peril. The Greeks were on the verge of defaulting and being kicked out of the Euro Club.

The decade that started in 1998 with the Russian and LTCM crises and ended with the 2008 crisis rolled into a new decade that promised more crowded crashes.

CHAPTER 17

The Flash Crash

> *The speed of the game has changed.*
>
> —Ivan Lendl

On the morning of May 6, 2010, the market was a little jittery. Traders had heard bad news about Greece's economic situation and ability to pay its debts. The VIX, a measure of the market's forecast about future short-term volatility, went from 25% to 40%, reflecting that volatility expectations had almost doubled during the course of the day. Gold rallied and Treasury yields decreased as the market scrambled for safer assets.

In the afternoon, the U.S. equity market—one of the most well-functioning, liquid markets in the world—went completely haywire. From 2:40 P.M. to 3:00 P.M. the market traded at ridiculous prices. Some bought Apple stock for $100,000 per share, some bought Accenture for $0.01 per share, and some pushed Procter & Gamble from $60 to $39.47 in less than four minutes (see Figure 17.1).[1] The markets weren't running smoothly. By 3 P.M., however, the markets suddenly went back to normal.

Stock prices moved in crazy ways for just a few minutes, giving this event its name: the Flash Crash. How could a well-functioning market spawn such chaos? What caused the Flash Crash? What happened to those poor souls who bought stocks at $100,000 per share or sold them for as little as a penny? Could crowd behavior be partly responsible for the distortions in the market movements of May 6?

FIGURE 17.1   Apple, Accenture, and Sotheby's Stock Prices

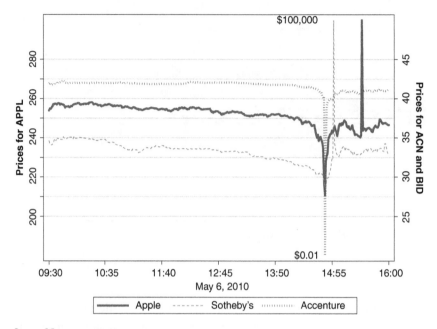

Source: Nanex.

Background

In the 1700s, stock traders met under a buttonwood tree on Wall Street. In 1792, they created the New York Stock Exchange (NYSE). For more than 200 years, individuals traded stocks face to face. Computer technology has since made trading blindingly fast and largely anonymous. In 2006, the NYSE became an electronic exchange, saying goodbye to the traditional floor brokers and specialists who ran around on those old wooden floors, screaming prices as they went.[2]

Stock purchases and sales can be completed through a variety of networks: a national exchange such as the NYSE, an electronic communication network (ECN), a large broker-dealer, or a dark pool. Most trading—64%—takes place on the exchanges. Broker-dealers account for another 18%, about 10% occurs through ECNs, and the remaining 8% occurs in dark pools.[3]

The exchanges consist of highly automated trading systems that respond to stock orders in less than one millisecond. ECNs are alternative trading systems that offer services that are very similar to those offered by the exchanges. They try to match buyers and sellers at the best bid and offer prices.

All the trades that occur on the exchanges and the ECNs must be posted on the consolidated tape, including price and quantity traded.[4] The consolidated tape is a real-time history of every trade in the U.S. markets. It provides marketplace transparency.

Dark pools can be a source of marketplace mystery, because their quotes are not reported to the CQS. A typical exchange order is 175 to 200 shares. Sometimes large institutions trade much larger share blocks—50,000 at a time, for instance. If they send such a big order to the marketplace, they may cause panic, get a horrible execution price, or generate questions about why they are selling or buying such a large amount. So institutions send these orders to one of the 56 U.S. dark pool providers, which try to match large buy and sell orders anonymously, limiting the impact on prices.

Pools report only the trade's size and price to the consolidated tape (CTS). They never report the buyer or seller's identity.[5]

Broker-dealers can route customer orders to the marketplace or internalize orders, using their own capital to settle customer trades. This is often more efficient and saves transaction costs. Broker-dealers must also report internalized trades to the consolidated tape.

Stock exchange laws say that all trades must be executed at the national best bid and offer at the time of execution. This is true for exchanges, ECNs, dark pools, and broker-dealers.

New technologies and interconnected trading systems have made trading much faster. Despite the high speeds and information flow, flash crashes have happened before. On May 3, 1906, and August 9, 1919, for instance, stock prices changed dramatically, then recovered.[6] The modern trading system had some flashes as early as April 28, 2010. Dendreon, a biotechnology company, dropped by 69% in less than two minutes; trading in the stock was halted. The stock returned to its previous price after the company released good results about its prostate cancer treatment drug Provenge. There is no definitive reason that the stock price moved so much, so quickly.[7]

On April 27, 2010, a failed basket trade on the Nasdaq resulted in about 80 broken trades.[8]

Flash Crash Theories

What causes a sudden drop or rise in market prices? There are many theories. Illiquidity is often present, with mismatched numbers of sellers and buyers. Too many sellers could cause a price drop, while too many buyers would push the price up.

Fat Finger Theory

The *fat finger* theory says that flash crashes happen when a mistakenly oversized order comes through the system. A trader might enter a buy order for a billion shares, when she really meant to buy a million shares. Because this large trade could not find enough sellers, it would cause a huge price spike.

High-Frequency Trader Theory

Another theory says that high-frequency traders (HFTs) caused the flash crash. HFTs represent about 73% of U.S. equity trading volume.[9] They program sophisticated algorithms that absorb massive amounts of market data, then quickly generate corresponding trades intended to profit from small price discrepancies while taking very little risk. These traders tend to close exposures at the end of each trading day. They help supply market liquidity and efficiency.

Some argue that these algorithms also manipulate the market to generate profits. In *quote stuffing*, for instance, algorithms post a large number of stock limit orders, then pull the orders before they are executed.[10] The idea is to flood the system with orders to slow down competitors' processing.

Suppose the best bid-ask in the market on a stock is $10 to $10.02.[11] An HFT might post a limit order to sell the stock at $10.01. Market makers can see this limit order.

A game of *slap hands* then takes place. A market maker decides whether to go for the limit order. Does he try to slap the other hand? Suppose he does, posting a new bid at $10.01 and making the market appear to move upward. The HFT could quickly remove the limit order before it's executed. The HFT moves its hand, in other words, and the market maker misses. But other market makers may move to the new bid-ask spread, actually causing the market to move up. Fast computer programs let HFTs play lots of games with the system. When traders place lots and lots of these limit orders to cause processing problems and confusion, the practice is known as quote stuffing. When they place just a few, it's known as *spoofing*.

Fast-moving algorithms can also manipulate the market through *fly fishing*.[12] HFTs want information on how market makers might move. They may throw a limit order for a small number of shares and see whether this moves market prices or not. This gives them valuable information about how a market might trend.

Painting the tape is yet another technique. This involves posting simultaneous buy and sell orders on large quantities of a given stock, giving the impression that the stock has significant volume and perhaps attracting other investors. Any sort of trading activity designed to alter other traders' perceptions of market prices could be called painting the tape. On the day of the Flash Crash, 5,000 quotes per second were sometimes sent on one particular stock. This alone does not pose any systemic challenge, but if computer programs made a large number of orders on every particular stock, it could cause communication delays between exchanges, which in turn would cause delays and uncertainties in the marketplace.

Quote stuffing and painting the tape are considered stock price manipulation and are illegal. Sometimes regulators uncover these games. For example, Trillium Brokerage Services placed a huge number of fake buy and sell orders and then canceled them quickly about 46,000 times in 2006 and 2007.[13] It was fined $1 million. It's not always easy, however, to regulate these fast-playing traders.

The theory is that HFTs may have flooded the system with orders. That created a slowdown in order processing, which led to delayed quotes and a loss in confidence around pricing on the day of the Flash Crash.

Jittery Markets

On the day of the Flash Crash, world developments made the market nervous. Market makers may have been shy about taking on sell volume on a day that was likely to have many sell orders. What made this jittery day different than other jittery days?

The Real Cause of the Flash Crash

A detailed investigation into Flash Crash causes showed what might have caused the market price chaos on that day in May.[14]

The market was already jittery on May 6, reacting to negative developments around the world, including the Greek and European debt crisis. By about 2:30 P.M., the market's assessment of future volatility had risen. Market participants' willingness to buy stocks declined by about 55% and sell order depth increased by about 40%.[15] Buyers stayed away from this market throughout the day and completely vanished around 2:45 P.M. Sell volume dropped sharply around 2:45 P.M., but not nearly as much as buy interest.

By 2:45 and 28 seconds, buy-side interest declined by about 99% compared to earlier that morning.

The Waddell-Reed Trade

At 2:32 P.M., the mutual fund company Waddell & Reed needed to sell a total of 75,000 S&P 500 futures contracts worth about $4.1 billion using the E-Mini. Waddell was making a futures overlay trade to reduce overall portfolio risk without the complications of selling individual securities. There are many ways a portfolio manager can trade shares: manually, through another firm, or with an automated execution algorithm. Waddell chose the algorithm.

Portfolio managers must consider the price impact of trading a large position. If a sell order is too large, too fast, there will not be enough liquidity and the price will drop. Sell algorithms use simple rules to make sure that only a small part of an entire position sells at any given time, so the market can handle the trade.

Waddell-Reed sent Barclays the sell order for execution. The SEC's Flash Crash report said the algorithm looked at only the trading volume over the preceding minute, and would initiate selling 9% of that minute's trading volume, independent of price. Vijay Pant, the Barclays trader, said that the algorithm did consider price.[16]

Whether the algorithm had a price trigger or not, the position was not large enough to cause chaos.[17]

In just four minutes, the S&P 500 E-Mini dropped by 3% (see Figure 17.2). At 2:45 and 28 seconds, the CME automatically halted E-Mini trading for five seconds. The delay let new buyers enter the market, and the E-Mini rallied as Waddell's order continued through the market system. Waddell sold all the contracts by 2:51 P.M. During the E-Mini's crucial drop, there were virtually no sell orders from the Waddell-Reed trade.[18]

Abnormal behavior spread to other parts of the stock market, primarily through cross-market trading firms, also known as program trading shops. These shops trade to keep markets that should be related through basic mathematics in alignment. For example, there is a natural relationship between the stocks in the S&P 500 and S&P 500 futures. If one declines rapidly, the other should as well. As the E-Mini S&P 500 futures moved, these program traders changed quotes for the SPY, the S&P 500 ETF, and other, related securities. Some of them were perplexed by the large moves and briefly ceased operations.

This seems a weak explanation for a collapse. A large sell order came through that was eventually absorbed. Why did buyers hide and why did liquidity dry up?

FIGURE 17.2 The Dow Jones, S&P 500 Futures, and SPY

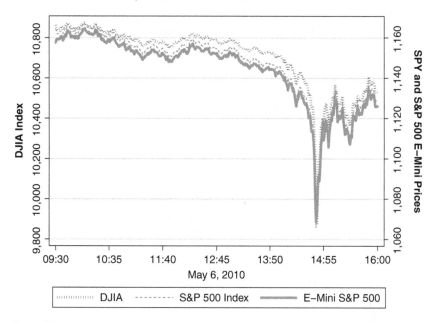

Source: Nanex.

The Computer Glitch

There are all kinds of equity market makers. Traditional market makers offer bid and ask quotes on individual stocks or ETFs and stand ready to buy or sell securities, making a profit over time from the spread. HFTs use high-speed computer systems, monitor market data, and submit both buy and sell orders to profit over shorter time periods. These two groups have different intentions, but both supply liquidity to slower traders.[19]

Broker-dealers who handle retail demand are the third type of equity market makers. They handle many trades internally or pass them on to other institutions that internalize the trades.[20]

These different traders typically provide market liquidity at any given moment. The market system is built so that traders always get the best available prices. If one exchange receives a buy order at less than the current best price, that exchange must either match the best price or route the order to the exchange that has the best price. There is one exception. If one exchange notices a communication problem with another exchange, the first exchange may declare a *self help* status, ignore the second exchange, and proceed with business as usual.[21]

At 2:30 P.M., the Chicago Board Options Exchange issued a communication:

> The CBOE has declared Self Help against the NYSE/ARCA as of 1:30 CT. The NYSE/ARCA is out of NBBO and unavailable for linkage. All CBOE systems are running normally.
> —CBOE Announcement, May 6, 2010, 2:30:00

At 2:37 P.M. Nasdaq announced:

> NASDAQ has declared Self Help against NYSE ARCA (ARCA) as/of 14:36:59 E.T. All NASDAQ systems are operating normally.
> —NASDAQ Member web site, May 6, 2010, 2:36:59

The OMX and BATS exchange followed suit at 2:38:40 and 2:49 P.M. respectively.[22]

The NYSE trading platform had some data reliability issues. From 2:30 P.M. to 3:00 P.M., the NYSE paused trading for more than 1,000 securities due to volatility issues. On a normal day, it might pause 20 to 30 securities.[23]

The NYSE also had processing errors. Because of the sustained high volume of market data that day, quotation and execution information was slow to disseminate to processors in 1,665 NYSE listed stocks, all traded on NYSE servers that had not been upgraded.[24]

Massive volume arrived at 2:42 and 44 seconds, clogging the systems even more.[25] These processing problems resulted in price delays of more than 10 seconds on all 1,665 stocks between 2:44 and 2:46 P.M. Between 2:45 and 2:50 P.M., more than 40 stocks had delays of over 20 seconds.

> Because of the incredibly high volume on that day, there were delays in the reporting on a number of stocks. We were in the process of updating our programs, and some areas that hadn't yet been updated [were unable to handle the increased load].
> —Ray Polleccia, NYSE Spokesman (Flood 2010)

These NYSE problems made the consolidated tape look strange. Some NYSE stock quotes appeared with a delay, and this gave the consolidated tape

TABLE 17.1 Consolidated Tape for Accenture on May 6, 2010

Time	Shares	Price	Exchange
2:47:25 P.M.	100	38.66	ISE
2:47:25 P.M.	100	40.22	FINRA
2:47:25 P.M.	100	40.22	FINRA
2:47:25 P.M.	100	39.06	NYSE Arca
2:47:28 P.M.	300	38.02	FINRA
2:47:29 P.M.	100	40.2	FINRA
2:47:34 P.M.	310	39.12	NYSE Arca

Source: Angel (2011).

a variety of jumping prices. Some NYSE bid quotes were higher than ask quotes, as was the case for Accenture.

For a major company such as Accenture, consolidated tape trades are executed at similar prices over several seconds. Prices move by (at most) one penny over several seconds. May 6 tape quotes did not follow this pattern (see Table 17.1). Accenture prices sometimes simultaneously traded at prices that differed by a dollar. That's virtually unheard of.

The market makers saw these data discrepancies on the consolidated tape and compared them to prices from their exchange proprietary feeds. They knew about the self-help declarations and began to mistrust market prices. Many market makers began to widen their bid-ask spreads, then completely withdrew from the markets.[26]

Gone Fishing

All market makers must maintain two-sided quotations at all times, as a condition of being a market maker. When market makers want to withdraw from the markets, they use *stub quotes*. Stub quotes, which can be generated automatically or manually, are unrealistically low bids and unrealistically high asks. Such quotes are intended to fulfill the market maker's obligation to quote, but effectively remove them from the marketplace by being so unrealistic. A market maker who would rather not make a market in Apple stock can post a bid of $0.01 and an ask of $100,000.

Many market makers didn't trust the market data and were further perturbed by high market volatility on May 6. They widened their bid-ask spreads or resorted to stub quotes. HFTs stopped trading and many of them increased the number of sell orders relative to buy orders.

Many internalizers got lots of sell orders from retail brokerages. Because of rapid price moves and large numbers of arriving sell orders, some internalizers routed sell orders to the exchanges rather than handle them internally. As market makers disappeared, these sell orders often found only stub quotes. An order to sell 100 shares of Accenture was executed at the stub ask price of 1 cent (see Table 17.2 and Figure 17.1), and a market order to buy 100 shares of Apple was executed at the stub order of $100,000.

The market was thin and liquidity was gone. Short sellers didn't make prices collapse—buyers in a market with no sellers and sellers in a market with no buyers did that job. Trading models ignored valuation and didn't trust information. Ultimately, prices depended on who was willing to buy or sell. At times, that was nobody.

Between 2:40 P.M. and 3:00 P.M., more than 20,000 trades representing a total of 5.5 million shares were executed at prices 60% away from their 2:40 P.M. value. About 50% of these erratic trades happened because one large internalizer sold positions and one large market maker acted as a buyer.[27] About half these crazy trades were due to retail sell orders that flushed into an illiquid system.

TABLE 17.2 Stub Quotes on Consolidated Tape for Accenture on May 6, 2010

Time	Shares	Price	Exchange
2:47:54 P.M.	100	1.84	Nasdaq
2:47:54 P.M.	100	0.01	Nasdaq
2:47:54 P.M.	100	0.01	CBSX
2:47:54 P.M.	100	1.74	Nasdaq
2:47:54 P.M.	100	0.01	CBSX

Note: CBSX is the CBOE Stock Exchange.
Source: Angel (2011).

The NYSE Arca caused most of the vanishing liquidity. The SEC-CFTC examination found that quote stuffers probably didn't cause the computer system glitches. When the quotes were delayed, much of the buy- and sell-side depth disappeared rather than increased. However, Nanex's analysis suggested that most of the high volume occurred at around 2:42:44 P.M. HFTs may have contributed, but it's hard to know, because no one has yet done a detailed analysis of this period.

A fat-finger mistake didn't cause the Flash Crash. The large Waddell-Reed trade was the intended size, and traders didn't spot any other large, peculiar orders.

HFT activity didn't seem to cause data problems during the severe liquidity drop, although a window of trading activity starting around 2:42 P.M. and 44 seconds has yet to be examined in detail. We can't completely rule out the possibility that HFT activity caused data overload in some of the NYSE Arca's out-of-date systems.

Jittery markets combined with a flood of orders and old computers to create a computer glitch at the NYSE Arca. This directly caused the Flash Crash. Chaos ruled those three minutes because faulty data scared off liquidity providers. Amazingly enough, the liquidity providers all ran for the exits at the same time. Crowd behavior erased liquidity just when traders needed it the most, and just as the market saw in the LTCM crisis, the Quant Crisis, and the subprime crisis.

> What caused the forest fire? It's easy to say it was the match, but it was really the dry kindling and gasoline all around the forest. The contracts that Waddell-Reed sold were infinitesimal compared to the market volume. So they weren't even the match. If there was a match, it was the activity at 14:42:44 and that still needs to be thoroughly examined, although no one has yet.
> —Eric Scott Hunsader, Nanex founder, December 9, 2011

The Aftermath

Don't feel too sorry for the traders who bought Sotheby's at $100,000 or sold Accenture for a penny. Both the exchanges and FINRA canceled all trades that moved by more than 60% from their last traded price between 2:40 P.M. and 3:00 P.M.[28] FINRA normally breaks trades with 10% to 20% moves. FINRA's decision was somewhat arbitrary and unfair to some market participants, while to others it was extremely helpful. Perhaps this is one of the lessons of the Flash Crash: The market system should establish a more transparent definition of what constitutes a broken trade.

The market learned other important lessons. In just seconds a crowd can disappear and take liquidity with it. Market interconnections were hidden within the system. As cross-market traders saw the S&P 500 E-Mini's price decline after a large sell order, they made corresponding trades in the underlying stocks and the S&P 500 ETFs, passing the E-Mini sell pressure on to other markets.

FINRA and the SEC have responded in part by implementing individual stock circuit breakers. If any stock price moves by 10% within five minutes, trading in that stock will stop for five minutes, until markets can digest the information or until system errors are corrected. Then trading can begin again.

Regulators have also established new trade break procedures. For high-priced stocks, a movement of 3% will establish the break level. Medium-priced stocks have a break level of 5%, and low-priced stocks have a 10% break level.[29]

In the end, the Flash Crash came and went with astonishing speed. The worst trades were erased, mending the situation—unless you sold a stock at a 59% loss or bought a stock at a 59% premium. Just a little data-feed delay caused a panic just when the market needed liquidity most. Liquidity providers have vanished in the past, before electronic trading was so dominant. In 1987, market makers just didn't answer their telephones, effectively refusing to provide liquidity. Maybe all liquidity is just a mirage and it never has changed.

Trouble in Europe, particularly Greece, caused the market's initial nervousness on May 6, 2010. It initially affected only a segment of the market, but it was bound to spread. Everyone would get greeked.

CHAPTER 18

Getting Greeked

> *So EMU has gone from being an improbable and bad idea to a bad idea that is about to come true. High unemployment, low growth, discomfort with a welfare state that is no longer affordable—all these issues have found new hope of resolution in a desperate bid for a common money, as if that could address the real problems of Europe.*
>
> —Rudiger Dornbusch, October 1996

Once upon a time, there were a bunch of independent countries that managed their own currency. These currencies included the Greek Drachma, the German Mark, the Italian Lira, the French Franc, the Belgium Franc, the Austrian Schilling, the Dutch Guilder, the Spanish Peseta, the Portuguese Escudo, the Luxembourg Franc, the Finnish Markka, and the Irish Pound.

On January 1, 1999, that all changed. All of these countries, except Greece, decided to give up their own money and share a common currency. It's not certain that the Greeks understood what they were doing, but they wanted to be part of the club. They kept submitting their application, but the Euro club told them they just didn't fit in. The Greeks promised they would get their undisciplined economy under control.

In 2001, the Euro club let in their irresponsible little cousin. Some countries that received a special club invitation, including Great Britain and Denmark, didn't care much for the club. After all, how could the British forget hundreds of years of animosity toward the Germans and allow a central bank run out of Frankfurt?[1]

Between 2007 and 2011, the Euro club let in other small countries, waving goodbye to the Slovenian Tolar, Cyprus Pound, Maltese Lira, Slovakian Koruna, and Estonian Kroon.

The European Union had been in the making for many years, starting with a customs union and then with the monetary union. The hope was that club members would have greater economic benefits. Some countries joined the Euro for political reasons, some for economic reasons. A few may not have really belonged at all—in particular, one little country named Greece.

Members Only

The idea of forming a currency union was not a new one. There are both advantages and disadvantages to giving up one's own currency. Some argue that the entire world should have just one currency.[2]

The Conditions

The more similar its members, the more successful a currency union will be. If only one central bank controls the group's interest rates and monetary policy, the group will be most harmonious if members have roughly the same economic circumstances. If there were a recession in one country, for instance, that country would want to lower interest rates and stimulate its economy. Dissimilar countries, however, might be doing quite well and would worry about stimulation and lower rates bringing rising inflation.

Similar economies make it more likely that members will experience synchronous business cycles. If the economies have different shocks, then it is important that the system can automatically handle shocks, without involving the common central bank.

U.S. states don't have identical economies, though they are more similar than are European countries. If people can move easily from one member country to another, for instance, they will flee high unemployment by moving to more prosperous countries. Unfortunately, Europe is not ideal for this. Each country has a different culture and language. In the U.S., by contrast, the common language is English. If there is a recession in one state, it is relatively easy for labor to migrate to another, more prosperous state.

Wage flexibility can help solve problems when one region is more competitive than another. The U.S. has far more wage flexibility than Europe, which might be due to labor mobility or to less-restrictive labor conditions. Europe has more protective labor laws and unions that restrict wage flexibility.[3]

The United States also has similar businesses. U.S. corporations tend to have stores in virtually every U.S. state. That's not true in Europe. Businesses can sometimes adjust profit margins to lower profit margins in depressed areas and raise them in booming areas, which offers another buffering mechanism. Institutional restrictions still make it difficult to locate a German business in Italy. These institutional restrictions mean lower shock absorption.[4]

U.S. financial markets are another leveling factor. U.S. investors typically buy mutual funds and companies all over the United States, diversifying their regional exposure. Europeans often buy companies from their individual countries.

The U.S. federal government helps all states weather shocks by using unemployment benefit transfers and even specific financial bailouts. The European Union doesn't have an equivalent.[5]

The EU's designers realized European countries are not as similar to each other as are the United States, and that there would be problems if individual countries were too different. They set up economic criteria for Euro membership (see Table 18.1). The requirements were designed to force member countries to have a minimum level of economic similarity. The first requirement is for low inflation. High inflation, compared with other members, is probably due to loose monetary policy, which wouldn't fit a conservative, low-inflation central bank.

The second requirement has to do with budget control. Every Euro country must transfer its monetary policy power to the European Central Bank (ECB). This removes one of the two policy tools countries use to manage their economies.

Each union country is left only with fiscal policy. This is the country's last form of policy discretion, but the club limits even this tool. If a country has

TABLE 18.1 Member Requirements

1. Price Stability	An average annual inflation rate not exceeding 1.5% of the three best performing states.
2. Budget Control	A budget deficit of less than 3% of GDP and a total public debt less than 60% of GDP.
3. Exchange Rate Control	No severe tensions due to currency movements prior to entrance.
4. Similar Interest Rates	An average nominal long-term interest rate not exceeding more than 2% of those of the three best performing members.

Source: ECB.

too much debt relative to the others, the country may not be able to pay its debt. It would then default, as it cannot devalue or inflate away debt through monetary policy. High debt may also lead to higher interest rates for that country, so the ECB might have little influence over the country's economy by interest-rate manipulation. A country with a very volatile exchange rate before joining the Euro must have an active and unstable monetary policy, which makes it too dissimilar. Too-high interest rates mean a country is not ready to be managed by a central bank with a much lower interest-rate target.

The Euro Club saw that members might behave well before entering the club and change their behavior later. They devised penalties for deviating from club rules. Countries that violated basic rules would be fined 0.2% of GDP. If they rectified their problems within two years, they would get a refund. If not, the funds would be distributed to other club members. The maximum amount that could be extracted was 0.5% of GDP, and fines would not be imposed on countries in recession.

Once a country has been admitted to the Euro, unfortunately, there is a strong desire to prevent them from leaving. Fines only make problems harder for misbehaving countries. There is no credible way to ensure good behavior.

Table 18.2 shows key economic statistics for a group of Euro countries, including Greece and Italy. In 1999, Greece did not qualify for membership, despite its desire to join. Its fiscal situation was horrible, with a debt-to-GDP ratio of 94%. Entry required 60% or less. Its annual deficit was −4.2%; entry required −3% or better. Its 10-year interest rates were 6.86%. The three best Euro countries had comparable average rates of 3.87%. Its inflation rate was a whopping 11%; the Euro zone's three best countries' average was 1.85%. Italy met some criteria and not others, but looked much better than Greece overall.[6] Except for Portugal, which was also much better than Greece, all other countries shown made the cut.

The European Union asked many nonqualifying countries to join anyway, politically spun as a chance for mismanaged countries to commit to doing better. They were like cigarette smokers who want to quit and join a social group that doesn't allow smoking. Economically, France didn't want the Italians to have their own currency and depreciate it anytime their goods were uncompetitive, increasing their exports at the cost of French exports. Italy was one of the EU's founding members and had a very large economy. Greece and other smaller countries probably were admitted for political reasons. Greece is home to a rich European history: the Olympic Games, the birthplace of Plato and Aristotle, the playground of Euclid and Pythagoras. And Greece was such a small place. How much harm could it do?

TABLE 18.2 Selected Euro Country Statistics

	Greece		Italy		Portugal		Ireland		Spain		Germany		France	
	1999	2010	1999	2010	1999	2010	1999	2010	1999	2010	1999	2010	1999	2010
Debt	122	329	1281	1842	59	161	44	144	362	642	1225	2062	805	1591
Percent Eurozone	2.7	4.2	27.9	23.5	1.3	2.1	1	1.8	7.9	8.2	26.7	26.3	17.5	20.3
Debt/GDP	94	145	113	118	50	93	48	93	62	61	61	83	59	82
Deficit/GDP	−4.2	−10.6	−2.7	−4.6	−3.5	−9.8	2.4	−31.3	−3	−9.3	−2.3	−4.3	−2.6	−7.1
Unemployment	11.6	15	11.2	8.3	5.6	12.9	6.5	14.4	14.9	20.4	9.4	6.6	11	9.9
9.9 Interest Rate (10-yr)	6.86	28.87	3.93	7.1	3.92	13.95	3.86	9.35	3.9	6.27	3.91	2.4	3.76	3.38
CA/GDP	−3.6	−10.10	1	−1.7	−8.7	−10	0.2	0.5	−2.9	−4.6	−1.3	5.7	3.1	−1.7
Labor Productivity	1.22	1.93	1.39	0.24	3.14	1.47	4.19	2.97	1.69	0.87	2.37	1.21	1.82	1.23
Real GDP Growth	1.89	2.27	1.44	0.67	3.45	0.93	6.58	3	2.77	2.34	2.14	1.12	1.82	1.36
Inflation	11.2	2.57	4.15	2.13	5.95	2.52	2.24	2.56	4.17	2.8	2.38	1.53	1.89	1.6
Qualify	No Way	No Way	Almost	No	No	No	Yes	No	Yes	No	Yes	No	Yes	No

Note: Debt is in billions of Euros. Percent Eurozone is the percentage of that country's debt as a fraction of all European debt. Debt/GDP and Deficit/GDP are in percent. Unemployment is the percent of the labor force unemployed. Interest Rate represents 10-year government interest rates in percent. CA/GDP is the current account as a percentage of GDP. Labor productivity is the average annual growth in GDP per hour worked over the period. Inflation for 1999 is measured as the average annualized inflation from 1990 to 1999 and inflation for 2010 is the average annual inflation from 1999 to 2010. Qualify indicates whether a country meets the Euro membership qualifications. For 1999, variables are measured as of end of 1998 if available, otherwise they are end of 1999 values. For 2010, variables are measured as of the end of 2010, except interest rates which are measured as of November 30, 2011.
Source: Eurostat IMF, and GFD.

The Benefits of Membership

In many senses, the Euro's creation was political, not economical. France and Germany were the core founders, uniting to provide stability in light of their long history of instability. Germany might have seen the Euro as its chance to export discipline to its less sophisticated neighbors.

Even so, club membership had some important economic benefits. Members can trade without the uncertainty of exchange rate movements and the costs of exchange rate commissions. These cost savings might be anywhere from 0.5% to 0.8% of GDP per year.

Membership promoted price transparency across similar goods from member countries. This reduces small uncertainties and costs associated with monitoring prices to find the best bargains.

By creating a strong, independent central bank, many countries could benefit from stable prices, which lead to better production, investment, and consumption decisions.

Many countries with irresponsible fiscal and monetary authorities gained discipline. This could lead to lower interest rates and more stable growth.

All members benefit from savings on exchange rate transaction costs and uncertainty. Gains from solid, disciplined monetary policy only apply to some. The German Bundesbank was already a well-tuned machine, ready to fight inflation and market excesses. The Euro offered France, Italy, Spain, Greece and others a cure for rotten public finance and ever-depreciating currencies. By giving up currency control, they also gave up the option of printing money to stimulate their economies through lower interest rates or depreciation.

The Drawbacks of Membership

Although a single-currency union offered cost savings, it brought a whole set of costs that come with giving up independence. Every country that joins the Euro must transfer its monetary policy power to the European Central Bank (ECB). Some countries couldn't sustain themselves without their own monetary policy and the ability to adjust their exchange rates. Many of these countries' economies depend heavily on trade. In 2010, trade accounted for 30% of Greece's economy and nearly 50% of Germany's economy.[7] Demand for goods depends on how competitive they are compared to other countries, with competitiveness measured by the price of a country's goods, adjusted for the exchange rate, compared to prices in other countries.

Suppose that Germany is very productive and can produce goods at low prices, while Greece is not very productive and its prices remain high. German exports will rise relative to Greek exports. This will dampen the

FIGURE 18.1 Competitiveness of Euro Countries in World Trade

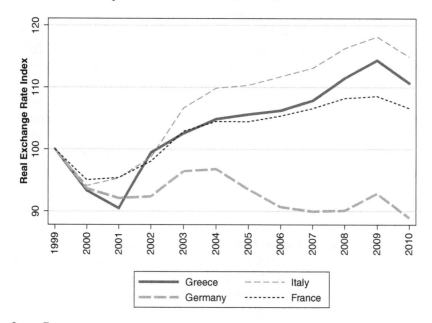

Source: Eurostat.

Greek economy and boost the German economy, as it should. A similar effect can happen, as the world grows more integrated. Much competition for low-skilled jobs comes from developing countries, and that makes Greek goods relatively uncompetitive in the world's markets.

Figure 18.1 shows Greece's real exchange rate versus those of Germany, France, and Italy.[8] The real exchange rate contains three elements: the average price of a country's goods, the average price of foreign goods, and the average exchange rate of a currency converting into the other countries' currencies. The real exchange rate increases if average prices in the country increase, foreign country prices decrease, or the country's exchange rate appreciates. If this real exchange rate increases over time, that country's goods are less competitive. Real exchange-rate decreases mean a country's goods are more competitive. Germany became more competitive while Greece, Italy, and France grew less competitive.

If Greece had its own currency, it could depreciate its exchange rate, making Greek goods cheaper than those of other countries. Or it could reduce Greek prices, which ultimately means decreasing uncompetitive Greek wages. Prices and wages are slow to adjust in many countries, but especially in European countries, which have lots of worker protections. (When the

Greek government announced plans to cut public spending and raise taxes in exchange for IMF and Eurozone bailout aid, demonstrations and general strikes broke out all across Greece. Greek protesters set fire to a bank and hurled petrol bombs as they marched toward parliament. On May 5, 2010, five protesters were killed.) Or Greece could borrow from the rest of the world and stimulate the Greek economy, albeit artificially. Because Greece is an EU member, it may do these things only within the club's deficit and debt limits.

Without an exchange-rate tool to increase Greece's short-term competitiveness, the Greeks would have to face a recession until prices and wages adjusted, or borrow money for as long as they can. Greece could also hand back its EU membership.

The Club's Early Years

The EU's first few years seemed calm and successful. As Europeans thought about launching the EU in 1999, countries scrambled to meet the inclusion criteria—especially countries like Greece. The European Monetary Union (EMU) plan was established in 1992, with the goal of having one currency in the near future. In 1992, it barely passed a French referendum, with a 51% vote.

Figure 18.2 shows interest rates in some major Euro countries. By 1992, rates in France and Germany had already converged, but Italy and Greece weren't ready. From 1992 to 1999, governments in various European countries struggled to make changes so they could join the club. The Greeks brought their fiscal deficit down from 15% in 1990 to 3.3% in 1999. Italy reduced theirs from 9% to 1.9%. The markets cheered and Euro countries' interest rates converged.

For Greece (and maybe Italy), meeting club requirements was an unrealistic economic strain. In fact, markets later learned that the Greeks had used clever schemes to disguise their debt's true value.

From 2002 to 2007, 10-year Greek debt traded at about the same level as German debt. That didn't make sense. A country's interest rates depend on repayment risk, which in turn depends on total debt, exchange rate risk, and the country's future prospects.

Interest rates are higher when:

- A country has more debt, because more debt is harder to pay back.
- A country has its own currency, because a depreciating exchange rate means that the locally denominated money owed to foreigners is worth less in the foreign currency, causing foreign lenders to lose money.

FIGURE 18.2 Ten-Year Government Interest Rates of Selected Euro Countries

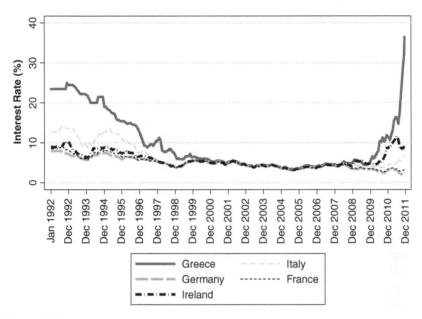

Source: GFD.

• A country's future ability to pay off debt decreases. A country's growth prospects, ability to collect taxes, and hopes for disciplined government spending all factor into this question.

When the Euro launched, foreign exchange-rate risk disappeared, but two other big risks remained. Greece's future payment ability and hopes for disciplined government spending were nowhere near those of Germany. In fact, the Greek government took advantage of low interest rates to borrow more money to spend and stimulate its lagging economy. From 1999 to 2008, the Greek annual deficit rose from 3.3% to 9.8% of GDP. The club failed to penalize Greece for these violations. In that same period, the German deficit improved from 1.6% to 0.1%.

Banks bought Greek debt for the same reason that banks and governments bought Freddie and Fannie's bonds at a 55 basis-point spread over Treasuries: they were certain that the European Union would bail out Greece. Greek bonds that paid 40 basis points above German bonds were a great deal if the EU would eventually rescue them. Crowd demand kept the spreads unrealistically low.

Getting Greeked

> The European single currency is bound to fail, economically, politically, and indeed socially, though the timing, occasion and full consequences are all necessarily still unclear.
> —Margaret Thatcher, former British prime minister, 2002

Greece kept borrowing to ease the strain of entering the Euro club. Greeks began importing more goods than they were exporting. This is measured by the current account deficit, which by 2008 was $35 billion Euro or 15% of GDP, compared to the 1.5% average for other EU countries. From when it adopted the Euro in 2001 until 2008, the Greek government spent more than it earned. By 2008, Greece spent 23 billion Euro more per year than it earned, or 9.8% of GDP. Other Euro countries had an average deficit of 2.1%, with Germany and France having deficits of −0.1% and −3.3% respectively. Greece's debt grew from 122 billion in 1999 to 263 billion Euro in 2010 or from 94% of GDP to 145% of GDP. It violated the EU's fiscal constraint, but was not penalized. The market thought Greece was too big to fail.

Things were already looking bad for Greece by 2009. In October of that year, Prime Minister George Papandreou made a startling announcement: Greece's 2009 deficit was more than double the amount that had been reported to the public. The deficit was 15.8% of GDP, not 6.7% of GDP.[9] The Greek government had used clever financing and accounting gimmicks to minimize its debt. The markets had been Greeked.

Soon after, bond yields on Greek debt began rising. Within one month of the announcement, 10-year interest rates went from 4.45% to 4.74% as investors began dumping Greek debt. Ratings firms downgraded Greek debt and the flight continued. By July 2011, Greek debt had a CC rating—super-junk status. Some runs on Greek banks had already started; depositors withdrew money before the possibility of frozen accounts. By December 2011, Greek 10-year debt traded at 36.37%, while German 10-year bonds traded at 2.23% (see Figure 18.2).

A host of banks have Greek debt exposure. Banks in many countries bought Greek debt, including Germany, France, Italy, Spain, the United Kingdom, Japan, and the United States. German and French exposures are estimated at as much as 34 billion Euros of Greek debt.[10] These were the crowds that rushed in to buy Greek debt, thinking it was as good as gold. Some banks and proprietary traders[11] bought Greek debt when interest rates skyrocketed, thinking that things had to get better. They forgot Dornbusch's adage: "Just because the patient is breathing harder, does that mean he's getting better?"[12]

Greek Choices

> It's a bit like the mafia: you probably shouldn't join. But after you join, it's a really bad idea to leave.
> —Pierre-Olivier Gourinchas, professor of economics at UC Berkeley

Greece had become a problem for Greek banks, banks around the world, and the Greek economy. Its economy declined 1.3% in 2009, −8.6% in 2010, and −8.1% in 2011.[13]

The Greeks have three choices. None of them are beautiful, but Greece must choose one of them.

Remain a Club Member and Order Finances

Greece has been spending more than it makes in revenues. The Greek economy has had reasonable productivity growth, but that masked the real problem: Greece was becoming less globally competitive (see Figure 18.1).

Government formed too much of the Greek economy. In 1999, the government sector represented about 18% of Greek GDP. This did not change much up to 2010, but while nominal GDP grew at 4.7% per year, Greek debt grew by 9.4% per year. The Greeks kept their economy afloat by borrowing.[14]

On May 6, 2010, Greece agreed to reduce its deficit level to 3% by 2014. It will cut spending by reducing civil service pensions and wages, and with a civil servant hiring freeze that allows only one new civil servant for every five retirees. In the long term, the Greek government hopes to reduce the number of local Greek municipalities. The Greek government has large pension liabilities—Greeks usually keep 80% of their last working year's salary payment in retirement—so it plans to raise the retirement age and may reduce pension amounts.

The Greek government has increased taxes on fuel, tobacco, liquor, and luxury products, and raised value-added taxes from 19% to 23%. It is trying to crack down on tax evasion. (Greece's underground economy is estimated between 25% and 30% of GDP.)

With all of Greece's problems, raising taxes and cutting government spending will lead to a sharp recession and higher unemployment. Greeks must accept that they are poorer than they thought and have been living on borrowed money. Reform may be very difficult if people won't accept it, as happened in Chile in the 1970s.[15] When Pinochet instituted tough reforms to bring down the deficit, output dropped and unemployment was high for several years. The military dictatorship forced citizens to accept the reforms and eventually Chile's economy recovered and did quite well.

Ditch the Club and Keep the Debt

If Greece leaves the Euro zone, it will still have problems. The country must issue its own currency and do everything it can to halt a bank run.[16] The drachma's new potential value is unknown, but it will most likely trade at a discount to the Euro, so residents will grab Euros before it's too late.

The 2001 Argentinian devaluation gives clues to Greece's future. A return to the drachma would mean converting many bank and government liabilities at a new exchange rate. Many savers would lose when savings in Euros convert to the depreciating drachma. Greece would have a large exchange-rate depreciation and probably lots of inflation. A depression would likely ensue, reducing real wages. Foreign goods would become prohibitively expensive.

Bank solvency would depend on how the Greek government handled deposits and assets.[17] Greek interest rates would move higher in the short run, so Greek debt value would decline, hurting Greek banks that own Greek debt. Debt devaluation would also hurt foreign banks, leading to bank insolvency problems in Greece and abroad.

Ditch the Club and Ditch the Debt

In 2010, Greece's total debt was 321 billion Euros. Foreigners still owned roughly 50% of this debt in 2011.[18] European bank exposure to all of Greece, including government and private sectors, was an estimated 206 billion Euros in 2011.[19]

An outright Greek default would pass a large chunk of the problem from Greece to foreign banks and investors. Greece would still suffer an indirect effect. Though devaluing would make Greek goods more affordable, the demand for Greek exports would decrease or stagnate to the extent that other Euro countries suffer. Ditching the club would devastate many contracts between Greek businesses and foreign businesses. Greece would also find it hard to borrow, bringing government expenditures to a screeching halt and causing a worse recession.

Greece's best plan may be to accept aid from the IMF and the EU while using austerity measures to get its house in order. A second-best solution is to leave the EU with an accompanying large depreciation, as Argentina did in 2001.

The IMF and Euro Packages

Greece's problems became increasingly worse in 2010 and 2011. The EU and IMF came to the rescue, just as the Fed rescued U.S. banks in 2008. In May 2010, EU leaders and the IMF announced Greek loans of 110 billion Euros over three years. EU countries are covering 80 billion and the IMF is covering the other 30 billion. These loans are contingent on Greek fiscal austerity. To stop the crowd from attacking other European countries, such as Italy, Ireland, and Portugal, the EU and IMF created a 500 billion Euro-lending facility for other Euro countries. In December 2010, Ireland borrowed 67.5 billion Euros. In May 2011, Portugal borrowed 78 billion Euros.

In July 2011, Euro leaders announced a second set of Greek loans, these totaling 109 billion Euros. The private markets will also contribute to Greece's bailout by taking losses on restructured Greek debt. Some estimate the losses at 21% of private holdings.

The Federal Reserve and the European Central Bank have tried to prevent panic by maintaining liquidity and keeping EU interest rates lower. This is extremely important, especially for countries such as Italy, which spends less than it collects in taxes (without considering interest payments on Italy's debt). If interest rates rise, borrowing nations will pay more, worsening their fiscal situations. Countries such as Italy, which is structurally on its way to a balanced budget, could also collapse if the crowd dumps Italian debt. Continuing low interest rates are important to every country's health. The ECB has also made large loans to European banks, loaning as much as $500 billion Euros as of December 2011.

The EU's Future

European banks rushed to buy Greek debt during the EU's early years, despite its small premium over German debt, because banks knew the EU would protect it. So far it has. Banks are interconnected throughout Europe and the world, so their Greek debt losses would pass through the system. The instability could lead to a run on Italy, though a new technocrat government could mitigate this. At 1,842 billion Euros, Italy's debt burden is much larger than that of Greece, but Italy's finances are better. An Italian crisis would cause large-scale problems everywhere, but it might be Portugal or Spain that find trouble first.

The EU is probably better without Greece, and Greece is probably better without the Euro. Not even a strong currency manager can solve Greece's fundamental problems: low growth and a lack of fiscal discipline. Some weakly managed countries joined the EU for disciplined economic management. The Greek crisis and emerging crises in other countries have shown that it's not that easy. No one likes relative poverty. If a country can borrow on the cheap to temporarily boost its economy, it will.

If Greece goes, Estonia, Slovakia, and Slovenia could follow, and the situations of deficit-ridden countries such as Turkey may persuade the EU to postpone new memberships for the foreseeable future. Italy seems committed to getting its house in order, but must also grapple with serious problems. Italians complain that they are poorer since joining the EU. The country's labor productivity has stagnated since it adopted the Euro, but the reasons are unclear. Italy must seek growth or accept that its standard of living will not improve rapidly.

Greece's situation happened because the EU took a member that didn't fit in. When times got tough, the Greeks borrowed to retain their standard of living. Banks around the world helped Greece go on its spending spree, believing that the EU would bail out Greece in the end. Everyone ignored the true risks. Greece also lied about its debt, so some investments in Greece were based on false information. The 2008 financial crisis brought massive deleveraging and a more thorough examination of risks, including the risks of lending to Greece.

With recessions in place all over the world, none of the large European countries qualify for EU membership as of December 2011.[20] Indirect Greek debt exposure is also high in Europe. European banks have sold a total of 178 billion Euros worth of credit default swap protection on the sovereign debt of Greece, Italy, Portugal, Ireland, and Spain.[21] Deutsche Bank alone has about 2.9 billion Euros in exposure. If Greece defaults, these European banks will have huge tabs.

Banks have hedged some of this exposure by purchasing protection. The diverse array of banks in the sovereign CDS market means that risks can spread more quickly through the financial system. It's hard to know how Greek debt problems would ricochet through the interconnected financial system. Though many banks have hedged their risks, the lack of transparency or a centralized swap platform make these interconnections potentially dangerous.

European countries have made preemptive plans in case the EU does fall apart. As of December 2011, Ireland's central bank has begun discussions about accessing printing presses, Montenegro is considering its own national currency, and investors are hedging their Euro exposures. The best investment in 2012 and 2013 might be a printing press.

The coming years will be interesting, as the world recession unwinds and Europeans grapple with their ailing club. The decade started with fairy tales, promises of new hope, a booming economy, an Internet revolution, and a strong and prosperous Euro. It ended with the 2008 financial crisis and Greek problems that continue into 2012. Do any parts of the fairy tale remain?

CHAPTER 19

The Fairy-Tale Decade

I do believe in fairies, I do, I do.

—Peter Pan

The Fairy-Tale Decade began in 1998 and came crashing down in 2008. Growth in housing, economies, the Internet, and technological gadgets made us think that we were getting richer. In the end all this was fluff, built on a massive housing bubble.

Two years after the Lehman collapse, it was October 23, 2010. I had arrived early at a favorite hangout for ex–LTCM partners to meet Chi-Fu Huang and John Meriwether, who planned to tell me more about the 2008 crisis. As I waited for them, I went over the past few years in my head.

I traveled back to 1994 and remembered the *Newsweek* cover story about the financial dream team and their years of success. We all thought the markets had finally found a group that could tame them. Then Bloomberg reported the shocking news that LTCM was teetering on the edge of bankruptcy. The press and the public debated whether there were issues to be fixed in finance. Despite all the discussion about interconnections and liquidity, nothing had really changed.

In fact, banks, large institutions, and even quasi-governmental organizations started behaving more like risky hedge funds during this period, all without telling anyone. That included AIG, Citibank, Goldman Sachs, Lehman Brothers, Bear Stearns, and most of all Freddie Mac and Fannie Mae. Some of these institutions used leverage that was as high as or higher than what LTCM used. They weren't making low-volatility spread trades, but outright bets in real estate and risky mortgages.

The real estate bubble began to grow, and investors and the general public behaved like sheep. They rushed to invest, using risk models that ignored valuations and interconnections. Everyone was to blame because everyone was part of the circle of greed, from home owners to bankers to insurance companies. The real estate market was overvalued in 2005, but there wasn't enough buzz to turn it around, so it kept going up.

In 2007 and 2008, the crowd couldn't sustain inflated values anymore. Investors headed for the exits. As actual and expected real estate prices went down, so did the value of mortgages, mortgage-backed securities (MBS), and commercial real estate. Most banks had real estate exposure, some more than others. Investment banks had real estate exposure through mortgage securitization, MBS ownership, and outright commercial and residential real estate ownership. Major U.S. companies such as AIG had written many insurance policies designed to protect against mortgage or company defaults. Commercial banks made mortgage loans to defaulting home owners, leaving banks with rapidly depreciating homes.

Defaults and declining housing prices changed crowd behavior, and with it the fortunes of major U.S. institutions. Individuals, investment banks, commercial banks, and major government institutions went bankrupt. Politicians didn't quickly understand the situation and so exacerbated problems. A banking freeze hurt Main Street, and the United States entered the biggest recession since the 1930s. The S&P 500 increased only 5.7% between December 31, 1999, and November 30, 2011.

In many ways, the United States is a country in decline. The end of the 1990s marked a beautiful mania for new ways to use information. The next decade's beginning saw the Internet bubble collapse. Government and the Federal Reserve struggled to resuscitate the economy by lowering taxes and interest rates. In part, this led to the housing bubble, which collapsed and had even more disastrous effects on the U.S. economy.

This fairy-tale decade was built, not on attaining the American dream through achievement, but on borrowing. Borrowing for consumption is usually a bad idea, especially with uncertain prospects for future income. The United States spent 10 years building fairy-tale houses and using fairy-tale finance—nothing that was real.

I Hate Wall Street

> Due to recent budget cuts, the light at the end of the tunnel has been turned off.
>
> —Occupy Wall Street sign

After the 2008 collapse, everyone seemed to pin the blame on Wall Street. The Occupy Wall Street movement spread from Zucotti Park as far west as Denver and Oakland, until cold weather and police shut it down. The protesters had a wide range of motivations. They think their hard work had not been rewarded. They were angry with big banks and rich bankers, who they believed caused this whole mess.[1]

Some protesters felt that the Federal Reserve and taxpayer bailouts should be abolished. As scapegoats, these are too simple.

Everyone shares the blame for the housing bubble, from greedy home buyers to greedy politicians to greedy Wall Street people. Without a housing bubble, the economy might have stagnated much earlier in the fairytale decade. Without irresponsible, greedy home buyers and politicians who promoted low-income loans, this bubble would never have gotten off the ground.

It is true that Wall Street employment pays better than the average U.S. job, and that some top managers made millions of dollars during the boom years. So did many mortgage brokers in every town in the United States, and some very talented athletes and performers. Talent and success don't make these people evil. Some people feel that some Wall Street bankers should go to jail or be fired, and some have been fired. None have gone to jail, because they did not do anything illegal. Should home owners that took out mortgages they could not afford also go to jail?

Another frustration is that Wall Street got a bailout while regular people struggled. There is no doubt that large banks received bailout money. Without it, they would have failed. However, many home owners were bailed out in a variety of ways, including by walking away from nothing-down mortgage obligations and through modification programs by the banks and the government. The latter are equivalent to the government's bank loans, and should perhaps be expanded. The largest bailouts came for Freddie and Fannie who were the leading providers of home loans, with a large percentage going to low-income housing.

Wall Street banks paid back government money with interest, so these loans cost taxpayers nothing. About $245 billion has not been repaid.[2] Debtors include many regular U.S. banks, Fannie and Freddie, and the automobile companies (see Table 19.1). Freddie and Fannie owe $151 billion alone.

If the Occupy movement wants the right place to locate its tents, it should consider Washington, DC, home to Congress, the White House, Freddie Mac, and Fannie Mae. However, this is probably not the most productive way to initiate change.

TABLE 19.1 Summary of TARP Program Profits and Losses

Category	Loan Amount	Paid Back	Return to Taxpayer (%)
Big Banks[a]	$160.86	$183.37	14.00
Fannie & Freddie	$182.80	$32.03	(82.48)
Auto Companies	$78.20	$38.35	(50.96)
AIG	$67.84	$18.22	(73.13)
The Rest[b]	$104.65	$77.85	(25.60)

Note: In billions. Return to taxpayer is as of November 28, 2011.
[a] Big Banks include Bank of America, Citibank, J.P. Morgan, Wells Fargo, Goldman Sachs, and Morgan Stanley, as well as the mortgage subsidiaries of J.P. Morgan and Bank of America.
[b] The rest are mainly smaller banks.
Source: http://projects.propublica.org/bailout/list.

We shouldn't criticize the Fed or the bailout too much. It prevented the lending markets from malfunctioning further, which would have meant a much larger burden for Main Street. Lehman's bankruptcy alone made it harder for Main Street businesses to borrow money.

> Many of our actions operated through financial institutions or financial markets, but were designed to help Main Street weather a crisis. . . . Main Street relies upon [the financial infrastructure] for credit, capital, and liquidity—an inherently frustrating scenario for citizens, to be sure. However, measures like the Fed's mortgage-backed securities purchase program have improved mortgage-market conditions, making it more affordable to obtain a loan for a home purchase or to refinance an existing mortgage. Our AMLF program was intended to support money market mutual funds at a time of great stress and, ultimately shore up the market for commercial paper—a market that makes credit cards, student loans, and home equity loans more affordable.
>
> —Eric Rosengren, CEO of Federal Reserve Bank of Boston,
> December 3, 2009

In recent years, many have argued that the financial sector is too big and doesn't bring anything productive to the economy.[3] It is true that much more innovation could take place in the financial markets and that the sector had grown rather large before the 2008 crash.[4]

The financial sector helps other businesses succeed directly and indirectly, in ways that are not always obvious. Alternative systems, including communism, have failed miserably at allocating wages and prices.

Finance is the oil that greases the economy's engine. Relative efficiency and ability to access capital are big reasons that Western economies have performed so well over time. Many firms, including Apple, Microsoft, Google, and others, use efficient capital markets to fund ongoing innovation. Even when finance isn't very innovative, its services are fundamentally linked to innovations on Main Street.

Finance has also innovated in ways that help society advance. The national mortgage market, despite its excesses, has let millions of people obtain mortgages that they might not have otherwise gotten. Securitized products such as mortgage-backed securities have allowed risk transfers from parties that do not want risk to those that do, and have helped make markets more liquid and interest rates lower. Every person who has ever taken out a mortgage has benefited.

Securitized lending across borders has helped the U.S. economy move forward. Some parts of the United States have had growth but little saving, and others have had little growth, but lots of saving. Matching these people has helped regional economies grow. The same is true of finance across national borders. Microfinance has a remarkable ability to help even extremely poor areas of the world develop and function.[5]

The mutual fund industry has offered millions of people efficient, affordable, accessible investing. The Internet-broker revolution allows even cheaper and more accessible investing. In 1988, it was prohibitively expensive to purchase a diversified security portfolio. Trading one stock might have cost as much as $350 per trade. Today's trades cost as little as $9 each in most standard brokerages, or even less in some innovative brokerages. The ETF revolution that has occurred since 1999 has made diversified investing accessible to many more people at a much lower cost. In less financially developed countries, individual investing is costly and grossly inefficient.

In the past, some corporations could borrow in one currency at a lower rate than in other currencies. The currency swap market lets these corporations trade with each other, reducing costs. Swaps also let corporations closely match their liabilities. Ultimately, swap facilities mean lower costs for individual savers. In the past 10 years, the financial industry may have abused swap contracts, especially the credit default swap, but swaps indirectly benefit everyone.

The investment banking industry has helped thousands of corporations finance new projects. It also lets people from all over the world share in company advances, just by purchasing the stock. The private equity industry has also funded thousands of small companies, advancing improvements that benefit everyone. There would be no Google, Apple Computers, Yahoo!, Bill and Melinda Gates Foundation, World Bank, or neighborhood banks without finance. Finance matters.

Some people misunderstand finance. Sports fans easily accept star athletes' high salaries, and customers rationalize Apple Computers' enormous profits because the iPhone is just so cool. The financial industry offers less obvious benefits, but has also done much to improve society even though it also sometimes engages in excesses.

In the future, most nations will try to stretch small tax bases to fund pensions for huge retiree populations. They'll need help from innovative finance. Too much financial regulation can kill this innovation. We must strike a balance between preventing abuses and excesses while also ensuring that talented people are rewarded for innovations that help Main Street face its future challenges.

The Real Costs of the Financial Crisis

People where you live, grow five thousand roses in one garden . . . yet they don't find what they're looking for . . .

—The Little Prince

Many people measure the real cost of the 2008 financial crisis as the decrease in the net worth of U.S. households. The real question is this: How far did this shock to the financial system take us from where we might have been without the financial crisis?

Many corporations, government, and citizens are obsessed with growth, an obsession that often does more harm than good. Sometimes growth stagnates, and spurring growth with low interest rates and implicit housing subsidies can create a house of cards that eventually collapses. This is part of what happened during the fairy-tale decade.

In 2000, household net worth was $43 trillion (see Table 19.2).[6] Household wealth is mainly the combined value of a home and stock market investments.

From 2000 to 2010, household financial wealth hit its peak at $66 trillion in the second quarter of 2007. It fell to a low of $49 trillion in the first quarter of 2009. As of the first quarter of 2011, it stood at $58 trillion. The world stock market dropped by 40% in 2008 and the United States lost $7.7 trillion from the peak. Without the 2008 crisis, Americans might still have that wealth.

This assumes that the United States was in the right position in 2007. If U.S. growth from 2000 onward was a house of cards, perhaps we should measure the change in net worth from 2000 to 2011. In the United States household net worth gained $15 trillion during this period. Or eliminate the period from 2004 to 2007, when the frothy real estate bubble went into hyperdrive. That change means more wealth, by $5.4 trillion.[7]

Unemployment tops many lists of worries around the world.[8]

Unemployment is tragic and destabilizing. From 2000 to 2011, the ranks of the unemployed grew by 8,796,000 people (see Table 19.2). During this period, the labor force also grew by 9,912,000, natural in a growing population. If an economy isn't currently growing, an increasing labor force means higher unemployment or a declining standard of living.

The financial industry alone lost a total of 711,000 jobs.[9] Resolving the unemployment problem will require new economic growth. Workers may also need new skill sets, ones that are relevant in a global economy.

Over most of the past century, U.S. economic growth has been about 3% per year. Growth in output per person has been about 1.88% annually.[10] By comparison, the past decade started out with promising 4% growth, then fell to overall growth of 2% and just 1.15% growth per capita.[11] The 2008 recession has been more pronounced than any other recession in the past 40 years, with a rebound that has been smaller than any other postrecession rebound.

TABLE 19.2 Net Worth and Unemployment in the U.S.

Date	Net Worth (trillions)	Unemployed (1,000s)	Labor Force (1,000s)
12/31/2000	43	5,264	143,110
12/31/2004	53	7,599	147,877
6/30/2007	66	7,295	154,253
3/31/2009	49	13,895	153,728
3/31/2011	58	14,060	153,022

Sources: Federal Reserve Flow of Funds and BLS.

These issues are particularly pronounced when it comes to income distribution. Since the 1970s, the gap between rich and poor has grown under both Democratic and Republican presidential administrations.[12] During the Clinton administration, the economy was prosperous, but the rich saw income growth of 30%. The poorest got income growth of 16%, while middle-class income grew just 15%. Since 1967, rich people's average incomes have grown by 70%. Poor people's incomes have grown by just 29%.

Wall Street and Washington didn't create this inequality. A variety of factors are at work. More-educated workers have reaped the rewards of technological progress to a greater degree than have less-educated workers. Opening world trade has meant fierce competition for low-skill jobs.

The fairy-tale decade misled us into thinking the economy was better than it was. Everyone is to blame.

Our next problem is already in the making. The U.S. government is taking on a huge amount of debt, which higher taxes will eventually have to repay. As of 2011, the total national debt is 93% of GDP, while debt held by the public is 62% of GDP.[13] As of May 2011, every one of the 311 million U.S. citizens would need to pay $31,000 to eliminate U.S. government debt. The United States could become another Greece. In these tough times, perhaps rather than sleep in crowded parks, we might remember Kennedy's old phrase, "And so, my fellow Americans, ask not what your country can do for you; ask what you can do for your country."

An Avatar's Life Force

> Now we're told there are going to be even higher capital requirements . . . and we know there are 300 rules coming. Has anyone bothered to study the cumulative effect of all these things?
> —James Dimon, CEO of J.P. Morgan, June 7, 2011

Small economic perturbations affect the whole, and that makes regulation difficult. There were and are problems with the financial and economic system, but it's hard to know how to improve it without creating unintended consequences that make things worse.[14]

It's the great challenge of all regulation. Oftentimes, we rush to offer a new regulation without thinking through all its potential flaws. Other times, we don't deeply analyze the action sequences that are connected to a piece of regulation. And sometimes we get it approximately right.

The Dodd-Frank rules put a lot of new regulation on the financial system.[15] To protect consumers, the new rules cap the fees that debit-card issuers charge merchants for purchases. Before the new regulation, the fee was an average of about 44 cents a swipe. The new rule caps the fee at 21 cents, or just less than half the original average. The new rule will reduce bank revenues by about $6 billion per year. This was better than earlier proposals, though banks still argued that it was below cost.

The new rules seem to be good advances, but they assume that the banking industry is not competitive and that bankers are colluding to keep fees high. This is a possibility, but generally there is a lot of competition in the United States.

The new rules also assume that new fees will create a new equilibrium. But the economic system is connected in all sorts of ways.[16]

After the fee hikes, banks began increasing monthly checking account fees and minimum balances to compensate for lost fees. As of 2011, J.P. Morgan charges customers a monthly fee if their balance is below $1,500. Commerce Bank in Kansas City will charge customers a fee per check if they don't meet certain requirements. The number of banks that offer free checking dropped by about half after the new rules took place. In 2011, banks also considered annual credit card fees, but dropped this idea when it led to complaints and a potential loss of customers.

These minimum fees hurt poorer people more than richer people. What seemed like a good proposal turned out to have unexpected problems that might make the overall situation worse, not better.

This occurs in other parts of the economy. Politicians in the past, for instance, have suggested raising oil company taxes.

> I'll make oil companies like Exxon pay a tax on their windfall profits, and we'll use the money to help families pay for their skyrocketing energy costs and other bills.
> —Presidential candidate Barack Obama, June 9, 2008

This statement sounds glorious and inspirational, but it misses the important links between economic agents. Gasoline demand is rigid, in that consumers must use some gasoline for travel no matter how high prices are. Oil company taxes are usually passed on to consumers in the form of higher prices.[17] Ironically, a gasoline tax hurts the poor through higher prices relatively more than it hurts the rich.

These basic ideas ignore economic interconnections, and so can certain regulations. When the BIS lowered the residential mortgage risk-weighting from 50% to 35% before the financial crisis, that may have increased banks' willingness to increase their own real estate exposure, because it counted less against their capital requirements.[18]

Another example of ignored interconnections is encapsulated in this question: "If financial innovation or derivatives have made us better off, then why aren't we safer today?"

> The question is not posed correctly. Suppose you're driving in Cambridge, Massachusetts, during the winter with your new four-wheel drive. Your police friend tells you that the data show that after 15 years with four-wheel drives, Cambridge still has the same rate of accidents per passenger mile. He tells you that four-wheel drives haven't made us safer. That doesn't sound right. That's because the policeman made the assumption that people behave the same way to the new technology. In reality, people alter their decisions. Thus, when it became safer to drive, people might have begun to drive on days when there was six inches of snow, which they wouldn't have done in the past. The amount of risk people take individually or collectively is not necessarily a constant. Thus, the question you should ask is "Are we better off?" To that, the answer is yes. E-mail is another example. With e-mail, we've saved so much time, we should take a few hours off each day. Is that what we do? No, we do more things.
> —Robert Merton interview, Nobel prizewinner in economics,
> July 9, 2011

New developments can change behavior.[19]

Some rules might make the system more trustworthy and stronger. An electronic clearinghouse for OTC products would probably offer a gain greater than its cost. Some constraints on standard or shadow banking leverage make sense. In the future, economists may more clearly understand the tradeoff between an economy's leverage and its growth, which will make it easier to set standards for the financial system.

In the past few years, policy makers have delayed changes and acted with uncertainty—both great mistakes. Business never functions well when the business landscape is uncertain. Businesses need resolutions to deficit reduction, corporate tax changes, derivatives-trading regulations, and whistleblower rules, but political gridlock, bureaucratic inertia, and inadequate resources stand in the way.[20] The policy makers have paralyzed the market system.

It may sometimes be better to make no regulations at all than to continue stalling the system. The CFTC handled as many as six new rules per week in 2011. That's the number it used to handle in an entire year. SEC Chairman Mary Schapiro summarized the clog when asked about corporate governance: "When we catch our breath from our Dodd-Frank responsibilities..."

No matter what economic choices we make, we will face trade-offs. We may ultimately choose a fast-paced, free system that produces innovation and growth, but also some big troughs. Or some level of regulation may offer a better trade-off between large recessions and growth. A small amount of directed regulation would have prevented the entire financial crisis of 2008, in particular limiting the amount of leverage that individuals and institutions could take on. Much of the other regulation in Dodd-Frank is probably unnecessary with respect to the financial crisis of 2008.

Economic System Choices

The sudden failure of a great firm which everybody trusted, and many similar events, have all caused a sudden demand for cash.

—Walter Bagehot, 1873

Economists have not really concerned themselves with the choice of economic systems since the 1960s and 1970s, when ideological debates were strong and economists weren't sure whether Communism was superior or inferior to the free-market system. The crumbling of the Soviet Union and China's generally free-market economy have caused this debate to fade away, and rightly so.

We need to make deliberate economic choices. The United States doesn't have a true free-market economy. The government sector controls a vast part of the market. We must decide how much government control is best. A system full of regulation might have fewer crises, but might also offer a slow route to long-term prosperity. A system with less regulation might have more agitated business cycles, more innovation, and higher long-term growth. We must consider the economic impact of universal health care, where the healthier and wealthier substantially subsidize the poor and less healthy, as well as the effects of affirmative action policies that may lead to less efficient workers in the workplace or less able students in the universities.[21]

Politicians should also concern themselves with system choices rather than easy, rhetorical sound bites that only distract and misinform the general population.

My own intuition is that there is a tradeoff. Innovation needs uncertainty. If you knew for certain that something was going to be successful, then you will build infrastructure to make it work. Infrastructure could stifle innovation. Look at things that are not very innovative, health care, education, aerospace, government activities, it is because all of the government regulation and infrastructure is so restraining. Internet is absent regulation and flourishes. The main question in our society is how do you marry together innovation and infrastructure? Innovation in finance goes way ahead of infrastructure and that becomes a problem. The development of CDOs outpaced infrastructure. Measurement, the legal structure, and senior management weren't prepared to control it. If you restrict banks, they will move into other societies or transform their structure. Society can grow but how does it garner the capital to do what they want to do? One of the reasons hedge funds have grown is due to regulation. In a regulated system, if Institution A can't do XYZ, then Institution B will form. It's like trying to plug a dike with multiple holes. If you plug one hole, water comes out from somewhere else.

—Myron Scholes interview, Nobel prizewinner in economics,
July 9, 2011

The Crisis of Crowds

The last 10 years of crises, from LTCM's failure to the Greek crisis, have shown both the market's fundamental interconnections and the problems inherent in risk models that don't account for both valuation and the relationship between individuals in a crowd.

In 1998, LTCM saw an opportunity and built a money machine. Other investors followed and soon the space was crowded. When a shock hit the system, the quant copycats ran for the exits. That dried up liquidity and sent LTCM crashing down.

In the 2000 Internet bubble, everyone in the crowd—from taxicab drivers to Wall Street analysts—bought Internet stocks, all trading at valuations that made absolutely no sense. The risk models used a short history and offered misguided comparisons that tempted greedy investors to buy more. From 2000 to 2008, a new levered bubble began forming, as home buyers, real estate agents, mortgage brokers, banks, investment banks, politicians, the media, rating agencies, and everyone else bought into the greatest levered trade ever: the housing bubble. Risk models ignored interconnections, crowds, and valuations. Eventually, housing prices collapsed, bringing the great recession of 2008.

After the 2008 financial crisis, the global economy is still suffering, but the crowds haven't gone away. Liquidity vanished for three minutes in 2010 in the most liquid market in the world: the U.S. equity market. In a flash, stocks traded at prices from as low as 1 penny to as high as $100,000 per share. Then came the Greek crisis, featuring a global web of banks—particularly European banks—all long Greek debt. They figured that, even though Greek debt paid just a little more than German debt, it was worth the extra yield. Uncle Bismarck would save the Greeks in case of trouble.

Crowd movements and interconnections are the most obvious signs that finance must improve. We need better models for financial securities that take market interconnections into account. We also need better security-pricing models that incorporate different agent types. These could lead to better risk management tools that are also more reliable in crises.

> There is a chance for big advancement in finance. Net present value methods that are commonly used can be improved upon. We know very little about uncertainty and trajectories. All the financial models deal with uncertainty by adding an error term. The models should start with an uncertainty first, not model the system and throw an error on it. In finance we assume there is no need to think about survivorship. All of our models usually have an ending period and you liquidate. This is not how hedge funds and private equity work. It's not a single-period world and not a single-opportunity world. In our current world of finance, we think of all the risks as exogenous. So there is room for tremendous growth.
> —Myron Scholes interview, Nobel prizewinner in economics,
> July 9, 2011

The Wine Arbitrage

As I sat with Meriwether and Huang that day, I realized that Meriwether was no longer the king of the hedge fund world. He didn't call me the "Italian Kid" any longer. He called me "the Professor." Should I have stayed in the Street, making the real money? These guys were still very rich, despite all that had happened. Before I became too depressed, it dawned upon me that this is what makes a free-market system so wonderful. Meriwether and his team were financial pioneers. They had converted an inefficient market into a much more efficient market—one so efficient that even they couldn't beat it any longer. Eventually, the rewards for all innovations die out.

What a messy decade it had been. I learned that no one can tame financial markets, even with sophistication and reasonable risk management. Greed and human actions sometimes work against collective wisdom. Price behavior is intrinsically related to interconnections and crowds. Ignore obvious lessons and you usually pay the price, sometimes more than once. We have so much more to learn as human beings.

As we sat and talked, we sipped the delicious wine that a few former LTCM partners had made. After the 2008 crisis, they began making

private equity investments in China, among other places. One of those investments was a U.S. vineyard that made a good Cabernet Sauvignon. They made
each glass for about $2 and sold each glass for $12. The boys just couldn't
give up looking for profitable opportunities. I wondered when the crowds
would follow.

A few days later, a former Blackrock principal called to say that he had
just bought a vineyard and was going to start selling wine.

Appendices

The Mathematics of LTCM's Risk-Management Framework

I suppose it takes maturity to know that models are to be used but never believed.
—Henri Theil

A General Framework

LTCM's traders were mathematically sophisticated individuals. The firm's trading approach involved choosing many diverse strategies that, though individually risky to varying degrees, were much less risky together. They chose about 50 weakly correlated trading strategies such that the group's collective risk was close to zero, but with a positive expected return.

Given the basket's low risk level, LTCM traders could then lever the strategies to their preferred risk profile.[1]

To understand this process in more detail, let's consider a simple two-trade strategy. In this case, the portfolio's expected return and variance are:

$$E(r_p) = \mu_p = w_x \mu_x + (1 - w_x)\mu_y \tag{A.1}$$

$$\sigma_p^2 = w_x^2 \sigma_x^2 + (1 - w_x)^2 \sigma_y^2 + 2w_x(1 - w_x)\rho_{xy}\sigma_x\sigma_y \tag{A.2}$$

where w_x is the weight placed in strategy x, $1 - w_x$ is placed in strategy y, μ_x and μ_y are the mean returns of strategy x and strategy y, respectively, σ_x^2 and σ_y^2 are the variances of strategy x and strategy y, respectively, and ρ_{xy} is the correlation between the two strategies.

The w_x that provides the lowest risk for the portfolio is given by:

$$w_x^* = \frac{\sigma_y^2 - \rho_{xy}\sigma_x\sigma_y}{\sigma_x^2 + \sigma_y^2 - 2\rho_{xy}\sigma_x\sigma_y} \tag{A.3}$$

Choose two trading strategies that are perfectly negatively correlated (i.e., $\rho_{xy} = -1$) and you'll have a riskless portfolio with a positive return.

Unfortunately, it is impossible to have an average correlation of -1 with more than two strategies in a portfolio. As you add more strategies, however, the conditions necessary for a very low-risk portfolio grow less stringent.

Consider a portfolio of n trading strategies. Assuming a similar variance for each strategy, σ^2, and that any pair of strategies has the same correlation coefficient, ρ. If all strategies are equally weighted (that is, $w_i = \frac{1}{n}$) and individual strategy returns are positive, the portfolio variance is:

$$\sigma_p^2 = \frac{\sigma^2}{n} + \left(\frac{n-1}{n}\right)\rho\sigma^2 \tag{A.4}$$

Construct a portfolio with a large number of positions that have an average correlation of zero, and the portfolio risk decreases toward zero. For the purposes of this analysis, assume that this was LTCM's driving concept.

It may seem that this is too simple an explanation of how LTCM operated. However, the art is not in the concept, but in picking and financing strategies so as to obtain an average correlation of zero.[2]

The average return for these positions is given by:

$$\mu_p = \frac{1}{n}\sum_{i=1}^{n}\mu_i \tag{A.5}$$

where μ_i is the average return of trade i.

The leveraged mean returns and variance are given by:

$$\mu_{p,l} = \frac{1}{n}\sum_{i=1}^{n}\mu_i + (l-1)\frac{1}{n}\sum_{i=1}^{n}(\mu_i - r_f) \tag{A.6}$$

$$= \mu_p + (l-1)(\mu_p - r_f) \tag{A.7}$$

$$\sigma_{p,l}^2 = l^2\left[\frac{\sigma^2}{n} + \left(\frac{n-1}{n}\right)\rho\sigma^2\right] \tag{A.8}$$

where l is the leverage factor and we make the transition from Equation (A.6) to (A.7) by assuming that the expected return of all trades is the same.[3] This assumes that there is no correlation between the financing rate and the risky strategies, and that the financing rate has a volatility of zero. In the real world, things are more complicated. When strategies are perceived to perform badly, banks may alter the terms of their financing agreements, pushing the correlations between financing rates and the strategy returns into negative territory (and creating a more complicated analysis).[4]

A Numerical Example

For illustration purposes, let's suppose that LTCM had roughly 50 types of trades on at any given moment. Also suppose that all trades had roughly the same monthly variance and mean ($\mu = 0.5583\%$ and $\sigma = 0.6723\%$).[5] Let's also assume an average financing rate of 5.65% or 0.4708% per month.

Because the mean return of these "low-risk" strategies is very low, traders need leverage to provide interesting returns on equity for them and their investors.[6]

For example, if we use these numbers and assume a correlation of zero between trades, we get a fund that, before leverage, would have been expected to deliver a 6.7% annualized return with a standard deviation of 0.33%.[7]

At the end of 1997, LTCM had a leverage ratio of 25. Using this value, the portfolio's expected annual return would have been 31.90%, with a standard deviation of 20%.[8]

Measuring Risk

Using this model of LTCM, the firm's risk management strategy is very clear. If we believe that the chosen trading strategies are distinctly uncorrelated, then LTCM wasn't taking much risk.

LTCM might have had a variety of reasons for believing that these strategies were uncorrelated or weakly correlated. They may have measured the historical correlations as very low. The company may have examined these strategies from a theoretical economics standpoint. Finally, LTCM was actively seeking trades with low correlations that fit its portfolio construction methodology.

The key to LTCM's aggregate risk was the average correlation between trades. If traders measured this correlation inaccurately and correlations across strategies were in fact higher than estimated, the fund's loss risk was much larger.

A simple value-at-risk (VaR) formula for the above structure is:

$$\text{VaR}_t = V_t(\mu_{p,l} - k\sigma_{p,l}) \qquad\qquad (A.9)$$

where $\mu_{p,l}$ represents the expected return of the levered portfolio, $\sigma_{p,l}$ represents the standard deviation of the levered portfolio, V_t represents the initial portfolio value, and k represents the confidence level critical value, assuming a normal distribution (i.e., $k = 1.96$ for a 97.5% confidence interval).[9]

Table A.1 presents the potential VaR calculations at a 99% confidence level for a normal distribution ($k = 2.33$) and a capital base of \$4.8B (the amount that LTCM had at the beginning of 1998). The VaR numbers are presented as monthly numbers. Given the correlation coefficient, this represents what might have been expected to occur in any given month at LTCM.

Table A.1 shows that an unlevered fund's standard deviation was 0.0951% per month and 0.6723% per month with a correlation of 0 and 1 respectively. The equivalent annualized volatility was 0.3294% and 2.3290% respectively. Generally this illustrates the portfolio that LTCM sought: a high Sharpe ratio and very low unlevered risk. The unlevered position's VaR for \$1 at the 99% confidence level would have been 0.34 cents and 1 cent for correlations of 0 and 1 respectively.

LTCM's leverage at the beginning of 1998 was 28, and we'll focus on this for the rest of the discussion.

In this situation, the fund's expected monthly return would have been 2.92%, or an annualized return of 35%. The monthly dollar VaR for a \$4.8 billion fund would have been \$160 million with a correlation of 0.

In our example, even a 0.3 correlation would have resulted in a monthly VaR of \$1.03 billion, which many would find quite acceptable.

If the correlations turned out to be incorrect and a period of correlations as high as 1 occurred, however, the monthly VaR could be as great as −\$1.96 billion dangerously high. In fact, two months of highly correlated

TABLE A.1 Sensitivity of VaR to Strategy Correlations

Baseline Parameters			$\rho = 0$	$\rho = 0.1$	$\rho = 0.3$	$\rho = 0.5$	$\rho = 0.8$	$\rho = 1$
σ_p^M			0.0951	0.2309	0.3767	0.4801	0.6028	0.6723
σ_p^A			0.3294	0.8000	1.3050	1.6632	2.0882	2.3289
VaR(\$1)			0.0034	0.0002	−0.0032	−0.0056	−0.0084	−0.0100
Leverage:	μ_p^M	μ_p^A	**Monthly Estimates VaR Losses from \$4.8B Portfolio**					
None	0.56	6.70	0.02	0.00	−0.02	−0.03	−0.04	−0.05
10	1.35	16.15	−0.04	−0.19	−0.35	−0.47	−0.61	−0.68
15	1.78	21.40	−0.07	−0.30	−0.54	−0.72	−0.92	−1.04
20	2.22	26.65	−0.11	−0.41	−0.73	−0.96	−1.24	−1.39
25	2.66	31.90	−0.14	−0.52	−0.92	−1.21	−1.55	−1.74
28	2.92	35.05	−0.16	−0.58	−1.03	−1.36	−1.74	−1.96
30	3.10	37.15	−0.17	−0.62	−1.11	−1.46	−1.87	−2.10

Note: VaR is computed at a 99% confidence interval (i.e., $k = 2.32$). The above computations assume a monthly mean return of each strategy of 0.5583%, a monthly standard deviation of each strategy of 0.6723%, a monthly financing rate of 0.4708%, $n = 50$ (50 strategies in the portfolio), and an initial capital base of \$4.8B (the amount that LTCM had at the beginning of 1998). μ_p^M, σ_p^M, μ_p^A, and σ_p^A represent the monthly and annualized expected returns and standard deviations for the portfolio based on the actual correlations between strategies. All numbers for means and standard deviations are reported in percentage terms, the VaR loss numbers are reported in billions of dollars, and the VaR(\$1) represents the losses of the unlevered portfolio for a \$1 position.

strategies could have led to 2.32 standard deviation losses of \$3.28 billion, or 68% of the fund. This would explain as much as 76% of LTCM's actual 1998 losses: a cool \$4.30 billion.

No matter how much correlations rose, each trade's ex-post standard deviations could also amplify losses if these turned out to be significantly higher than estimated. For example, if the typical standard deviation of each trade doubled from 0.6723% per month to 1.3446, the one-month VaR would rise to \$2.37B for a correlation of 0.3 and \$4.34B for a correlation of 1.

The Mechanics of the Swap Spread Trade

If you work at that which is before you, following right reason seriously, vigorously, calmly, without allowing anything else to distract you, but keeping your divine part pure, as if you should be bound to give it back immediately; if you hold to this, expecting nothing, fearing nothing, but satisfied with your present activity according to nature, and with heroic truth in every word and sound which you utter, you will be happy. And there is no man who is able to prevent this.

—Marcus Aurelius

LTCM constructed many strategies to trade swap interest rate spreads over government security interest rates. The firm implemented these within countries, across countries, and across different parts of the yield curve. In trading terms, a bet that the spread between swap interest rates and government interest rates will widen is called being long the spread.[1] A bet that the spread between swap interest rates and government interest rates will shrink is called being short the swap spread. The mechanics of going long or short a spread apply to any spread, not only to those between swaps and government yields.

The Long Swap Spread Trade

A long swap trade profits when swap spreads widen.

Box B.1 shows the basic steps in constructing a long swap trade. The transaction flows are shown in Figure B.1 and represent the steps in creating

361

FIGURE B.1   Example of Flows from Long Swap Spread Trade

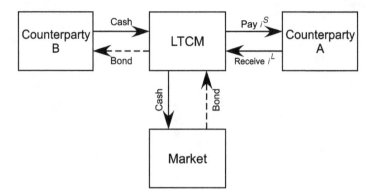

the position. The diagram's left shows LTCM's repo transaction with coun-terparty B. LTCM borrowed cash in exchange for a bond. The diagram's right shows LTCM's swap agreement with counterparty A. LTCM will pay a fixed interest rate over time of i^S and receive a floating interest rate determined at the time of i^L's payment.[2]

At the figure's bottom, LTCM buys the bond with the cash from the repo transaction. Typically, dealers require haircuts on these transactions— the buyer's collateral value is more than the cash value. LTCM, however, paid nothing extra on its positions, so financing this trade was very cheap.

Box B.1   Steps to Creating a Long Swap Spread Position on $100 Million Notional

Step 1: Enter into a 10-year swap position to pay fixed (i^S) and receive LIBOR (i^L) on a notional of $100 million.

Step 2: Use $100 million to purchase a 10-year U.S. Treasury bond.

Step 3: Repo the U.S. Treasury bond to a counterparty for a (1-ϵ) $100 million loan at the repo rate (i^R), where ϵ is the haircut.

The Short Swap Spread Trade

A short swap spread trade profits when swap spreads narrow. Traders create one by following steps that are exactly the opposite of those used to make a long swap trade (Box B.2). To execute a short swap spread trade, LTCM does a reverse repo with counterparty B and receives the repo rate, then short sells the government bond. LTCM pays floating interest and receives fixed interest on a swap with counterparty A.

Box B.2 Steps to Creating a Short Swap Spread Position on $100 Million Notional

Step 1: Enter into a 10-year swap position to pay floating (i^L) and receive fixed (i^S) on a notional of $100 million.

Step 2: Reverse repo to obtain a U.S. Treasury bond from a counterparty and pay cash of (1-ϵ) $100 million in exchange for the repo rate (i^R), where ϵ is the haircut.

Step 3: Short $100 million of 10-year U.S. Treasury bonds. Use proceeds to pay cash position in reverse repo.

Derivation of Approximate Swap Spread Returns

In the case of a zero-coupon curve for both swap fixed-rate yields and government bond yields, the return over a given horizon h from going short the swap spread is given by:[1]

$$r^{SS}_{S,t,t+h} = \left[\frac{\left(1 + y^S_{m,t}\right)^{m/z}}{\left(1 + y^S_{m-h,t+h}\right)^{(m-h)/z}} - 1 \right] - \left[\frac{\left(1 + y^B_{m,t}\right)^{m/z}}{\left(1 + y^B_{m-h,t+h}\right)^{(m-h)/z}} - 1 \right] \tag{C.1}$$

$$= \left[\frac{\left(1 + y^S_{m,t}\right)^{m/z}}{\left(1 + y^S_{m-h,t+h}\right)^{(m-h)/z}} \right] - \left[\frac{\left(1 + y^B_{m,t}\right)^{m/z}}{\left(1 + y^B_{m-h,t+h}\right)^{(m-h)/z}} \right] \tag{C.2}$$

where $y^S_{m,t}$ and $y^B_{m,t}$ represent the yields of the swap and bond at time t for maturity m, $y^S_{m-h,t+h}$ and $y^B_{m-h,t+h}$ represent the yields of the swap and bonds of original maturity m after time h, m represents the initial maturity of the bond or swap contract, h represents the holding period of the trade, and z represents the basis for computing the yields.

Take a typical bond and swap curve as illustrated in Figure C.1. Define the following variables. $y^S_{m,t} = y^B_{m,t} + \epsilon$, $y^S_{m,t} - y^S_{m-h,t} = \eta$, $y^B_{m,t} - y^B_{m-h,t} = \psi$, where ϵ represents the initial spread between the two m-maturity instruments, η represents the expected roll down return from the swap curve, and ψ

FIGURE C.1   Typical Swap and Government Curve

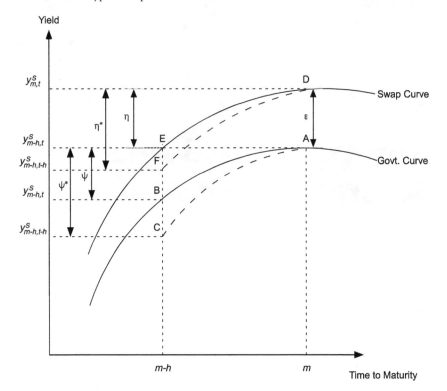

represents the expected roll down return from the bond instrument. Also define $y^S_{m,t} - y^S_{m-h,t-h} = \eta^*$, $y^B_{m,t} - y^B_{m-h,t-h} = \psi^*$, where these represent the realized roll down respectively. These equations also imply that $\epsilon - \eta^* + \psi^*$ is the realized spread change, and $\epsilon - \eta + \psi$ is the expected spread change, and that the actual spread change is $(\eta - \eta^*) + (\psi^* - \psi)$.

Combine these definitions with two approximations to simplify the returns to being short the swap spread. The first approximation is that $\frac{(1+x)}{(1+y)} \approx 1 + x - y$ for small x and y and that $(1+x)^n \approx (1 + nx)$ for small x.

Thus, equation (C.1) can be simplified to

$$r^{SS}_{S,t,t+h} \approx \left[\frac{m}{z} y^S_{m,t} - \left(\frac{m-h}{z}\right) y^S_{m-h,t+h}\right] - \left[\frac{m}{z} y^B_{m,t} - \left(\frac{m-h}{z}\right) y^B_{m-h,t+h}\right]$$

$$(C.3)$$

Making the following substitution of variables, $y^S_{m,t} = y^B_{m,t} + \epsilon$, $y^S_{m-h,t+h} = y^B_{m-h,t} + \psi + \epsilon - \eta^*$, and $y^B_{m-h,t+h} = y^B_{m-h,t} + \psi - \psi^*$, we can rewrite equation (C.3) as

$$r^{SS}_{S,t,t+h} \approx \frac{1}{z}\left[m\epsilon - (m-h)(\psi + \epsilon - \eta^* + (m-h)(\psi - \psi^*)\right] \tag{C.4}$$

$$\approx \frac{1}{z}\left[m\epsilon - (m-h)\left(\epsilon - \eta^* + \psi^*\right)\right] \tag{C.5}$$

$$\approx \frac{1}{z}\left[\underbrace{m\epsilon}_{\text{Carry}} - \underbrace{(m-h)\left[\epsilon - \eta + \psi\right]}_{\text{Expected Roll Down}} - \underbrace{(m-h)\left[(\eta - \eta^*) + (\psi^* - \psi)\right]}_{\text{Realized Spread Change}}\right] \tag{C.6}$$

where the first term represents the trade carry, the second terms represents the expected roll return, and the third term represents the return due to a change in realized spreads from expected spreads.

This formulation ignores financing concerns. On a plain-vanilla swap and a term repo that matched the timing of swap payments, however, LTCM would be exposed to financing costs at every regular interval. In fact, LTCM's basis for taking on such trades was related to its views of both swap spreads going forward and financing terms going forward. Modify the equation for the approximate return to the swap spread trade by adding these financing costs. Being short the swap spread has returns over a period h that are approximately equal to:

$$r^{SS}_{S,t,t+h} \approx \frac{1}{z}\left[m\epsilon - (m-h)\left[\epsilon - \eta + \psi\right] - (m-h)\left[(\eta - \eta^*) + (\psi^* - \psi)\right]\right]$$
$$+ \frac{h}{z}\left(y^R_t - y^L_t\right) \tag{C.7}$$

where y^L_t is the annual interest yield on the LIBOR for the reset period after h, and y^R_t is the repo or reverse repo rate at reset period h.[2]

Consider some extreme parameter values to get an idea of the decomposition of returns from being short the swap spread in simple circumstances.

First examine the situation where $\eta = \eta^* = \psi = \psi^*$. This is essentially a flat yield curve that does not change over the investment horizon. In this case, equation (C.7) simplifies to $\frac{h}{z}\left[\epsilon - (y^L_t - y^R_t)\right]$, which is just the positions' carry minus the financing costs.

Suppose that the initial swap spread is 17 basis points ($\epsilon = 0.0017$) and suppose that for the period (or typically) LIBOR traded 20 basis points higher than the repo rate, then the trade's expected return would be -3 basis points annualized (or approximately $-3\frac{h}{z}$ for the period).[3]

Being short the swap spread would have what LTCM called negative carry, while being long the spread would have positive carry. Being long this trade was preferable from a financing perspective, all other things being equal.

Consider another situation, this one with an initial flat yield curve, but interest rates that go down and government yields that move much more than swap yields. In other words, interest rates decline in general, but the swap spread widens. This could be a flight to quality where $\eta = \psi = 0$ and $\psi^* = 2\eta^*$. The return formula simplifies to:

$$r^{SS}_{S,t,t+h} \approx \frac{1}{z}h\epsilon - \frac{(m-h)}{z}\eta^* + \frac{h}{z}\left(y^R_t - y^L_t\right) \qquad (C.8)$$

A short swap spread loses money in a flight to quality depending on the magnitude of η^* versus ϵ. If the flight to quality occurs fast (i.e., h is close to 0), the mark-to-market losses are roughly $r \approx -\frac{m}{z}\eta^*$.

Examine the theoretical risk of this swap spread position. Take the variance of the returns and see that:

$$\text{Var}\left(r^{SS}_{S,t,t+h}\right) \approx \left[\frac{m-h}{z}\right]^2 \text{Var}\left(\psi^* - \eta^*\right) + \left(\frac{h}{z}\right)^2 \text{Var}\left(y^L_t - y^R_t\right)$$
$$+ 2\frac{m-h}{z}\frac{h}{z}\text{Cov}\left(\psi^* - \eta^*, y^L_t - y^R_t\right)$$

APPENDIX D

Methodology to Compute Zero-Coupon Daily Returns

Bloomberg supplied data for zero-coupon yields for a variety of maturities from 3 months to 30 years, for both swap and government bonds in a variety of countries on a daily basis. To compute daily returns from movements in the swap yields and government bond yields, we also need to interpolate and construct zero-coupon yields for each instrument minus k days. For this, $k = 1$, or one day. The following methodology describes computing these rates and consequently the daily returns on these instruments.

On any given day, t, we have zero-coupon yields for the maturities 3-month ($t_k = 0.25$), 6-month ($t_k = 0.50$), and 1-year all the way to 10-years by 1-year increments, a 15-year, a 20-year, and a 30-year. For every one of these maturities, we know the time to maturity for each yield. The time to each maturity is exactly the number of years or fraction of years. Convert these rates to their respective discount rates, δ_k, by using the formula:

$$\delta_k = \frac{1}{(1 + y_k)^{t_k}} \tag{D.1}$$

where y_k is the yield of the respective zero-coupon rate occurring at time k and t_k is the time from date t to time k, expressed in years and fractions of a year. Compute these for every instrument on every day.

Then use these discount rates to interpolate and find the discount rates for the constant maturity minus one day. For every date, adjacent discount

TABLE D.1 Example of Zero-Coupon Return Computation

Date	y_9	y_{10}	δ_9	δ_{10}	$\delta_{10-1day}$	P_9	P_{10}	$P_{10-1day}$	$r_{10, t, t+1}$
4/5/1989	9.37200	9.34000	0.44652	0.40946	—	44.65238	40.94579	—	—
4/6/1989	9.40700	9.37400	0.44524	0.40819	0.40828	44.52398	40.81869	40.82837	−0.00287

Note: The above table uses actual zero-coupon government bond yields to compute the daily return from holding a 10-year zero-coupon bond for one day. The prices for intermediate periods are computed by exponential interpolation of the discount rates.

rates are exponentially interpolated in order to obtain intermediate discount rates that will then be used to generate new zero-coupon yields.

Calculate the discount rate for a k-year bond on day t, where the maturity is in between the maturity of two other bonds with maturity t_1 and t_2, using the following formula:

$$\delta_k = \delta_1^{\left[\frac{t_k}{t_1}\left(\frac{t_2-t_k}{t_2-t_1}\right)\right]}\delta_2^{\left[\frac{t_k}{t_2}\left(\frac{t_k-t_1}{t_2-t_1}\right)\right]} \tag{D.2}$$

With the new discount factor, we can immediately compute the price of the zero-coupon bond on the next business day. For example, suppose we wish to compute the return of the 10-year zero-coupon bond from day t to day $t+1$.[1] The price of bond with maturity m on day t would be given by $P_{m,t} = \delta_{m,t} \cdot 100$.[2] The same bond's price one day later would be given by $P_{m-1,t+1} = \delta_{m-1,t+1} \cdot 100$, where $\delta_{m-1,t+1}$ is calculated on day $t+1$ according to the interpolation above. The return of the bond for that constant maturity series is given by:

$$r_{m,t,t+1} = \frac{P_{m-1,t+1}}{P_{m,t}} - 1 \tag{D.3}$$

Consider an example of this methodology. Suppose that on April 5, 1989, and April 6, 1989, the 10-year and 9-year zero-coupon bond yields were 9.34, 9.372 and 9.374, 9.407, respectively.

Table D.1 uses the methodology described above to compute the price of the 10-year on April 5, 1989, the price of the 10-year minus 1-day on April 6, 1989, and the daily return of the 10-year from April 5 to April 6. In this particular example, the return is −0.00287, or −0.287%.

APPENDIX E

Methodology to Compute Swap Spread Returns from Zero-Coupon Returns

Once the zero-coupon swap and government bond returns are computed, it's straightforward to compute the returns from being long or short the swap spread. A position that is long the swap spread at the 10-year maturity will profit if swap spreads widen. That is, the trader is essentially paying fixed (or short the hypothetical bond equivalent of the swap) and long the bond. The financing costs are LIBOR minus repo.

Compute the strategy's daily returns as follows:

$$r^{SS}_{L,t,t+h} = r^{B}_{m,t,t+1} - r^{S}_{m,t,t+1} + \frac{1}{360}(y^{L}_t - y^{R}_t) \qquad \text{(E.1)}$$

where $r^{B}_{m,t,t+1}$ is the daily return of the bond of maturity m as computed in the previous section, $r^{S}_{m,t,t+1}$ is the daily return of the swap of maturity m, y^{L}_t is the previous day's yield of the LIBOR rate, and y^{R}_t is the previous day's yield of the repo rate. The formula for the short swap spread is the minus of these returns, with the reverse repo replacing the repo rate.

The methodology described above for computing approximate swap spread returns can be applied to a combination of swap spread trades by combining the different returns. For example, a trade that is short one part of the swap spread curve and long another would offer a combination of these two returns.

The Mechanics of the On-the-Run and Off-the-Run Trade

When LTCM made an on-the-run and off-the-run trade, the firm needed to short the on-the-run bond (the expensive bond) and buy the off-the-run bond (the cheap bond). This trade offers a very small return for an even smaller risk, so LTCM needed to use capital very efficiently, to reduce costs and leverage the trade sufficiently.

To limit the capital involved, LTCM created a two-sided transaction. It purchased the $29^1/_2$-year bond and funded it in the repo market, then did a reverse repo with the 30-year bond and sold that bond short. See the flows in Figure F.1.

LTCM received a variety of trade payoffs. LTCM paid the repo rate and received the reverse repo rate. (The difference between the two was small.) LTCM also received the yield spread between the two bonds. In a declining interest rate environment, the OFR bond usually had the higher coupon and so represented a yield pickup. After the 30-year bond became an OFR bond and dropped in price, LTCM also received the profit from this transaction.

With a small modification, equation (C.7) is a good way to analyze this strategy's approximate returns. In this trade, the financing is not $\frac{h}{z}(y_t^R - y_t^L)$, but rather $\frac{h}{z}(y_t^{RR} - y_t^R)$, where y_t^{RR} is the reverse repo rate and y_t^R is the repo rate as before.

Making this modification to equation (C.7), starting with a flat yield curve of $\psi = \eta = 0$, assuming that $\psi^* = 0$, and letting the off-the-run

FIGURE F.1 The Classic On-the-Run, Off-the-Run Arbitrage Transaction

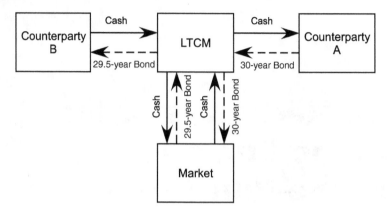

security adjust shows that this convergence trade returns approximately $\frac{h}{z}\epsilon + \frac{m-h}{z}\eta^* + \frac{h}{z}(y_t^{RR} - y_t^{R})$.

With an initial spread of 12 basis points, a convergence of 10 basis points, a reverse repo minus repo spread of 10 basis points, and a maturity of about 10 years, this trade returns approximately 56 basis points over six months, or about 1% over one year. This is a very small return, so LTCM substantially leveraged the trade.

APPENDIX G

The Correlations between LTCM Strategies Before and During the Crisis

Table G.1 shows the correlations between the top eight trading strategies in LTCM's portfolio before and during the crisis. The precrisis correlations are the top number and the crisis correlations are the bottom number.

Trade 1, which corresponds to the U.S. short swap trade, and Trade 3, the long mortgage trade, had a correlation of 0.05 before the crisis and 0.79 during the crisis.

TABLE G.1 Correlations Among LTCM Strategies Pre-August, 1998 and Post-August, 1998

	Trade Number							
	1	**2**	**3**	**4**	**5**	**6**	**7**	**8**
Trade 1	1.00	0.11	0.05	0.08	0.02	0.14	0.04	0.13
	1.00	0.04	0.79	−0.03	0.36	0.51	0.14	0.42
Trade 2	0.11	1.00	0.06	0.00	0.01	0.13	−0.07	0.05
	0.04	1.00	0.12	0.40	0.28	0.27	0.09	0.02
Trade 3	0.05	0.06	1.00	−0.04	0.20	0.15	0.12	0.21
	0.79	0.12	1.00	0.06	0.42	0.45	0.12	0.16
Trade 4	0.08	0.00	−0.04	1.00	0.07	0.04	0.05	−0.18
	−0.03	0.40	0.06	1.00	0.11	0.16	−0.18	0.27
Trade 5	0.02	0.01	0.20	0.07	1.00	0.36	0.16	0.45
	0.36	0.28	0.42	0.11	1.00	0.56	0.45	0.42
Trade 6	0.14	0.13	0.15	0.04	0.36	1.00	0.17	0.25
	0.51	0.27	0.45	0.16	0.56	1.00	−0.05	0.42
Trade 7	0.04	−0.07	0.12	0.05	0.16	0.17	1.00	0.25
	0.14	0.09	0.12	−0.18	0.45	−0.05	1.00	0.29
Trade 8	0.13	0.05	0.21	−0.18	0.45	0.25	0.25	1.00
	0.42	0.02	0.16	0.27	0.42	0.42	0.29	1.00

Note: Correlations were computed from the inception of LTCM in February 1994 until July 31, 1998 and then from August 1, 1998, until October 1, 1998. Trade 1 is the short U.S. swap trade, Trade 2 is the European cross swap trade, Trade 3 is the long mortgage trade, Trade 4 is the Japanese box trade, Trade 5 is the short equity volatility trade, Trade 6 is risk arb trade, Trade 7 is the equity relative-value trade, and Trade 8 is the long emerging markets trade.

APPENDIX H

The Basics of Creative Mortgage Accounting

The mathematics of creating the cash flows on a mortgage loan are quite straightforward. For a 30-year fixed-rate mortgage, find the monthly mortgage payment required by finding the mortgage payments that equate the value of the loan with the present discounted value of the mortgage payments.

$$V = \frac{M_1}{(1 + y_m)} + \frac{M_1}{(1 + y_m)^2} + \cdots + \frac{M_{360}}{(1 + y_m)^{360}} \qquad \text{(H.1)}$$

where V is the value of the loan, M_1 is the monthly mortgage payment for month 1, M_{360} is the mortgage payment due at the end of year 30 (i.e., in month 360), y_m is the monthly mortgage rate, which is just the yearly rate divided by the monthly rate. For a standard fixed-rate mortgage, all the payments are the same every month, thus $M_1 = M_2 = \cdots = M_{360} = M$, so this can be written as:[1]

$$V = \frac{M}{1 + y_M} \left(1 + \frac{1}{(1 + y_m)} + \cdots + \frac{1}{(1 + y_m)^{359}} \right)$$

$$V = M \left(\frac{1}{y_M} - \frac{1}{y_M(1 + y_M)^{360}} \right) \qquad \text{(H.2)}$$

Rearrange to find the monthly mortgage payment required for this particular loan.

Now take a specific example. Suppose a realtor representing a company or home owner sells a \$600,000 house to a buyer who borrows the entire amount from a bank or mortgage lender at an annualized mortgage rate of 4.5%, or the monthly equivalent rate of 0.375%. The mortgage payment must equal:

$$M = \frac{V}{\left(\dfrac{1}{y_M} - \dfrac{1}{y_M(1 + y_M)^{360}}\right)}$$

$$= \frac{600,000}{\left(\dfrac{1}{0.00375} - \dfrac{1}{(0.00375)(1.00375)^{360}}\right)} \tag{H.3}$$

$$= 3,040.11$$

This basic tool can create an endless number of mortgage cash flow schemes. The cash flows can be manipulated such that the flows in the first few years are low, then rise in later years. Given a lower payment for the first three years, the value of the later payment comes from rearranging the original equation.

$$M_2 = \frac{V - M_1\left(\dfrac{1}{y_M} - \dfrac{1}{y_M(1 + y_M)^{36}}\right)}{\dfrac{1}{(1 + y)^{36}}\left(\dfrac{1}{y_M} - \dfrac{1}{y_M(1 + y_M)^{324}}\right)} \tag{H.4}$$

where M_1 is the monthly low payment for the first three years and M_2 is the higher payment required from year 4 onward.

For example, one can buy the $600,000 house with a monthly mortgage payment of just $500 ($M_1$) for the first three years. But wherever you take away, you must add. After year 3, monthly mortgage payments rise to $3,561 ($M_2$) to keep the equation balanced.

If the borrower's income had not substantially increased, this person could no longer afford the house and would have to sell or default. This was one of the many schemes that helped mortgage lenders put home owners into houses that were beyond their means, but looked affordable in the short run.

APPENDIX I

The Business of an Investment Bank

Most investment banks have similar functions, though they differ in their exposures to different lines of business. This appendix describes the investment banking business by exploring Lehman Brothers as a specific example.

Lehman Brothers was involved in several lines of business, as shown in Figure I.1.

Investment Banking

Investment banking included acquisitions and strategic advisory services. In this division, Lehman Brothers advised companies that were considering strategic purchases of other companies or business interests.

The mergers and acquisitions strategic advisory group was another division within investment banking. This division also offered advice and handled financing for firms that were purchasing other firms in deals that included mergers and acquisitions, restructurings and spin-offs, targeted stock transactions, share-repurchase strategies, government privatization programs, takeover defenses, and other strategic advice.

Lehman was involved in underwriting, helping private companies become public companies by selling their shares to the public. Underwriting also involves helping companies borrow by selling debt to the general public. Lehman helped public companies raise capital and was involved in the housing market, underwriting agency securities (i.e., Fannie and Freddie bonds) and mortgage-backed securities.

FIGURE I.1 The Business of Investment Banking and Its Connection to Main Street

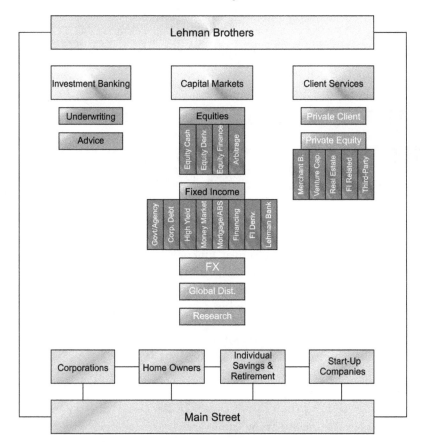

Capital Markets

Lehman's second line of business was in the *capital markets*. This is a vast area for the typical investment bank; it involves selling, trading, and researching investment products.

Equities

Equity Cash

The equities group and its subdivision *equity cash products* acted as a *market-maker* for clients to trade equity securities all around the world. A market-maker is willing to buy or sell any security an investor would like to buy or sell.

Because a market-maker is a known liquidity source, investors don't need to search for someone who wants to buy what they're selling or sell what they're buying. Lehman's market-making area served a variety of investors, including institutions and individuals.

Equity Derivatives

Some people consider *equity derivatives* the "evil area" of Wall Street. Warren Buffett labeled these "financial weapons of mass destruction."[1]

As a group, equity derivatives are virtually anything that trade based on underlying equity value. Investors trade every imaginable derivative, including derivatives based on equity, bonds, real estate, foreign exchange, commodities, and even the weather. That's right: Investors can trade a contract that depends on future weather conditions.[2]

Forward contracts and options contracts are the most common derivatives. A futures contract works like this. Suppose a coffee company must deliver coffee beans to its wholesale buyer in three months, when the crop will be ready. The company's profits are very sensitive to actual coffee prices at harvest time. Company management may not want to deal with the uncertainty of coffee prices, especially when a sudden decrease in demand or increase in supply could cause a sudden drop in price. The business would like to remove the risk associated with movement in coffee prices.

This is where derivatives come in. The coffee company might reduce its risk by selling a futures contract on coffee due three months from now. To do this, the coffee company agrees to sell the equivalent of its entire crop at a given price. An investor on the other side of the futures contract agrees to buy the coffee at that price. If coffee prices drop, the coffee company wins on the futures contract, but loses when selling the actual beans to the wholesaler, and is unaffected overall. If coffee prices rise, on the other hand, the coffee producer loses on the futures contract, but wins when selling the actual beans to the wholesaler, and is still unaffected overall. The futures contract lets the coffee producer lock in profits now regardless of future movements in the price of coffee.

Options are slightly more complicated. They give the holder the right, but not the obligation, to buy or sell an underlying equity security.

Suppose an investor has $100,000 invested in the stock market, saving the money for a down payment on a house. The investor worries that the stock market might decline in the next year or two. The investor could buy a *put option* on the equity investment for one year, two years, or longer. The put option gives the investor the right to sell the entire U.S. stock market at a given price, an option that becomes more valuable as the equity market declines. In fact, if the investor bought the right amount of put options, the nest egg would lose nothing, even if the equity market declined by 100%. The only cost would be the option's purchase price.

The market is full of various forwards, futures, and option contracts. Lehman Brothers helped investors buy both *listed* and *over-the-counter* (OTC) futures and options. Listed derivatives are traded on exchanges, are standardized, and have greater risk controls. Investment banks typically customize OTC derivatives to investors' specific preferences. For example, Coca-Cola might purchase a rainbow option, which pays the company its top competitors' performance. That hedges some of Coca-Cola's business risk. However, OTC options are less transparent than listed options.

Lehman Brothers further divided its equity derivatives area into two businesses, one handling standardized volatility-related options and the other dealing with structured products. The structured product area created a lot of very customized, complicated derivatives.

Equity Finance

Equity finance works to find financing for investors and firms, making it possible for clients to purchase equities and other securities on margin or short-sell securities.[3]

This group included the *prime brokerage unit*. Prime brokerage has grown in many investment banks over the past 20 years to support the trading activities of money management firms, especially hedge funds. Prime brokerage operations handle clearing and trade settlement, as well as other back-office operations, for hedge funds and other money managers.

Arbitrage (Proprietary Trading)

An *arbitrage* group, sometimes called the *proprietary trading* group, is the part of any investment bank that most closely resembles a hedge fund. Investors in this very diverse area look for equity market imbalances and trade accordingly, using internal money to make proprietary profits.

For example, an arbitrage group might find two companies that should trade at the same value, but don't. (Remember the example of LTCM's trades around Royal Dutch and Shell?[4] They're not the only ones who look for such opportunities.)

Lehman Brothers believed that its presence in the global capital markets; its access to advanced information technology, in-depth market research, proprietary risk management, and its general assessment experience under rapidly changing market conditions gave it a comparative advantage in finding profitable trading opportunities.

Fixed Income

Fixed income is another large part of the capital markets division. Fixed income was particularly important at Lehman Brothers, which was known as one of the leading fixed-income specialists in investment banking.

Fixed-income instruments pay a fixed, known stream of future income—hence the term "fixed income." Bonds are the most common example.

Buy a stock, and you have no idea what the future returns will be. The stock could go up or down by any amount, making the income from it variable, not fixed. Bonds and other fixed-income instruments, by contrast, commit to paying a known payment on specified future dates.[5]

As a broker, Lehman helped investors trade fixed-income instruments, 24 hours a day and around the world. The fixed-income area had several subdivisions. One of these was the fixed-income research department, which was one of the top such departments anywhere. It created bond indices that investors used to gauge bond segment performance.[6]

Government and Agency Obligations

The *government and agency obligations* group at Lehman Brothers worked with multiple government bonds, as well as bonds issued by Freddie Mac and Fannie Mae. Lehman Brothers was a *primary dealer*, with the privilege of being the first to purchase U.S. government bonds for its own account and for clients.[7]

Lehman was also a market-maker in U.S. government bond securities and all major government bond securities. It stood ready to buy or sell when portfolio managers, hedge funds, or investors needed to buy or sell government bonds.

Through this group, Lehman was also an underwriter and market-maker for bonds issued by Freddie and Fannie. As an underwriter, Lehman helped Freddie and Fannie publicly issue their debt.

Corporate Debt Securities and Loans

The *corporate debt securities and loans* group served a function similar to that of the government and agency group, but for corporations rather than for governments. Lehman helped companies issue and sell fixed- and floating-rate debt, as well as preferred equity.

Suppose General Motors, or another large company, needs to raise cash to run or expand its business. It can borrow the money by selling bonds. Fixed-rate bonds pay investors a fixed interest rate at specified intervals. Floating-rate bonds pay a variable interest over the bond's life, based on some determined mechanism. Companies in need of funds turned to Lehman Brothers and other investment banks to help them design, issue, and sell both types of debt. This is one of the primary links between Wall Street and Main Street.

High-Yield Securities and Leveraged Bank Loans

Lehman's *high-yield securities and leveraged bank loans* group dealt with company debt that's less than investment grade. Investment banks help companies with credit ratings below BBB issue debt. Lehman Brothers also offered such firms loans for purchasing or acquiring other companies, and was a market-maker in high-yield securities.

Money Market Products

At Lehman, the *money market products* group dealt with short-term fixed income. Money market securities typically have less than one-year maturities.

Lehman was a leader in originating and distributing medium-term notes and commercial paper. Companies use commercial paper to borrow money for less than 270 days. Both banks and large corporations often use it to meet short-term obligations, such as payroll or inventory. It is not backed by collateral, so it's usually issued by large, stable businesses that are very likely to pay back the loan. Many businesses in the world rely on short-term commercial paper to fund their operations, and rely on Wall Street to facilitate borrowing. This is another important link between Main Street and Wall Street.

Mortgage- and Asset-Backed Securities

The *mortgage- and asset-backed securities* group generated lots of profits for Lehman Brothers throughout the decade, but would also be the reason for Lehman's demise. In 2006, Lehman Brothers was the world's number-one underwriter of subprime mortgages.

Freddie and Fannie bought mortgage portfolios, securitized them, and sold them to investors. Investment banks, including Lehman, did the same thing. They packaged these mortgage pools—especially subprime mortgage pools—and sold them to investors. They also traded mortgage-backed securities on behalf of clients and for their proprietary trading groups.

At Lehman, this group was also heavily involved in securitizing and trading *asset-backed securities* (ABS). An asset-backed security, not surprisingly, is any security backed by an asset. A mortgage-backed security (MBS) is a kind of ABS. Other ABS include securities backed by auto loans, student loans, or credit card loans. An investment bank might purchase a group of these loans—perhaps 100,000 auto loans of similar credit quality—then package them into a security and sell that security to an investor. The investor then receives the payment stream from that group of auto loans.

Creative finance can make the basic security more complicated. For example, an investment bank might split the auto-loan portfolio into a CDO of various tranches with different characteristics designed to appeal to various investors.[8]

Lehman Brothers participated in both the commercial and residential mortgage market. It also originated mortgage loans directly through its subsidiary savings bank, Lehman Brothers Bank. Lehman purchased mortgage lenders, including BNC in Irvine, California, and Aurora Loan Services in Littleton, Colorado, which helped them originate and securitize mortgages.

All the investment banks were involved in the mortgage market, but Lehman was more involved than any of the others in creating, trading, and investing in residential and commercial mortgages and real estate.

Municipal and Tax-Exempt Securities

Lehman's *municipal and tax-exempt securities* group participated in all aspects of the municipal bond business, from origination to trading. States, cities, and local governments issue municipal bonds to finance their activities, from improving the roads or schools to building a new football stadium. It's another important link between Main Street and Wall Street.

Financing

The *financing* department was involved in facilitating financing for Lehman Brothers and its customers. It managed the company's matched-book activities, supplied customers with secured financing, and funded the company's activities.

Matched-book funding involves borrowing and lending cash on a short-term basis to institutional customers. Marketable securities or government or government-agency securities in reverse repos typically collateralized these loans. Lehman made these agreements in various currencies and sought to generate profits from the difference between interest earned and interest paid.

The financing unit worked with Lehman's institutional sales force to identify customers with cash to invest and/or securities to pledge to meet the firm's (and its customers') financing and investment objectives. Financing also coordinated with the company's Treasury area to provide collateralized financing for a large portion of the company's securities and other financial instruments.

Lehman was a major participant in the European and Asian repurchase agreement markets, which provided secured financing for the firm's customers in those regions.

The firm's short-term financing provided an important link between Lehman and other investment and commercial banks. The financial system is fundamentally linked through this web of connections.

Fixed-Income Derivatives

The *fixed-income derivatives* group created, traded, made markets, and invested in the derivatives that are based on the underlying value of fixed-income products, including swaps, options, and futures. This area also included highly levered CDO and CDS fixed-income derivatives, which were based on underlying mortgages. Lehman lost a lot of money on these derivatives.

Lehman Brothers Bank

Lehman owned an actual bank, *Lehman Brothers Bank*. Like most other banks, it issued mortgages for commercial and residential real estate. Lehman believed that owning a bank let it move more easily into the mortgage securitization business, but the bank was also outside Lehman's core expertise.

Foreign Exchange

Lehman operated in global equity and fixed-income markets, so its clients needed foreign currency transactions. The *foreign exchange* division let clients trade foreign currency in both spot and derivative markets around the world. Lehman Brothers also provided crucial advisory services regarding foreign exchange to central banks and other clients.

A corporate client might have business offices in Germany, but headquarters in the United States. Company profits depend on how well products sell in both countries. Profits made in Germany also depend on currency movements between the Euro and the U.S. dollar. Profits are reported in U.S. dollars and many shareholders are U.S. investors, so the firm may want to stabilize exchange-rate fluctuations. Lehman Brothers could help the company buy or sell futures or options on the Euro versus the U.S. dollar, hedging future foreign-division profits.

Global Distribution (Global Sales)

The *global distribution* unit, or global sales, worked to sell and promote fixed-income and equity products to clients all over the world. Salespeople used Lehman's well-known research reports to help them.

Research

Lehman's *research* business was among the most elite, especially in fixed income, which distributed its reports all over the world.

The group did quantitative, qualitative, economic, strategic, and trade-related research in equity and fixed income. A typical economic research piece might have discussed the economies of one or more countries, offering forecasts about inflation, GDP growth, and other important economic fundamentals. A typical trade research piece might have offered ideas on how to profit from a market anomaly, such as situations in which two companies are mispriced but should converge to the same value, or discussed how to use a foreign-exchange option to hedge foreign-currency risk.

These reports were supposed to help clients, but far too often investment banks use their research as a way to push products. For example, a piece that J.P. Morgan published in the late 1990s showed that clients who traded more frequently made higher profits. The argument helped Morgan generate more trades and increase trading-division profits. The idea was enticing, but only valid if every trade was a good trade—and it's hard to make only good trades.

Client Services

Private Client Services (Private Wealth Management)

Private client services is an area within many investment banks, including Lehman. Some banks call it private wealth management. This group focused on the investment needs of very wealthy individuals and small to mid-sized institutions worldwide. Private client service groups perform all kinds of functions, designing special investment vehicles for high-net-worth investors and managing clients' money to achieve their goals.

As an example, suppose a small company's CEO had a concentrated stock position in that company—an undiversified and risky investment. Lehman (and other investment banks) worked to diversify the CEO's portfolio, trading company returns for returns on a more diversified index. Lehman could offset this risk through other customers with different goals, or use the portfolio as a natural hedge against the bank's broad holdings and obligations.

Private Equity

The *private equity* group worked with investments related to private companies on behalf of clients, the firm, and company employees. Private companies don't trade publicly in the stock market, so their needs are different than those of publicly traded firms.

This group included several areas of specialization: *merchant banking, venture capital, real estate, fixed income,* and *third-party funds.* The main areas were the venture capital unit, which invested in start-up companies, and the real estate area, which made commercial and residential real estate investments. This area's real estate investments later caused Lehman Brothers lots of problems. The venture capital unit helped provide financing for many new and innovative firms.

Technology

Through its LehmanLive platform, this unit distributed information and facilitated execution over the Internet. It also had strategic investments in various institutional trading networks throughout the world, including TradeWeb, Arca, and others.

Corporate and Risk Management

Corporate business handled the details of running Lehman Brothers; *risk management* was in charge of monitoring and managing Lehman's principal risks, including market, credit, liquidity, legal, and operational exposure.[9] This unit missed the massive risks in Lehman's real estate positions.

Summary

Lehman Brothers and other investment banks are linked to Main Street by performing intermediary and financing functions for businesses. For example, Lehman's capital markets division bought Fannie and Freddie debt, which in turn facilitated Fannie and Freddie's growth, which made mortgages possible for millions of Americans. Lehman also originated and securitized mortgages through its fixed-income division and through Lehman Bank. Lehman provided short-term and long-term financing for U.S. corporations through its fixed-income unit. Through its client services area, Lehman provided venture capital funds for start-ups and other companies.

Investment banks, including Lehman, can also became heavily involved in proprietary positions, including real estate. It's not clear whether this makes other businesses within Lehman more liquid and better functioning or if it improved financial system operations. It did, however, financially ruin Lehman Brothers.

The Calculation of the BIS Capital Adequacy Ratio

Merely corroborative detail, intended to give artistic verisimilitude to an otherwise bald and unconvincing narrative.
—Pooh-Bah, Gilbert & Sullivan's *The Mikado*

The General Calculation

The formula for CAR is:

$$\text{CAR} = \frac{\text{Capital}}{\text{Risk-Weighted Assets}} = \frac{\text{Capital}}{\sum_{i=1}^{N} A_i w_i} \tag{J.1}$$

where A_i represents the value of the ith asset, and w_i is the risk weighting of the ith asset.

According to Basel I and Basel II, banks should have a CAR of no less than 8%, and 4% of that should be in the form of Tier 1 capital. Table J.1 describes what constitutes Tier 1 and other types of capital.

The details are numerous, but the basic idea is simple. If a bank has $100 million in assets, it should have a minimum amount of capital to cover potential losses. That minimum level was thought to be 8%. Basel III amended the minimum ratio to 13% of total capital in certain conditions. This includes

TABLE J.1 Basel I Types of Capital

Type of Capital	Type of Asset
Tier 1	Common stock, preferred shares, and disclosed bank reserves
Tier 2	Undisclosed bank reserves, hybrid capital instruments, and subordinated short-term debt
Tier 3	Short-term subordinated debt

Note: Basel I has many more details about these sources of capital.
Source: BIS.

9.5% of common equity capital. Systemically important financial institutions (SIFI) may require an additional 1% to 3.5% of capital.

Not all assets are considered equivalent. The rules weight each asset by its level of risk. A very risky asset should be counted fully against the capital requirement, so it has a weighting of 100%. A very safe asset, such as cash, gets a weighting of 0%.[1] Basel II modified the risk weightings to account for the credit rating of an asset (see Table J.2).

TABLE J.2 Basel II Risk Weightings (%) Based on Ratings

	AAA to AA−	A+ to A−	BBB+ to BBB−	BB+ to BB−	B+ to B−	Below B−	Unrated	Past Due
Corporates	20	50	100	100	150	150	100	150
Sovereign Entities	0	20	50	100	100	150	100	—
Banks	20	50	50	100	100	150	50	—
Residential Mortgages	35	35	35	35	35	35	35	100
Nonresidential Mortgages[a]	50–100	50–100	50–100	50–100	50–100	50–100	50–100	150

Note: Rating agencies determine these ratings. Past Due loans are 90 days or more overdue.
[a] These can vary according to the decision of national supervisory authorities.
Source: BIS.

Basel I and II recommendations also require that Tier 1 capital make up 4% of the ratio and that the total 8% must consist of Tier 1, Tier 2, and Tier 3 capital. The different capital tiers have differing liquidities and abilities to protect third parties from bank losses. Tier 1 is the most useful capital. It consists of common equity and disclosed bank reserves, put aside against future losses. Irredeemable noncumulative preferred shares and retained earnings are also part of Tier 1 capital.[2]

Tier 2 capital is less tangible capital, such as undisclosed reserves (solid, but not shown in firm financial statements), and subordinated debt, which may also appear in Tier 3 capital. Tier 2 capital includes supplementary capital, also categorized as undisclosed reserves, revaluation reserves, general provisions, hybrid instruments, and subordinated term debt.

Undisclosed reserves are uncommon, but some regulators accept them when a bank has made a profit that has not appeared in normal retained profits or in the bank's general reserves.

Revaluation reserves are created when a company asset is revalued at a higher price. Perhaps a bank owns its headquarters, having bought it for $100 a century ago. A current revaluation will likely show a large increase in value, which is added to a revaluation reserve.

A general provision is created when a company knows a loss may have occurred but does not know the loss's exact nature. Under pre-IFRS accounting standards, general provisions commonly provided for expected future losses. Because they did not represent incurred losses, regulators often let banks count them as capital.

Hybrids have both debt and equity characteristics. They may count as capital if the bank can take losses on their face value without triggering a liquidation. Preferred stocks are hybrid instruments.

Subordinated debt is debt that ranks below ordinary bank deposits. Tier 3 capital debts may include more subordinated issues, undisclosed reserves, and general loss reserves than Tier 2.

In normal times, Basel III requires a higher amount of Tier 1 capital (11%) and a higher amount of common equity in Tier 1 capital (9.5%) than Basel II.[3]

An Example

Suppose a bank has $100 million in deposits at the beginning of the year. It has $5 million in equity. It has invested $50 million in residential real estate loans, $20 million in BBB + government debt, and $20 million in A + bank debt, holding $10 million in cash. Under Basel I, the bank's CAR would equal 13.33%. Under Basel II, its CAR would equal 17.24%. The difference is mainly due to the reduced weight that mortgages receive under Basel II.

At the end of the year, mortgage assets have dropped by 10% in value. Bank A recognizes these losses accurately, but Bank B does not. Bank A's CAR will be 6.67% and Bank B's CAR will be 13.33%. Investors might incorrectly conclude that Bank B is better capitalized than Bank A. This is one of the problems with interpreting capital ratios with stale asset markings.

Notes

Chapter 2

1. For more information, see Livingston (2007).
2. Hawk is from Arkansas. He spent his senior year away from school, helping another young man become Arkansas attorney general. That man was President Bill Clinton.
3. From 1990 to September 1995, Salomon Brothers separated out the pretax profits from its proprietary trading business.

    Although Meriwether left Salomon in 1991, his entire trading team kept operating the proprietary trading group, so we use this as a performance proxy. In Figure 2.1, LTCM's profits from 1994 to 1998 are computed as end-of-year capital multiplied by gross returns.
4. In April 1991 Mozer submitted two false customer bids to the three-year Treasury note auction. These false bids of $3.15 billion each, along with one made by Salomon for its own account, let the firm capture over $5.1 billion of a three-year note sale totaling $9 billion.
5. Goldman changed this policy and caught criticism for it during the 2008 financial crisis.
6. On a particularly amusing capital raising campaign in the Middle East, the team of Rosenfeld and Hilibrand and the team of Meriwether and Leahy tried to decide which group would visit Israel and which would visit Saudi Arabia. Ultimately the Jews went to Saudi Arabia and the Irish went to Israel.
7. Siconolfi et al. (November 16, 1998).
8. Rumor had it that Fischer Black was also invited to join LTCM and leave Goldman Sachs (Mehrling [2005], p. 297). LTCM partners say they never invited Fischer Black to join them.
9. Not everyone agrees with their conclusions, including well-known option theorist Mark Rubinstein.
10. Another, more academic way to consider LTCM's performance is by using an asset pricing model for security returns and measuring whether LTCM had a positive return after accounting for their exposure to that model. Measure LTCM's returns against one of the standard academic models for assessing hedge funds' excess performance and you'll find that LTCM provided an

excess return or *alpha* of 2.93% per month. The commonly used academic model for hedge funds is the Fung-Hsieh model (2001, 2004), which regresses fund returns against a series of benchmark returns. The model is of the form $\bar{r}_{it} = \alpha_{iT} + \beta_{1iT}\text{RMRF} + \beta_{2iT}\text{SMB} + \beta_{3iT}\text{HML} + \beta_{4iT}\text{MOM} + \beta_{5iT}10\text{yr} + \beta_{6iT}\text{CS} + \beta_{7iT}\text{BdOpt} + \beta_{8iT}\text{FXOpt} + \beta_{9iT}\text{ComOpt} + \beta_{10iT}\text{EE} + \epsilon_{it}$ $t = 1, 2, ... T$, where $\bar{r}_{it}(= r_{it} - r_{ft})$ is the net-of-fee return on a hedge fund portfolio in excess of the risk-free rate, RMRF is the excess return on value-weighted aggregate market proxy, SMB, HML, and MOM are the returns on a value-weighted, zero-investment, factor-mimicking portfolios for size, book-to-market equity, and one-year momentum in stock returns as computed by Fama and French, 10 yr is the Lehman U.S. ten-year bellwether total return, CS is the Lehman aggregate intermediate BAA corporate bond index return minus the Lehman 10-year bond return, BdOpt is the look-back straddle for bonds, FXOpt is the look-back straddle for foreign exchange, ComOpt is the look-back straddle for commodities, and EE is the total return from an emerging market equity index.

11. It is not practically investable because it consists of many hedge funds. That would complicate investment, as would the fact that many of those hedge funds are closed to new investments.

12. In 1928, Frederick McCauley offered one of the first mathematical bond descriptions in academia. Almost every young analyst on Wall Street read through the Liebowitz team's fixed-income research publications.

13. Meriwether even purchased pictures and the rights to pictures of himself from the media that owned them, to limit the number of stories written about him.

Chapter 3

1. See the mathematics of this model in Appendix A of this book.

2. The use of historical numbers and the assumption of normality are not required for VaR. In fact, more sophisticated VaR techniques do not assume normality, or they modify the VaR estimates for more complicated distributions. See Dowd (1999) or Jorion (2006) for more information.

3. The details of this calculation are contained in Appendix A.

4. Other funds were being told "LTCM made $2B last year. Can't you?" John Meriwether interview on November 14, 2000. One financial participant said in an interview on June 22, 2001, "The arbitrage community ... are quite a bright lot, so if they see a trade happening—even if you're as secretive as LTCM— they'll analyze them and realize there's an opportunity for themselves ...." See MacKenzie (2003).

5. Convergence Asset Management raised $700 million in a single month.

6. This is explained in Chapter 7.

7. Various discussions with Dr. Eric Rosenfeld.

8. See MacKenzie (2003), p. 358.

9. This is discussed in detail in Chapters 4 and 5.

10. For more information, see Culp and Miller (1994, 1995).

11. This is discussed in further detail in Chapter 7.

12. Henry Davison started Bankers Trust, a leading investment bank, in 1903. Deutsche Bank purchased it in 1998.

13. A "dead swap" involves one swap with a counterparty, plus a new swap that's designed to neutralize the first swap's market exposure, giving an overall position risk that's very small. This is explained in more detail in Chapter 5. Consider an analogy from the equity market. A trader who is short $100 IBM and long $100 IBM has a risk of zero and $200 in off-balance-sheet items.

14. These are discussed in more detail in Chapter 13.

15. A bank holding company is a company that has control of a bank.

Chapter 4

1. As examples, this chapter re-creates some of LTCM's standard trades, focusing in particular on the trades in LTCM's portfolio just before their collapse in 1998. This was challenging. Reconstructing complicated, over-the-counter, fixed-income arbitrage trades requires accurate historical data. Some of this data was exceptionally hard to collect. As a result, some of these examples exactly reflect actual trades; others are approximations that give a sense of how LTCM trades behaved before, during, and after the LTCM crisis. (LTCM did not keep original trade data after LTCM and JWMP closed. Perold [1999] and direct conversations with former LTCM principals provided some information.)

2. Appendix B describes the mechanics of a swap spread trade, as well as a method to compute the approximate returns from such a trade. This terminology can be confusing in the rare circumstance when swap spreads are negative. One should think of a spread widening as the swap minus bond yield getting more positive.

3. See Appendix B for more details.

4. A reverse repo transaction is collateralized lending: One party lends cash to another party in exchange for a bond. The reverse repo rate is the interest rate LTCM received on the cash it loaned a counterparty in exchange for a bond when LTCM entered into a short swap spread transaction.

5. LTCM might even consider a swap spread trade with negative carry if the opportunity looked interesting enough.

6. For this chapter, 750 business days was used to compute the 3-year moving average and 250 days was used to compute the 1-year moving average.

7. These are generic swap spreads and hence on the run. The off-the-run securities may have been more attractive.

8. The mean of this swap spread from January 1991 to July 1998 was 43 basis points, with a daily standard deviation of 8 basis points. It was two standard

deviations from its mean at the beginning of August. It went out another four standard deviations compared to the historical daily mean.

9. LTCM also made trades using underlying mortgage-backed securities (MBS).

10. One can't really short a swap. The term refers to initiating a swap to receive a fixed interest rate and pay a floating interest rate.

11. Bonds issued by Freddie or Fannie, or mortgages that either one had securitized, had an implicit government guarantee.

12. In bond terminology, this is known as negative convexity.

13. This number is option-adjusted. The actual trade yield may have been more in the absence of typical defaults.

14. The mean spread and the spread standard deviations are not computed on the actual spread, but rather the percentage of the underlying Treasury yield that the spread represents. In the past, interest rates were quite high and so spreads were also significantly higher. Even so, it's probably more accurate to assume that, as interest rates rise, so does investor desire for a larger spread premium: a percentage return over the prevailing Treasury yields. Calculate the average percentage spread and apply it to the value of current interest rates to obtain the current mean spread and upper and lower two standard deviation levels.

15. There are arguments for and against using more historical data. One could argue that the spreads of many years ago were not as relevant, because the mortgage markets were less sophisticated and less liquid, making spreads much higher. The counter-argument is that a longer history gives some idea of what can happen in a liquidity squeeze.

16. LTCM partners preferred to use the terms "cheapen" and "richen." They believed swaps were expensive compared to government bonds in the 7-year area and that swaps were cheap versus the government bonds in the 10-year area.

17. See Chapter 15.

18. This can be accomplished using the same spread techniques discussed earlier. If the firm were short the box spread, in 10-year maturities, LTCM would pay floating interest, receive fixed interest, and short the 10-year Japanese government bond (JGB). This was naturally hedged against interest rate movements (i.e., duration neutral). In the 7-year area, LTCM would enter a swap to pay fixed interest, receive floating interest, and go long a 7-year JGB. This was also naturally hedged against interest rate movements.

19. At the time that the contract was settled, this was a fair exchange for the swap contract. The additional 40 basis points gave the swap a theoretical value of zero for both sides on the day the swap began.

20. LTCM could have also unwound the trade at a large profit.

21. LTCM was generally long bond volatility throughout Europe, not just in Germany.

22. In 2011, financing the U.S. deficit became big news, with disagreement over the budget and worries that the U.S. would not be able to borrow to finance its interest payments.

23. Appendix F discusses the transactions LTCM used to create this trade.
24. The OFR bond matures on February 15, 2023, and the OTR bond matures on August 15, 2023.
25. In fact, it had moved more than two monthly standard deviations, or 25.68 basis points. Shown in the figure, this was measured by computing the trade's average daily historical spread and the average historical daily standard deviation since 1994. Convert the daily standard deviation to a monthly standard deviation, assuming no mean reversion, using the formula $\sigma_m = \sigma_d \sqrt{20}$. Two monthly standard deviations equal the mean plus two times the monthly standard deviation. It's hard to use statistical tools to measure these deviations, because they are absent valuation, which in this case is very important.
26. The March 1998 30-year trade started with an unusually small spread and contracted less than normal—perhaps an early indicator that the space was getting crowded.
27. Using the Black-Scholes model, a short position in one call and one put option garners a premium of $36 on a notional amount of $100, with a strike price at the 5-years forward price of $122, with maturity 5 years, interest rate equal to 4%, and volatility equal to 20%. This position has a delta equal to −0.18, a gamma equal to −0.02, a rho of 88, a theta of 2.78, and a vega of −174. Thus, for every one percent increase in volatility this position will lose 5% of the premium ($1.74 of the position value).
28. Illiquidity would become a huge problem for many institutions during the 2008 crisis.
29. The cash would typically be kept to hedge the position, but LTCM may have used it to pay off investors at the end of 1997. Partners did not confirm this speculation.
30. As an LTCM partner said to me, "Another lesson is that you've got to have enough capital to hold these trades until convergence."
31. In a stock deal, a hedge fund would buy the target company and short the acquiring company to hedge out stock price movement risk. In a cash deal, a hedge fund would typically just buy the underlying target company.
32. If the market declines, stock deals don't necessarily cost the company more money. The number of shares that pay for the deal holds steady even when its dollar value drops. Cash deals, on the other hand, can place a higher burden on a company, especially if the market is declining.
33. This index is based on returns from the mutual fund MEFRX. The fund invests at least 80% of assets in the equity of companies that are involved in publicly announced mergers, takeovers, tender offers, leveraged buyouts, spin-offs, liquidations, and other corporate reorganizations.
34. LTCM used two other common types of equity relative-value trades. One type of trade involved non-voting shares that trade at a discount to voting shares. For example, LTCM traded BMW's preferred and common shares because voting rights had put a wedge between their prices. Another relative-value trade

depended on holding companies that traded at a discount to their underlying holdings. LTCM looked for the discrepancy's source, then shorted some of the underlying holdings while buying the holding company and waiting for prices to converge.

35. Former Salomon Brothers bond trader and PIMCO trader who requested anonymity.

36. Although the trade seems simple enough at first, thinking about the reason for price discrepancy gets quite complicated in a multicurrency world. The companies shared the cash flows 60/40. Determining whether the share prices were overvalued or undervalued necessitates converting both prices into a common currency. The exchange rate could potentially affect the misvaluation's direction. One might even think that the valuation difference's appropriate value should actually be related to the present discounted value of future earnings streams, represented in the exchange rate of the investor making the trade. Thus, the price ratio of the two firms will be equal to $\frac{P_{RD}}{P_S} = \left(\frac{\Psi}{1}\right)\left[\frac{E_{\$/\text{Guilder},t+1}\delta}{E_{\$/\text{Pound},t+1}\delta} + \cdots + \frac{E_{\$/\text{Guilder},t+N}\delta^N}{E_{\$/\text{Pound},t+N}\delta^N}\right]$, where δ is the discount rate (i.e., $\delta = \frac{1}{1+r}$), N is the number of periods into the future to which the discounting applied, and Ψ is the conversion factor. In the case of the actual shares in 1996, the factor is 9.2744 for shares listed on the home exchanges. In some cases, current and future expected exchange rates might affect this premium. For example, traders might expect the guilder to appreciate ahead of the Euro's anticipated arrival, leading to the Royal Dutch premium.

37. A total-return swap of this sort is quite simple. LTCM pays a counterparty the Royal Dutch return and the counterparty pays LTCM the Shell return.

38. This was calculated using the ADR prices trading in NYC to avoid exchange-rate complications. Around 1996 one share of Royal Dutch was equivalent to 9.2744 shares of Shell.

   In addition, while the Royal Dutch shares traded on par with Amsterdam (once the exchange rate is considered), the Shell ADR was worth one sixth the value of Shell shares traded on the London stock exchange. Take the share equivalent of 9.2744 and divide by 6 to get the Shell equivalent, which was 1.54 before June 30, 1997. On June 30, 1997, Royal Dutch had a 4-for-1 stock split and Shell had a 3-for-1 stock split, thus making one share of Royal Dutch worth 6.9557 shares of Shell (from a cash-flow rights perspective) and yielding an ADR relationship of 1.1593. Compare the price of one share of Royal Dutch with the price of the Shell ADR multiplied by 1.1593. If the results are not the same, buy the cheaper one and short the more expensive one. In 1998, this would have meant that, for every 1.1593 shares of Shell LTCM was long, the company was short one share of Royal Dutch.

39. This includes the financing cost of 70 basis points per year. Without this, the trade would have made 16% over the period.

40. The company merged into one company, but with A class and B class shares due to tax differences. The B class shares were for Shell owners and the A class shares

were for Royal Dutch owners. As of October 2011, B shares still carried a small premium.

41. See Chapter 3.

42. Organization for Economic Cooperation and Development, a group of about 25 industrialized democracies.

43. In 2008, this turned out to be false when Lehman Brothers collapsed and intermediaries were washed away with the tide.

44. Harvard Management Company, which manages Harvard's endowment, would go long the swap spread when it looked cheap. When it looked expensive, however, they took no position and waited instead of shorting it, according to an anonymous LTCM partner.

Chapter 5

1. According to a member of the executive team, Salomon didn't sell the other half until 1999. Dimon went on to become the conservative CEO of J.P. Morgan. Deryck Maughan went on to become partner at KKR.

2. At the time, the MICEX set a daily official exchange rate through a series of iterative auctions that were based on written bids submitted by buyers and sellers. Reuters published this rate. Banks and currency dealers worldwide commonly use the MICEX rate as the reference exchange rate for transactions involving the Russian ruble and other foreign currencies.

3. This is not Cramer's only incorrect argument. Cramer advises hundreds of thousands of small investors through his TV show. Reports from *Barron's* and others show the poor performance of Cramer's stock picks. His worst recommendations are frightening. He suggested: (i) Bear Stearns as a buy on 10/17/2005 at $55.18 per share, selling at under $6 on 03/20/08; (ii) a buy on Morgan Stanley on 09/15/06 at $70.95, trading at $24 by 10/27/10; (iii) a buy on Lehman Brothers on 10/17/05 at $55.18, then a "screaming buy" on Lehman Brothers at $16 on 09/05/08, saying that "things could not get any worse for the company," when just 10 days later it sold for pennies on the share after going bankrupt; (iv) a buy on AIG at $66.34 on 11/07/05; and many others. Unfortunately, his TV show has real consequences for real people. There are others. Jim Glassman, with no finance experience, wrote the book with the title *Dow 36,000*. Since the publication date of the book on October 1, 1999, the Dow dropped to a low of 6,547 on March 9, 2009 (−36%) and more than 10 years later has grown by only 8% (or 0.75% per year). With all the talk of hedge fund regulation, it's amazing that no one has spoken about financial journalism regulation, where these people are much more likely to affect the portfolios of lower-income investors.

4. Much of this came from Siconolfi (1998).

5. A copy of that letter is in this chapter's appendix.

6. I remember sitting at my trading desk in Basel, Switzerland, and reading the letter in total disbelief. Why would an LTCM investor release this material to the press? Wasn't it against their self-interest? Perhaps their position in LTCM was smaller than the trades they had initiated on the other side? But then who would that have been? Goldman? Bear Stearns? Salomon?

7. A similar situation occurred in 2008, when rumors spread that Lehman Brothers might be in trouble. In their case, however, it was counterparties and customers that began a run on the bank.

8. Witnesses at LTCM believe that a Goldman trader named Jacob Goldfield learned of their trades and may have used the information.

9. Chase complained to the Fed about the risk of the emergency loans to LTCM.

10. A copy of the letter is in the appendix to this chapter.

11. Material about the Buffett offer comes from Rosenfeld (2010) and conversations with Rosenfeld.

12. Despite Cayne's legitimate reasons for not contributing, it may have hurt Bear in terms of the long-term relationships within the Wall Street club.

13. Many market participants, including LTCM partners, were upset that Lehman and Bear did not contribute as much as the other banks. According to a lawyer at the SEC at the time, the SEC prohibited Lehman from contributing more due to their fragile circumstances.

14. The analysis is based on this representative collection of trades.

15. An extension of this work would use new econometric techniques designed by Engle and Sheppard (2001) to create a dynamic view of the strategies' daily correlation, then examine whether spikes occurred on the days of events described in Appendix 5, such as the day Meriwether's letter leaked to the press.

16. These portfolio statistics are equally weighted between trades, using a three-day return. The entire set of pair-wise correlations between strategies is shown in Appendix G.

17. It is difficult to accurately measure the daily standard deviations and correlations of very short-term returns.

Chapter 6

1. A down round of financing is a financing in which the firm's valuation in the financing round is substantially less than it was when previous investors put money in the firm.

2. Vinny Mattone and Jimmy Cayne were original investors that were handed back a portion of their investment. Vinny said to Jimmy at the time, "I can't believe they're doing this to us."

3. These returns were computed from end of February 1994 to end of March 1999.
    An investor that gave LTCM $1 at launch and never removed the money would have had $2.8 by end of 1997. LTCM paid a $1.8 dividend to departing

investors, leaving them with $1 still in the fund. Those investors received only 10 cents of that $1, giving them an annualized return of 14.6% for this period.

4. The warrants, sold in June, August, and October 1997, gave fund managers the right to buy more shares from UBS. The options could only be exercised after seven years.

5. Originally UBS wanted to invest more in the fund, but LTCM's partners did not want to increase new investor money. This scheme was a compromise.

6. The ratio of the option's price to the notional value was roughly 39%. The fund's historical volatility was around 8% to 9%, LTCM partners recall, but they priced the option using a volatility around 14%. Using a Black-Scholes model to price an option with a 14% volatility, risk-free rate of 7.5% (Treasury Yield + 50 basis points of swap spread + 100 basis points borrowing fee), with 100 as the current fund value and 110 as the strike price (slightly in the money), and seven years to maturity gives a price of 35.93 and a ratio of 36%.

7. Even if UBS had tried to dynamically hedge the position, it wouldn't have worked. Dynamic hedging relies on small stock price movements. The large jumps in LTCM's underlying value in August and September 1998 would have made it nearly impossible for UBS to use this hedge type.

8. Interestingly enough, this injection of cash was likely used by LTCM to pay off other investors at the end of 1997. This was not confirmed by LTCM partners.

9. UBS heard a lot of criticism, most of it around the idea that its call option had been impossible to hedge. UBS, however, had just wanted an investment in LTCM—so they wrote a put on LTCM and added some additional direct exposure.

10. Later, the U.S. Congress read a letter from Democrat Richard Neal that criticized these transactions as tax aversion techniques. At the time, Neal wanted to pass new legislation to prohibit tax avoidance potentials. See "U.S. Congress Considers LTCM Investment Technique," *Wall Street Journal*, October 18, 1998.

11. A key figure at the Bank of England, who wished to remain anonymous, disagreed and believed it was negligent for the Bank of Italy to invest in LTCM because it had no idea what LTCM was doing with the investment. "It was too secretive," he said. LTCM did share information with the Bank of Italy and had frequent trainee programs for Bank of Italy analysts.

12. Funds of funds prefer hedge funds in which management has personally invested, but this case shows that it's no guarantee.

13. This information came from Raghavan (1998) and was not verified by LTCM partners.

Chapter 7

1. Draw from others the lesson that may profit yourself.
2. For an example, see Lux (1995).

3. Fischer Black used to do this on an ad hoc basis, using the Black-Scholes option pricing model for special circumstances. When people said that tails were fat, he replied, "Just make your volatility input higher."

4. Ultimately, more theoretical and empirical research is needed in the area of endogeneity.

5. More advanced research examines VaR's measures when returns are not normal.

6. Amaranth Advisors LLC is the multistrategy hedge fund that collapsed in 2006. It made large bets in the natural gas futures market and ended up losing billions of dollars and closing its hedge fund. For more information, see Chincarini (2006, 2007).

7. This corresponds to an annual average return of 10% and an annual standard deviation of 20%. The VaR measurement uses an expanding rolling window.

8. Both Meriwether and Merton stated in interviews that this marking against LTCM was occurring during September 1998 (MacKenzie 2003).

9. Lehman Brother's 10-Q statements.

10. Normally, this need not be a cause for alarm. A stock-price decrease reduces shareholder wealth, but is not necessarily a business impediment. However, when a company needs to raise capital, a declining stock price means that, in order to raise a given amount of capital, the firm will have to sell many more shares, thus diluting existing shareholders' positions. If the declining share price becomes a focal point for counterparties and customers and leads to a crowded exit, this also will adversely affect the company.

11. I am unaware of any study that has analyzed this in detail. See Chapter 11 for a more in-depth discussion of Lehman Brothers.

12. I generally do not subscribe to a prohibition on leverage or on any strict controls on the free market, unless a specific discussion of the pros and cons can be pointed out accurately.

13. Their constraints might force them to accept the situation. These constraints could include intellectual constraints (they don't see this discrepancy), institutional constraints, and/or individual biases.

14. Of course, many of these loans are auto loans, credit card loans, and mortgage loans, which have default probabilities and other uncertainties.

15. See www.fdic.gov/bank/individual/failed/banklist.html.

16. There is a vast literature discussing alternative banking systems, including mutual fund banks (where depositors own the bank) and narrow banks.

17. See "Hedge Funds, Leverage, and the Lessons of Long-Term Capital Management" (April, 1999).

18. In reality they would not have been the same, but very close. Nevertheless, the general point is still valid.

19. If the individual banks hedge their outright risks, prices should not move too much, because (if LTCM's book were carefully balanced) every buyer should have a natural seller. But if they can't match up in the marketplace at the right time, every bank's mistimed marketplace entry would create excess volatility.

20. This situation is discussed in more detail in Chapters 11 and 12.
21. Two-way mark-to-market was discussed in detail in Chapter 3. Marking-to-market means that at the end of each day, counterparties valued LTCM's position with them. If the position did well, the counterparty gave cash back to LTCM. If the position went against LTCM, the counterparty demanded extra cash from LTCM. This is a standard way to control risk when traders take leveraged positions. Traders keep funds in case a counterparty cannot pay and a firm has to liquidate the position. Something similar occurs at a standard brokerage account when one margins equities.
22. LTCM partner conversations.
23. LTCM's requests may have had other detrimental effects on its portfolio.
24. As discussed earlier, some strategic investors kept their full investment shares. Jimmy Cayne described the forced dividend as the " . . . friends and family plan." Author Interview, February 15, 2012.
25. Fischer Black did not win, because he died in 1995.
26. In reality, the trader might short the 10-year futures contract, instead of U.S. Treasury bonds.
27. This is known as a duration-hedged portfolio.
28. Black published a 1998 article titled "How to Use the Holes in Black-Scholes," which described some practical ways to improve the model's reliability in various situations. Black writes, "Since these assumptions are wrong, we know the formula must be wrong. But we may not be able to find another formula that gives better results in a wide range of circumstances."
29. The regulators in the United States were the CFTC and the NFA. In the UK, it was the SFA and the FSA, and in Japan it was the MoF.
30. LTCM's regulatory reports regularly included the audited annual report for the master fund and each feeder fund to CFTC/NFA, the CFTC/NFA Annual Update of CPO (Form R-7) Registration to NFA, the NFA annual CPO Financial Questionnaire for the master Fund and each feeder fund to NFA, the Securities Exchange Commission (SEC) Form 13F to SEC to U.S. authorities.

    For the UK, the CFTC/NFA Annual Update of CTA (7-R) registration, the NFA Annual CTA Financial Questionnaire, and the Annual Audited financial Statements for Fund. For the SFA, LTCM filed the Annual Compliance review, the Annual Confirmation of Registered Persons & Category, the Annual reporting Statement, the Annual Auditor's Report, the Annual Internal Control Letter, the Annual Reconciliation, the Bi-annual Consolidated Reporting Statement, the Quarterly Large Exposure Monitoring Report, the Quarterly Reporting Statement. For Japan, the CFTC/NFA Annual Update of CTA (7-R) registration, and the NFA Annual CTA Financial Questionnaire. They reported to the MoF, the Annual Result of Operation and the Quarterly Status of Fund Management Form 7. To the Japanese Securities Investment Advisory Association (JSIA), they filed the Annual Result of Operation, the Annual Kaisha Gaiyo Form 1–1, the Annual Shouken Torihiki Gaiyou Form 1–2, the Annual Financial Ratios Form, the Annual Personnel Status Form 3, the Quarterly Balance Form 5, and the Quarterly Portfolio Balance Forms 2–1 and 2–2. In addition, they filed other reports in the United States for the Cayman Limited Partnership, the Audited Annual Fund Report, the NFA Annual CPO Financial Questionnaire on each Spoke, the SEC Form 13F-U.S. Equities, and the Commodity Futures Trading Commission (CFTC) Form 40 Statement of Reporting Trader to CFTC. They also filed reports to the U.S. Treasury, including the U.S. Treasury Auction Net Long Position report to Respective Dealers, and the U.S. Treasury Auction Award Notification to the Federal Reserve Bank of New York. They also reported to the Cayman Island Monetary Authority (CIMA) and an Audited Annual report to CIMA.

Chapter 8

1. Cioffi was also the head of the 11 CDOs that Bear had originated, some of which the fund bought. His dual roles created a disturbing sense of conflict of interest. Deloitte & Touche, the firm's auditor, warned investors in the 2006 audited financial statements that the fund's own managers had estimated the majority of the fund's net assets. Bear Stearns did not release this report until May 2007 (FCIC Report 2010).
2. Subprime securities are collateralized mortgages or other securities that depend on the behavior of subprime loans. Subprime loans are loans to borrowers that do not qualify for the lowest, or "prime" interest rates, because of poor credit histories, high debt relative to income, high loan-to-value ratios, or other risk factors.
3. This was very similar to the repo concepts discussed in Chapter 4, but instead of Treasury securities, the collateral here was CDOs and mortgage-backed securities.
4. Goldstein (June 25, 2007). In another sign of management failure, Chairman Jimmy Cayne was not aware when the hedge funds first got into trouble, and Warren Spector, co-President of Bear Stearns, agreed to invest another $25M in the funds (FCIC Report, page 446).
5. Investors commonly use these contracts to speculate on or hedge against the risk that the underlying mortgage securities may not be repaid as expected. The ABX, CMBX, and CDX underlying CDS offer protection if the securities (MBS or company debt) are not repaid as expected, in return for regular insurance-like premiums, called coupons.
6. This was for the January 2007 vintage compiled by Markit. The ABX index is also separated into different indices based on the credit rating of the underlying mortgages in the pool. The lower the rating, the lower the credit quality of those mortgages.
7. Sowood's name came from South Woodside Avenue, the street in Wellesley, Massachusetts, where Larson lived when he started at Harvard Management.

8. Citadel Investment Group, a large investment management firm with $14 billion under management at the time, also assumed what remained of Amaranth's natural gas financial swap book in October 2006. Amaranth, another hedge fund, spectacularly went bust in September 2006.

9. Mathematician James Simons, who earned his BS from MIT and his PhD from UC Berkeley, started Renaissance Technologies in 1982. As of late 2011, it managed around $15 billion. Its most famous offering is the Medallion Fund, which is closed to outside investors. Rumors say it consistently returned 35% net of fees from 1989 to 2007, though there's no way to really know. The funds charge much higher fees than do typical hedge funds, relying on great performance to attract investors. Medallion charges management fees of 5% and incentive fees of 36%. It trades all sorts of financial instruments around the world. The fund uses complex mathematical models to execute trades, which are often automated and generated on a model's signal. One-third of the fund's employees have PhDs in fields such as statistics, economics, mathematics, and physics.

    The firm depends on models built by mathematician Leonard Baum, co-author of the Baum-Welch algorithm, which determine probabilities in (among other things) biology, automated speech recognition, and statistical computing. Simons hoped to harness Baum's mathematical models to trade currencies. The models and techniques were modified over time, but stayed rooted in the quantitative discipline. Some of Medallion's staff eventually left to start their own hedge funds. Sandor Strauss, for instance, started Merfin LLC using a similar methodology.

10. Zuckerman et al. (2007) and Sender et al. (2007).

11. Other quantitative hedge funds, particularly quantitative macro hedge funds, actually performed well during this period. See Chincarini (2010).

12. For more information on quantitative equity funds, see Chincarini and Kim (2006).

13. Stat arb can be thought of as a short-term mean-reversion strategy.

14. Quantitative equity managers seek opportunities all over the world. It would be enlightening to examine quant factors constructed in different currency markets.

15. Asness (2007).

16. On August 6, 2007, American Home Mortgage Lenders filed for bankruptcy. Although many other mortgage lenders had filed for bankruptcy already, this was one of the first bankrupt lenders that had hardly any link to subprime mortgages.

17. The short-term contrarian indicator is a return index that shows the returns of previous negative return stocks minus previous positive return stocks. If this continues to decline, it suggests that there are very few suppliers on the other side of these equity transactions, indicating low liquidity. This theory is largely speculative.

18. As a rough rule of thumb, the formula for obtaining the return of a zero-investment factor, such as the value factor, to a position that is dollar-levered equivalently by l on each side is $l \cdot r_{factor}$.

19. The historical period used to compute standard deviations was January 1990 to August 2007. For the value factor, every day from August 2 to 8 brought results within the worst 5% of all returns from January 2005 to August 15, 2007. This was true for four days in August for the momentum factor, two days in August for the size factor, and four days in August for the market factor.

    Compared with results from a much longer time period—January 1980 to August 15, 2007—August brought the market factor three exceptional down days, the size factor two, the value factor only one (August 8, 2007), and the momentum factor four, including August 6 and August 8.

20. "In the usual quant equity portfolio, the Fama-French factors might play a 15% to 25% role, while the other 75% is made up of other factors," says a trader from Goldman Sachs.

21. Goldman Sachs Asset Management (2007) and conversations with traders at BGI. To verify this claim, I constructed 20 portfolios separated by price to book at the beginning of every year, then created a factor portfolio of the first bucket minus the twentieth bucket. From August 3, 2007, to August 9, 2007, this factor declined every day, for a cumulative move of 16 standard deviations during a one-year look-back period, or a cumulative five standard deviations over a look-back period to 2000. This concentration seems to explain some of the differences between professional and standard quant factors.

22. Caxton did not return calls requesting comment.

23. SAC, the hedge fund run by Steve Cohen, also likely liquidated its quant portfolio.

24. Khandani and Lo (2008) argue that market makers reduced their liquidity from August 7 to 13, and had a larger effect on price impact as quantitative equity funds sold similar factor positions. Their evidence is based on creating a contrarian strategy and observing its daily and hourly behavior. Despite all their evidence, their case is very weak and speculative, ultimately saying nothing about the unwind's actual causes.

25. The prime broker typically sets a maximum allowed leverage, after which a quantitative equity firm must liquidate or post additional collateral.

26. GSAM is Goldman Sachs Asset Management, BGI is Barclays Global Investors, AQR is Applied Quantitative Research.

27. It's not clear why these particular positions were moving. Copycat funds may have been liquidating their positions, or broker-dealers may have been "front-running" the funds. As Goldman and other large quant funds made trades, broker-dealers may have heard that large orders were coming their way, then taken positions to profit from the unwinding. Or market makers may have been protecting themselves with larger bid-ask spreads.

28. AQR's Asness and Morgan's Muller called Goldman during the day to ask what was happening.

29. This term originates from the expression "tool" as a term for a loser or uncool person. A "tool shed" represents a collection of tools. A shed show happens when

the individual tools work together to blow up the system. This term can be applied to life's other areas as well, whenever collective action causes trouble for all involved.

30. According to traders at Goldman, Global Alpha made around 12% annually during its 14-year history. Some years were very good. In 2003 and 2005, for instance, returns were in the high 30s and high 40s. A combination of bad returns and redemptions caused the fund to go from $10 billion at the beginning of 2007 to about $2 billion by 2010. Global Alpha was up 30% in 2009 and still held about $2 billion when the fund officially closed in 2011.

31. Data for analyzing quant equity portfolio managers can be obtained from four sources. Equity mutual fund data for quantitative type funds is publicly available. The eVestAlliance database contains data on institutional separate account performance. One can build pro-forma returns from quantitative managers' 13-F statements or use hedge fund databases such as Hedge Fund Research, Dow Jones Tremont, or TASS.

32. Hedge Fund Research.

33. This decline makes intuitive sense. The momentum factor picked up stocks that declined the least in 2008 and shorted those that declined the most, and so was very defensive. As the market rallied in 2009, this factor dramatically underperformed.

34. BGI trader.

35. GSAM trader.

36. Asness still believes in the power of quantitative equity hedge funds. "I've seen these strategies hold up very well in the Asian currency-inspired stock market plunge of October 1997; in the LTCM and Russian debt crisis of August 1998; in September 2001; and during the whole post-internet-bubble bear market," he writes. He also thinks that, as of September 21, 2007, the value spread was still very attractive.

37. Researchers might attempt to model the opportunity space to determine if a strategy has become crowded. For a factor like value, one might measure the opportunity by the current average value of top decile P/B stocks minus the bottom decile of P/B stocks. Run a regression on subsequent value-space returns for the next t periods. If there is a relationship, consider reducing positions as the opportunities get smaller in real time, perhaps with more complicated techniques as well or even with other factors or combinations of factors. One can also try to estimate the relative assets under management of same-space players versus the amount of assets under management in the general asset space. Another possibility might be to take the cross-sectional standard deviation of the signals within a factor category. The higher this value, the more opportunities might exist.

38. GSAM trader interview. Some traders are making minor changes by adding fundamental views to quantitative analysis. Others are using a top-level process to decide when they'll use or ignore certain factors.

Chapter 9

1. "Parking securities" means transferring stock positions to another party so that the stock's true ownership is hidden. For example, in a company takeover, an investor may park company securities with other investors so that the target company's management won't know the extent of the investor's company ownership, giving the investor the advantage of surprise. This practice is against security regulation laws. The SEC and Justice Department filed several lawsuits against Bear Stearns for these practices; all were settled.

2. Cayne's bridge team won the Reisinger national bridge championship in the Fall of 2011, as well as in 1977, 1988, 1992, 2007, and 2010. He tutored Warren Buffett and many other high profile people in bridge.

3. Of this, $38.5 million was paid to the SEC, $10 million was paid to the Manhattan District Attorney's office plus $2.5 million in costs to the D.A. The Bear Stearns executive in charge of the relationship with A.R. Baron, Richard Harriton, was fired.

4. When Jimmy Cayne retired his post as CEO, the Board urged him to stay on. As he announced his resignation, he received standing ovations on three separate occasions from the President's Advisory Committee, the entire retail sales force, and in the partners' meeting consisting of around 400 senior managing directors.

5. Bank competition for customer assets determines these rates.

6. In fact, banking used to follow the 3-6-3 rule, paying depositors 3%, then lending to them through some other arrangement at 6% and being at the golf course by 3 p.m. See a more complete description of banking in Appendix I and the online appendix on banking at www.wiley.com/go/crisisofcrowds.

7. Also known as the capital intermediation business.

8. Monoline insurers provide guarantees to issuers of securities.

9. Many relative-value hedge funds observe this institutional bias and exploit it. They typically load up on risk as the year ends. Banks reload risk in the first months of the new year, and the hedge funds benefit from this with first-quarter relative-value fund returns that are usually very good. In 2008, this was not the case, in large part due to the unexpected collapse of Bear Stearns (see Chapter 15). Chincarini and Kim (2006) discuss how to exploit profit opportunities created by the behavioral biases of investors and institutions. Sometimes this bias can be a reaction to institutional constraints.

10. See Rapoport (2010). In an April congressional hearing, Rep. Gregory W. Meeks said, "It appears investment banks are temporarily lowering risk when they have to report results, [then] they're leveraging up with additional risk right after." The banks in this study were primary dealers: banks and securities broker-dealers that trade in U.S. government securities with the Federal Reserve Bank of New York. As of October 18, 2010, primary dealers were: BNP Paribas Securities Corp., Banc of America Securities LLC, Barclays Capital Inc., Cantor Fitzgerald & Co., Citigroup Global Markets Inc., Credit Suisse Securities (USA) LLC, Daiwa

Capital Markets America Inc., Deutsche Bank Securities Inc., Goldman, Sachs & Co., HSBC Securities (USA) Inc., Jefferies & Company, Inc., J.P. Morgan Securities LLC, Mizuho Securities USA Inc., Morgan Stanley & Co. Incorporated, Nomura Securities International, Inc., RBC Capital Markets Corporation, RBS Securities Inc., and UBS Securities LLC. (For more information about primary dealers, see www.ny.frb.org/aboutthefed/fedpoint/fed02.html.)

11. FCIC (2010), p. 281.
12. Repo contracts in LTCM trades are discussed extensively in Chapter 4.
13. This rate is usually lower than other borrowing rates, because the borrowing is collateralized borrowing and therefore less risky for the counterparty.
14. J.P. Morgan had privileges with the Fed as a bank that Bear did not.
15. FCIC (2010), p. 288.
16. Cohan (2010), p. 49.
17. FCIC (2010).
18. Bear separated their assets by Level I, II, or III. Level I: Quoted market prices in active markets for identical assets or liabilities. Level II: Observable market-based inputs or unobservable inputs that are corroborated by market data. Level III: Unobservable inputs that are not corroborated by market data.
19. FCIC (2010), p. 284.
20. Thomas (2007).
21. The mortgage-related assets represented 38% of Bear's nonderivative trading assets at the beginning of 2008.
22. The Bear financial statements reported only $200 million, but an SEC investigation later found the actual write-down to be $500 million. Bear did not disclose this to investors for fear that markets would react badly to the value of subprime mortgages. The eventual loss may have even been higher than the $500 million. See United District Court Southern District of New York (2009).
23. The late Rudiger Dornbusch used to joke that when the leaders announce that everything is okay, that's the cue for their friends to start unloading.
24. Goldman had done this to LTCM in 1998.
25. The supervision program started in March 1994 and ended in September 2008 because SEC Chairman Christopher Cox concluded that it clearly hadn't worked.
26. An anonymous market participant revealed to me that in early March, with the stock trading around $80 per share, there were requests by investors to the Chicago Board of Trade to list $20 strike put options—very unusual activity. There may also have been a lot of naked shorting of Bear's stock—an illegal activity that has not been fully investigated.
27. Using prices on May 16, when the deal was originally struck, it was only $7.94 per share. Thus, in dollar terms, the deal was only four times larger.
28. Lots of other big Bear Stearns holders also took a dive. The stock's largest holders were Barrow Hanley Mewhinney & Strauss (9.73%), Joseph Lewis (9.36%), Morgan Stanley (5.37%), James Cayne (4.94%), Legg Mason Capital

Management (4.84%), Private Capital Management (4.69%), Barclays Global Investors (3.60%), State Street (3.01%), Vanguard Group (2.67%), Janus Capital Management (2.34%), Legg Mason Funds Management (1.93%), Fidelity Management (1.93%), Putnam Investment Management (1.90%), Neuberger Berman (1.55%), and UBS (1.54%). Most of these are mutual funds that held these stocks on the behalf of millions of ordinary American savers.

29. The source wished to remain anonymous.

30. This underlines another problem in the financial system: People sometimes rise to the top without real experience in the areas they regulate.

Chapter 10

1. The budget surplus was $69 billion, $126 billion, and $236 billion respectively from 1998 to 2000.

2. These averages are from January 1998 to January 2008. Spreads for Fannie Mae bonds are similar. These are not actual yield spreads, but option-adjusted spreads (OAS).

3. Originally, these were the nicknames professional investors gave to the institutions. The official names: Federal Home Loan Mortgage Association is Freddie (Ticker Symbol: FMCC.OB), the Federal National Mortgage Association is Fannie (Ticker Symbol: FNMA.OB), and the Government National Mortgage Association is Ginnie (no ticker symbol, because it is government owned). Many years ago the markets gave them these nicknames, and eventually the companies' board of directors allowed the use of these names for official business.

4. This is not entirely true, of course. The spread trade carries a risk that the spread widens, but on average if the spread is not too volatile, the extra yield more than compensate for the risk.

5. In 1987, for example, when another government-sponsored enterprise (GSE), the Farm Credit System, became insolvent, Congress and the administration developed and implemented a $4 billion bailout plan, confirming the capital markets' view of what the government would do if Fannie and Freddie had financial difficulty.

6. A mortgage originator is any institution that makes mortgage loans to individuals.

7. The servicing fee for doing the paperwork on the monthly mortgage payments may or may not be subtracted depending on whether the original bank continues to service the loans. This fee is typically about 25 bps. The G-fee represents the fee that the GSEs take for "guaranteeing" the interest and principal payments and is typically between 20 and 25 bps. The fair value calculation is actually quite complicated, but can be found in Fabozzi (1999).

8. It is roughly the 30-year mortgage rate minus the G-fee, the servicing fee, and the rate Freddie or Fannie pay on their bonds.

9. Freddie and Fannie also specialize in moving these liabilities off their balance sheets through qualified special purpose entities.

10. In addition to buying and creating housing mortgage pools, Freddie and Fannie also buy mortgage-backed securities (MBS) from other institutions that securitize them.

11. In simple terms, they hedge interest rate risk by using interest rate futures, bonds, and swaps to adjust duration exposure to interest rates from the difference in duration between the mortgage pool and the bonds they issue. They typically hedge their anticipated lender commitments 30 to 90 days in the future and use derivatives to account for the mortgages' prepayment behavior. These tactics are similar to LTCM's short swap trade. See more details about hedging the interest rate risk on a mortgage pool in Fabozzi (1999) or Jaffee (2005).

12. A CMO can distribute defaults across tranches in various ways, not all of them as straightforward as this example. Tranches can have ratings across the spectrum, from AAA to AA+, AA, AA−, A+, A, A−, BBB+, BBB, BBB−, BB+, BB, BB−, B+, B, B−, CCC+, CCC, CCC−, CC, C, and D, according to the rating agency's opinion. Ratings are based on the general probability of default. In theory, all the tranches could have a AAA rating.

13. The market calls a CDO created from another CDO "CDO-squared."

14. Of course, the assumption that only some home owners will default may itself be wrong. If the pool consists of very similar borrowers, they may all default at once, causing a loss for the whole pool. If all home owners were perfectly correlated in their behavior when housing prices declined, a pool could not have different rating tranches.

15. For more details on the structure of synthetic CDOs as well as Goldman's involvement, see FCIC (2010), p. 143. Goldman was later sued and settled for $550 million for some of the conflicts of interest associated with synthetic CDOs, such as the Abacus 2004-1 lawsuit.

16. Off-balance sheet is an accounting term meaning that certain assets do not need to be shown on a firm's balance sheet.

17. Ironically, off-balance-sheet MBS had a lower capital requirement, even though the notional value of these was much larger and posed the same degree of credit risk.

18. The risk-based capital standards are intended to ensure that Fannie Mae and Freddie Mac can survive a sustained period of economic distress. The Federal Housing Enterprises Financial Safety and Soundness Act of 1992 specifies that the risk-based capital requirement be calculated to withstand two hypothetical stress tests. Both tests cover a period of 10 years. In one test, interest rates rise by 75 percent over a 12-month period and then remain at that level for the remaining nine years. In the other test, rates fall by 50 percent. In each test, the rate change is generally capped at 600 basis points. Both tests have a credit risk component: Real estate prices fall throughout the country by 11 percent during the first five years of the stress period and then recover to their initial level during

the last five years. Both Fannie Mae and Freddie Mac must hold capital sufficient to survive the worst of those stress tests, plus an extra 30 percent in capital to cover operational risk. Under the law, GSEs must hold capital equal to the minimum requirement or the risk-based requirement, whichever is larger. The risk-based capital requirement was typically significantly lower than the 2.5 percent of assets plus 0.45 percent of off-balance-sheet obligations for both Fannie Mae and Freddie Mac, as the risk-based standard was adopted in 2002. As a result, the risk-based standard didn't increase the two firms' capital requirements.

19. This was the average for Merrill Lynch, Morgan Stanley, Goldman Sachs, Lehman Brothers, Citi, Deutsche Bank, UBS, J.P. Morgan, and Bear Stearns.

20. The calculation is simple. Suppose the loans were completed at $100, for a total of 100 $1 loans. Each house costs $1. Now suppose all housing prices drop by $x\%$ in value and $p\%$ default. Freddie is stuck with the underlying collateral: the houses of those who default. Forget any transaction costs associated with this and just focus on the portfolio's mark-to-market value. Freddie will have losses of $\$100 \cdot x \cdot p$. To figure out the size of x that forces Freddie into bankruptcy, find the x such that $\$100 \cdot x \cdot p =$ Shareholder Equity. The critical x is given by $x = \dfrac{\text{Shareholder Equity}}{\$100 \cdot p}$. This is an illustrative example, using approximations. In the real world, only mortgages issued in 2006 would have dropped by the full 27%. If we look at all the mortgages Freddie Mac originated from 2002 to 2008 and consider the average price drop of housing during this period using the Case-Shiller index, total losses are around −$167 billion. A minimum 17% default rate would make the firm insolvent. Costs would likely be much higher, as Freddie would be at least temporarily without cash to pay investors on its securitized portfolios. The example also ignores Freddie's insurance protection. This protection, however, did not cover all mortgages and only covered defaults up to a certain level.

21. There is much history on this, but some summary sources are Pinto (2010, 2011) and Wallison (2010).

22. HUD Glossary. FICO scores summarize a person's credit riskiness. FICO is an acronym for the Fair Isaac Corporation, creator of the FICO score. A person's FICO score can be between 300 and 850. In general, a FICO score above 650 indicates a very good credit history.

23. Pinto (2010).

24. Jaffee (2010).

25. FCIC (2010), p. 181.

26. HUD wrote that "As the GSEs become more comfortable with subprime lending, the line between what today is considered a subprime loan versus a prime loan will likely deteriorate, making expansion by the GSEs look more like an increase in the prime market." HUD (2000).

27. Fannie and Freddie acquired large amounts of subprime private-label securities (PLSs) because these securities were "goals rich" (Lockhart, 2009). The

agencies were required to meet affordable housing goals, set annually by the Department of Housing and Urban Development (HUD) in accordance with the Federal Housing Enterprises Financial Safety and Soundness Act of 1992. Buying PLSs backed by subprime mortgages counted toward meeting these goals because the underlying mortgages tended to be made to borrowers earning less than the median income, or were backed by properties in "underserved areas" (HUD, 2004). According to Freddie Mac's 2006 annual report, 99.9% of the PLS purchases had AAA credit. Parts of this report are also extremely interesting. For example, the statement "While the securities that the GSEs guarantee, and the debt instruments they issue, are explicitly not backed by the full faith and credit of the United States, and nothing in this rule should be construed otherwise..." The constant pressure from HUD to serve the lower-income housing community is apparent. "The GSEs have room for growth in serving the affordable housing mortgage market. The Department estimates that the two GSEs' mortgage purchases accounted for 55 percent of the total (single-family and multifamily) conventional, conforming mortgage market between 1999 and 2002. In contrast, GSE purchases comprised 48 percent of the low- and moderate-income market, 48 percent of the underserved-areas market, and a still smaller 41 percent of the special affordable market. Thus, the remaining 52 to 59 percent of the goals-qualifying markets have not yet been touched by the GSEs."

The GSEs saw tension between these goals and safe lending practices. Freddie Mac stated that the "... increased affordable housing goals created tension in its business practices between meeting the goals and conducting responsible lending practices." Some statements are extremely worrying, suggesting that Freddie and Fannie should manage their businesses according to perceived future forecasts. "Evidence suggests that there is a significant population of potential homebuyers who might respond well to aggressive outreach by the GSEs— immigrants and minorities, in particular, are expected to be a major source of future homebuyers. Furthermore, studies indicate the existence of a large untapped pool of potential home owners among the rental population." It's almost comical that the government wanted Freddie and Fannie to make bets on this imagined future.

28. Those banks included Lehman Brothers, Bear Stearns, Goldman Sachs, J.P. Morgan, Merrill Lynch, UBS, and Deutsche Bank. For a breakdown of profits, see Figure 11.1 in Chapter 11.

29. Freddie's 2002 employment numbers were not available, so I've used the 2006 number, which is higher. In 2006, Freddie employed 5,040 people.

30. We know a lot more about these firms' compensation practices today, but in the past the government gave them an exemption from filing SEC-compliant quarterly statements and annual reports. It is mindboggling that a public company in the United States was given this exemption but allowed to take large bets on the housing market. Fannie Mae voluntarily submitted 10-K statements since

2002, while Freddie Mac voluntarily submitted their first 10-Q statement in August of 2008, right before they imploded. Freddie did produce annual reports for shareholders throughout the period.

31. The 10-city composite index is the Case-Shiller housing index, published monthly by Standard & Poor's. It uses the Karl Case and Robert Shiller method to compute a house price index using a modified version of the weighted-repeat sales methodology. This method can adjust for the quality of homes sold, unlike simple average-based indices. The CSXR is a three-month moving average, as are the indices that compose it. The cities included in the 10-city index are Boston, Chicago, Denver, Las Vegas, Los Angeles, Miami, New York, San Diego, San Francisco, and Washington DC.

32. See Frank (2005), Henderson (2005), Reynolds (2005), and Setzer (2005).

33. As Mark Twain said, "Suppose you were an idiot. And suppose you were a member of Congress. But I repeat myself."

34. Another measure can be found in Himmelberg et al. (2005).

35. The mortgage cash flow is adjusted for both property taxes and interest rate deductions. It reflects a 0.97% property tax and the appropriate marginal tax rate given the average income in the U.S. in that year.

36. From 2002 to 2005, residential construction contributed three times more to the economy than it contributed on average since 1990. FCIC (2010), p. 84.

37. This bubble was particularly harmful because it shifted resources away from potentially more productive economic areas and may have led to an unnecessary inflow of low-skill immigrant workers.

38. The largest national drop in real estate prices occurred between 1912 to 1920, when the national indices plunged by 35%. This took eight years, however, and the data quality is questionable. The worst annual drop in housing prices before 2008 and 2009 was in 1896, when national prices dropped by 14%.

39. I even complained on Austrian television on July 23, 2007. See Chincarini (July 23, 2007).

40. Every time a house is bought or sold, the buyer's realtor gets 3% of the house value and the selling realtor gets 3% of the house value. Buy a $600,000 house, and $36,000 of that goes to the two real estate agents. Thus, realtors have an incentive to sell houses at higher prices and sell as many as they can. Herb Sandler, CEO of Golden West Financial Corporation, called real estate agents the "whores of the world." There are no doubt many helpful real estate agents. There are also those who, rather than guide homebuyers appropriately, are just concerned with selling houses. One would think that the Internet would help create a more efficient mechanism for selling houses, reducing the need for a middleman.

41. Between 1999 and 2006, the number of U.S. real estate agents almost doubled, going from 761,181 to 1,357,732. See National Association of Realtors.

42. Other peripheral players also had a financial incentive to keep the bubble going: appraisers, building inspectors, title companies, and other real estate industry players. Some may have practiced unethical behavior. For example, a 2003 survey

found that 55% of appraisers had felt pressed to inflate the value of homes. By 2006, the percentage had climbed to 90%. FCIC (2010), p. 91. Young (2011) proposes that real estate agents need a new set of legal rules.

43. In practice there were numerous schemes. For instance, Countrywide offered approximately 250 loan programs to potential home owners. Consumers could obtain a loan either through one of Countrywide's thousands of retail storefront locations or through a mortgage broker.

44. Some home buyers use a cash down payment, which reduces the amount borrowed to buy the property. Appendix H describes the mathematics of creating a mortgage plan.

45. Generally, be skeptical of home buyers who now claim that lenders took advantage of them.

46. There is no formal definition for prime and subprime mortgages. The Federal Reserve Bank of San Francisco considers loans given to borrowers with FICO scores below 620 in the subprime category. A FICO score considers a person's new credit, old credit, payment history, credit history length, and amounts owed. For more information, see myFICO.com. In general, prime mortgages go to borrowers with low default probability, which bankers associate with low loan-to-value ratios, high FICO scores, low debt-to-income ratios, and lots of assets. Subprime loans go to borrowers with a higher probability of default. Alt-A mortgages fit somewhere in between.

47. In fact, some of the alt-A mortgages that Freddie and Fannie bought were not subprime by credit-quality standards. Instead, these were no-documentation loans made to high-quality borrowers. Alt-A mortgages are often characterized by borrowers with incomplete documentation, lower credit scores, higher loan-to-value ratios, and more investment properties.

48. Morgensen and Rosner (2011).

49. Some recent research argues that housing goals aren't enough to explain Freddie's losses (Thomas and Van Order [2011]), and that credit risk was the primary culprit. Wallison (2011) and Pinto (2010) make a convincing argument for the fact that lower-income housing goals were a major housing bubble determinant.

50. Prevost (2006).

51. During the housing bubble, many politicians hoped to gain votes by promising home ownership. They didn't want to halt the major economic generator of 2001 to 2007, and buckled under pressure from special interest groups such as ACORN. See Morgensen and Rosner (2011), p. 32. One remedy for politicians' frequent misunderstanding of vital economic issues would be to stipulate that, to run for elected office, candidates should have advanced degrees in economics or pass an equivalent economics exam, with partial credit for a degree in a hard science.

52. FCIC (2010).

53. Appelbaum et al. (2008).

54. OFHEO (2006).

55. Hedge funds based a great pairs trade on the idea that Fannie was sure to have accounting issues after Freddie did. For more details, see Chincarini and Kim (2006).
56. An article foreshadowing the crisis appeared in the Wall Street Journal on October 4, 2004, with the amusing title "Fannie Mae Enron?".
57. See Guberman (2002).
58. They did securitize many mortgages with FICO scores of 660 and less, which some classify as high-risk mortgages.
59. These numbers are from Thomas and Van Order, who used the OFHEO 2008 Report to Congress and the companies' financial statements. Freddie Mac had supplied very little to the market before 2006. These estimates have changed slightly since their publication, but the exposure is approximately the same.
60. Total Common Equity.
61. Many hedge funds and other investors have exploited holes in the rating system. In 2003, the market knew that many German Landesbanks would lose their implicit government backing beginning in July 2005, which would reduce their credit rating from AA to something in the B range. The new law's phase-in date was known, but the major rating agencies hadn't yet updated their ratings. Hedge funds and other investors short sold the Landesbank bonds and bought other bonds. Institutions were slow to react, so these bonds were mispriced for quite a while.
62. Although no one knows the exact reason for the switch, White (2009) gives some hypotheses.
63. Andrew Kimball, executive vice president at Moody's, wrote a memorandum in October 2007 confirming this sentiment. "It turns out that ratings quality has surprisingly few friends: issuers want high ratings; investors don't want rating downgrades; and bankers game the rating agencies for a few extra basis points on execution." See FCIC (2010), p. 211.
64. FCIC (2010), p. 149.
65. SEC Release (2003).
66. FCIC (2010), p. 149.
67. Gary Witt, a former managing director of Moody's CDO unit. See FCIC (2010), p. 147.
68. Moody's actually uses Aaa and Baa for these equivalent ratings, but I'ved used the S&P ratings format throughout for consistency.
69. Subsequent chapters offer detailed discussions of investment banks and hedge funds.
70. Banks could also buy insurance on the retained mortgages' credit risk or hedge the risk using tradable baskets such as ABX or CMBX.
71. WaMU also serviced a total $689 billion in loans for other organizations as well as for their own.
72. A lawsuit later claimed that the bank had not been in such dire straits.

73. In the four quarters leading up to August 22, 2008, Fannie and Freddie recorded combined losses of $15 billion. It prompted Warren Buffett in a CNBC interview to say that Freddie and Fannie " . . . don't have any net worth . . . the game is over . . . they were able to borrow without any of the normal restraints. They had a blank check from the Federal government." Although Buffett was absolutely right, why had he not vocalized this sentiment earlier and louder when it might have been more useful? Perhaps he also enjoyed the profits on the way up.

74. These losses would have sent the firms into bankruptcy many times over had the government not stepped in on September 7, 2008.

75. In conservatorship, a person or entity is appointed to establish control and oversight of a company and move it into sound and solvent condition.

76. Technically, the Treasury pumped $183 billion into the agencies, but received a dividend on its preferred debt of $32 billion, thus making the total $151 billion. Source: http://projects.propublica.org/bailout/list.

77. Thomas and Van Order (2010).

78. Although Ginnie is completely government owned, it produces annual financial statements. In 2006, its market share was only 4%, whereas Freddie and Fannie had 38% of the market. After Fannie and Freddie's collapse, Ginnie took on more loans. In 2010, its market share jumped to 29% of mortgage issuance. During 2008, 2009, and 2010, it had positive profits. However, its steady profits (which go to the government) declined by half in 2009 and 2010. The total of mortgages that Ginnie supports grew from $409 million in 2006 to $1.046 billion in 2010. Ginnie's capital ratio also dropped from 2.94% in 2006 to 1.47% in 2010, altering its leverage ratio from 34 to 68. Could Ginnie Mae be the next levered housing company to cost the taxpayers money?

79. FCIC (2010), p. 321.

80. And it wasn't the people that you might think. Nobel prizewinner Joseph Stiglitz did a study in 2002 that concluded that Freddie and Fannie posed very little risk to the economy. He wasn't extremely familiar with housing issues, but people listened to him because he had won a Nobel prize. Later he said, "I'd like to think that if we'd done the same stress test in 2007 . . . we would have said, 'You ought to be worried.'" See Stiglitz et al. (2002).

81. Guberman (2002).

82. FCIC (2010), p. 4 and 21.

83. Freddie and Fannie cherished the lobbyists that secured them favorable deals. For example, Robert Mitchell Delk, a key Freddie lobbyist, was a crucial part of the GSE's efforts to remain on good terms with Congress. He was one of the company's highest-paid executives, earning more than $6 million in deferred compensation. The Federal Election Commission issued its largest civil penalty– $3.8 million–against Freddie Mac on April 18, 2006.

84. Bonuses that went to GSE executives should have really gone to the U.S. taxpayer. See Passmore et al. (2005, 2006). Wallison (2005) said that if Congress did not

do something to curb Freddie and Fannie's expansion that they "will continue to grow and one day–as Alan Greenspan has predicted–there will be a massive default with huge losses to taxpayers and systemic effects on the economy."

85. FHFA, October 2011.

Chapter 11

1. Commercial banks that are part of the Federal Reserve system must hold 10% of their deposits in reserves and follow broad capital adequacy guidelines that naturally limit their leverage.

2. It is difficult to get a precise estimate of a bank's exposure because bank financial statements aren't transparent. Even calling the banks and reading analyst reports doesn't help a lot. Banks can also disguise information intentionally. Ironically, Lehman Brothers was one of the most transparent investment banks.

3. For a full description of what investment banks do and the particular investment banking business of Lehman Brothers, see Appendix I.

4. See Lehman Brothers' financial statements.

5. McDonald and Robinson (2009), p. 213.

6. A balance sheet is an accounting item that public firms are required to report to the SEC. It describes the things the business owns (assets) and the things the business has borrowed from others (liabilities). Unfortunately, bank balance sheets are usually difficult to understand and analyze; investment bank balance sheets are even more complicated, in both cases because they tend to focus on legal boilerplate rather than on the intricate details of the company's business. The private sector should reform this voluntarily with better disclosure rules.

7. Repo agreements between two banks are a fancy form of collateralized borrowing.

8. In reality, there would be a small haircut on this trade, since collateral is not exactly equivalent to cash. The borrower might get a loan of $98,000 for the bond.

9. The difference between total and net real estate exposure is that total mortgage assets and ABS include a portion of securitized loans that would have eventually gone to investors.

10. All of these numbers are in Table 11.4.

11. In Lehman's annual statement these are referred to as Level II and Level III assets. Lehman Brothers wasn't the only bank with these difficult-to-value securities. In the first quarter of 2007, Bear had $19 billion of Level III assets against $13 billion in equity, Morgan Stanley had $60 billion against $38 billion in equity, and Goldman had $48 billion against $37 billion in equity. See FCIC (2010), p. 227.

12. Lehman purchased six domestic mortgage lenders and three international ones between 1998 and 2004. FCIC (2010), p. 88.

13. This was net real estate exposure. Total exposure was 35%.

14. Much of the information in this section came from the official report written by the Lehman collapse's legal examiner, who looked for the most promising materials about Lehman. The examiner had documents from Lehman and from numerous third parties and government agencies, including the Department of the Treasury, the SEC, the Federal Reserve, FRBNY, the Office of Thrift Supervision, the SIPA Trustee, Ernst & Young, J.P. Morgan, Barclays, Bank of America, HSBC, Citibank, Fitch, Moody's, S&P, and others. In total, the examiner collected more than five million documents and interviewed many of the principal people at Lehman, the Fed, the Treasury, and other institutions. Unfortunately, many of these interviews were done ex-post, so the material may have hindsight bias.

15. Lehman Brothers had subsidiaries that focused on mortgage origination, such as BNC Mortgage Inc. and Aurora Loan Services, LLC.

16. "Double down" comes from the gambling game blackjack. In blackjack, after receiving the first card, a player can double the initial bet by committing to accept only one more card. This is a typical move for a player who has a card with a face value of 10 showing. The term migrated to investing, where it typically describes a situation in which an investor puts additional capital into a losing position.

17. Net assets grew from $269 billion to $373 billion and total assets grew from $504 billion to $691 billion. Both peaked in the first quarter of 2008, at $397 billion and $783 billion.

18. Fuld, Gregory, and McGee believed that every dollar that Lehman made from a leveraged loan would lead to five dollars of follow-on profits.

19. McDonald and Robinson (2009).

20. Sorkin (2009), p. 125.

21. His termination letter, dated May 7, 2007, gave him a severance package of $20 million provided he did not compete with the firm before January 2008. When he left Lehman on May 2, 2007, "there was a sustained and heartfelt burst of applause . . . he was such a big part of our strength and standing in the corporation." McDonald and Robinson (2009).

22. Nagioff told examiners that it took time to "stop the machine" because a lot of deals were already in the pipeline or under negotiation and he didn't believe Lehman could just terminate those deals.

23. The total breakdown of the Lehman exposure was Permanent equity $250 million, Bridge equity $2.14 billion, Mezzanine loan $240 million, Term loan $2.47 billion, and Senior debt $850 million.

24. Many traders shorted Lehman on March 17, 2008, not because they had a precise knowledge of its exposures, but simply out of contagion.

25. Matthew Eichner, a Federal Reserve employee, said that the SEC had monitors on site at Lehman almost all the time. Jan H. Voigts, also a supervisor at the Fed, monitored Lehman's liquidity position. According to an interview on November 24, 2009, Geithner was worried about Lehman's funding structure. He said he

was consumed with figuring out how to push Lehman toward more conservative funding.

26. Valukas (2010).

27. Buffett never invested in Lehman Brothers. He invested $5 billion in Goldman Sachs on September 24, 2008, but not before the $700 billion bailout plan was announced and Goldman was converted to a bank holding company. Buffett's investment wasn't a sign of confidence in Goldman. He bought preferred shares, which paid him a 10% return every year regardless of what other shareholders got.

28. The March 25, 2008, board minutes and handwritten notes taken by Lehman corporate secretary Jeffrey Welikson do not reflect that management advised the board of ICD's interest.

29. See Table 11.4.

30. James Grant produces a regular publication on the financial markets for investors, *Grant's Interest Rate Observer*. He also speaks in public and organizes the Grant Conferences, which many practitioners attend.

31. Einhorn was on the Board of New Century Financial Corporation, a large subprime mortgage lender, and thus had some firsthand insight into the real estate industry.

32. Some on Lehman's board of directors doubted the Koreans. John D. Macomber and John F. Akers had warned Fuld that Lehman never would sign a deal with KDB because Korean companies historically dragged out discussions without ever completing a deal. Valukas (2010).

33. Lehman's McDade and McGee had arranged a deal with KDB, but when Fuld arrived at the negotiation, he bargained harder, perhaps causing the deal to collapse. Min said, "I'm not comfortable with this." Sorkin (2010).

34. According to Fuld, short sellers were "kicking the daylights" out of Lehman.

35. Lehman's officers believe that KDB's disclosures had strongly decreased Lehman's stock price, which in turn was a driving force behind the decision to accelerate the third-quarter earnings announcement. In a November 16, 2009, interview, Min said, "We missed a very good opportunity . . . I think we could have avoided a situation where Lehman collapsed so rapidly." During the interview, Min said that he had been prepared to raise his offer as high as $9 per share. Min blamed the confidentiality agreement for preventing KDB from explaining the proposed transaction to Korean regulators while negotiations were ongoing.

36. Valukas (2010).

37. Ben Bernanke was not at this meeting. Bernanke told the legal examiners that he remained in Washington, DC, during Lehman's final weekend in part because Bernanke might have needed to convene a meeting of the Federal Reserve Board to exercise the Federal Reserve's emergency lending powers under Section 13(3) of the Federal Reserve Act.

38. Gregory L. Curl, Bank of America's executive responsible for global strategic planning, later told legal examiners that during the weekend's negotiations, the

government gave conflicting signals regarding the availability of some form of federal assistance.

39. Sorkin (2010), p. 305 and p. 313.

40. Paulson thought Fuld would stall any solution he didn't like.

41. Throughout the day on Saturday, September 13, 2008, Fuld mentioned that he continued to call Lewis without getting a response. Lewis' wife eventually answered the phone and said that if her husband wanted to talk to Fuld, he would return the call. Fuld thought that perhaps Lewis was using Lehman as a bargaining chip with the FRBNY regarding assistance the Federal Reserve had apparently promised but never delivered in connection with Bank of America's purchase of Countrywide.

42. Later, in testimony to the House Committee on Oversight and Government Reform, Lewis said that pressure from federal regulators played an important part in the company's decision to continue its planned acquisition of Merrill Lynch. He said that threats by regulators to remove management or board members were not only credible, but indicated just how important the government felt it was to carry out the acquisition. In fact, when Lewis had wanted to terminate the merger in December 2008, Paulson told him that if he did so he would be making a "colossal loss of judgment" and that the Fed, as its regulator, had the legal authority to replace Bank of America's management and board. FCIC (2010), p. 384.

43. On Saturday, September 13, Barclays asked Buffett whether Buffett would guarantee Lehman's operations until a Lehman-Barclays deal closed. Barclays and Buffett discussed a scenario in which Buffett would provide $5 billion of protection. Buffett expressed interest in that possibility, but Barclays did not pursue it.

44. Lehman tried to get around this, asking Paulson and then-president George W. Bush to call Prime Minister Gordon Brown. Paulson did not call Brown, but did call Chancellor of the Exchequer Alistair Darling. This deal, and perhaps a deal with another suitor, would have been much more likely had the U.S. guaranteed it.

45. Mozilo, Countrywide's CEO, pointed to a *Los Angeles Times* article that caused depositor panic. The next day depositors withdrew $8 billion from the bank. In nine days, depositors withdrew $16.7 billion, forcing the bank out of business.

46. This didn't prevent bank runs in 2008, partly because many depositors had more than the $100,000 account limit and partly because, even with the guarantee, people were nervous or didn't understand the rules. The FDIC subsequently raised the account limit to $250,000.

47. Transparent, stress-tested financial statements detailing Lehman's exposure would have helped a great deal in the weeks leading up to Lehman's collapse. For instance, financial statements could have contained scenario tests, such as the effects on Lehman's portfolio if real estate prices drop by 30% in all of markets and subsequent defaults are 10%. The results could have given market participants a

clearer understanding of the real risks they were taking. Of course, the trust issue would still have been a problem for everyone.

48. According to Lehman CFO Paolo Tonucci, Lehman financed the majority of its balance sheet in the short-term repo market, borrowing more than $200 billion a day in 2008. It needed short-term, secured financing to conduct its daily operations. For more information on repos, refer to Chapter 9.

49. This computes losses based on $54 billion of total real estate exposure shown in the third-quarter financial release and assumes $4 billion more real estate exposure, which Lehman was in the process of transferring.

50. This is according to Case-Shiller Composite 10 and Composite 20 indices. Commercial real estate prices dropped by much more than this in the months following September 2008.

51. Interview with *60 Minutes* on December 5, 2010. Bernanke (2010).

52. In a call, Senator Chris Dodd told Paulson, "Fuld is a friend. Try to help, but don't bail Lehman out." Sorkin (2010), p. 284.

53. Ignorance might have been part of the problem, but Paulson seemed aware of the dangers. In a July 2, 2008, speech at Chatham House in London, titled "The U.S., The World Economy and Markets," Paulson noted that "[b]ankruptcy [can] impose[] market discipline on creditors" but that "in a time of crisis, [bankruptcy] could involve undue market disruption."

54. Their increased transparency, ironically, may have led to more second guessing by investors of their valuations.

55. The market was not aware of this practice, so it's hard to know if it affected trust in Lehman. Some market participants questioned whether Lehman's financial statements told the entire story.

56. See page 177 of the Examiner report for more details.

57. Stress tests are done to make sure a firm has adequate capital if things go bad. Typically, a firm assumes that prices of their investments move against them and see how much they would lose.

58. Lehman's Lawrence McDonald believed a rubber-stamp board of directors allowed Fuld to run the firm as he wished. Nine of the 10 members were retired and the board included a theater director, the former head of the Red Cross, and an actress.

59. In one e-mail from Dimitrious Kritikos to Jeffrey Goodman on January 31, 2007, he wrote about the Archstone real estate company that Lehman had bought. "Looking at the trends on originations and linking them to first payment defaults, the story is ugly: The last four months Aurora has originated the riskiest loans ever, with every month being riskier than the one before—the industry meanwhile has pulled back during that time."

On May 7, 2007, Goodman e-mailed Antoncic about the Archstone transaction and said that O'Meara, then the CFO, "ha[d] significant concerns regarding overall size of [the real estate] book and how much of the firm's equity [was] tied up in such bridge equity deals."

60. McDonald mentioned that the risk committee favored AAA CDOs versus the long position the group had in Delta bonds (McDonald and Robinson 2010). The missing link was a lack of valuation in the historical VaR model.

61. Merrill Lynch raised $6.2 billion toward the end of 2007 and early 2008 by selling stock at a discount to the stock price. In January 2008, Merrill also issued $6.6 billion of convertible preferred shares with a dividend yield of 9% to KIA, the Korean Consortium, and Mizuho. Similarly, during late 2007 and the first quarter of 2008, after announcing losses during 2007, Citibank issued $30 billion of preferred stock, trust-preferred, and forward-purchase contracts. The sale included $7.5 billion of equity units. In December 2007, after posting its first-ever quarterly loss, Morgan Stanley raised $5 billion through an investment by the China Investment Corporation. Morgan Stanley sold equity units, including futures contracts to buy common shares. Following an income decline in 2007, on January 24, 2008, Bank of America sold $6 billion in depositary shares, each representing a 1/25th interest in a share of fixed-to-floating preferred stock. That same month, Bank of America also sold $6.9 billion of convertible preferred securities. On March 5, 2008, after announcing a CHF 4.4 billion loss (roughly $3.9 billion) on January 30, 2008, UBS issued CHF 13 billion (roughly $11.7 billion) in convertible stock to the government of Singapore Investment Corporation and an undisclosed investor from the Middle East.

62. Just after Labor Day, September 4, 2008, Morgan asked for more collateral—up to $5 billion—from Lehman.

63. A colorful claim is one for which the examiner has found that there is sufficient credible evidence to support a finding by a trier of fact. Valukas (2010).

64. See Chapter 12.

65. Sorkin (2010), p. 438.

66. Sorkin (2010), p. 460–462.

67. These values were calculated using each business segment's asset exposure as described in the third-quarter 2008 AIG financial statements. Amazingly enough, this insurance company even had an aircraft leasing business, which had $38 billion in Airbus and Boeing airplanes that it leased to airline companies.

68. AIG was an "innovative" insurance company, just as Enron had been an innovative energy company.

69. FCIC (2010), p. 347.

70. According to Goldman, it had acquired most of the collateral on the AIG positions and would not have lost much from AIG's default.

71. Now called Blackrock.

72. If the Fed would have lent to me personally, I would have bought Lehman Brothers at those prices, too.

73. Morgan Stanley also started making some of its financial statements more transparent by specifying the contents of corporate and other debt, which it had not done in previous financial statements.

Chapter 12

1. The details of the Fed programs are contained in the online appendices at www.wiley.com/go/crisisofcrowds.
2. Broker-dealers are institutions, such as the major investment banks, that act as both brokers and dealers. When executing trade orders on behalf of a customer, the institution is said to be acting as a broker. When executing trades for its own account, the institution is said to be acting as a dealer.
3. Refco was a major commodity and futures broker whose CEO concealed substantial debts. Refco filed for Chapter 11 for a number of its businesses on October 17, 2005. It also looked for buyers for its regulated futures and commodity business, to limit the disruption to financial markets. On November 10, 2005, Man Financial bought it. At the time, Refco was rather small, with $75 billion in assets and debts totaling $430 million. The brokerage portion of Refco's business traded through the CME, so the OTC portion of the firm was small. As a result, Refco's bankruptcy created relatively fewer market imbalances.

   In February 1990, after a large insider-trading scandal and other problems, Drexel Burnham Lambert filed for Chapter 11 bankruptcy. It had hoped to be bailed out by the U.S. government, but Treasury Secretary Nicholas Brady had old animosity against Drexel for its involvement with a Unocal deal and left that option off the table. The Drexel bankruptcy hugely disrupted the high-yield debt market, but this was overall a very small market (around $200 billion). The SEC facilitated the orderly transfer of 30,000 customer accounts, with $5 billion in customer property, to several securities firms. None of Drexel's customers lost money because of the bankruptcy. Regulators unwound millions of dollars in Drexel financial positions, mostly with minor disruptions to the other firms that had done business with Drexel. More research may clarify why Refco and Drexel's failures did not create as large a disruption as Lehman's did. Perhaps it was because Refco really played the role of a broker working through a futures exchange, or maybe it was the small size of Refco and Drexel's market, or maybe it had to do with some of the International Swaps and Derivatives Association (ISDA) procedures used to exit Lehman positions.
4. Forty-four percent of Lehman's assets were collateralized lending agreements. As of November 2007 Lehman had $691 billion in assets. Of these, $301 billion were in collateralized lending agreements (e.g., repos and such); the firm also had $258 billion in collateralized financing. Lehman was a net lender of cash. Some traders believe Lehman may have taken initial margin from its prime broker business and used that cash in reverse repos.
5. In a 30-year liability with a given interest rate, the liability is like a zero-coupon bond with a duration of 30. $P = \frac{100}{(1+y)^{30}}$, where y is the bond yield and P is the bond price.

6. Duration is a bond portfolio management concept that expresses how much a portfolio's value will move for a given change in interest rates. If interest rates go down, a position with long duration makes money. If interest rates go up, the position loses money.

7. When a government issues a bond, it is essentially a fixed-rate payer and has a short or negative duration. Generally, shorter-maturity bonds have lower duration.

8. Some of the swap spreads' odd movement may have been linked to the government-sponsored bank bailout and banks' subsequent reluctance to lend long term.

9. Myron Scholes would argue that this is one of the main reasons behind an intermediary's success. A relative-value hedge fund acts as an intermediary, absorbing excess supply and demand and retrieving a premium for this.

10. Since the 1930s, more than 150 laws and regulations have sprung up that require banks, brokerage firms, insurance companies, pension plans, and money-market funds to hold only securities that rating agencies consider investment grade. A study released in 2007, on the eve of the financial crisis, found that 76% of fund managers wouldn't invest in bonds below certain credit ratings, even though fewer than a third of them thought that was a good investment strategy (Zwieg 2010).

11. The number 228 refers to the 228 house representatives who did not pass the bill.

12. This was a major hedge fund at Goldman Sachs. The story places more doubt on the rumor that Goldman wanted Lehman to fail.

Chapter 13

1. Its official name is the Basel Committee on Banking Supervision. The committee's members come from Argentina, Australia, Belgium, Brazil, Canada, China, France, Germany, Hong Kong, India, Indonesia, Italy, Japan, Korea, Luxembourg, Mexico, the Netherlands, Russia, Saudi Arabia, Singapore, South Africa, Spain, Sweden, Switzerland, Turkey, the United Kingdom, and the United States. Countries are represented by their central bank and also by the authority with formal responsibility for the prudential supervision of banking business, where this is not the central bank.

2. Employees call the BIS the Golden Cage. There are some very good economists at the BIS, but usually they have little impact on the Basel Committee.

3. See Appendix J for more details on the calculation.

4. This is for overall capital. There is also a minimum ratio of 4% for a more strict form of capital.

5. Market risk was eventually added to Basel I.

6. Stale means that assets and liabilities don't reflect the most recent actual market values.

7. A document released in April of 1995 specified some detailed ways to handle market risk.

8. The group couldn't reach specific conclusions in these areas.

9. VaR measurements include daily estimation, a 99% confidence interval, holding periods of at least 10 business days, a one-year minimum historical measurement period for variance and covariances, estimates updated at least quarterly, and models that properly assess different types of risks, such as the delta risk of option contracts.

10. Basel II proposals started in 1999. The predominant documents related to Basel II were titled "International Convergence of Capital Measurement and Capital Standards A Revised Framework" (June 2004) and "A New Capital Adequacy Framework" (June 1999). All of these documents are available at www.bis.org/list/bcbs/index.htm.

11. See Resti and Sironi (2007) for a good diagram of this.

12. See the discussion in Lall (2009).

13. See Blundell and Atkinson (2008).

14. FCIC (2010), p. 206. Basel III was issued in September 2010 to correct for the problems in Basel I and II.

15. Some BIS research hinted at macroeconomic imbalances, but it was buried and the BIS did not do enough to emphasize it, maybe because they didn't know what it meant or were being constrained in what they could say. The BIS Secretary General Dittus said, "We didn't manage to portray the global and financial imbalances in a convincing fashion." See Balzli and Schiessl (2009).

Chapter 14

1. Many people will wonder how a failed hedge fund can raise more money. LTCM is just one of the many hedge funds that have done this. Rosenfeld (2007) argued that the new money depended on three factors. First, LTCM partners stuck around to clean up their mess. Second, market participants have very short memories. Third, the partners' new prudence suggested that they had learned something from the crisis. It was still difficult to raise money. Some investors believed that the partners were scarred and would never take enough risk again, while others believed that they were still too risky.

2. Mean reversion describes the idea that prices eventually revert to their average. In fixed-income spread trading, it is the idea that the spread between two securities will move toward its historical average.

3. Some investors took advantage of this offer indirectly, through feeder accounts. A representative of a Swiss private bank that was offered the high-water mark deal, for instance, asked investors to put money in that company's fund, which would then invest in JWMP and offer a special high-water mark, with profits to be split between the bank and investor.

4. Giovannini earned his PhD from MIT and was a professor of economics at Columbia University from 1983 to 1995. From 1993 to 1995 he worked for the Ministero del Tesoro (the Italian Treasury). He was a senior strategist at LTCM from 1995 to 1999. As of 2011, he was the CEO at Unifortune Asset Management SGR SpA in Italy.

5. The firm charged management fees at the beginning of every month (0.167%) after January 2002; before that, the charge came at the beginning of every quarter.

6. The table compares performance from June 2000 to December 2007, as this is the longest period for which all hedge funds have return information. Copycat funds are discussed in more detail later in this chapter.

7. The Sortino is a risk-adjusted performance measure that adjusts the standard deviation for nonnormal returns.

8. The HFR Relative Value hedge fund index is equal weighted, not asset weighted, and may not be entirely investable. It has the benefit of diversification across many hedge funds. Some academics think this database has more survivorship bias than do other databases.

9. Statement made on April 30, 2008, while giving a guest lecture in Claremont, California.

10. Five is nearly the square root of 24, multiplied by the biweekly standard deviation to obtain the annualized standard deviation. A few years after PGAM was launched, it changed this to the expected 0.5% tail gain or loss using a bootstrap. To calculate the bootstrap, take perhaps 10 years of data and write a program that draws random returns from that historical sample.

    The user then must decide how frequently crises may occur. Assume that a crisis happens every 10 years, let random draws create many simulated two-week intervals, draw a histogram, and compute the losses in a 0.5% tail. Assume that LTCM-size crises happen more frequently, perhaps twice every 10 years, then one could copy the 1998 data into the 10-year data, representing it twice in the 10-year sample. PGAM could compare risk measures using all these methods. For more details on this type of risk management, see Litzenberger and Modest (2008).

11. Hawkins left Caxton in part because McEntee, Hawkins's business partner and a former LTCM principal, had a stroke. When he returned to Caxton after his stroke, the two closed their portfolio.

12. Before running his own hedge fund, Sanford Grossman was a professor of finance at the University of Chicago. He wrote one of the best-known papers in finance, "On the Impossibility of Informationally Efficient Markets," with Joseph Stiglitz.

13. The term "copycat" really refers to firms that copied Salomon's successful strategies. III and Smith Breeden launched before LTCM.

14. See returns in Table 14.1.

15. See Button (2004).

Chapter 15

1. His stay as president of the large hedge fund Paloma Partners was short lived, and he eventually teamed up with LTCM alum Robert Shustak and the fund's former controller, Bruce Wilson, to start Quantitative Alternatives LLC, in Rye Brook, New York. Their plan was to use statistical models for trading strategies much like those employed by LTCM. The fund never raised enough funds, and the three partners folded the operation at the end of 2008. Rosenfeld is now retired, but teaches part-time at MIT's Sloan School of Management.

2. This phenomenon was discussed in Chapter 9.

3. This was later revised to $8 after various shareholder complaints and threats to sue J.P. Morgan.

4. Traders also take the opposite position, depending on circumstances.

5. These hedge funds represent the shadow banking system. Swaps are in net-zero supply, whereas Japanese government bonds have positive supply. As yields decrease or are low, natural buyers for long-term government bonds—pension funds and insurance companies—might wait or invest elsewhere, because yields are unattractive. As a result, these bonds get cheap relative to swaps. Hedge funds buy these securities, hedge them with interest-rate swaps, and hold them as inventory.

    Eventually, the pension funds want to buy these bonds and the hedge funds can sell them at a profit. Trade timing depends on experience and lots of information from pension funds, life insurance companies, and other Japanese investors.

6. The annual meeting in Jackson Hole, Wyoming, is a mecca for financial experts. Leading economists, central bankers, and finance practitioners come to discuss the state of the global economy. It is preceded by a meeting of financial leaders at the Global Economic Forum at the Aspen Institute.

7. Crockett quipped to Maughan, "I hope we're not one of the twelve."

8. This is discussed in more detail in Chapter 11 on Lehman Brothers.

9. John Holloway, the head of risk control at JWMP, left the firm in September.

10. O'Hara (2008).

11. One lesson from this is that it is wise to choose two different institutions as custodian and counterparty.

12. J.P. Morgan sued Parkcentral in New York State Supreme Court. J.P. Morgan argued that the fund should repay Morgan $753 million for fees associated with the early termination of many of its counterparty contracts. The court ruled that J.P. Morgan could not be paid before other creditors, and that liquidators must handle all Parkcentral assets. Parkcentral and J.P. Morgan settled the case privately. Public documents offer more detailed information.

13. I attempted to speak with fund representatives, but they declined to talk about collapse details.

14. Other hedge funds had locked up clients' money to protect the funds. PGAM felt it was right to let distressed investors pull out funds.
15. The Smith Breeden numbers are unverified.
16. Parkcentral third-quarter newsletter.
17. This is an equal-weighted index of the 125 companies.
18. Calculate this as $n = \frac{125 \cdot 0.30}{1 - 0.40}$, where n is the number of companies that must default for a 30% dollar loss.
19. Compute this figure by taking the actual coupon on the CDS for the 30 to 100 tranche and compute the percentage change versus the November 5, 2007 reference date. Do the same for tranches 3–7, 7–10, 10–15, and 15–30. Compute the average of the four other tranches. Subtract that average from the 30 to 100 tranche. No data was available for the 0–3 tranche.
20. That is, a trade that was long AAA-rated and short A-rated instruments. Of course, this trade has several variations. A trader could be long AAA and short BBB and so on.
21. Bank of America Commercial MBS yields.
22. This trade would have made money if it had a 1-1 hedge. Based on information at the time of the trade, a 1-1 hedge would not have been a risk-neutral trade.
23. As of June 2009, the positions came back completely and would have been profitable. The trade's performance from August 29, 2008, to June 30, 2009 was 12.6%. (The AAA CMBS lost 16.35% and the CMBX A lost 78%.) As of July 2011, some relative-value hedge fund traders think the BBB group will collapse to zero when principal payments come due on the interest-only loans.
24. According to interviews with relative-value hedge fund principals.
25. Conversations with PGAM trader.
26. See Chapter 12 for a detailed discussion.
27. The index shows the combination of swap yields as $y_{30} - 1.55y_{10} + 0.6y_5$, where y_{30}, y_{10}, and y_5 are the 30-, 10-, and 5-year swap yields. Weights are duration and curve slope neutral. As this yield index increases, the position loses money, but in 2008 these hedge funds used a butterfly trade that was short this yield index, which made money when the index increased and lost money when the index declined.
28. Many funds stopped reporting before their worst monthly returns, because they were going out of business.

Chapter 16

1. Also called market endogenity.
2. See the Turner Review (2009).
3. More theoretical and applied research is needed to examine the relationship between leverage in the financial system, long-run growth, and short-run fluctuations.

4. For example, Citigroup's management admitted that it should have made mortgage market deterioration known throughout the firm. While some divisions were creating new mortgages, others were avoiding or taking positions against them. See FCIC (2010), p. 261.

5. Bernie Madoff had a legitimate broker-dealer business, which was separate from his money management business. It was the money management business that committed fraud and brought down the legitimate business. MF Global was a cash and derivatives broker-dealer led by Jon Corzine that went bankrupt due to large bets placed on Greece and other countries.

6. This is essentially the Volker rule. It should be noted that what caused these investment banks trouble was exposure to real estate mortgages, the same things that caused plain vanilla banks across the United States to fail. It wasn't the mixing of their businesses. Even a standard bank might decide to hedge its real estate exposure, which is not proprietary trading. If this hedge goes wrong, the plain vanilla bank could still lose lots of money. We must think carefully about the Volker rule.

7. The FDIC did have to charge banks for future fees, otherwise the crisis would have wiped out the fund.

8. See Cassidy (2010).

9. See Chapter 7.

10. Palyi mentioned many of these problems in 1938 (see Chapter 10).

11. Bebchuk et al. (2009).

12. See Giovannini (2010).

13. See Bieri and Chincarini (2005).

14. Interview with former CEO who wished to remain anonymous. December 20, 2011.

15. See Merton and Bodie (1995).

16. Although if bond holders had more closely scrutinized their corporate borrowers, there might have been no bailout. Bond interest rates may have been higher and the firms would probably have borrowed less money.

17. This principal at a major quant firm asked to remain anonymous.

Chapter 17

1. The Apple trades actually occurred later in the day, at 3:29 P.M. Sotheby's (BID) traded for $100,000 at 2:57 P.M. and 8 seconds.

2. The NYSE's transition to an electronic exchange took several years.

3. SEC and CFTC (May 18, 2010).

4. This is more formally known as the Consolidated Tape System (CTS). ECNs and exchanges must also post their best bid and ask quotes on the Consolidated Quotation System (CQS). With the implementation of Regulation NMS in 2006 and 2007, ECNs and exchanges perform essentially the same functions.

5. The more buyers and sellers that participate in the dark pool, the better chance of a successful execution. Many services try to ping through different dark pools.

6. Angel (2010).

7. This price move may have been due to a large sell order and low liquidity. On August 4, 2011, the company announced that the drug would not sell as well as it had thought. The stock dropped by 67%, or about the same amount. Perhaps the initial drop actually reflected the true fundamentals.

8. A broken trade happens when the exchanges determine that any trades in a particular security are canceled. The troubled securities trades happened between 4:00 P.M. and 4:01 P.M. See Angel (2010).

9. See Rose (2011).

10. A limit order is a stock order that includes the number of shares a trader would like to buy or sell at a given stock price or better. In a buy limit order at $12 per share, the order is only executed at a price of $12 or less. Otherwise, it isn't executed at all.

11. This is known as the NBBO, or the national best bid and offer. A market maker is willing to buy the stock at $10 and another market maker will sell the stock at $10.02. The spread is compensation for the risk market makers take in providing liquidity.

12. Jim Angel, a professor at Georgetown University, used these terms in our conversations about trading.

13. This qualifies as *spoofing*.

14. See SEC and CFTC (2010). The company Nanex, www.nanex.net, has also done a lot of research on the Flash Crash.

15. These numbers are based on the willingness to trade the S&P 500 E-Mini futures contract. We measure this by looking at the total amount of buy limit orders available near the last quoted price.

16. Based on discussions with Eric Hunsader, Nanex co-founder. Apparently, the SEC had not even called the trader at Barclays until after it had written the final version of the Flash Crash report. In my phone call with the SEC, they said this story was consistent, but pointed out that the CFTC had jurisdiction over this part of the report.

17. Preliminary evidence suggests that the SEC was incorrect in its claim that the algorithm did not have a price component. Barclays claimed this was not true and an independent analysis by Nanex suggests that the algorithm did slow down when the price dropped. In a phone call with the SEC on December 29, 2011, an SEC representative explained that its report may have been confusing. The report meant to say that Waddell did not have a price limit for the order specified, even though the actual algorithm used may have considered price.

18. See www.nanex.net/FlashCrashFinal/FlashCrashAnalysis_W&R.html.

19. It is becoming more difficult to distinguish traditional market makers from HFTs, as they are both using similar technology.

20. Internalizers are OTC market makers who execute trades for their customers, which might include large retail brokerage houses such as TD Ameritrade or Charles Schwab. TD Ameritrade has used Citadel as an internalizer and Charles Schwab frequently used UBS.

21. Rule 611(b)(1) provides an exception for trading when the trading center displaying a quotation is experiencing a systems or equipment failure, material delay, or malfunction.
22. BATS stands for Better Alternative Trading System. The Nasdaq OMX BX is an electronic exchange. Problems started early in the day. Nasdaq declared self-help against the Amex and the CBOE Stock Exchange (CBSX) at 9:31:28 A.M. and 11:34:51 A.M., respectively.
23. The technical name for this action is Liquidity Replenishment Point (LRP).
24. Since the Flash Crash, the NYSE has upgraded all server systems.
25. According to Nanex members, this was the main problem source for data systems. Neither the SEC nor any other regulatory body has examined in detail what might have occurred at this particular time.
26. In my conversation with the SEC, a representative explained to me that when the SEC interviewed market makers about their liquidity withdrawal, market makers pointed first to the rapidly moving prices and said they had worried that trades would later be canceled. To them, the data feed delays confirmed potential problems. This is why the SEC believes that the data glitches were not crucial. An experienced trader sarcastically quipped, "So the SEC is saying the price drop caused market makers to stop quoting, which caused the price drop? That makes a lot of sense."
27. The SEC did not release this confidential information.
28. FINRA is the Financial Industry Regulatory Authority, the largest independent regulator for all the securities firms that do business in the United States.
29. Professor Jim Angel argues that, in addition to these rules, trading should stop when there are data disruptions or technological issues with data feeds. Some human mechanism should determine when to interrupt trading. In general, halts should be short-lived, because markets function precisely because traders are available.

Chapter 18

1. There was also huge animosity between Great Britain and France, including the 100 years war (period of conflicts between 1337 and 1453) and the second 100 years war (period of conflicts between 1689 and 1815).
2. The idea is very old (Smith 1776). For a modern treatment, see Mundell (2003).
3. See PIMCO (2011).
4. Of course, the idea was to eventually reduce these barriers and some of this has already occurred across Europe.
5. Nobel prizewinner Robert Mundell (1961), who first described the idea of optimal currency unions, believed that flexible labor and capital factors were essential ingredients for a currency union to properly function.

6. Italy had a higher debt ratio than Greece, yet was admitted into the club in 1999. The club focused mainly on the deficit criteria, since that represented current behavior while debt levels represented the accumulation of past behavior.

7. This is measured as the average of exports and imports divided by GDP.

8. This is computed by comparing the prices of Greek goods, adjusted for the exchange rate, against 36 other countries. See Eurostat.

9. On the day of the announcement it was revised to 12.7%, but later bumped up again.

10. See Avdjiev et al. (2010).

11. MF Global, for example.

12. The late Rudi Dornbusch, MIT's famous international economist, said this to a group at MIT after the Mexican Peso crisis, when interest rates were very high and people were considering investing.

13. Helenic Republic Press Release.

14. Even these numbers must be treated cautiously, because much Greek data is suspect.

15. The Greek people voted heavily for the anti-austerity party in the May 6, 2012 elections. In surveys, 70% of the Greeks do not want to leave the Euro, but also don't want the austerity measures.

16. On May 14, 2012, 700 million Euros were removed from Greek banks due to worries about the future of Greece.

17. For example, a mortgage loan to a Greek citizen might be an asset, and a bank might have deposits to back it. Convert both to the new drachma at the same exchange rate, and immediate solvency is unchanged.

18. See Enrich and Fidler (2011). That figure was as high as 75% at the end of 2009, but dropped dramatically when foreigners dumped Greek debt.

19. See Avdjiev (2010).

20. See Table 18.2.

21. As of September 30, 2011. Enrich and Stevens (2011).

Chapter 19

1. Many protest signs indicated frustration with the richest 1% of Americans. The financial industry is home to only 14% of this group. Nonfinancial executives and managers, doctors, lawyers, and professionals in computer, math, and engineering make up most of the group (60%). See Bakija et al. (2010).

2. As of November 2011.

3. Even Paul Volker said that "the only useful banking innovation was the invention of the ATM."

4. At the end of the 1990s, I was involved in creating a technology to make investing cheaper and more accessible. See Chincarini and Wallman (2000).

5. Muhammad Yumus won the 2006 Nobel Peace Prize for his work in this area.

6. These numbers are from the Federal Reserve Flow of Funds data. See Table B.100. www.federalreserve.gov/RELEASES/z1/Current/data.htm.

7. Measured as the change between 2004 and 2011.

8. Only about 15% of the Occupy Wall Street crowd is unemployed, according to surveys. Schoen (2011).

9. FCIC (2010), p. 401.

10. See the online appendix to this book titled "The U.S. Economy: Before and After the Crisis" at www.wiley.com/go/crisisofcrowds.

11. From 1998 to the third quarter of 2011.

12. The rich are defined as the top 20% of income earners, the middle class are defined as the middle 20%, and the poor are defined as the bottom 20%. The other 40% are in the second and fourth quintiles, but aren't part of this calculation.

13. Total debt includes debt held by U.S. government institutions and others. Publicly held debt does not include debt held by government institutions.

14. For a detailed analysis of the new Dodd-Frank rules, read the online appendix "The Policy Reaction" www.wiley.com/go/crisisofcrowds.

15. The new rules were passed before most people even understood the financial crisis's causes.

16. Even the Federal Reserve admitted that "it is difficult to predict the overall effect" on consumers. Representative Barney Frank illustrated his misunderstanding of the economic system when he remarked that "I think [the banks] were fighting to raise their revenue."

17. The more inelastic the demand for goods is, the more costs are passed along.

18. The Basel rules are discussed in detail in Chapter 13.

19. This concept of the danger of creating new policy without considering individual reactions is called the Lucas Critique, commonly credited to Robert Lucas of the University of Chicago. Some people call the human behavior Merton discussed the Peltzman Effect, named after economist Sam Peltzman, who first showed that regulatory changes do not always lead to the intended consequences. The No Child Left Behind Act is another example. This seemingly good rule had led to undesirable changes in behavior. On July 13, 2011, the Atlanta school system found widespread cheating among teachers and administrators, who wanted an easier way to keep up with educational standards (Timothy 2011).

20. See McDermott (2011).

21. Another commonly used term for this is "diversity."

Appendix A

1. In Chincarini (1998), I called this the *magic wand* of a firm like LTCM.

2. It's similar to MIT's famous group of blackjack traders. They didn't invent card counting, but they did invent a new way to approach card counting: by having spotters and other people to help determine when a deck was really hot.

3. That is, $\mu_i = \mu \; \forall i$. This is not a necessary part of illustrating this argument, but makes the mathematics much simpler.

4. This is probably the more relevant formula to use, given the dynamic nature of risks in financial markets. In addition, one could make the model more realistic by assuming a different r_f for every trading strategy, which might very well be the case, depending on the financing terms. For simplicity, we assumed that all the financing was done at a rate of r_f.

5. In this example the mean return is chosen to be similar to the on-the-run/off-the-run trade's annual mean, with about three times its standard deviation.

6. In theory, a strategy with almost zero risk should be almost equal to the financing rate, because of arbitrageurs in the market. But we are considering the arbitrageurs themselves, so we can allow for these riskless possibilities.

7. Multiply the monthly mean by 12 and the monthly standard deviation by $\sqrt{12}$ to see the annualized numbers.

8. This is close to the actual LTCM returns. In 1995 and 1996, the firms' net-of-fee profits were 42% and 41% respectively. Fees were 2% flat fee and 25% of profits.

9. For a non-normal distribution, one could use the Cornish-Fisher expansion for VaR or some other method. See Chincarini (2008).

Appendix B

1. This terminology is confusing when swap markets trade below bond markets, but the basic ideas are the same.

2. The floating swap interest rate changes throughout the contract's life, based on current LIBOR rates. The parties won't make full interest payments on swap contracts. They make net payments. If LTCM owed $5 million in interest at quarter-end and the counterparty owed $6 million, the counterparty would pay LTCM $1 million. Furthermore, both parties posted variation margin throughout the duration of the swap contract if valuations changed on either side. If interest rates rose by a significant amount, the swap position would be worth more to LTCM than to the counterparty. Increased variation margins would reflect this change. See Galitz (1995) for a more in-depth discussion of swaps.

Appendix C

1. This ignores any immediate financing concerns, which we will add later.

2. The returns for being long the swap spread are computed as -1 multiplied by these returns.

3. These numbers were constructed to coincide with the example in Perold (2000).

Appendix D

1. Over a weekend, one would have to adjust this formula, since actually it would be from day t to day $t + 3$.
2. Choose any normalization for the price of the bond. Here it is 100, but this is unimportant for computing returns, provided it is consistent.

Appendix H

1. To get the simplified expression, start with a series of the form $S_n = 1 + \delta + \delta^2 + \cdots + \delta^n$. Then $S_n - \delta S_n = 1 - \delta^{n+1}$, and thus $S_n = \frac{1-\delta^{n+1}}{1-\delta}$. Then plug in $\delta = \frac{1}{1+y_M}$ and obtain the expressions in Equation (H.2).

Appendix I

1. See Buffett (2003). A more useful statement was in the same Buffett letter. "When Charlie and I finish reading the long footnotes detailing the derivatives activities of major banks, the only thing we understand is that we don't understand how much risk the institution is running." This is still a problem, and not just for Buffett. Understanding net risk is genuinely difficult. The companies Buffett owns use derivatives, and Buffett's Berkshire Hathaway sold Lehman Brothers lots of credit default swaps on municipal-bond debt.
2. See Chincarini (2010).
3. Investors short-sell when they promise to sell a security that they don't already own. The brokerage house—Lehman Brothers, in this case—handles the logistics of short-selling.

    Short-selling can bring efficiency to the market. Think of buying and selling as ways to vote on a security's appropriate price. If no one ever short-sold a security, stock prices might be higher than appropriate, because no investor could vote for them to be lower.
4. See Chapter 4.
5. Of course, if the borrower on a bond defaults, then even this income is variable. Investors realized this in spades when the mortgage market fell apart and "fixed-income" mortgage-backed securities turned out to be not so fixed.
6. A bond index is composed of many bonds in the same class. It gives an indication of how that part of the bond world is performing. For example, a short-term German government bond index would be a portfolio of many German government bonds with maturities of less than three years.
7. Primary dealers can buy a limited number of new U.S. government bonds for their own accounts, to limit the potential for abuse of monopoly power.
8. See Chapter 16.

9. See a full description of the firm's risk management procedures in management's discussion and analysis in the Lehman Brothers 2002 Annual Report.

Appendix J

1. The broad risk weightings were shown in Chapter 13.
2. See Table J.1 for the types of capital.
3. These values include a countercyclical buffer of 2.5%, which may not always be at full value.

Glossary

alpha The value added of a portfolio manager over simple ways of investing. Measures portfolio manager skill.

arb spread The difference in price between the price at which a company will be purchased by another buyer and the actual traded price. The spread reflects a return that an investor can make for taking on the risk that the merger may not be consummated.

asset management fee A base fee of assets under management that is charged by hedge funds and other money managers. Typical fee is 2%.

bank holding company A company that has control of a bank. Must register and become part of Federal Reserve system. During the financial crisis, certain companies converted to this form of structure so as to gain borrowing ability from the Federal Reserve.

bootstrap Bootstrapping is the practice of estimating properties of an estimator (such as its variance) by measuring those properties when sampling from an approximating distribution. One standard choice for an approximating distribution is the empirical distribution of the observed data. In the case where a set of observations can be assumed to be from an independent and identically distributed population, this can be implemented by constructing a number of resamples of the observed dataset (and of equal size to the observed dataset), each of which is obtained by random sampling with replacement from the original dataset.

bridge equity Equity contributed by financing banks in order to help an LBO fund to close a deal. This equity is normally sold to other investors by the lending banks after the LBO deal is completed.

call option The right, not obligation, to buy a security at a specified price in a specified time interval.

capital intermediation The process of channeling funds between savers and borrowers across a variety of venues.

CDO A collateralized debt obligation is any kind of security whose payments are divided into tranches and depend on the behavior of an underlying collateral. A CMO is a type of CDO that depends on an underlying pool of mortgages. There are other CDOs including those backed by auto loans, credit card loans, and student loans.

CDO^2 A CDO constructed based on another underlying CDO. It amplifies the exposure of market participants to a given underlying security. For example, during the mortgage crisis, there were collateralized mortgages offered as CMOs and then some banks constructed CDOs out of the individual tranches of those CMOs and sold them to another group of investors.

CDS A method of insurance to protect the buyer of a bond from a company in the event it goes bankrupt or does not pay its loan back. The buyer of the insurance pays a fee to the seller of the loan for the entire duration of the credit default swap in exchange for the insurance that, if the insured bond falls below a certain value, the insured will be made whole. For example, during the financial crisis, Goldman Sachs was worried that some of the mortgage securities it owned would default, thus it purchased a CDS from AIG, whereby Goldman paid AIG a fee in return for AIG insuring Goldman against any losses if the mortgages collapsed in value.

CMO A mortgage-backed security whose payments have been split up into several tranches. For example, in a three-tranche CMO, the tranches might be split up such that Tranche 1 gets paid first if there are prepayments and also loses first if there are defaults on the underlying pool of mortgages. Tranche 2 is next, and Tranche 3 is last to be affected by changes in the behavior of mortgage owners.

comparative advantage When one compares one's efficiency at doing one task versus another as compared to others doing the similar task versus other tasks, those with a better relative ability to do one task are said to have a comparative advantage in that task.

conflict of interest A condition where a manager or company has two or more objectives that conflict with each other, such as being appointed attorney for your wife at your divorce hearing.

convergence trade A trade that is long an overvalued security and short an undervalued security with the expectation that prices would converge by a specific date.

convexity A measure used in the bond market to measure the sensivity of both the bond price and duration to changes in interest rates. In general, the higher the convexity, the more sensitive the bond price is to decreasing interest rates and the less sensitive the bond price is to increasing rates.

countercyclical buffer An extra amount of capital that banks must hold during booms to restrain excessive leverage and to act as a buffer in case of a recession. Part of the Basel III guidelines for banks.

credit risk The risk that a borrower may not pay back a loan.

crowded trade A crowded trade or crowded trading space is one in which many traders of similar type have taken the same positions. Risk models must be even more sensitive to measure the presence of the traders in the space.

dead swap When a swap is bought to offset the position from another swap, the two swaps have become dead swaps. They are active, but from an exposure point of view are neutralized or dead.

default risk The risk that a borrower may not pay back a loan.

directional trade A trade that is long or short a particular security in the anticipation that the security prices move in a favorable direction.

duration A measure used in bond markets to measure how much bond prices change from a 1% change in interest rates. Most commonly referred to as modified duration.

endogeneity Refers to variables that are not external to the system. For example, prices of certain securities are influenced by the types of investors that are trading them. Effects on some traders or players cannot be taken as external; they will influence everyone else in the system. Prices and risk can also be endogenous.

fat fingers A term used to denote a mistake made by a trader when making a trade. For example, making a trade of one billion shares rather than the intended one million.

fly fishing The process of placing small limit orders on a security to see how the market reacts.

GSE Government-sponsored enterprise, like Freddie Mac and Fannie Mae were prior to their conservatorship in 2008.

hedge fund gates The control of the withdrawal of money from a hedge fund.

HFT High-frequency traders use automated electronic trading systems to trade instantaneously in the marketplace in an attempt to make small profits repeatedly.

high-water mark A level of net asset value that a hedge fund must return to before it can collect incentive fees from its customers.

implied volatility A measure of the expectation of the return volatility the market expects in the future derived from the prices of traded options.

incentive fees Fees that hedge funds collect as a percentage of the performance of their clients. Thus, the hedge funds get paid more when they provide better returns for their clients. Typical fee is 20% of the performance.

index art The process of using basket indices and futures to construct an arbitrage trade for a small group of securities.

interconnectedness Refers to the interconnections in the financial system. It can include traders in a similar space, counterparties linked to traders, and banks. The interconnectedness makes events in one part of the system very correlated with other seemingly independent parts.

level I, II, and III assets Level I: Quoted market prices in active markets for identical assets or liabilities. Level II: Observable market-based inputs or unobservable inputs that are corroborated by market data. Level III: Unobservable inputs that are not corroborated by market data.

liquid trade A trade that can be executed easily with little impact on market prices and where market prices before trading are quite reliable.

liquidity premium Refers to the extra return an investor receives when taking investments that aren't as easily converted into cash.

liquidity trap A situation where monetary policy is unable to stimulate an economy by lowering interest rates or increasing the money supply. For example, if short-term interest rates are already at zero percent, the Fed must resort to other policies since they cannot reduce the interest rate any further. May also occur in other situations, such as when investment does not respond to interest rates.

long the spread A long spread trade is positioned to profit if the spread widens. For example, if swap yields are 10% and bond yields are 5%. A long spread trade profits when swap yields increase relative to bond yields. Some traders refer to this as betting that bonds will richen versus swaps.

Main Street A common term used to describe nonfinancial businesses, like supermarkets and clothing stores, as opposed to banking or the financial businesses of Wall Street.

mark-to-market The process of valuing one's portfolio or one's assets and liabilities based on the current market value of the securities.

MBS Mortgage-backed security refers to a security whose value depends on a group of mortgage loans.

monoline insurer An insurance company that provides guarantees to issuers, often in the form of credit wraps, that enhance the credit of the issuer. For example, insuring of mortgage-backed securities and collateralized debt obligations.

moral hazard A situation in which a party that doesn't bear any risk results in them behaving differently than they would otherwise. For example, during the financial crisis, the fact that mortgage lenders could sell off their mortgages, and hence their risk, to banks led them to be less scrutinizing of the people that they lent to.

mortgage cash business In the cash transaction, a company pays cash for a mortgage pool. The company then securitizes the loans, selling them in pools to investors—usually pension funds and insurance companies.

mortgage swap business In the swap transaction, a mortgage originator gives the entire mortgage pool to the company in exchange for a security that is backed by the pool of mortgages, minus the credit risk.

multiplier Measures the change in GDP from a given change in either government spending or a reduction in taxes. Liberal economists tend to believe it is greater than 1, while conservative economists believe it is less than 1. Most empirical studies find the multiplier to be less than 1 both in the short and long term.

P/L Standard usage for profit and loss.

painting the tape A practice in which traders make numerous buy and sell orders for a security in order to create the appearance of high trading volume.

potential holders Prospective holders of a security or future buyers of a security.

preferred habitat The preferred group of securities that a particular individual or institution would like to own due to their own particular circumstances. For example, a pension fund generally likes to own long maturity bonds.

price impact The movement in price that results when a trade is executed. A very large trade in a thin market may move the price a lot and result in poor execution.

primary dealer A formal designation of a firm as a market maker of government securities. In the United States, a primary dealer is a bank or securities broker-dealer that is permitted to trade directly with the Federal Reserve. These firms are required to participate regularly in auctions of U.S. government debt.

proprietary trading group A group within a company devoted to trading the bank's capital to make profits for the bank.

put option The right, not obligation, to sell a security at a specified price in a specified time interval.

quantitative easing A central bank program whereby the Fed attempts to influence longer-term interest rates by direct purchases of government bonds or mortgage-backed securities or other securities.

quote stuffing The trading tactic of quickly entering and withdrawing large orders in an attempt to flood the market with quotes that competitors have to process, thus causing processor delays and gaining an advantage over others. It's a much more elaborate form of spoofing.

regulatory arbitrage The exploitation by traders of poorly specified government regulations so as to make arbitrage returns. For example, a bank could hold much riskier assets and hope to achieve a higher return in normal times, but the capital ratio would not reflect it and thus their borrowing rates would be artificially low.

relative-value trade A trade that is long an overvalued security and short an undervalued security with the expectation that prices would converge eventually, but with no certain time frame.

repo Short for repurchase agreement. It is a common method for investment banks and money managers to borrow money short term with posted collateral. In a repo agreement, the borrowing party gives a security to the lending party in exchange for cash with an agreement that at the end of the term, the borrower will take back the security and return the cash plus an amount of interest. It is a common form of borrowing, because the collateral makes the interest rate slightly less than with an outright loan.

repo 105 A repo that Lehman engaged in to avoid reporting the transactions on the balance sheet. They involved repo deals with haircuts of 5% or greater, hence the name.

RWL Residential whole loans.

securitization The act of taking several individual securities or loans and bunching them together and selling the whole pool as a security.

shadow banking system The banking system that is performed by investment banks, insurance companies, and other types of companies that are in the business of some form of short-term borrowing and long-term lending.

Sharpe ratio Measures the return of a portfolio minus the risk-free rate divided by the portfolio's standard deviation. It is a risk-adjusted return measure that assists in comparing different portfolios or investments, even in the presence of leverage.

short the spread A short spread trade is positioned to profit if the spread narrows. For example, if swap yields are 10% and bond yields are 5%. A short spread trade profits when swap yields decrease relative to bond yields.

slap hands The game, within the larger game of spoofing, where a trader places a limit order and removes it before the market can hit it.

Sortino ratio Similar to the Sharpe ratio but divides excess return by the semistandard deviation rather than the standard deviation.

spoofing A fraudulent trading practice that occurs when a trader that owns a particular security places a large buy limit order through an electronic trading system and it cancels within seconds. The trader's objective is to influence the market to trade higher as market participants see the large limit order in the limit order display.

stub quotes Default quotes that market makers resort to when they would like to not participate in the marketplace as a liquidity provider, but are required to by security laws.

subprime securities Securities that are based upon the behavior of subprime borrowers who typically have weakened credit histories that include payment delinquencies, and possibly more severe problems such as charge-offs, judgments, and bankruptcies.

swap trade There are a variety of types. The typical swap trade is either long or short the spread versus Treasuries, but it could also be versus agency securities, mortgage-backed securities, corporate securities, and others.

tail risk Refers to the risk of a portfolio return being very negative and far from the typical return. In other words, a very unlikely but large negative return. If the return distribution is normal, it usually refers to larger than three standard deviation events.

term financing An agreement to obtain financing or borrowing for a specific time period related to the needs of the particular investment that the financing is used for.

term repo Rather than being a typical overnight repo, a term repo has a longer maturity. For example, LTCM engaged in many term repos of three to six months in maturity.

VaR Value at risk is a measure of the potential losses of a portfolio if very large market deviations occur.

vega The sensitivity of an option or an option position to a change in the volatility of the underlying asset. Typically, it represents the price change in an option position due to a 1% change in the volatility of the underlying asset.

Volker rule The rule proposed under Dodd-Frank to limit investment bank activities, including limited ownership of hedge funds and private equity, and the absence of proprietary trading.

Bibliography

"A Guide to FRB/US. A Macroeconomic Model of the United States." *Macroeconomic and Quantitative Studies Federal Reserve Note*, October 1996.

"Bear Stearns' Jimmy Cayne's Profane Tirade Against Treasury's Geithner." *Wall Street Journal*, March 4, 2009.

"Berkshire Hathaway Report 10-Q." June 30, 2008.

"Budget Report: H.R. 5140: Economic Stimulus Act of 2008." *Congressional Budget Office*, February 11, 2008.

"Consumer Assistance to Recycle and Save Act of 2009 Report to the House Committee on Energy and Commerce, the Senate Committee on Commerce, Science, and Transportation and the House and Senate Committees on Appropriations." Report to Congress National Highway Traffic Safety Administration, December 2009.

"Department of Housing and Urban Development (HUD)."

"DLJ States Exposure to Hedge Funds Is Total of $106 Million." *Wall Street Journal*, October 8, 1998.

"Drowning or Waiving." *The Economist*, October 21, 2010.

"Endeavor Takes $725M Loss on Japanese Debt." *Wall Street Journal*, March 20, 2008.

"Fannie Mae Enron." *Wall Street Journal*, October 4, 2004.

"FDIC Sues Former IndyMac Bank CEO Michael Perry To Recover $600M." *Huffpost Business*, July 7, 2011.

"Financial Audit: Resolution Trust Corporation's 1995 and 1994 Financial Statements." *United States General Accounting Office Report to the Congress*, July 1996.

"Former CEO Says Bear Stearns' Collapse Unavoidable." *Right Vision News*, May 7, 2010.

"Fuld of Experience." *The Economist*, April 24, 2008.

"German Landesbanks: Deep Impact. A Revealing Dispute over Credit Ratings." *The Economist*, November 27, 2003.

"Group of Governors and Heads of Supervision Announces Higher Global Minimum Capital Standards." Basel Committee on Banking Supervision Press Release, September 12, 2010.

"Hedge Funds, Leverage, and the Lessons of Long-Term Capital Management." *Report of the President's Working Group on Financial Markets*, April 1999.

"HFR Global Hedge Fund Industry Report Year-End 2010." *Hedge Fund Research Publication*, 2011.

"III Fund Ltd Restructuring of the Fund." *London Stock Exchange Aggregated Regulatory News Service*, March 4, 2009.

"III Readies Credit Derivatives Fund." *Derivatives Week*, October 14, 2005.

"In Search of Certainty." *Wall Street Journal*, June 27, 2011.

"Obama says he would impose oil windfall profits tax." Reuters, June 9, 2008.

"OTS Fact Sheet on Washington Mutual Bank." *Office of Thrift Supervision Fact Sheet*, September 25, 2008.

"Parkcentral Capital Management L.P. Leverage Report." Parkcentral Capital Management Letter to Investors, September 2008.

"Parkcentral Capital Management L.P. Monthly Performance Update." Parkcentral Capital Management Letter to Investors, September 2008.

"Parkcentral Capital Management L.P. Risk Summary Report." Parkcentral Capital Management Letter to Investors, September 2008.

"Quarterly Banking Profile: First Quarter 2011." *FDIC Quarterly*, 2011.

"Quarterly Banking Profile: Fourth Quarter 2010." *FDIC Quarterly*, 2011.

"Rules. And More Rules." *Wall Street Journal*, June 27, 2011.

"The Next Fannie Mae." *Wall Street Journal*, August 11, 2009.

"U.S. Congress Considers LTCM Investment Technique." *Wall Street Journal*, October 16, 1998.

"What Would Keynes Have Done?" *Wall Street Journal*, November 21, 2010.

Acharya, Viral, Thomas Cooley, Matthew Richardson, and Ingo Walter. *Regulating Wall Street: The Dodd-Frank Act and the New Architecture of Global Finance*. John Wiley & Sons, November 2010.

Acharya, Viral V. and Matthew Richardson. *Restoring Financial Stability: How to Repair a Failed System*. John Wiley & Sons, Inc., 2009.

Acharya, Viral V., Lasse H. Pedersen, Thomas Philippon, and Matthew Richardson. "Measuring Systemic Risk." NYU Working Paper, May 2010.

AIG. "Annual Report." AIG Annual Report, September 30, 2008.

Alpert, Bill. "Shorting Cramer." *Barron's*, August 20, 2007.

Anderson, Jenny. "Survivor." *New York Times*, October 28, 2007.

Angel, James. "Examining the Efficiency, Stability, and Integrity of the U.S. Capital Markets." Testimony to Senate Subcommittee on Securities, Insurance, and Investment and the Senate Permanent Subcommittee on Investigations, December 8, 2010.

Angel, James. "Open Letter to the SEC Regarding Market Rules After Flash Crash." *Georgetown Letter*, October 25, 2011.

Appelbaum, Binyamin. "Fannie and Freddie May Need Infusion." *New York Times*, October 21, 2010.

Appelbaum, Binyamin, Carol D. Leonnig, and David S. Hilzenrath. "How Washington Failed to Rein in Fannie, Freddie as Profits Grew, Firms Used Their Power to Mask Peril." *Washington Post*, September 14, 2008.

Ascraft, Adam, Paul Goldsmith-Pinkham, Peter Hull, and James Vickery. "Credit Ratings and Security Prices in the Subprime MBS Market." *American Economic Review: Papers & Proceedings*, May 2011.

Asness, Cliff. "The August of Our Discontent." AQR Capital Management Working Paper, September 2007.

Atanasov, Maria and Carol J. Loomis. "Warren Buffett's Wild Ride at Salomon a Harrowing, Bizarre Tale of Misdeeds and Mistakes that Pushed Salomon to the Brink and Produced the 'Most Important Day' in Warren Buffett's Life." *Fortune*, October 27, 1997.

Avdjiev, Stefan, Christian Upper, and Nicholas Vause. "Highlights of International Banking and Financial Market Activity." *BIS Quarterly Review*, December 2010.

Bakija, Jon, Adam Cole, and Bradley Heim. "Jobs and Income Growth of Top Earners and the Causes of Changing Income Inequality: Evidence from U.S. Tax Return Data." Working Paper, November 2010.

Balzli, Beat and Michaela Schiessl. "Global Banking Economist Warned of Coming Crisis." *Spiegel Online*, July 8, 2009.

Barr, Alistair. "Sowood loses more than $1 billion in July. Facing margin calls, hedge fund firm sells portfolio to Citadel." *MarketWatch*, July 30, 2007.

Barraclough, Theresa. "Buy Japan's 'Cheap' Inflation-Linked Bonds, Says ABN." Bloomberg, April 2, 2008.

Barro, Robert J. and Charles J. Redlick. "Macroeconomic Effects from Government Purchases and Taxes." Harvard Working Paper, February 2010.

Bart, Katharina. "Rules will Push UBS to Cut Exposure." *Wall Street Journal*, October 1, 2010.

Barta, Patrick, John D. McKinnon, and John R. Wilke. "Leading the News: Freddie Mac Gives Large Parachutes—Ex-CEO Gets $24 Million, While Another Officer Is to Receive $5.3 Million." *Wall Street Journal*, July 12, 2003.

Basel Committee on Banking Supervision. "Principles for Sound Liquidity Risk Management and Supervision." *BIS Publication*, September 2008.

Basel Committee on Banking Supervision. "Basel III: A Global Regulatory Framework for More Resilient Banks and Banking Systems." *BIS Publication*, December 2010.

Basel Committee on Banking Supervision. "Basel III: International Framework for Liquidity Risk Measurement, Standards and Monitoring." *BIS Publication*, December 2010.

Bebchuk, Lucian A., Alma Cohen, and Holder Spamann. "The Wages of Failure: Executive Compensation at Bear Stearns and Lehman 2000-2008." Harvard Law Economics Discussion Paper, November 24, 2009.

Becker, Bernie and Ben White. "Lehman's Chief Defends His Actions as Prudent for the Time." *New York Times*, October 7, 2008.

Bernanke, Ben. "Fed Chairman Bernanke On The Economy." www.cbsnews.com/video/watch/?id=7120553n, December 5, 2010.

Bernanke, B., V. Reinhart, and B. Sack. "Monetary Policy Alternatives at the Zero Bound: An Empirical Assessment." Brookings Paper on Economics Activity, 2004.

Bernstein, Jared and Christina Romer. "The Job Impact of the American Recovery and Reinvestment Plan." Chair of Economic Advisors Release, January 10, 2009.

Bieri, David and Ludwig B. Chincarini. "Riding the Yield Curve: A Variety of Strategies." *Journal of Fixed Income*, September 2005.

Black, Fischer. "How to Use the Holes in Black-Scholes." *Risk*, March, 1988.

Blasnik, Steve and Peter Karmin. "Parkcentral Global Fund Quarter Review." Parkcentral Capital Management Letter to Investors, July 17 and November 3, 2008.

Blasnik, Steve, Peter Karmin, and Michael Presley. "Parkcentral Global Fund Quarter Review." Parkcentral Capital Management Letter to Investors, January 30, 2008.

Blasnik, Steve, Peter Karmin, Michael Presley, and Jason Pizer. "Parkcentral Global Fund Quarter Review." Parkcentral Capital Management Letter to Investors, April 15, 2008.

Blinder, Alan S. "Two Cheers for the New Bank Capital Standards." *Wall Street Journal*, September 30, 2010.

Blitz, James. "Storm over Bank of Italy Investment in LTCM: Central Bank Members of Italian Parliament Call for Inquiry into How High-Risk Exposure Was Allowed." *Financial Times*, October 3, 1998.

Blitz, James and Gillian Tett. "Bank of Italy Put $250M into LTCM." *Financial Times*, October 2, 1998.

Bloomberg News. "UBS Says Mathis Cabiallavetta to Step Down as Chairman." *Bloomberg News*, October 1, 1998.

Blundell-Wignall, Adrian and Paul Atkinson. "The Subprime Crisis: Causal Distortions and Regulatory Reform." Working Paper, July 2008.

Blundell-Wignall, Adrian and Paul Atkinson. "Thinking Beyond Basel III: Necessary Solutions for Capital and Liquidity." *Financial Market Trends*, 2010.

Bodie, Zvi and Robert Merton. "Financial Infrastructure and Public Policy: A Functional Perspective." Chapter 8. *The Global Financial System: A Functional Perspective*, 1995.

Boskin, Michael J. "Five Lessons for Deficit Busters." *Wall Street Journal*, June 20, 2011.

Boskin, Michael J. "Get Ready for a 70% Marginal Tax Rate." *Wall Street Journal*, July 18, 2011.

Bourassa, Steven C. and Martin Hoesli. "Why Do the Swiss Rent?" Swiss Finance Institute Research Paper No. 07-04. Available at SSRN: http://ssrn.com/abstract=964637, December 27, 2006.

Boyd, Roddy. "The Last Days of Bear Stearns." *CNN Money*, March 31, 2008.

Bray, Chad, Liz Rappaport, and Nick Timiraos. "U.S. Says Deutsche Bank Lied." *Wall Street Journal*, May 4, 2011.

Brinkley, Tracy. "Lehman Brothers Termination Letter." Lehman Brothers Confidential Document, May 7, 2007.

Brinsley, John. "Paulson Says No Plans to Add Cash to Fannie, Freddie." *Bloomberg News*, August 10, 2008.

Bruno, Joe Bel and Marty Crutsinger. "Barclays pulls out of Lehman deal, talks continue." *Associated Press Online*, September 14, 2008.

Buffett, Warren. "Berkshire Letter to Investors." Berkshire Annual Report, February 23, 2003.

Burhouse, Susan, John Feid, George French, and Keith Ligon. "Basel and the Evolution of Capital Regulation: Moving Forward, Looking Back." *FDIC Publication*, January 14, 2003.

Butler, Shaun, Dick Fuld, Ian Lowitt, and Bart McDade. "Lehman Brothers Holdings Inc. Earnings Conference Call." *Thomson StreetEvents*, September 10, 2008.

Button, Keith. "Best When Stressed." *MAR/Hedge*, January, 2004.

Card, David and Ethan G. Lewis. "The Diffusion of Mexican Immigrants During the 1990s: Explanations and Impacts." *Mexican Immigration*, 2007.

Case, Brendan and Gary Jacobson. "Revisiting Final Frantic Days of a Hedge Fund: Perots' Global Hub Spiraled Down Quickly, Court Filings Show." *Dallas Morning News*, April 26, 2009.

Case, Brendan M. "Hedge Fund with Ties to Perots to Start Liquidating Parkcentral Global's Assets Fell as Much as 40 Percent to $1.5 Billion in October." *Dallas Morning News*, November 26, 2009.

Cassidy, John. "What Good is Wall Street?" *The New Yorker*, November 29, 2010.

Cha, Ariana Eunjung. "Lehman 'Was Forced into Bankruptcy' by Regulators, Former CEO Testifies." *Washington Post*, September 2, 2010.

Chincarini, Ludwig B. "The Failure of Long Term Capital Management." BIS Banking Paper, pages 1–15, October 8, 1998.

Chincarini, Ludwig B. "The Failure of LTCM." Presentation at the Bank for International Settlements. http://pages.pomona.edu/lbc04747/videos.html, October 8, 1998.

Chincarini, Ludwig B. "Segment on Private Equity with Ludwig Chincarini." Interview with ORF2 on Private Equity. http://pages.pomona.edu/lbc04747/videos.html, July 23, 2007.

Chincarini, Ludwig B. "Segment on Private Equity with Ludwig Chincarini." Interview on Private Equity on ORF2. http://pages.pomona.edu/lbc04747/videos.html, July 23, 2007.

Chincarini, Ludwig B. "The Amaranth Debacle. Failure of Risk Measures or Failure of Risk Management." *Journal of Alternative Investments*, pp. 91–104, Winter 2007.

Chincarini, Ludwig B. "A Case Study on Risk Management: Lessons from the Collapse of Amaranth Advisors L.L.C." *Journal of Applied Finance*, pp. 152–174, Spring/Summer 2008.

Chincarini, Ludwig B. "Readers & Thinkers: 228 Wasted Resources." Memo. http://pages.pomona.edu/lbc04747/, 2008.

Chincarini, Ludwig B. "The World Financial Crisis." Presentation at Pomona College. http://pages.pomona.edu/lbc04747/research.html#, September 17, 2008.

Chincarini, Ludwig B. "Banks, Bonds, and Bailouts: Government Policy and the Financial Market." Presentation at Pomona College. http://pages.pomona.edu/lbc04747/research.html#, February 14, 2009.

Chincarini, Ludwig B. "On the Government's Stimulus Package: Banking." Presentation at Pomona College. http://pages.pomona.edu/lbc04747/research.html#, February 26, 2009.

Chincarini, Ludwig B. "The Review of the Financial Markets in 2008." Presentation at Pomona College. http://pages.pomona.edu/lbc04747/research.html#, January 26, 2009.

Chincarini, Ludwig B. "A Comparison of Quantitative and Qualitative Hedge Funds." Available at SSRN: http://ssrn.com/abstract=1532992, January 2010.

Chincarini, Ludwig B. "No Chills or Burns from Temperature Surprises: An Empirical Analysis of the Weather Derivatives Market." *Journal of Futures Markets*, January, 2011.

Chincarini, Ludwig B. and Alex Nakao. "Measuring Hedge Fund Timing Ability Across Factors." Available at SSRN: http://ssrn.com/abstract=1544452, January 2010.

Chincarini, Ludwig B. and Daehwan Kim. *Quantitative Equity Portfolio Management: An Active Approach to Portfolio Construction and Management*. McGraw-Hill, 2006.

Chincarini, Ludwig B. and Steven Wallman. "Method and Apparatus for Trading Securities or Other Instruments on Behalf of Customers." U.S. Patent # 7,047,218 B1, March 1, 2000.

Chung, Kaimon, Joseph Mack, and Meredith Whitney. "Lehman Brothers Holdings Inc.: LEH Likely Forced Into Liquidation." Oppenheimer Equity Research, September 14, 2008.

Cohan, William D. *House of Cards. A Tale of Hubris and Wretched Excess on Wall Street*. Anchor Books, 2009.

Cook, Nancy. "The Rise and Fall of Bear Stearns. Alan "Ace" Greenberg, the Wall Street firm's defiant former CEO, discloses his regrets, his beef with mortgage brokers, and why he thinks financial reform isn't necessary." *The Daily Beast*, June 21, 2010.

Corbett, Jennifer and John Connor. "New Agency Gears Up to Scrutinize Fannie Mae, Freddie Mac Officials' Pay." *Wall Street Journal*, April 8, 1996.

CoreLogic. "2011 Mortgage Fraud Trends Report." *CoreLogic Report*, September 2011.

Cowen, Tyler and Randall Kroszner. "Mutual Fund Banking: A Market Approach." *Cato Journal*, Spring/Summer, 1990.

Cramer, James. "A Reporter's Primer." TheStreet.com, September 28, 1998.

Culp, Christopher and Merton Miller. "Hedging a Flow of Commodity Deliveries with Futures: Lessons from Metallgesellschaft." *Derivatives Quarterly*, Fall 1994.

Culp, Christopher and Merton Miller. "Metallgesellschaft and the Economics of Synthetic Storage." *Journal of Applied Corporate Finance*, Winter 1995.

Doering, Christopher. "CFTC proposes clearing rules, lawmaker challenge looms." *Reuters*, July 19, 2011.

Dornbusch, Rudiger. "Free Markets Work Best—But They Need a Little Tweaking." *Business-Week*, December 18, 1995.

Dornbusch, Rudiger. "Euro Fantasies." *Foreign Affairs*, September–October, 1996.

Dowd, Kevin. *Beyond Value at Risk: The New Science of Risk Management*. John Wiley & Sons, Inc., 1999.

Dunbar, Nicholas. "LTCM and the Dangers of Marking to Market." *Risk*, October 1999.

Eaglesham, Jean and Dan Fitzpatrick. "Bank Fine Hints at Fed's Playbook." *Wall Street Journal*, June 22, 2011.

Editorial. "Bush Spanks Fannie." *Wall Street Journal*, February 10, 2004.

Editorial. "Systemic Political Risk." *Wall Street Journal*, September 30, 2005.

Editorial. "Warren Buffett says 'game is over' for Freddie and Fannie." *New York Times*, August 22, 2008.

Editorial. "Systemic Risk and Fannie Mae: The Education of Joseph Stiglitz and Peter Orzag." *Wall Street Journal*, December 1, 2009.

Edwards, Chris. "Cash for Clunkers: Dumbest Program Ever?" *Cato Insitute Blog*, August 21, 2009.

Edwards, Franklin and Michael S. Canter. "The Collapse of Metallgesellschaft: Unhedgeable Risks, Poor Hedging Strategy, or Just Bad Luck?" *Journal of Futures Markets*, May 1995.

Eichenwalk, Kurt. "Low-Price Settlement in Big Salomon Scandal." *New York Times*, December 4, 1992.

Eisinger, Jesse. "The Debt Shuffle: Wall Street Cheered Lehmans Earnings, but There Are Questions about Its Balance Sheet." *Portfolio.com*, March 20, 2008.

Ellis, David. "BofA's Ken Lewis defends Merrill deal." *CNNMoney.com*, June 11, 2009.

Ely, Bert. "The Narrow Bank. A Flawed Response to the Failings of Federal Deposit Insurance." *Cato Review of Business and Government*, Spring 1991.

Ely, Bert. "How to Stop Fannie and Freddie." *Wall Street Journal*, February 5, 2004.

Engle, Robert F. and Kevin Sheppard. "Theoretical and Empirical Properties of Dynamic Conditional Correlation Multivariate GARCH." University of San Diego Working Paper, December 12, 2001.

Enrich, David, Deborah Ball, and Alistair MacDonald. "Banks Prep for Life After Euro Countries Study Printing Their Own Notes in Case Monetary Union Unravels." *Wall Street Journal*, December 8, 2011.

Enrich, David and Laura Stevens. "Europe Banks Sit in a Tangled Web." *Wall Street Journal*, December 12, 2011.

Enrich, David and Stephen Fidler. "Ties that Bound Europe Now Fraying." *Wall Street Journal*, December 16, 2011.

Fabozzi, Frank J. *Bond Markets: Analysis and Strategies*. Prentice Hall, 1999.

Financial Crisis Inquiry Commission. *The Financial Crisis Inquiry Report*. Public Affairs, 2011.

Financial Services Authority. "The Turner Review: A Regulatory Response to the Global Banking Crisis." March 2009.

Fisk, Margaret Cronin. "JPMorgan, Bank of America Face 'Hydra' of Foreclosure Probes." *Bloomberg*, October 6, 2010.

Fitzpatrick, Dan. "BofA Nears Huge Settlement." *Wall Street Journal*, June 29, 2011.

Fitzpatrick, Dan and Jean Eaglesham. "Wachovia Targeted Over Sale of CDOs." *Wall Street Journal*, April 4, 2011.

Flood, Joe. "NYSE Tech Delays Contributed to the May 6 Flash Crash." *The Atlantic*, August 10, 2010.

Foley, Stephen. "Goldman Accused of Spreading Rumors about Rivals." *The Independent*, July 17, 2008.

Fontevecchia, Agustino. "PIMCOs Bill Gross Shorts Treasuries As Experts Eye Inflation." *Forbes*, April 11, 2011.

Frank, Barney. "Speech on House Floor." www.youtube.com/watch?v=iW5qKYfqALE, June 27, 2005.

Froeba, Mark. "Testimony to Financial Crisis Inquiry Commission." FCIC Document, June 2, 2010.

Gagnon, Joseph, Matthew Raskin, Julie Remache, and Brian Sack. "Large-Scale Asset Purchases by the Federal Reserve: Did They Work?" Federal Reserve Bank of New York Staff Report No. 441, March 2010.

Galitz, Lawrence C. *Financial Engineering*. Irwin Publishing, 1995.

Gaspari, Al. "Uncommon Interview with Mark Carhart." *The Chicago Maroon*, April 23, 2010.

Gerth, Jeff. "Cause of Ginnie Mae Losses Said to Be Lax Supervision." *New York Times*, July 17, 1989.

Gibson, Brett G. and Arun N. Kumar. "American International Group: Valuations Look Attractive, but Company has Miles to Go; Downgrading to Neutral." J.P. Morgan Credit Research, August 13, 2008.

Ginnie Mae. "Annual Report." Ginnie Mae Annual Report, November 2009.

Giovannini, Alberto. "Financial System Reform Proposals from First Principles." *Centre for Economic Policy Research Policy Insight #45*, January 2010.

Global Quantitative Equity Group. "The Quant Liquidity Crunch." Goldman Sachs Asset Management Paper, August 2007.

Goldman, Russell. "Little Sympathy for Financial Fat Cats." *ABC News*, March 18, 2008.

Goldman Sachs Asset Management. "The Liquidity Crunch in Quant Equities: Analysis and Implications." Goldman Sachs Asset Management Presentation, December 13, 2007.

Goldman Sachs Asset Management. "The Quantity Liquidity Crunch." Goldman Sachs Global Quantitative Equity Report, August 2007.

Goldstein, Matthew. "Bear Stearns to the Rescue—Sort Of." *Bloomberg Businessweek*, June 22, 2007.

Goldstein, Matthew. "Bear's Big Loss Arouses SEC Interest." *Bloomberg Businessweek*, June 25, 2007.

Gongloff, Mark. "'QE2' in the Dock: Some Yields are Going Up." *Wall Street Journal*, November 11, 2010.

Gordon, Marcy. "Franklin Raines to pay $24.7 million to settle Fannie Mae lawsuit." *Seattle Times*, April 18, 2008.

Griffin, John M. and Dragon Yongjun Tang. "Did Credit Rating Agencies Make Unbiased Assumptions on CDOs?" *American Economic Review: Papers & Proceedings*, May 2011.

Grynbaum, Michael M. "Bear Stearns Profit Plunges 61% on Subprime Woes." *New York Times*, September 21, 2007.

Guberman, Ross. "Balancing Act." *The Washingtonian*, August 2002.

Hagerty, James R. "Freddie Mac Ousts Lobbyist Amid Election-Law Probe." *Wall Street Journal*, March 12, 2004.

Hamilton, James D. *Time Series Analysis*. Princeton Press, 1994.

Hamilton, James D. and Jing Cynthia Wu. "The Effectiveness of Alternative Monetary Policy Tools in a Zero Lower Bound Environment." UCSD Working Paper, May 2011.

He, Jie, Jun Qian, and Philip E. Strahan. "Credit Ratings and the Evolution of the Mortgage-Backed Securities Market." *American Economic Review: Papers & Proceedings*, May 2011.

Henderson, Nell. "Bernanke: There's No Housing Bubble to Go Bust; Fed Nominee Has Said 'Cooling' Won't Hurt." *Washington Post*, October 27, 2005.

Herman, Tom. "Historians Marvel at Rescue's Size, Twists." *Wall Street Journal*, September 25, 1998.

Hilsenrath, Jon. "Fed Fires $600 Billion Stimulus Shot." *Wall Street Journal*, November 4, 2010.

Hilsenrath, Jon and Mark Whitehouse. "Markets Defy Fed's Bond-Buying Push." *Wall Street Journal*, December 9, 2009.

Himmerlberg, Charles, Christopher Mayer, and Todd Sinai. "Assessing High House Prices: Bubbles, Fundamentals and Misperceptions." *Journal of Economic Perspectives*, Fall 2005.

Hirtle, Beverly. "Bank Holding Company Capital Ratios and Shareholder Payouts." *Current Issues in Economics and Finance*, September 1998.

Homer, Sidney and Martin Liebowitz. *Some Theoretical Problems Suggested by the Movements of Interest Rates, Bond Yields and Stock Prices in the United States since 1856*. Prentice-Hall, 1972.

Hubbard, Glenn and Chris Mayer. "First, Let's Stabilize Home Prices." *Wall Street Journal*, October 2, 2008.

HUD. "HUD's Regulation of the Federal National Mortgage Association (Fannie Mae) and the Federal Home Loan Mortgage Corporation (Freddie Mac)." *Federal Register*, October 31, 2000.

HUD. "Reforming the U.S. Mortgage Market Through Private Market Incentives." University of Berkeley Working Paper, November 15, 2010.

Ilzetzki, Ethan, Enrique Mendoza, and Carlos Vegh. "How Big Are Fiscal Multipliers?" CEPR Policy Insight Number 39, October 2009.

Infovest21 Staff. "Endeavor Close to Shutting Flagship Fund." *Infovest21 News*, February 16, 2009.

Jaffee, Dwight. "On Limiting the Retained Mortgage Portfolios of Fannie Mae and Freddie Mac." AEI Presentation, April 20, 2005.

Jorion, Philippe. *Value at Risk*. McGraw-Hill, 2006.

Kacperczyk, Marcin and Philipp Schnabl. "When Safe Proved Risky: Commercial Paper during the Financial Crisis of 2007-2009." *The Journal of Economic Perspectives*, Winter 2010.

Keynes, John Maynard. *The General Theory of Employment, Interest and Money*. Macmillan Cambridge University Press, 1936.

Khandani, Amir E. and Andrew Lo. "What Happened to the Quants in August 2007?: Evidence from Factors and Transaction Data." http://ssrn.com/abstract=1288988, 2008.

Kirilenko, Andrei, Albert S. Kyle, Mehrdad Samadi, and Tugkan Tuzun. "The Flash Crash: The Impact of High Frequency Trading on an Electronic Market." http://ssrn.com/abstract=1686004, January 12, 2011.

Klyuev, Vladimir, Phil de Imus, and Krishna Srinivasan. "Unconventional Choices for Unconventional Times: Credit and Quantitative Easing in Advanced Economies." IMF Staff Position Note, November 4, 2009.

Kopecki, Dawn. "Freddie Paid Big Bonuses in '04." *Wall Street Journal*, June 5, 2005.

Kopecki, Dawn. "New Fannie Mae Violations Surface." *Wall Street Journal*, September 29, 2005.

Krasker, William S. "The Rate of Return to Storing Wines." *Journal of Political Economy*, December 1979.

Krishnamurthy, Arvind and Annette Vissing-Jorgensen. "The Effects of Quantitative Easing on Long-Term Interest Rates." Northwestern Working Paper, November 8, 2010.

Kumar, Arun N. "American International Group: A View Through the Looking Glass as the World Turns." J.P. Morgan Credit Research, October 1, 2008.

Kuykendall, Lavonne. "AIG to Sell Asset-Management Unit." *Wall Street Journal*, September 5, 2009.

Lacko, James M. "The Failure and Promise of Mandated Consumer Mortgage Disclosures: Evidence from Qualitative Interviews and a Controlled Experiment with Mortgage Borrowers." *American Economic Review*, May 2010.

Lall, Ranjit. "Why Basel II Failed and Why Any Basel III Is Doomed." GEG Working Paper, October 2009.

Lehman Brothers. "Annual Report." Lehman Brothers Annual Report, December 31, 2007.

Lewis, Michael. "How the Eggheads Cracked." *New York Times*, January 24, 1999.

Lipin, Steven. "Long-Term Capital Pressured by Underlying Bets." *Wall Street Journal*, September 8, 1998.

Livingston, Jessica. *Founders at Work. Stories of Startups' Early Days*. Apress, 2007.

Lockhart, James B. "FHFA's First Anniversary and Challenges Ahead." FHFA Speech, July 30, 2009.

Long-Term Capital Management. "Long-Term Capital, Ltd. Private Placement of Ordinary Shares." Confidential Private Placement Memorandum #225, October 1, 1993.

Lowenstein, Roger. *When Genius Failed. The Rise and Fall of Long-Term Capital Management*. Random House, 2000.

Luce, Edward. "Bank of Italy Governor Defends LTCM Position." *Financial Times*, October 5, 1998.

Lux, Thomas. "Herd Behavior, Bubbles, and Crashes." *The Economic Journal*, July 1995.

Macauley, Frederick. *Some Theoretical Problems Suggested by the Movements of Interest Rates, Bond Yields and Stock Prices in the United States since 1856*. NBER, 1938.

MacKenzie, Donald. "Long-Term Capital Management and the Sociology of Arbitrage." *Economy and Society*, 32:349–380, August 2003.

Margasak, Larry. "Some Firms Get Bailouts, Some Don't. Unfair?" *Associated Press Online*, September 15, 2008.

Martin, Timothy. "Atlanta School Scandal Sparks House Cleaning." *BusinessWeek*, July 13, 2011.

McDermott, Daniel. "In Search of Certainty." *Wall Street Journal*, June 27, 2011.

McDonald, Lawrence G. and Patrick Robinson. *A Colossal Failure of Common Sense: The Inside Story of the Collapse of Lehman Brothers*. Crown Publishing Group, 2009.

McGeehan, Patrick. "Lehman Offers a Rare Glimpse of Risk Profile." *Wall Street Journal*, October 6, 1998.

McGrane, Victoria and Deborah Salomon. "CFTC Chief Feels Need for Speed." *Wall Street Journal*, December 14, 2010.

McGrane, Victoria and Robin Sidel. "Fed Softens 'Swipe' Fees." *Wall Street Journal*, June 30, 2011.

McGrane, Victoria, Dan Fitzpatrick, and Randall Smith. "Fed's New Debit-Card Fee Rules Hit Hard; Issuers Howl." *Wall Street Journal*, December 16, 2010.

McKinnon, John D. and Dawn Kopecki. "Greenspan Issues Another Warning on Fannie, Freddie." *Wall Street Journal*, September 15, 2005.

Mehrling, Perry. *Fischer Black and the Revolutionary Idea of Finance*. Wiley, 2005.

Mello, Antonio S. and John E. Parsons. "Maturity Structure of a Hedge Matters: Lessons from the Metallgesellschaft Debacle." *Journal of Applied Corporate Finance*, Spring 1995.

Meriwether, John W. "Relative Value Opportunity Fund Letter." JWMP Letter to Investors, December 2007–May 2009.

Meriwether, John W. "Global Macro Fund Letter." JWMP Letter to Investors, December 31, 2009.

Mezrich, Ben. *Bringing Down the House: The Inside Story of Six M.I.T. Students Who Took Vegas for Millions*. Free Press, 2003.

Mian, Atif and Amir Sufi. "The Effects of Fiscal Stimulus: Evidence from the 2009 Cash for Clunkers Program." NBER Working Paper, No. 16,351, September 2010.

Miles, David, Jing Yang, and Gilberto Marcheggiano. "Optimal Bank Capital." The Bank of England Discussion Paper No. 31, January 2011.

Miron, Jeffrey. "Cash for Clunkers Is a Clunker." *Cato Insitute Blog*, August 3, 2009.

Modest, David M. and Robert H. Litzenberger. "Crisis and Non-Crisis Risk in Financial Markets: A Unified Approach to Risk Management." Available at SSRN: http://ssrn.com/abstract=1160273, July 15, 2008.

Morgensen, Gretchen. "Bear Stearns Says Battered Hedge Funds Are Worth Little." *New York Times*, July 18, 2007.

Morgenson, Gretchen and Joshua Rosner. *Reckless Endangerment. How Outsized Ambition, Greed, and Corruption Led to Economic Armageddon*. Henry Holt, 2011.

Muehring, Kevin. "John Meriwether by the numbers; Long Term Capital Management Results Moves Fund into Top Tanks and Founder's Status has Grown." *Institutional Investor*, November 1996.

Mundell, Robert A. "The International Monetary System and the Case for a World Currency." Leon Kozminski Academy of Entrepreneurship and Management and TIGER Distinguished Lectures Series 2003, 2003.

Nocera, Joe. "Markets Quake, and a 'Neutral' Strategy Slips." *New York Times*, August 18, 2007.

OFHEO. "Report of the Special Examination of Fannie Mae." *OFHEO Report*, May 2006.

O'Hara, Neil. "Finding deals in the downtrodden mortgage market." *Alpha*, October 2008.

Orzag, Jonathan M., Peter R. Orzag, and Joseph E. Stiglitz. "Implications of the New Fannie Mae and Freddie Mac Risk-Based Capital Standard." Fannie Mae Papers, March 2002.

Pacelle, Mitchell, Leslie Scism, and Steve Lipin. "How Buffett, AIG, and Goldman Sought Long-Term Capital, but Were Rejected." *Wall Street Journal*, September 30, 1998.

Palyi, Melchior. "Bank Portfolios and the Control of the Capital Market." *Journal of Business*, pp. 70–111, January 1938.

Passmore, Wayne, Gillian Burgess, Diana Hancock, Andreas Lehnert, and Shane Sherlund. "Federal Reserve Research on Government-Sponsored Enterprises." Federal Reserve Working Paper, May 2006.

Passmore, Wayne, Shane Sherlund, and Gillian Burgess. "The Effect of Housing Government-Sponsored Enterprises on Mortgage Rates." *Real Estate Economics*, September 2005.

Peltzman, Sam. "The Effects of Automobile Safety Regulation." *Journal of Political Economy*, August 1975.

Perold, Andre. "Long Term Capital Management (A-D)." Harvard Business School Case Study, 1999.

Phillips, Matt. "Do Jim Cramer Stock Picks Beat the Market? Finance Profs Investigate." *Wall Street Journal*, May 20, 2009.

PIMCO. "Evaluating Optimum Currency Areas: The U.S. versus Europe." www.pimco.com/EN/Insights/Pages/Evaluating-Optimum-Currency-Areas-The-US-versus-Europe-.aspx, December 2011.

Pinto, Edward. "The Subprime Mortgage Market National and Twelfth District Developments." Federal Reserve Bank of San Francisco Annual Report, 2007.

Pinto, Edward. "Government Housing Policies in the Lead-up to the Financial Crisis: A Forensic Study." AEI Working Paper, August 14, 2010.

Pinto, Edward. "Government Housing Policy: The Sine Qua Non of the Financial Crisis How did the financial system accumulate an unprecedented number of risky mortgages?" *AEI Online*, September 16, 2011.

Platinum Grove Asset Management. "March 2009 Review." Platinum Grove Contingent Capital Fund Investor Report, March 31, 2009.

Pojarliev, Momtchil and Richard M. Levich. "Detecting Crowded Trades in Currency Funds." *Financial Analysts Journal*, January/February, 2011.

Prevost, Lisa. "Homeownership Is Next to Godliness." *New York Times*, May 28, 2006.

Public Citizen. "Rewarding Failure." www.citizen.org, December 14, 2009.

Raghavan, Anita. "Long-Term Capital's Partners Got Big Loans to Invest in Fund." *Wall Street Journal*, October 6, 1998.

Raghavan, Anita. "Salomon Shuts Down A Bond Unit—Arbitrage Group's End Aimed at Cutting Risk." *Wall Street Journal*, July 7, 1998.

Raghavan, Anita and Michael R. Sesit. "Fund Partners Got Outside Financing — Move to Boost Investments in Long-Term Capital Adds to Financial Woes." *Wall Street Journal*, September 28, 1998.

Raghavan Anita and Mitchell Pacelle. "To the Rescue? A Hedge Fund Falters, So the Fed Persuades Big Banks to Ante Up—Firms to Lend $3.6 Billion As Long-Term Capital Loses on Its Bond Bets—'Star Power' and Red Ink." *Wall Street Journal*, September 24, 1998.

Rapoport, Michael. "Regulators to Target 'Window Dressing'." *Wall Street Journal*, September 16, 2010.

Reddy, Sudeep. "Criticism Hinders Fed's Easing Plan." *Wall Street Journal*, November 22, 2010.

Reinhart, Carmen M. and Belen Sbrancia. "The Liquidation of Government Debt." NBER Working Paper #16893, March 2011.

Resti, Andrea and Andrea Sironi. *Risk Management and Shareholder's Value in Banking*. Wiley-Finance, 2007.

Reynolds, Alan. "No Housing Bubble Trouble." *Washington Times*, January 9, 2005.

Reynolds, Alan. "Ben Bernanke's Impossible Dream." *Wall Street Journal*, November 9, 2010.

Rose, Chris. "The Flash Crash of May 2010: Accident or Market Manipulation?" *Journal of Business and Economics Research*, January 2011.

Rosenfeld, Eric. "LTCM and the Role of the Federal Reserve." Presentation at Georgetown McDonough School of Business. http://pages.pomona.edu/lbc04747/videos.html, April 17, 2007.

Rosenfeld, Eric. "Long Term Capital Management." *Encyclopedia of Finance*, pp. 1–15, 2010.

Rothman, Matthew S. "Rebalance of Large Cap Portfolio." *Lehman Brothers Equity Research*, September 5, 2007.

Rothman, Matthew S. "Turbulent Times in Quant Land." *Lehman Brothers Equity Research*, August 9, 2007.

Rothman, Matthew S. "Where Do We Go Now?" *Lehman Brothers Equity Research*, August 15, 2007.

Rothman, Matthew S. "August Redux/Redo?" *Lehman Brothers Equity Research*, January 25, 2008.

Sargent, Carolyn. "Savvy Bets in MBS Pay Off for Bear; It Tops U.S. Tables on Strength of Subprime and New Channel for Product Loans." *Investment Dealers Digest*, January 10, 2005.

Schenkelberg, Heike and Watzka Sebastian. "Real Effects of Quantitative Easing at the Zero-Lower Bound: Structural VAR-based Evidence from Japan." Working Paper, February 3, 2011.

Schlesinger, Jacob M. "Long-Term Capital Bailout Spotlights a Fed 'Radical'." *Wall Street Journal*, November 2, 1998.

Schlesinger, Jacob M. and Michael Schroeder. "Greenspan Defends Long-Term Capital Plan—More Threats Lurk in Market, Fed Chairman Testifies; Lawmakers Are Critical." October 2, 1998.

Schoen, Douglas. "Polling the Occupy Wall Street Crowd." *Wall Street Journal*, October 18, 2011.

Scholes, Myron. "Crisis and Risk Management." *AEA Papers and Proceedings*, pp. 17–21, May 2000.

SEC. "Concept Release: Rating Agencies and the Use of Credit Ratings under the Federal Securities Laws." www.sec.gov/rules/concept/33-8236.htm, 2003.

SEC and CFTC. "Findings Regarding the Market Events of May 6, 2010." Report of the Staffs of the CTC and SEC to the Joint Advisory Committee on Emerging Regulatory Issues, September 30, 2010.

SEC and CFTC. "Preliminary Findings Regarding the Market Events of May 6, 2010." Report of the Staffs of the CTC and SEC to the Joint Advisory Committee on Emerging Regulatory Issues, May 18, 2010.

Seiler, Michael J., Mark A. Lane, Vicky L. Seiler, and David M. Harrison. "Can Real Estate Agents Influence Homebuyer Property Perceptions Through Their Appearance and Hyperbolic Rhetoric?" Old Dominion Working Paper, August 2010.

Sender, H., K. Kelly, and G. Zuckerman. "Goldman Wagers on Cash Infusion to Show Resolve." *Wall Street Journal*, August 14, 2007.

Setzer, Glenn. "Housing Bubble to Bust? FDIC Certainly Hopes Not." *Mortgage News Daily*, May 17, 2005.

Shin, Annys. "Capital Grilling for Lehman CEO; Fuld Says Crisis 'Overwhelmed' Him." *Washington Post*, October 7, 2008.

Siconolfi, Michael. "How Merrill Lynch Aided Both the Birth and the Bailout of a Powerful Hedge Fund." *Wall Street Journal*, September 25, 1998.

Siconolfi, Michael, Mitchell Pacelle, and Anita Raghavan. "All Bets Are Off: How the Salesmanship and Brainpower Failed at Long-Term Capital." *Wall Street Journal*, November 16, 1998.

Sidel, Robin. "At Banks, New Fees Replacing Old Levies." *Wall Street Journal*, January 5, 2011.

Sidel, Robin. "Big Banks Blink on New Card Fees." *Wall Street Journal*, October 28, 2011.

Sidel, Robin. "Secret to Bank's Comeback: A Rich Uncle Named Sam." *Wall Street Journal*, January 28, 2011.

Sidel, Robin and Dan Fitzpatrick. "Debit-Fee Retreat Complete." *Wall Street Journal*, November 2, 2011.

Sloan, Allan. "The Hedgies' Tide Rolls Out." *Newsweek*, July 17, 2000.

Smith, Adam. *The Wealth of Nations*. Edwin Cannan, 1776.

Solomon, Deborah and Randall Smith. "Banks May Need More Capital." *Wall Street Journal*, June 4, 2011.

Sorkin, Andrew Ross. *Too Big to Fail: The Inside Story of How Wall Street and Washington Fought to Save the Financial System—and Themselves*. Penguin Group, 2009.

Spilimbergo, Antonio, Steve Symansky, and Martin Schindler. "Fiscal Multipliers." IMF Staff Position Note, May 2009.

Spiro, Leah Nathans. "The Trader Dream Team." *BusinessWeek*, August 29, 1994.

Story, Louise. "At Lehman, Chief Exudes Confidence." *New York Times*, June 17, 2008.

Stossel, John. "Scrap the Traffic Lights, Give Private Enterprise the Green Light." *FoxNews.com*, August 4, 2010.

Strasburg, Jenny. "Hedge Fund Snapshots: Surviving the Financial Crisis." *Wall Street Journal*, April 18, 2011.

Strasburg, Jenny and Katherine Burton. "Sowood Funds Lose More Than 50% as Debt Markets Fall." *Bloomberg*, July 31, 2007.

Syron, Richard F. "Rebuilding Confidence. Leading Responsibly." Freddie Mac Annual Report, 2004.

Talley, Ian. "IMF Finds Rules for Banks Lacking." *Wall Street Journal*, October 4, 2010.

Taylor, John B. "Getting Back on Track: Macroeconomic Policy Lessons from the Financial Crisis." *Federal Reserve Bank of St. Louis Review*, May/June 2010.

Taylor, John B. "Evaluating TARP." Written Testimony for the Committee on Banking, Housing, and Urban Affairs, March 17, 2011.

Thomas, Jason and Robert Van Order. "A Closer Look at Fannie Mae and Freddie Mac: What We Know, What We Think We Know and What We Don't Know." George Washington Working Paper, pp. 1–50, March 2011.

Timiraos, Nick. "Banks Hit Hurdle to Foreclosures." *Wall Street Journal*, June 1, 2011.

Tirole, Jean. "Illiquidity and All Its Friends." *Journal of Economic Literature*, June 2011.

Tyson, Eric. "The Worth of Jim Cramer's Advice." www.erictyson.com, September 22, 2009.

United States Department of the Treasury. "Troubled Asset Relief Program: Two Year Retrospective." *Treasury Department Publication*, October 5, 2010.

Valukas, Anton R. "Chapter 11 Case No. 08-13555 (JMP). Lehman Brothers Holdings Inc." United States Bankruptcy Court Southern District of New York, March 11, 2010.

Wallison, Peter J. "Dissent from the Majority Report of the Financial Crisis Inquiry Commission." *FCIC Publication*, January 2011.

Wallison, Peter J. "Regulating Fannie Mae and Freddie Mac: Now It Gets Serious." *American Enterprise Institute Financial Services Outlook*, May 2005.

Wallison, Peter J. "Regulating Fannie Mae and Freddie Mac: Now It Gets Serious (Continued)." *American Enterprise Institute Financial Services Outlook*, September 2005.

Weil, Gotshal, & Manges, L.L.P. "An Overview of the Dodd-Frank Wall Street Reform and Consumer Protection Act." Financial Regulatory Reform Working Paper, 2010.

Weisbecker, Lee. "Hedge-fund woes sink Brightleaf Capital, smack Morgan Creek, Smith Breeden, Silverback." *Triangle Business Journal*, March 20, 2009.

Whelan, Robbie. "Reports of Mortgage Fraud Reach Record Level." *Wall Street Journal*, May 10, 2011.

White, Ben. "Buffett Deal at Goldman Seen as a Sign of Confidence." *New York Times*, September 24, 2008.

White, Lawrence J. "The Credit Rating Agencies." *Journal of Economic Perspectives*, Spring 2010.

Woodward, Susan E. and Robert E. Hall. "Consumer Confusion in the Mortgage Market: Evidence of Less than a Perfectly Transparent and Competitive Market." *American Economic Review*, May 2010.

Wuffli, Peter. "Salomon Global Banking Conference." UBS Presentation by CFO, October 28, 1998.

Young, Ashley N. "The Real Estate Agent's Role in the Housing Crisis: A Proposal for Ethical Reform." *Georgetown Journal of Legal Ethics*, Summer 2011.

Zingales, Luigi. "Overall Impact of TARP on Financial Stability." Oral Testimony before the Congressional Oversight Panel, March 4, 2011.

Zuckerman, G., J. Hagerty, and D. Gauthier-Villars. "Impact of Mortgage Crisis Spreads; Dow Tumbles 2.8% as Fallout Intensifies; Moves by Central Banks." *Wall Street Journal*, August 10, 2007.

Zweig, Jason. "The Man Who Called the Financial Crisis–70 Years Early." *Wall Street Journal*, November 6, 2010.

About the Author

Ludwig Chincarini is an Associate Professor of Finance in the School of Management at the University of San Francisco and Director of Quantitative Strategies at United States Commodity Funds and a financial consultant to money managers and hedge funds. He was a professor of finance at Georgetown University. He was on the academic council of Index IQ from 2007 to 2015. He was also Director of Research at Rydex Global Advisors, where he codeveloped the S&P 500 Equal-Weight Index and ETF, and at FOLIO*fn*, helping to build its innovative basket trading and portfolio management platform. He also worked in the portfolio management group of the Bank for International Settlements (BIS) and in the investment research department of Schroders.

Chincarini teaches finance to both undergraduates and MBA students. He earned a PhD from the Massachusetts Institute of Technology and an AB from the University of California at Berkeley.

Index

467